GENDER
&
COMMUNICATION

GENDER
&
COMMUNICATION

SECOND EDITION

JUDY CORNELIA PEARSON
Ohio University at Athens

LYNN H. TURNER
Marquette University

WILLIAM TODD-MANCILLAS
California State University, Chico

 Wm. C. Brown Publishers

Book Team

Editor *Stan Stoga*
Developmentai Editor *Jane F. Lambert*
Production Coordinator *Carla D. Arnold*
Photo Editor *Carrie Burger*

 Wm. C. Brown Publishers

President *G. Franklin Lewis*
Vice President, Publisher *George Wm. Bergquist*
Vice President, Publisher *Thomas E. Doran*
Vice President, Operations and Production *Beverly Kolz*
National Sales Manager *Virginia S. Moffat*
Senior Marketing Manager *Kathy Law Laube*
Marketing Manager *Kathleen Nietzke*
Executive Editor *Edgar J. Laube*
Managing Editor, Production *Colleen A. Yonda*
Production Editorial Manager *Julie A. Kennedy*
Production Editorial Manager *Ann Fuerste*
Publishing Services Manager *Karen J. Slaght*
Manager of Visuals and Design *Faye M. Schilling*

Cover design by Elaine G. Allen

The credits section for this book begins on page 297, and is considered an extension of the copyright page.

Library of Congress Catalog Card Number: 90–80346

ISBN 0–697–03021–0

Printed in the United States of America by Wm. C. Brown Publishers, 2460 Kerper Boulevard, Dubuque, IA 52001

10 9 8 7 6 5 4 3 2 1

Contents

9   Gender and communication in public contexts   216

10 Gender and communication in mediated contexts 250

Preface

Interest in the communication relationships between women and men has progressed at a geometric rate during the past 15 years. While the origins of this interest in gender and communication date to the beginning of the century, gender scholars have only recently amassed enough data for a systematic examination of this area.

A variety of models have guided the research on gender and communication. The initial lack of investigations on women promoted stereotypical images and effective communication models derived from the interactions of men. Implicitly, communicative success was equated with male practice. Today the communicative behaviors of both women and men are examined with behavioral research replacing "folk linguistics."

The purpose of *Gender and Communication* is to synthesize the research findings into a single, manageable source. Although the text includes hundreds of citations, at least as many were deleted from inclusion. An attempt has been made to include the various findings on each issue, to include at least one or two citations from the major researchers, and to suggest the breadth of research in this area. At the same time, manageability of the text, considerations such as book length, and concern about the teaching value of the text suggested some restraint.

We have made an effort to cite the most up-to-date research on each issue. However, when we refer to research written several years ago, we do so because it still stands as the best work on a given subject.

The organization and orientation of this text

Gender and Communication is both theoretical and pragmatic in orientation. It is theoretical in that attempts are made to construct conceptual maps useful to understand how and why men's and women's communication behaviors are similar to one another in some instances, yet different in others. In addition, this book is pragmatic in that it suggests how men and women can communicate more effectively.

The text is divided into three major sections: Section I defines the domain of gender and communication studies and considers how men's and women's self-perceptions evolve as a function of cultural influences; Section II considers differences and similarities in the ways women and men are described and the communication patterns they use; Section III concerns differences and similarities in men's and women's communication within a variety of contexts.

Teaching gender and communication

This text is of interest to any person interested in understanding how gender is related to communication phenomena; however, it is particularly relevant to the reader with a behavioral science orientation. What follows is based substantially on what is known to us as a result of systematic empirical research and a plausible interpretation of findings obtained thereby.

The authors are aware of the considerable controversy surrounding gender and communication studies. Some consideration of this controversy is needed to understand more fully the authors' orientations. This controversy is premised largely on four arguments: 1) that much gender and communication research is class-, culture-, and historically bound; 2) that gender and communication studies are largely atheoretical, i.e., research undertaken in this area consists of unconnected—or, at best, only loosely connected—variable-based studies, with no effort to integrate this research into a meaningful whole; 3) that gender and communication studies underemphasize communication dynamics, focusing disproportionate attention on gender per se; and 4) that unhealthful divisiveness too often accompanies discussions of gender's impact on human communication.

In the authors' opinions, none of the above arguments carry sufficient weight to justify abandoning research in gender and communication. In response to the first criticism, the authors must acknowledge that they are reporting and experiencing gender and communication issues from a white, middle-class perspective. However, there are many other ways of seeing gender roles and communication. The reader is urged to reflect on these other points of view to gain an understanding of the complex relationships existing among class, culture, and gender.

Concerning the second argument, while it is certainly true that much of the research done today has been atheoretical, it does not necessarily follow that the subject matter, in and of itself, precludes the development of sound theory. Quite the contrary. If anything, the absence of sufficient theory simply indicates the need to "fix what is broken," not to discard the subject matter altogether. The development of a theory to allow better understanding of how and why gender relates to communication would explain much about human behavior. That we have not yet developed such a theory should be recognized as a challenge to be met, not a problem without resolution.

The third argument that gender and communication studies are often undertaken with a view to expanding what is known about gender rather than communication per se, is also an argument premised on what has happened in the past rather than on what can happen in the future. Because some researchers have disregarded the importance of focusing attention on communication, it does not follow that all others will continue to do so. *Gender and Communication,* however, emphasizes the importance communication plays in explaining those similarities and differences between men and women.

The last argument concerns the divisiveness so often accompanying discussions of communication and gender. Courses on gender and communication sometimes focus on differences rather than similarities reflecting our social scientific methodology and our research in this area; however, most researchers and instructors encourage the enlargement of behavioral repertories, not the prescription of continued difference. Money and Tucker (1975) are probably accurate when they write, "When it comes down to the biological imperatives that are laid down for all men and women, there are only four: Only a man can impregnate; only a woman can menstruate, gestate, and lactate" (p. 38). The long history of psychological research on sex differences, however, has demonstrated a variety of personality, attitudinal, and behavioral differences between women and men.

Most recently psychologists have questioned their position on examining differences between people on the basis of anatomical, physiological, or intrapsychic bases and have begun to assess gender differences within a social context. Perhaps the strongest appeal came from Weisstein (1971) who authored the monograph, *Psychology Constructs the Female, or the Fantasy Life of the Male Psychologist.* In her article, Weisstein effectively argues that many psychological correlates for biological differences could be explained by invoking such concepts as conformity to social pressure, expectancy effects, differential socialization practices for females and males, and experimenter bias. We have noted, since the Weisstein article, a sharp upswing of research interest in the social variables that underlie sex differences.

The emphasis on differences between women and men is probably disheartening for most people who write or teach in the gender-and-communication area. We find ourselves constantly emphasizing that which we symbolically and pragmatically wish to deemphasize: the differences between females and males. Ambert and Ambert (1976) wrote,

> For, in spite of current research trends and ideologies, the sexes are more alike than dissimilar. We are in the presence of a range of human potentialities and qualities and the more important observation resides in the overlap of human traits between the sexes in spite of a socialization process that encourages cleavage (p. 7).

While we write and talk of differences, our emphasis reminds us of the great overlap of human traits and the large range of human potential. Notions of psychological androgyny, behavioral flexibility, and communication competence mark most of our recommendations for improving both women's and men's communication.

Acknowledgments

Gender and Communication is a cumulative effort by publishers, editors, critic-evaluators, students, fellow teachers, and the authors. Judy Pearson was initially encouraged by Louise Waller who signed the contract for the first edition of this book and the birth of Rebekah Kristina Pearson-Nelson who provided her six weeks of maternity leave on which to write a large part of the manuscript. The text was completed through long and loving hours of research and writing and Rebekah is nine years old as the second edition is published. Kim Hause, Amy Thieme, Chun Wah Lee, Amy Haskins, and Sue Manderick, all at Ohio University, assisted in the preparation of the second edition. A sincere thanks to each of you.

Lynn Turner would like to acknowledge Marquette University, especially Marci Berlin in the College of Communication, Journalism, and Performing Arts for her patience and excellent typing. She would also like to express thanks to her husband Ted and daughter Sabrina for their love, support, and the thousands of object lessons demonstrating the relationship of gender and communication.

The people at Wm. C. Brown Company Publishers have earned our appreciation, and so have the reviewers they have selected: First edition—Dencil K. Backus, Purdue University at Calumet; Mary Anne Fitzpatrick, University of Wisconsin at Madison; H. Lloyd Goodall, Jr., University of Alabama; Patricia Riley, University of Southern California at Los Angeles; Don W. Stacks, University of South Alabama; Constance M. Staley, University of Colorado at Colorado Springs. Second Edition—Teresa Chandler, University of Cincinnati; Adele L. Lenrow, William Paterson College; Maria Loffredo, State University of New York at Oneanta; Pat McEvoy, University of Iowa; Carol Valentine, Arizona State University.

GENDER
&
COMMUNICATION

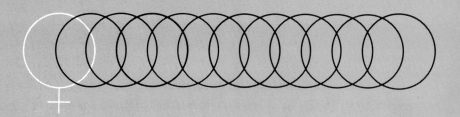

Section 1

You are about to begin the exploration of one of the most fascinating topics in contemporary life: an examination of the communicative behavior of women and men. To accomplish this task, certain basic considerations must be discussed. This first section of the text lays the groundwork for the material to follow. In this section you will be introduced to some new terms and will learn to define some familiar terms in specific ways.

This section includes three chapters. Chapter 1 provides an introduction to gender and communication, defines relevant terms, and presents a model by which we may view the communication between women and men.

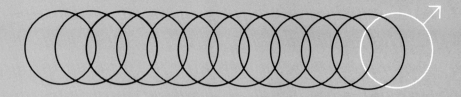

Fundamentals

Chapter 2 considers the research on the proposition that men and women think and perceive differently from one another. As you will see, although people believe that information processing is different for women and men, the research does not always support this conclusion. In chapter 3, we move from a general discussion of the perception process to an examination of the ways in which women and men perceive themselves. This chapter analyzes the self-concepts that women and men form by interacting with others.

1 An introduction to gender and communication: what's it all about?

Introduction

When you learn that a friend or acquaintance has had a baby, what is the first question you are likely to ask about the infant? When you see a person walking on the street ahead of you and cannot determine his or her biological sex immediately, why do you strive to find out if it is a man or a woman? When you learn that an individual has made an important discovery, has achieved a remarkable feat, or has lived an incredibly long life, are you curious if they are male or female? Every day you consider and ask questions about people's biological sex. Your curiosity is stimulated, at least in part, by your interest in knowing how to communicate with them.

You make observations and predictions about whether people are male or female based on their communicative behavior and their roles in society. You may be surprised when someone does not conform to your beliefs about how biological sex and communicative behavior are related.

While gender and communication are intimately related, the relationship is not as simple and straightforward as it once may have been. Because our society is changing, it is no longer easy to predict a person's occupation or family role based on his or her gender. For example, women are becoming increasingly successful in managerial roles and in attaining high status in a variety of organizations. Fathers are becoming more involved with their children from the moment of birth.

The changing roles of women and men are inescapable, and the topic of gender and communication is relevant today because of these vast sociological and psychological changes. Virtually every medium—books, magazines, newspapers, film, television, and radio—carries stories about the central and yet changeable issues of men's and women's roles and the manner in which they communicate them.

The nature of these changes in male/female roles can be likened to Kuhn's discussion of "paradigm shifts." Kuhn (1974) introduced the concept of a paradigm shift to explain how, within any given field, truly significant advances are indicated by the introduction of new belief structures (called paradigms) that, if true, would imply a completely different way of thinking from that previously endorsed. For instance, as a result of adopting the paradigm of a "round" rather than a "flat" earth, explorers discovered new continents, and the history of the world changed dramatically. Similarly, the changes in men's and women's roles and their manner of enactment through communication clearly signal important cultural paradigm shifts.

We note that it is more appropriate to speak in terms of "shifts" rather than a "shift" for the simple reason that it is not entirely clear which, among competing paradigms, is the most preferred or effective for thinking about women and men in our culture. We now have more ways to live our lives as men and women than previously thought possible. In fact, we have so many different possibilities that much contemporary stress is caused by our not being able to select from the many available options. Quite literally, many of us do not know what constitutes "proper" communication behavior for men and women.

In large part, this stress is associated with not being able to predict which behaviors are preferred in which given contexts. Previously, for instance, it was assumed that when dating, a man would take the initiative, asking a woman out and paying for the date. While this continues to be the norm for many, it is now much more common to find women who prefer to "pay their own way" and who sometimes take the initiative to ask a man out for a date. This change in norms has caused no small degree of stress for both men and women in attempting to predict which dating behaviors are most acceptable.

In the past it was easy. The game was clearly understood, at least by the more experienced players. It was often the stuff of which movies were made, especially movies focusing on the difficulties young adults had mastering the game. Note that no such simple plots occur in contemporary movies. The dynamics are much more complicated in *Mystic Pizza* or *Saint Elmo's Fire* than they ever were in any Andy Hardy movie.

The dating context is not, of course, the only arena in which men and women are confused about how to behave with one another. In fact, much confusion also occurs when simply interacting with people of your own sex. The problem is not simply one of how people generally interact with other people. Sex does make a significant difference. Note, for instance, Melanie Griffith's line in *Working Girl* when she first learns Sigourney Weaver is her new boss. Griffith, somewhat surprised, tells Weaver that she has never worked for a female boss. Griffith asks for clarification of what is expected of her, and from the tone of this interaction, we know this question is different from what would be asked a male employer.

Why the difference? Clearly, the fact that Weaver is a woman has made the difference. And just as that makes a difference in Griffith's approach toward Weaver, so does it make a difference in the working relationships of many women, especially women in so-called "men's" positions. With so few role models to guide them, women and men are often at a loss to enact their roles and relate to those playing new roles. Such issues continue to trouble both men and women struggling to make sense of their respective roles (both in and out of the workplace) and determining ways to communicate those roles to others.

In the face of this confusion, considerable research has attempted to understand the nature of various sex-role shifts and the ways those roles are interpreted and communicated. This research has been undertaken for essentially two reasons. First, it helps us better to understand the nature of our own human condition and how it is we make sense of the world we live in. Second, from this understanding we attempt to predict how better to live in our complicated and continually changing world. Thus, this research is of immediate and personal concern to us all. To assist us in understanding this research, we must first define the terms central to it.

"Gender" versus "sex": what's the difference?

Sex refers to biological categories, male and female, determined by the presence of XX chromosomes for females and an XY chromosome pattern for males. The chromosomes provide genetic information which produces sex characteristics, such as the penis and scrotum in the male and the clitoris and vagina in the female. As Smith (1985) points out, these categories, male and female, "are understood by most people as an inherent and/or God-given attribute of individuality, an inalienable, incontrovertible fact of human existence" (p. 20).

Gender, on the other hand, is usually thought of as the learned behaviors a culture associates with being male or female. The ideal of masculinity is communicated to males, whereas, the feminine ideal is communicated to females in our culture. Often this process fuses sex and gender together, although theoretically they are separate concerns.

It is our position that biological sex converges with gender so that, practically speaking, it becomes difficult to disentangle the two. Although people believe biological sex to be a relatively simple and unchanging attribute, it is never unaffected by the overlay of social learning we call gender. Some researchers refer to this interaction as "achieved" sex.

Kopkind (1986) discusses this commingling of the psychological, sociological, and biological categories in his review of a television drama, "Second Serve," based on the life of Richard Raskind. Raskind was an ophthalmologist and amateur tennis player who through surgery became a woman, Renee Richards.

Kopkind concludes that though the accouterments of masculinity and femininity are logically distinct from a person's essence, our culture stresses their fusion. Richards felt compelled, after the operation, to be a *feminine* woman "to gain the social acceptance that would confirm her transformation" (p. 802). Social expectations of masculinity and femininity are so closely tied to biological sex that Kopkind refers to society as "gender police" on the lookout for nonconformists and transgressors who wish to escape the "sexual slammer."

Other related terms

Another term frequently used in the text is "sexism." **Sexism** denotes a particular type of discrimination or manner of unfairly and/or inappropriately treating others. Sexism pertains to the manner in which either men or women are sometimes discriminated against (or, in some instances, inappropriately favored), merely because it is believed their biological sex ensures or significantly predisposes them to manifest some competencies more than others (Morris, 1975; Pearson, 1975). Thus, sexism is discrimination based on sex-role stereotypes—those oversimplified ideas of what constitutes masculinity and femininity.

For instance, Trenholm and Todd-Mancillas (1980) report an example of one young man's being disallowed an opportunity to address shipping labels because his employer thought men incapable of printing neatly. Women, on the other hand, were thought by this employer to be innately capable of printing legibly.

In a second example, a male teacher recently wrote Miss Manners (Martin, 1989) for advice on politely telling the female teachers at his school that he and his one other male colleague were tired of being expected to set up the tables every month for the staff meetings. Miss Manners suggested that he say, " 'Oh, are we distributing the work assignments by gender? O.K., then sure, we'll set up the tables, if you women do all the cooking. Or would you rather we all just pitch in and help without considering some tasks male and some female?' " (p. 76).

Sexism has been extensively researched and found to be systematically associated with a number of constructs pertinent to discussions about gender and communication. First, women have been found to be significantly less sexist than men (Pearson, 1980; Whitehead & Tawes, 1976). Second, sexism has been found to be related to a number of personality constructs: 1) men and women holding sexist attitudes toward women (*misogynists*) also tend to be overly defensive (Albright & Chang, 1976); 2) misogynists also tend to be excessively dogmatic (Whitehead & Tawes, 1976); 3) while age and educational level seem not to be associated with differential sexism among men, older and less educated women tend to differ from younger and more educated women in their being less supportive of women in general (Unger, 1979); 4) sexist men tend to have lower self-esteem (Miller, 1974); 5) sexist men and women tend to hold, as might be expected, more conservative attitudes toward sex, particularly a greater inclination to disapprove of homosexual behavior (Minnigerode, 1976). In general, it appears that persons holding more negative attitudes toward women are also more likely to stereotype others in general as well as define acceptable sexual behaviors more narrowly.

The meaning of the term communication

The word "communication" comes from the Latin *communicare* which literally means, "to make common." Thus, **communication** takes place whenever two people interact and, intentionally or unintentionally, negotiate the meaning of any phenomenon.

Earlier definitions of communication have identified messages or thoughts as the objects of communication. Neither of these terms is as accurate as "meaning." The term "message" does not imply any level of understanding. We may listen to a radio station which transmits its signal from Istanbul and be able to repeat words and phrases that we hear (the message), but have no

To have the opportunity of experiencing different sex-role behaviors, this exercise is useful. As you engage in the exercise, observe how people respond to you in your selected or assigned role and how you feel about portraying the particular role. You can participate in this exercise with members of your class or friends in an informal setting.

Each person should select, or be assigned to, one of the following roles.

Female Roles

1. **Good Old Mom**   You are an older woman who enjoys nurturing and helping others. You enjoy listening to other peoples' problems and offering advice.

2. **Mrs. Anybody**   You are dedicated to the traditional ideal. You are a wife and mother who puts the needs of your children and husband before yourself. You do all of this unselfishly.

3. **Ms. Somebody**   You have internalized all of the ideals of feminism. You are concerned about women being treated as sex objects. You want equality with men. Some people accuse you of being strident and pushy.

4. **Sensuous Woman**   You have a terrific figure and you like to show it off. You dress in a manner to attract attention—no neckline is too low and no skirt is slit too high. You flirt overtly with all of the men and have little time for the women.

5. **Little Girl**   You have found that the best strategy in gaining what you desire is through never growing up. You dress in a juvenile manner and generally act helpless.

6. **Professional Person**   You perceive your role as a professional and behave accordingly. You dress in business suits, even for social occasions. You want to be taken seriously and, to accomplish this, you always appear goal-oriented and business-like.

Male Roles

1. **Playboy of this world**   You view yourself as highly sophisticated and very subtle in the seduction of women. You enjoy capturing the

attention of the women you meet. Your relationships with women are primarily sexual; every woman is a conquest, regardless of her marital status.

2. **Ted Traditionalist**   You believe that women have a limited role in our society and that they should maintain it. Men should be men and women should be women and no confusion between sex roles should occur.

3. **Helpless Harry**   You have found that women like to "mother" you and you enjoy it. You continually forget important items, but you know that someone will take care of you.

4. **Feminist Male**   You are highly sympathetic with the struggle of women. You demonstrate genuine interest and concern. You perceive biological gender to be less important than other factors about a person.

5. **"Jock" Ewing**   You have been an athlete all of your life. You have a very strong and well-developed body and you are proud of it. You believe that men should work out every day and should be physically fit; you are less convinced of the importance of exercise for women.

6. **Dandy Dad**   You see yourself as someone who can offer years of experience to younger people that you meet. You are eager to provide advice on any topic. You tend to be patronizing sometimes, paternalistic always.

After you have selected one of these roles or been assigned a role to play, consider how you will dress, walk, talk, and behave. After you have had some opportunity to experiment with the new behavior, interact with the others in a social situation, or a role-playing social setting, in which you play your new role. Interact with others at a "party." After you have mingled with the other "people," discuss your feelings. What did you learn about the role you were playing, what did you learn about other sex roles, and how do people respond to the variety of roles presented? Do you think these sex roles actually occur? Which of the roles are preferable? Which ones do you normally play? Which roles would you like to avoid?

notion of the meaning if we do not speak Turkish. The term "thought" is problematic since thoughts are difficult to define and analyze. How do we know another person's thoughts? The term "meaning" is more accurately the object of communication.

Meanings are, in significant degree, a function of shared history among communicants. Thus, for example, people sharing the same larger culture (e.g., Americans from Milwaukee sharing a dinner with Americans from San Francisco) are likely to be able to communicate on a wide variety of topics because their common cultural world, by definition, imposes upon them extensive rules for how messages are shared and what constitutes recognizable messages. However, they would be limited on matters of unique character to their particular geographic regions. San Franciscans may not, for instance, call water fountains "bubblers," or understand a reference to Summerfest, a summer music festival in Milwaukee.

Families often construct private communication systems allowing family members to understand one another's inside (family) jokes not ordinarily and systematically understood by nonfamily members. Communication can only take place when there is a reasonable expectation that communicants have common experiences allowing them to arrive at the same or highly similar meanings associated with messages. Gender is one of the factors that creates a shared history between interactants and, thus, influences communication. Many researchers (i.e., Rakow, 1985) consider gender as *a* (if not *the*) primary social organizer.

Axioms of communication

Communication is a process
The word "communication" can mean both a product and a process. For instance, if we refer to a letter we have recently received as a communication, we are using the word "communication" as a noun, as a thing. We can also use the word "communication" to refer to the process by which that letter was written. For the purposes of our discussion, we use the term "messages" when referring to the noun form of communication and the term "communication" when referencing the process or verb form of the word. This distinction is important to use because were we to discuss communication as a product, our task might then be reduced merely to discovering a "correct" message intended to elicit a "correct" response. This orientation imposes a fixed and predetermined relationship between message sender and receiver that prevents us from recognizing and adapting to changes in human behavior. Since our goal is to understand changes in human communication behavior, we reject

the communication-as-product perspective. Accordingly, we accept as a fundamental axiom of communication the presumption that, while understanding message patterns and structures is important, it is far MORE important to understand the dynamics through which shared understanding is realized.

We also make the additional presumption that while communication-as-product may change dramatically from one instance to the next, the underlying process of communication is fundamentally the same across contexts. It is the sameness in this process that allows us to develop a field of study. This, or course, is not to imply that discovering this sameness is easy. Quite the contrary. It is extremely difficult to discover commonalities in the ways people mutually influence and understand one another; until now we have made only partial progress in developing theories useful for understanding communication-as-process. Nonetheless, that objective continues to be the fundamental one underlying communication research and theory development. It is because of this largely agreed-upon objective that we, in fact, entitle our academic departments as Departments of "Communication" rather than "Communications."

Communication involves bargaining and negotiation

When we negotiate a matter, we attempt to reach a common agreement about the phenomenon. A sound argument can be made for the assertion that over three billion languages exist in our world; in other words, each of us has a different notion of what particular words mean. While we may hold similar conceptions of words, we also have unique experiences with them which alter our perceptions. For instance, you may share with others the denotative meaning that a mouse is a small, brown rodent, but not share the connotative idea that they are cute and fun to hold. The word "mouse," then, elicits simultaneously both similar and different responses from different people.

Although each one of us has a unique language, we must rely on a common code to communicate with others. How do we do this to interact effectively with others? We negotiate the meaning of the words which we must use and the order in which we arrange them. When we are using more descriptive language or concrete words, such as "desk," "chair," "Santa Claus," "walk," "drink," or "type," we have less trouble in establishing a common meaning for the terms than when we use abstract or ambiguous words, such as "beautiful," "honest," "kind," "ugly," "loving," "warm," or "phony." You may find that many of the disagreements you have with others come from a lack of negotiating the meaning of such terms.

Bargaining and negotiating are obvious in those communication settings where people are arguing over a particular phenomenon, behavior, or person.

Children learn how to negotiate meaning in their interaction with each other.

It may be less obvious to consider that bargaining occurs, to some extent, in nearly every interaction. Consider the following conversation that occurred between a ten-year-old girl and her four-year-old brother.

B I'm really smart.
G What is 2 times 3?
B I know what a giraffe is.
G What is 2 times 3?
B I know all about giraffes—where they live, what they eat, and what they do all day.
G What is 2 times 3?
B What is 2 times 4?

In this conversation, the two children are attempting to negotiate some meaning for the concept of "really smart." For the ten-year-old girl, the concept meant that a person could do multiplication problems; for the four-year-old boy, it meant that a person had some understanding of animals. The boy correctly perceived that his sister was going to maintain her position regardless of his knowledge about giraffes and clearly attempted to change the focus of the application of the definition of "really smart" from him to her.

Some bargaining and negotiation may be nearly invisible in interactions. For instance, in the following conversation, the two people have a different conception of the word "several," although they never appear to disagree.

wife Don't hurry—we have several minutes before we need to go.
husband Do I have time to water the plants?
wife No, unless you can do it quickly.
husband It usually takes about ten or fifteen minutes.
wife We need to go sooner than that.
husband Okay, I'll be right down.

The wife in this instance perceives "several minutes" to mean about "five minutes," while the husband perceives it to be about "fifteen minutes." The two bargain, but in this instance, they never appear to become angry or sharply disagree.

We also negotiate the meaning of phrases and sentences by the order in which we put them together. For instance, we commonly place adjectives before the words they modify. If someone asserts that, "It's a beautiful day, but I have a terrible cold," we assume that "beautiful" modifies the kind of day it is and "terrible" modifies the condition of the cold. Sometimes we put words together in less clear ways, however. Suppose the person interacting with you states, "It's a beautiful day today, isn't it?" Would you assume they are asking a question or making an assertion? The other person's anger or apparent frustration when you do not answer may tell you that your conclusion that the person had made an assertion was incorrect. Your sensitivity to feedback will help you in the negotiation process.

A **bargain** is an agreement between two parties determining what each should give and receive in a transaction between them. Bargains may be explicit and formal, such as the kinds of agreements we reach with others to share tasks, attend social events, or behave in particular ways. Bargains may also be as implicit and informal as an agreement to avoid profane language around your parents. You may not be aware of some of the implicit, tacit agreements you have with others.

Two researchers in a study on interpersonal bargaining found that three essential features of a bargaining situation exist. They include:

1. The possibility of reaching an agreement in which both parties will be better off, or no worse off, than if no agreement is reached;

2. Both parties perceive that there is more than one agreement which could be reached; and

3. Both parties perceive each other to have conflicting preferences or opposed interests regarding the different agreements which might be reached. (Deutsch & Kraus, 1962, 52).

Some researchers conclude that all relationships are bargaining ones. Thibaut and Kelley believe

> The point should be made . . . that whatever the gratifications achieved in dyads, however lofty or fine the motives satisfied may be, the relationship may be viewed as a trading or bargaining one. The basic assumption running throughout our analysis is that every individual voluntarily enters and stays in any relationship only as long as it is adequately satisfactory in terms of his [sic] rewards and costs (Thibaut & Kelley, 1959).

These writers stress the central role of bargaining in interpersonal relationships and underline a notion of cost-benefit analysis that appears to occur.

Communication includes costs and benefits. When we choose to interact with another person, we are free to select from those behaviors that will have the most positive outcomes for us. In other words, we attempt to maximize the benefits or rewards and minimize the costs. The rewards may be personal gratification, satisfaction of ego needs, or demonstration of status. The costs include anxiety, mental and physical effort, and possible embarrassment.

To illustrate the cost-reward consideration in communication, suppose that you have an acquaintance who is going through the dissolution of her marriage. After she has confided in you and has asked for your understanding, you decide to disclose to her that you, too, had a marriage that ended. You may never have considered talking about your own divorce with her because the relationship had not been very close, and you may have determined that she would have judged you negatively if she had known about this incident. The cost, prior to this interaction, was higher than any potential reward you could determine. After she had disclosed to you, you reassessed the situation and determined that it was appropriate to tell her about your own unsatisfying marriage. In this instance, you perceived the cost (her negative judgment of you) to be minimal, while the reward (her perception of you as someone understanding and experienced in dealing with difficult relationship termination) to be maximized.

Communication begins with self and others simultaneously

Communication begins simultaneously with ourselves and others. Carl Rogers wrote, "Every individual exists in a continually changing world of experience of which he (or she) is the center" (Rogers 1951, 483). All of our communication behavior is viewed from the perspective of ourselves. Chapter 3 discusses the central role of self in communication and stresses the importance of self-awareness and self-concept in communication.

Give and Take

In this exercise you will experience the negotiation inherent to communication. Write down something which another person could do for you that you would enjoy. For example, you might write down that you would like someone to give you a backrub, that you would like someone to type a paper for you, that you would enjoy someone preparing a meal for you, or that you would like someone to babysit for your children. Select a partner from your class with whom to interact. During your conversation, you each need to negotiate your wishes. The other person may want you to go to a movie with him or her and you may want the other person to go on a run with you. Engage in bargaining to gain agreement for both of your goals. For this exercise to work effectively, you must honestly engage in the interaction. In other words, do not simply respond that you will do something unless you actually will engage in the behavior. You may find that you reach agreement fairly quickly if you want something that is relatively easy for the other person to do, but rather slowly if you want something that is relatively difficult for the other person to do, or not at all if you want something which the other person would not, or could not, perform. After your interaction with the other person, discuss what has occurred. What strategies appear to facilitate agreement? What communication attempts appear to result in failure to negotiate? What have you learned about two-person interactions from this exercise?

How does our self-centered perspective affect our communication with others? Dean Barnlund, a communication scholar, suggested that "six people" are actually involved in every "two-person" communicative situation. The six people include (1) how you see yourself; (2) how the other person sees himself or herself; (3) how you see the other person; (4) how the other person sees you; (5) how you believe the other person views you; and (6) how the other person believes you view him or her. Barnlund's model implies that we "create" views of ourselves and of others in our transactions with them (Barnlund 1970).

As we negotiate meaning with others, we need to keep in mind that our skills in establishing common meanings are limited by our unique perspectives. As we describe, explain, and evaluate the communication transactions in which we take part, we reflect a great deal on ourselves. As communicators, we are limited by our own view of the situation. Yet, in another sense, communication begins with others. Although we view communication from our own perspective and with our unique perceptual processes, the self we know is learned from others. George Herbert Mead explains that the self originates in communication. The child, through verbal and nonverbal symbols, learns to accept roles in response to the expectations of others (Mead, 1977). We establish our self-image, the sort of person we believe we are, by the ways other people categorize us. The positive, negative, and neutral messages others offer us enable us to determine who we are. Our self-definition, then, arises through our interactions with others.

Communication also begins with others in the sense that the effective communicator considers the other person's needs and expectations as he or she selects appropriate messages to share. The effective communicator understands that a large number of messages can be shared at any time, but sensitivity and responsiveness to the other communicator is essential. Thus, we observe that communication begins simultaneously with the self (defined by others) and with others (defined by self).

Communication occurs in a context

Communication occurs in a context. We do not communicate in a vacuum. Sometimes we communicate with one other person in an intimate setting; at other times, we communicate with a small number of people in a task-oriented small group; and occasionally we give public speeches to large groups of people. The changes in these contexts affect our communication. We sit, stand, and move differently, depending upon the context. When we are talking to someone we love, we use different words from when we are speaking to a crowd. The levels of formality, the amount of preparation, the places where communication can occur, the topics which are appropriate, and the purposes it serves, all vary as a result of differences in context.

Communication involves codes

Communication involves codes and consists of encoding and decoding. Codes are systematic arrangements or comprehensive collections of symbols with arbitrary meanings and are used in communication. The codes used in our interactions with others may be classified as either verbal or nonverbal. Verbal codes are the words we use and their grammatical arrangement. Nonverbal codes are all the symbols used that are not words; they include bodily movements, space, time, clothing and other adornments, as well as sounds that are not words.

The communication process can be viewed as the process of encoding and decoding. **Encoding** is the act of putting a message or a thought into a code; **decoding** is the assignment of meaning to a message. If you are feeling morose and you want to explain your feelings to a small child, you might encode your message by stating, "I feel sad today," or "I feel like a day when the skies are cloudy, and the rain drizzles all day long." The child would then decode your message by considering the word "sad" or the meaning of a gray day. Your ability to encode your message and the child's ability to decode it are essential in establishing common meanings.

Communication is a transaction

As you considered the example above, you might have felt that the communication process did not sound like a process at all, or that it sounded somewhat slow-moving and artificial. The relationship between encoding and decoding has been viewed in three ways by researchers. Historically, people viewed communication as action. An **action perspective** meant that one person sent a message (encoded) and the other person received it (decoded). This perspective is comparable to a juggler tossing a ball to a second person.

A second, more recent view of communication involves the idea that communication is an **interaction** in which one person sends a message to a second person (encodes), the second person receives it (decodes), and then sends a message back (encodes). When we view communication as an interaction, we perceive communicators taking turns encoding and decoding messages. This point of view is comparable to two jugglers throwing a ball to each other. However, one juggler cannot throw the ball until he or she has caught it from the other person.

The final, most recent perspective on communication is that communication is **transactional.** This point of view suggests that communicators are both receiving (decoding) and sending (encoding) messages. The jugglers each have multiple balls tossed to each other simultaneously. In addition, they might be receiving balls from other sources (the environment, other persons), and they may be sending balls to other sources (to others in the environment, to no one in particular). Finally, some of the balls may be intended for the communicator, yet they may never reach their destination.

When we consider communication to be a transaction, we do not perceive one person to be the sender of messages and another person to be the receiver of messages. Both people are simultaneously senders and receivers, and neither has the status of the initiator of the message. Two communication scholars coined the term "transceivers" (Zelko & Dance, 1965) to describe the communicators in a transactional perspective. According to this point of view, people are continually sending and receiving messages; they cannot avoid communicating with others. This perspective is adopted in this text.

Communication is composed of complementary and symmetrical transactions

Communication transactions are either symmetrical or complementary. Watzlawick, Beavin, and Jackson (1967) in their classic book on communication offer the principle that, "All communicational interchanges are either symmetrical or complementary, depending on whether they are based on equality or difference" (p. 70). They explain that symmetrical interchanges are those where the two people tend to mirror each other's behavior. Complementary interactions occur when one partner's behavior is the complement to the other's. Symmetrical interactions minimize differences, while complementary

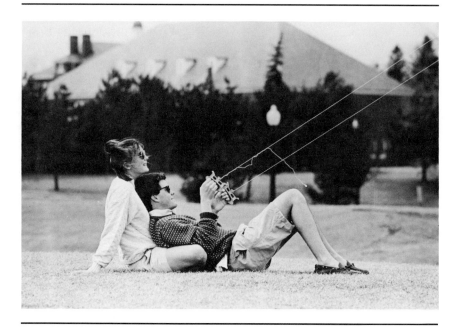

interactions maximize differences. Complementary interactions include communicators who are of different status, within the confines of the interaction. One person is perceived to be superior, primary, or the initiator; the other person is perceived to be inferior, secondary, or the responder. Some complementary interactions occur because of social or cultural norms about various roles. For instance, a doctor may be perceived to be of superior status to her or his patient. A parent may be viewed as superior in an interaction with his or her child. Complementary relationships may also exist in interpersonal exchanges as a result of an implicit agreement between the communicators. One person cannot be superior unless the other agrees to be inferior, and vice versa. The complementary relationship is dependent upon both people engaging in what becomes an interlocking pattern.

Watzlawick, Beavin, and Jackson (1967) emphasize that the symmetrical or complementary definitions of interaction are descriptive and that persons should not associate them with "naturally" good or bad relationships. Either can be satisfying to the participants, and either can be used for good or ill. They conclude that "the symmetry-complementarity paradigm comes perhaps closest to the mathematical concept of function, the individual's positions merely being variables with an infinity of possible values whose meaning is not absolute but rather emerges only in relation to each other" (p. 71).

Women and men both hold a number of stereotyped beliefs about the other sex, and they are both frequently curious about how it might feel to be the other sex. In this exercise you will gain an opportunity to ask questions you have always wondered about, but never felt comfortable asking. First, make a list of questions you would like to ask members of the other sex. Then, share these questions with members of the same sex, creating one master list. After you have completed this, join with all the others and take turns asking each other questions. For example, one of the men and one of the women might serve as spokespersons and take turns asking the questions generated by the individual lists and by the groups. Some examples of questions might be, "How does it feel to be pregnant?" "How do you cope with feelings of emotional inadequacy?" "Do men want to be fathers?" "Do you like to initiate conversations?" "What communication skills are most important for a member of your sex?" Although this exercise may begin in a fairly structured and uncomfortable manner, you will probably find that it loosens up as the discussion ensues. All of the men and all of the women should feel free to add comments about their own feelings; however, individuals should be discouraged from judging the feelings of others. For instance, if a man discloses that he tries to be understanding and sensitive in his relationships with women, none of the women should disagree or argue with him. As you engage in this exercise, observe how **talking** and listening appear to be essential in understanding and relating to others.

To recapitulate the essential features of the definition of communication discussed in this section of the chapter: Communication is the process of bargaining and negotiating meaning which begins with ourselves and others, has costs and benefits, occurs in a context, involves codes and consists of encoding and decoding, is transactional, and occurs in transactions either symmetrical or complementary. This definition with its unique features will guide our understanding of the communication occurring between and among women and men.

Gender and communication research: an historical perspective

One of the continuing threads woven through this chapter has been the idea of the changing nature of our society, resulting in confusion and a certain amount of chaos in relationships between women and men. In the same way, persons who have been interested in understanding, explaining, and predicting communication behaviors between women and men have tried alternative approaches, differing methods, and distinctive philosophies. Let us briefly review the research on gender-related variables and communication.

Early research

The origin of research on gender-related variables in communication probably can be traced to studies in which researchers included biological sex as a category to determine whether or not it affected the particular area of communication under consideration. Most of these studies treated biological sex as an accidental feature, rather than as the primary area of interest in the study (cf. Ball, 1958; Bryan & Wilke, 1942). Further, these studies operated under a paradigm that suggested men and women were, indeed different, and that we should expect to see differences in every instance.

About twenty years ago researchers began to examine biological sex differences in communication as a central concern. During this first wave of research, a number of differences in communication were determined (cf. Bostrom & Kemp, 1968; Brooks, 1974). This work on sex differences in communication proceeded until 1974 when Bem reintroduced the concept of *androgyny*, the internalization of both masculine and feminine characteristics. The term *androgyny* was used by the ancient Greeks with essentially the same meaning, although it had little currency in modern history until Bem rediscovered it.

Bem's approach was to conceptualize masculinity and femininity as two independent dimensions rather than as opposite ends of a continuum. In Bem's system, a person could be high or low in both masculinity and femininity as opposed to the older notion that high levels of one would mean low levels of the other.

Bem approached androgyny, masculinity, and femininity as sex-roles or psychological orientations. Thus, sex-role could be combined with biological sex (as in an androgynous male, a feminine male, a masculine female, etc.) to achieve a more precise measure than the two-part category system afforded. This then represented a paradigm shift, a new way of thinking about men and women. Research in communication after 1974 replaced biological sex with psychological gender-role orientation (cf. Greenblatt, Hasenauer & Freimuth, 1980; Talley & Richmond, 1980).

The Bem Sex-Role Inventory (BSRI: Bem, 1974) was the questionnaire most often used by researchers to measure masculinity, femininity, and androgyny. Criticism of the instrument (cf. Locksley & Colton, 1979; Pedhauzur & Tetenbaum, 1979; Spence, Helmreich & Strapp, 1975; Strahan, 1975; Uleman & Weston, 1986) resulted in the development of new methods of tapping the androgyny component (cf. Heilbrun, 1976; Spence, Helmreich &

Strapp, 1975; Stern, Barak & Gould, 1987; Wheeless & Dierks-Stewart, 1981; Wheeless & Wheeless, 1981). Thus, communication researchers accordingly shifted their understanding of gender-role orientation.

The early studies using psychological gender rather than biological sex appeared to hold some promise. While the use of biological sex resulted in mixed findings, the utilization of the new psychological gender instruments appeared to clarify the findings and sharpen the issues. However, research using gender role began to break down, too, so that people became increasingly unclear about the meaningfulness of their findings. In addition, reexamining all of the previous research on communication by replacing biological sex with psychological gender became tedious and tiresome.

Researchers began to ask themselves about the purpose and goal of their work. They began to realize that the research on gender and communication had little conceptual basis. In other words, after having completed a study, they were no closer to an explanation of people's communication behaviors than before, and could offer no useful or clear predictions. In short, the research did not answer basic questions about women's and men's communication, nor did it point to a purpose to be served once the answers were found.

The theorists and practitioners

Some communication theorists have worked on constructs to provide a theoretical framework for organizing the sex and communication literature. Hart and his associates developed the Rhetorical Sensitivity construct (cf. Hart & Burks 1972; Hart, Carlson & Eadie 1980) and defined the rhetorically sensitive person as one who characterizes herself or himself as a changing, fluctuating person appropriately adapting to situational environmental variations.

Norton (1978) created the Communicator Style construct which offered an integrated scheme for organizing communication behavior into specific-style categories. Among the styles he identified are the dominant, contentious, precise, attentive, friendly, open, relaxed, animated, and dramatic. Of importance in communicator style is the general assessment of the effectiveness of an individual's style of communication.

Other researchers considered the importance of communication competence (Bochner & Kelly, 1974; Brunner & Phelps, 1980; Cegala, 1981; Duran & Wheeless, 1982) which included an element of adaptability or flexibility. In general, these researchers acknowledged the importance of sensitivity to oneself, to the other communicator(s), the context, and the message variables inherent in communication. Overriding these concerns was the importance of flexibility, adaptability, and situational appropriateness.

"I'm paying. I'll taste the wine."

Other researchers tried to integrate several constructs into theories to explain the results of gender and communication studies. Kramarae (1981) suggests four different perspectives: (1) looking at women as a muted group; (2) psychobiological differences; (3) language as a marker of in-group status; (4) or language as a socially situated strategy. These perspectives are advanced for understanding issues of gender and communication.

Gilligan (1982) suggests that, based on different relationships to a female caregiver (mother), boys and girls develop different psychologies and different ways of perceiving the world. By adulthood, the difference is maximized. Men, she claims, think in terms of vertical hierarchies and women in terms of horizontals and webs.

None of these theories is perfectly satisfactory for understanding the array of behaviors we observe in male/female communication. However, researchers continue theorizing to gain a clearer understanding of gender and communication.

At the same time researchers were considering theoretical constructs, practitioners were offering prescriptive advice to people about how they should behave. Some of them simply stated that women and men communicate differently and *vive la difference*. Marabel Morgan's bestseller, *The Total Woman* (1974), for instance, promised fulfillment to women who were willing to limit

24   Fundamentals

"I really enjoyed dinner at your place last night, Marge. Your husband is a marvelous cook."

themselves to stereotypically feminine behaviors. (An excellent rhetorical analysis of *The Total Woman* is available by Solomon, 1981.) More recently, Grant (1988) suggests that being completely feminine is the way for women to find happiness and love.

Others have pointed up the difficulties women in our culture have had in achieving success and have suggested women adopt some male behaviors. For instance, John Molloy's *Dress for Success Book* (1975) and its companion, *The Women's Dress for Success Book* (1977), recommended that men and women dress in prescribed ways which would lead to success in the business world. Women were also encouraged to become more assertive; to say no; to be outspoken, aggressive, and shrewd (cf. Bloom, Copburn & Pearlman, 1975; Briles, 1987; Phelps & Austin, 1975).

Other people observed the highly technological culture and suggested that all of us should adopt women's behaviors. By becoming more cooperative, more emotional, more supportive, and more nurturing, our culture would become qualitatively better. These suggestions were consistent with communication prescriptions for empathic understanding and active listening skills.

The largest group of people, however, suggest we become more behaviorally flexible (cf. Pearson, 1983; Schaef, 1985), i.e., exhibit the ability to change and alter behavior to adapt to new situations and relate in new ways as necessary. Persons who were behaviorally flexible listened actively with empathic understanding when it was appropriate and were similarly able to self-disclose and be assertive in their communication when these communication behaviors were demanded. The competent communicator was sensitive to the other person, or people, with whom she or he was communicating, the situation in which they were communicating, the level of intimacy in the relationship, and other variables. Behavioral flexibility, however, is a difficult skill calling for an attendance to all environmental stimuli, an ability to sort them out, consider alternative behaviors, and then respond appropriately.

The basis of this text

Gender and Communication rests on these historical developments in the study of women's and men's communication. We believe the most useful research in communication dealing with gender variables is well grounded in a philosophy or theory which offers a framework for understanding, explaining, and predicting communication between women and men. We reject the notion that men and women should be encouraged to communicate differently. We support the belief that a continuation of distinctive patterns of communication will encourage the superordinate/subordinate status existing between men and women. We reject the idea that women should simply become men. When women adopt the communication behaviors of men and reject the communication behaviors of their own sex, they limit their behavioral options. Similarly, men who simply adopt the behaviors of women are limited by an incomplete set of communication skills.

We propose that behavioral flexibility holds the most promise for success in communication between women and men; however, we recognize the complexity of the notion of behavioral flexibility. Behavioral flexibility is not simply a matter of selecting "three behaviors from Column A and three behaviors from Column B." It is not merely a matter of mixing a few behaviors from those stereotypically associated with males and females. It does not offer simple prescriptions for complex communicative problems.

Behavioral flexibility requires that each of us develops extensive repertoires of communication skills to provide the tools we need for the complex and varied communication situations we have with others. The development of these skills will allow us to become more effective communicators only if we recognize the basic principles of communication presented in this chapter. We must recognize that communication is the process of negotiating meaning.

None of us alone can determine the meaning of an interaction. We must enter into an exchange with another person to determine a meaning we can share. Similarly, the process notion of communication requires that we continue to redefine and renegotiate shared meanings.

We need to appreciate and understand that communication interaction begins simultaneously with ourselves and with others. We must be sensitive to the sociological characteristics we possess, the stereotypical representations we offer, and the unique personal characteristics affecting our communication with others. Our awareness and appreciation of the various "selves" offered by the other person must be taken into consideration in our interactions with them. The roles we play are largely determined by others; whereas, the roles others play are largely defined by us.

We recognize that communication occurs in a context and that change in context results in changes in communication types. For instance, a married couple who works in the same organization must recognize the differences in appropriate behavior in each context. The influence of other people and environment, alterations occurring because of the passage of time, or changes in culture affect appropriate communication.

We know that communication consists of codes and involves encoding and decoding behaviors. We will see in later chapters that women and men are socialized to learn different sets of codes, and that they may actually decode differently. The essential nature of encoding and decoding in communication, as well as the historical and sociological differences between women and men, must be considered as we observe the communication behavior across these subcultures.

We understand that communication is transactional. We cannot assume that because we have offered a message to another person, they have received it. The other person may not have been able to "catch" our message, may have been preoccupied with "throwing" one of her or his own, or may have been distracted by other bombarding stimuli. Similarly, we can not allow one person to be perceived as the exclusive initiator of ideas, while the other person is viewed as the sole respondent, or receiver of ideas. Both parties can initiate and can respond.

We accept the idea that communication involves costs and rewards, that we risk exposing ourselves, experiencing personal hurt, being frustrated, becoming angry, or feeling embarrassed when we communicate with others. At the same time, we stand to gain a better understanding of ourselves, a better understanding of others, closer personal relationships, and more satisfying occupational careers through our communication.

Finally, we know that communication interactions are either symmetrical or complementary. We recognize that men may be in "one-up" positions in relation to women's "one-down" situations in conversations, just as men and women may be viewed as symmetrical equals. Women may be the superiors in interactions with men as the subordinates. Neither sex should be "naturally" complementary or symmetrical to the other. At the same time, we understand the historical traditions placing men and women in complementary relationships and continuing to affect their relationships.

To the extent this text helps people develop extensive repertoires of communication behaviors not limited by their particular sex, it will have achieved its purpose. To the extent it allows all of us to describe, explain, and predict communication between women and men in the complex, changing world in which we live, it will have met its goal.

Conclusions

In this chapter, you have been introduced to the subject matter of the book. You are now probably more aware of this topic's relevance to you as a communicator. You have examined a variety of ways to use the term "gender," learned about "communication," and combined these two concepts to determine the variety of topics considered here.

Research in the last decade has altered our conceptions of masculinity and femininity, while emphasizing the notion of *androgyny*. Although some changes have occurred in the characterizations of women and men, stereotypical notions still predominate. Communication research and theory in the area of gender-related variables is new and somewhat fragmented. In this text we maintain that behavioral flexibility is the most useful framework in which to consider the communication between women and men.

We are living in a highly exciting time in the history of our culture. New ideas are occurring all around us. The curricula in academic institutions are rapidly changing to meet the need for future career paths. In mass communication, electronic "newspapers" are replacing those printed on papers, and movies of every type are available in people's homes whenever they choose to see them. In interpersonal communication, the changes are no less dramatic. Women and men who were once offered prescriptions for communicating effectively with each other, now find them outdated. Your ability to understand the material in this text and to put into practice the skills suggested will help you create new guidelines for communication helpful to your personal relationships and to the successful accomplishment of your goals.

2 Information processing: gender variation

Introduction

Information processing, or giving meaning to that which comes to us through our senses, is the topic of this chapter. Information processing is a complex process which consists of a number of interrelated activities that allow us to think, learn, and remember.

Many people believe that information processing is different for women and men. Virginia Woolf argued in *A Room of One's Own* (1957) that the creative power of women, though highly developed, "differs greatly from the creative power of men" (p. 91). We have all heard the comment, "She thinks like a man." This comment may be variously interpreted as either praise for a clear-thinking woman, or another example of how women are devalued in language and society. However, regardless of the interpretation, the comment illustrates the underlying assumption that women and men think differently. This belief persists despite much evidence to the contrary. In reviewing cognitive gender differences, the only consistent findings are the following: 1) a small female superiority in verbal abilities; and 2) a small male superiority in quantitative and visual-spatial abilities (Basow, 1986). Even these differences may not be constant. A recent article reports after reviewing 165 studies of gender differences in verbal ability, that there are no significant differences between girls and boys on that variable. The researchers conclude that if girls once had an advantage over boys in verbal skills, boys have caught up by age 11.

In this chapter we will review the sex difference literature in three areas of information processing relevant to communication: perception, listening, and empathy. We will also discuss the controversy that continues as we try to explain sex differences in these areas.

The nature of perception

Perception is a highly complicated process by which we understand ourselves, others, and our environment. We all use our senses to perceive, and most researchers agree that the perceptual process is a creative, interpretive one. People add to and subtract from the stimuli to which they are exposed. Thus, perception is a creative process to which individuals bring their physiological factors, experiences, and present circumstances.

We engage in at least three activities when we perceive a phenomenon: selection, organization, and interpretation. However, we are generally not aware of engaging in separate activities because they occur quickly, almost simultaneously. They do not appear in a neat, linear manner as they are presented here. However, each of these activities is involved in our perceptions of people and events.

Selection

We do not perceive all of the phenomenon in our environment. Instead, we select some stimuli and ignore others. A distant conversation sounds like mumbling until you hear your name mentioned. You have the radio on for an hour, but you can only recall one song. We attend selectively to stimuli, remember selectively, and selectively expose ourselves to stimuli.

Selective attention refers to our tendency to focus on some stimuli and ignore others. If you are in a room in which a number of people are conversing, you may hear only what your conversational partner says, although the voices of the others are loud enough for you to hear. You may hear part of a news broadcast, but miss what a friend tells you at the same time.

Selective retention means that we categorize, store, and retrieve some information, yet fail to categorize, store, or retrieve other information. Consider the first memory you have of your childhood. For many people, the event may have occurred when they were as young as three or four years of age; for others, it may be earlier or later. However, in almost every case, the occurrence was one of significance. You may recall the birth of a baby brother or sister, an accident that occurred, or some other traumatic event. Some research (Furnham & Singh, 1986) indicates that memory is a function of attitudes toward that being remembered. For example, Furnham and Singh found that men and those with more negative attitudes towards women, recalled fewer pro-female and more anti-female items heard on a tape recording; whereas, women and those with more positive attitudes toward women, recalled more favorable items.

Selective exposure means that we tend to seek out stimuli to which we wish to be exposed and avoid coming into contact with stimuli we do not wish to experience. Most investigations considering selective exposure have demonstrated that persons tend to expose themselves to messages consistent with their own attitudes and interests.

However, "boomerang effects" may also occur when people expose themselves to information consistent with their beliefs and attitudes. Paletz, Koon, Whitehead, and Hagens (1972) demonstrated that people who listened to messages consistent with their previously stated attitudes actually became less committed to them than before they heard them. In other words, continual exposure to messages with which we already agree may result in our questioning those agreements. For instance, if you feel that the right to abortion should be available to all women and you regularly attend meetings where speakers espouse this position, you may begin to question your own attitude.

Organization

A second activity in perception is organization. After selecting the stimuli to which we will attend, we attempt to organize it in some way. Some of us are prone to organize stimuli in a linear, logical way, while others will organize stimuli in an holistic manner. To the extent that we organize phenomena differently, we perceive them differently. Some examples may help to clarify this point.

Figure and background method of organization means that we may perceive one thing as the figure, or most important part, and the rest of the stimuli as the background, or less important part. If you glance into a physician's waiting room and observe the receptionist at the desk but do not notice one of your friends is sitting in the room, you are perceiving the receptionist as the figure and the rest of the stimuli in the room as background. Another person less task-oriented and more relationally oriented, might notice the friend but not observe the receptionist.

Closure is a type of organization that calls for us to fill in missing elements or parts. Suppose you sit down in the physician's waiting room and decide to strike up a conversation with one of the other people in the room. You observe that the other person is favoring his or her left arm. You might assume that the person is seeing their physician about an arm injury. While you cannot be certain the arm is injured, you observe the cues and fill in what you believe to be true. Or, you perceive an older couple sitting together and touching each other in a familiar way. Your conclusion? The couple has had a long and happy married life.

Proximity is another method of organizing stimuli and refers to the fact that we group things which appear close together. The couple was perceived to be together because of their physical proximity to each other. Three children playing in the corner in the waiting room are perceived to be siblings because of their grouping together.

Similarity means that we organize stimuli because of resemblance in size, color, shape, or other attributes. You may notice that the little children playing together in the waiting room are all blonde and brown-eyed and, therefore, conclude that this is further evidence they are siblings. When you meet someone who shares your economic views, you may assume that person will also appreciate your taste in music or clothing.

Perceptual constancy as an organizational principle refers to the idea that we tend to maintain the same perception of a phenomenon over time. You might have a view of your parents when they were ten years younger or have a picture of the house that you grew up in, which is quite different from the actual house. This principle explains why it is so difficult for us to change our perception of another person even when that individual has changed. If you

Proximity provides us information about the relationships between and among people.

have a friend who used to be chemically dependent and behaved in inconsistent ways, you may have trouble adapting to new, consistent behavior, even though the new behavior is preferable. You may still worry about whether he or she will show up on time, whether he or she will go to work, attend classes, and fulfill other commitments. A long period of time may pass before you trust the changes your friend has made.

We risk error when we organize stimuli. We may find that the person favoring his or her arm in the physician's waiting room had just received an allergy injection in the arm and was waiting to determine whether he or she would have a reaction; or that the arm injury was a congenital birth defect, and the person was waiting to see the doctor about the stomach flu. The couple in the waiting room may have only recently met; may be living together, but not be married; or may be siblings rather than a married couple. People who are similar in some ways may be very different in others; besides, people do change over time.

After we have selected and organized stimuli, we interpret it. Interpretation is perhaps more creative than is selection and organization. Generally, the more ambiguous the stimuli, the more room there is for creativity in our interpretation of it. When we meet a new person in an unfamiliar place, we have more freedom to interpret what the person may be like than we do when she or he is introduced to us by a friend who provides information about this individual.

Both context and comparison are used in our interpretation of stimuli. If we meet a new person in a class, we assume that he or she is a student, is interested in the subject matter of the course (unless it simply fulfills a requirement), and has certain attitudes and beliefs shared by many college students. The context of the classroom helps you to draw these conclusions, although they may be incorrect. Similarly, you use the method of comparison to draw conclusions about the person, observing whether she or he looks older than the other students, appears to be more alert, and is more talkative. You may decide that she or he is a returning student, intelligent, and friendly. Again, you could be incorrect, but you are using the method of comparison to draw these conclusions.

Gender differences in perception

Harris (1984) asserts that since perception is the creative process we have described, dependent on individual differences, past experiences and present circumstances, we would expect women and men to perceive differently. Although sex differences in information processing is not an area that communication researchers have studied extensively, some evidence of difference exists in other disciplines. For example, some studies indicate that there are differences in males' and females' color preferences, with females preferring yellow to orange and males having the reverse preference. Men seem more constant in color preference than women, who fluctuate somewhat from year to year (Harris, 1984). Further, Oeser (1932) and Caldwell (1982) found that women are more influenced by color than form, while men are more influenced by form than color in making interpretations.

In addition, some studies have looked at preferences for complexity versus simplicity in stimuli. In general, females preferred more complexity than males (Eisenman & Johnson, 1969; Looft & Baranowski, 1971). Andrews' (1985) findings offer some application for women's apparent preference for complexity. Andrews asked people to read "The Kidney Machine" problem where five candidates are vying for one spot on a life-preserving kidney machine. Participants read the descriptions for the five candidates and were told to choose one based on age and emotional stability. Then they were to present to a judge an oral argument for their choice.

Andrews observed that men were more likely than women to stick to the stated criteria when they made their arguments. Women made fewer references to the criteria and, when they did refer to them, it was often to take exception to them. Andrews suggests that "complex decision making often requires one to forsake rules and procedures[,] . . . to question them if they seem to be standing in the way of a sound, equitable or humane decision" (pp. 22–23). In this instance, for good or ill, women respondents preferred to consider the problem less literally, and more complexly than the men did.

Some research in literary criticism and theory (Flynn, 1983; Schweickart, in press) indicates that women and men read, and thus, process information differently. Flynn notes that women are more receptive to the text than men. Bleich (cited in Dobris, 1986) suggests that men are more literal in reading than women, who tend to enter the world of a novel and are, therefore, freer to include inferences when retelling the story. Bleich believes his findings point to perceptual differences between the sexes.

Finally, Fabes and Laner (1986) found that men and women tend to perceive each other differently, at least in terms of relative advantages and disadvantages. They found that, although males and females perceived the same number of advantages for each other, males perceived significantly more disadvantages for females than females did for males.

Largely, perception is a complex process in which men and women seem to differ somewhat. We will now turn our attention to a specific perceptual component—listening.

Listening

The nature of listening

We defined **perception** as the process of experiencing stimuli through any one of our five senses. **Listening** focuses exclusively on hearing: the process of receiving and interpreting aural stimuli. All the factors discussed relevant to perception are equally applicable to our understanding of listening. In listening, we attend selectively to some sounds and ignore others; we recall some things we have heard and forget others; we expose ourselves to particular aural messages and avoid others. We organize the sounds that we hear into meaningful units. For instance, when someone asks, "Are you going?" we may fill in the object of the sentence and conclude they are asking whether we are going to the football game, thus using the principle of "closure." Or, we may use figure and background to determine that the words, "Are you going" are not as relevant as the frustrated manner in which the question is stated. Finally, we interpret what we hear in creative ways.

As you can see, listening is just as complex as other types of perception and involves far more than simply hearing a sound. Hearing is a natural, physiological function all can perform, unless we suffer from a physical deficit. Listening is an activity involving both the physiological reception and the psychological interpretation of aural stimuli. Contemporary researchers are trying to determine the specific skills involved in listening (cf. Bostrom & Bryant, 1980). The complexity of listening is apparent as you consider your own experiences. You may have heard a popular song a dozen times, but never have listened to the words. You may hear the content of what another person has to say, but not understand adequately the intent of his or her message. Listening is also complex because we engage in it for a variety of reasons: appreciation, discrimination, comprehension, evaluation, empathy, and therapy (cf. Wolff, Marsnik, Tacey & Nichols, 1983; Wolvin & Coakley, 1982).

Listening is a fundamental component of communication that engages a great deal of our time. One classic study found that we spend more than 40 percent of our time listening (Rankin, 1926). Contemporary studies have found that we listen to a greater extent than we engage in any other form of communication. Weinrauch and Swanda (1974) found that business personnel, including those with and without managerial responsibilities, spend nearly 33 percent of their time listening, almost 26 percent of their time speaking, nearly 23 percent of their time writing, and almost 19 percent of their time reading. When Werner (1975) investigated the communication activities of high-school and college students, homemakers, and employees in a variety of other occupations, he determined that they spent 55 percent of their time listening, and only 23 percent speaking, 13 percent reading, and 8 percent writing.

If these studies were to be repeated today, with the addition of various forms of mass communication, the listening quotient might even be larger. We spend time listening to people in social situations, classrooms, and at work. We listen to the radio, the television, records, cassette tapes, movies, cable programs, and word synthesizers. Thus, a large portion of our time is spent in listening.

Gender differences in listening

A common impression is that men do not listen well to women. In an article on listening for *Ms.* magazine, Chassler (1984) recalls that his wife sent him to the ear doctor because she suspected he was hard of hearing. After the doctor told him his hearing was perfect, Chassler said that he had only come because of his wife. The doctor responded, "Most of my male patients . . . are here on the advice of their wives" (p. 99).

However, at this time, the research evidence is inconclusive as to whether men or women are better listeners. The findings of a few studies have suggested that men and women do not differ significantly in their listening behavior (Buchli & Pearce, 1974; Hollow, 1956; King, 1959). While the findings of a few others have suggested that women have better listening skills than men (Lundsteen, 1963; Palamatier & McNinch, 1972; Winter, 1966). A preponderance of research findings suggest that men's listening skills are superior (Caffrey, 1955; Goldhaber & Weaver, 1968; Hampleman, 1958; Irvin, 1953; Nichols, 1948; Winter, 1966). We hasten to add, however, that while these studies suggest that men are better listeners, there are many limitations associated with the listening research done to date. First, most of these studies have relied on paper-and-pencil tests, the validity of which has been seriously challenged (Bostrom & Waldhart, 1980).

Another problem with listening research has been the lack of consistency in research participants used in the studies. Some of the studies have used elementary-school children, while others have used high-school or college students. Inasmuch as it is unclear whether the listening abilities of these populations are the same, or if gender differences in listening abilities change developmentally, it is unwise simply to lump findings together from disparate studies.

Because of the concerns we have about the ways listening abilities have been measured in research and the difficulty in generalizing across different participant populations, we do not know at this time whether one sex is consistently and substantively better at listening than the other. Weaver (1972) argues that men and women may listen differently; men listen to find out how to solve a specific recognizable problem, while women listen to understand something they did not understand before.

This notion of males' goal orientation is illustrated in a listening study. College students were told to listen to one of two stories presented simultaneously. When they were tested on their assigned story, males were found to extract more information than females (Halley, 1975). The study shows that females were more easily distracted by the irrelevant story, while males were more goal-oriented. Although women are more easily distracted by competing details, men focus only on certain segments and ignore others. Males tend to restructure observations in terms of their own goals, whereas, females tend to accept the pattern as it is to determine relationships. The female hears more of a message because she rejects less of it, while the male derives more coherent meaning from the message because he is building a structure of the general message as he listens. In addition, the female style allows emotions and unclear impressions to govern selective attention more than the male style.

How do these differences in listening behavior affect our interactions? A recent situation illustrates the effect. One evening another couple was sitting with the first author and her husband in the family room watching television. The other woman was doing some needlepoint which she always carried with her in her oversized bag. She was also "listening for" the front door to open, which would mean that some of the children had come back from a neighborhood park. She also "heard" the sound the coffee pot makes when it is done brewing, since she immediately asked if anyone wanted a second cup of coffee. After she returned with the coffee, she asked her husband about the movie's plot. He seemed annoyed and suggested she watch the movie if she wanted to follow the fairly complex plotline. A little later she seemed exasperated when he did not hear the children return from the park. Was either member of the couple a poor listener? No, they were simply demonstrating the listening differences between women and men which occur daily.

Empathy

The nature of empathy

Given that perceptions can differ markedly from person to person, **empathy** is the skill of understanding another's perceptions. When someone asks you to put yourself "in his or her shoes," that person is figuratively asking you to empathize with him or her. In the 1920s, research on empathy was performed by physiological measures of muscle tension and movement. The concept has changed from that time, and empathy is now regarded as a perceptual variable.

Our ability to measure empathy has changed as the meaning of the term has altered. When empathy was defined as a physical response to stimuli, it was a relatively easy matter to measure. But when we define it as a perceptual variable, we encounter the same problems in measurement we observed in the listening literature. Pearson and Spitzberg (1990) have explained the complexity of empathy as it is currently conceptualized:

> First, you must be sensitive to yourself and be able to vividly recall your past experiences. Empathy involves the process of recalling our past emotions and feelings in order to see common experiences with others. Second, you must be able to recall how particular feelings were translated into behaviors for you. To the extent that we can relate particular behaviors to specific feeling states within ourselves, we can recognize the same or similar behaviors suggesting shared feelings. Third, you must be a sensitive perceiver of those cues offered to you by another person. The empathic person is alert to subtle, as well as blatant, cues in the environment. An empathic person possesses insight, perseptiveness, and social acuity. Fourth, you must be able to separate your own intellectually reflective response and your emotional or feeling response from those of the person with whom you are empathizing, and hold your responses in temporary suspension. In other words, inferences about self and others are kept distinct. Fifth, you must interpret the available cues assisted by your past knowledge of the other person, similar experiences, and cognitive ability. The empathic person is able to generate creative hunches. Adequate explanations, and correct inferences. Finally, you must communicate your understanding to the other person through clear and specific feedback (pp. 220–21).

As you examine this list of skills, you begin to understand the complexity and difficulty of responding empathically to others.

Too often we assume that other people perceive the world in exactly the same way we do, or, at least, in a very similar manner. However, great variations in perception exist particularly between people of different subcultures. There are countless ways in which women and men are socialized differently in our culture, and how the two sexes consequently perceive the world differently. At the same time, empathy is a particularly important skill to have when we wish to communicate effectively with a person of different perceptions. Let us consider some of the differences in empathic ability that have been identified in the literature.

Gender differences in empathy

If you surmised that women are more empathic than men, you are not alone. Generally, women are perceived as more sensitive and perceptive empathizers than men. The literature, however, is less simplistic in its implications.

Maccoby and Jacklin (1974) argue that while measures of empathy have been limited, the available evidence would indicate men and women do not differ significantly in their empathic ability. In addition, at least two subsequent studies failed to find significant differences in men's and women's empathic ability (Brehm, Powell & Coke, 1984; Breisinger, 1976). In fact, when gender differences have been noted, it has sometimes been the male research participants who have evidenced greater empathy, as in MacDonald's (1977) findings indicating that male nurses evidenced greater empathy than female nurses. MacDonald's study also indicated that the male nurses were more empathic than males who were not also nurses, which might imply that the job required the development of empathic ability or that men oriented toward jobs requiring empathy were disproportionately represented in the research sample. That people learn empathy as a function of employment demands is clearly indicated in research demonstrating that people are best able to decode non-verbal communication if they are employed in positions requiring nurturing, expressiveness, or artistic ability. Furthermore, this finding obtains both for men as well as women (Rosenthal, Archer, DiMatteo, Koivumaki & Rogers, 1974).

Some evidence indicates that males and females achieve empathy in different ways. Hughey (1984) found that when males were talking to other males, they were more successful empathizers after they adapted to their partner. In female pairs, trust-gaining was the best method for succeeding at empathy.

Psychological gender may be a better predictor of the skill of empathy than biological sex (Bem, 1975). Bem asked students to listen to the apparently spontaneous conversation of another person (who was actually a confederate delivering a prepared statement). When the confederate disclosed

The goals of empathy include accepting ourselves and accepting others. However, stereotypes affect our ability to empathize with others. For instance, if you believe men are insensitive, you may never express intimate feelings because you think they won't understand them. Or if you think women are overly emotional, you may refrain from sharing highly emotional information with them for fear they cannot cope with it adequately.

This exercise will help you understand stereotypes which you may have, and will provide an opportunity to demonstrate empathy to another person. Before you are paired off, write down at least five sex-typical behaviors in which you engage and at least five sex-atypical behaviors in which you engage. For instance, you might include knitting, sewing, or cooking as sex-typical behaviors if you are a woman, and weight lifting, sports-car racing, and bartending as sex-atypical behavior. Men might include jogging, motorcycle racing, and small-motor repair as sex-typical behavior, and babysitting, crocheting, and baking as sex-atypical behaviors. With your partner, take turns sharing your lists of activities. You will probably find that your partner can easily understand why you participate in the sex-typical behaviors, but may have some difficulty understanding why you pursue some of the sex-atypical activities. Try to explain why you engage in the sex-atypical behaviors to your partner's satisfaction until you feel that he or she genuinely understands your behavior. As you listen to your partner discuss his or her behaviors, try to demonstrate empathy. Consider the complexity of empathy and the number of steps involved. Consciously attempt to go through these steps, demonstrating sincere and honest understanding for the other person's behaviors.

With the entire class, discuss your feelings about this exercise. Did you find it relatively easy or difficult to demonstrate empathy? Why or why not? Did you learn anything about your own communication skills? What stereotypes tended to interfere in your ability to understand the other person? What steps in the empathy process seemed particularly difficult for you? Which steps were relatively easy? How can you improve your ability to empathize with members of the same and other sex? This exercise can be repeated so that each person has an opportunity to interact with members of the same sex and members of the other sex. Results can be compared and contrasted to determine whether empathy is more difficult or easier when discussing sex-atypical behaviors with people of your own gender or those of the other sex.

"I'm married. I have three sons. My boss is a man. I sell Jockey shorts. And I just need a woman to talk to!"

personal problems, the investigators recorded the number of times each student listener nodded or made sympathetic comments. The more traditionally feminine female participants, as measured by Bem's sex-role inventory, reacted with greater concern (empathy) than did female participants having a less traditional orientation. Further research indicates that more androgynous individuals are more empathic—regardless of their biological sex—than less androgynous individuals (Fong & Borders, 1985; Watson, 1976), although training can improve the empathy skills of people of other psychological genders.

Explanations

In review, research has demonstrated some differences between women and men in perception, listening, and empathy. Although these differences are not always pronounced, women and men differ somewhat in color preference and color-versus-form preference. Women prefer more complexity in stimuli than men, and women tend to make more inferences when perceiving stimuli than men. Finally, men and women perceive each other somewhat differently, with men perceiving significantly more disadvantages for women than vice versa.

Despite prevalent stereotypes, the evidence is unclear as to whether men or women are better listeners. Women and men may listen differently, with women concentrating on detailed understanding and men focusing on picking up information to allow them to reach a goal. In terms of empathy, men and women may not differ significantly, although psychological gender may be associated with differences in the skill. Feminine females and androgynous individuals seem to be the most empathic listeners, although anyone can be trained to become a more skillful empathizer.

Researchers have searched for explanations for these findings. In Chapter 1, we noted that both biology and culture (i.e., nature and nurture) affect people's behavior. The relative importance of physiological and psychological factors has been the subject of much debate. Often, people who believe that women and men are more different than alike rely on physiological explanations of differences. Those who believe that women and men are more similar than different emphasize the importance of socialization and psychological differences which are learned rather than "natural." Contemporary theorists now agree that both "nature" and "nurture" affect our behavior; hence, it is unreasonable for us to deny either perspective and its potential for explaining behavior.

Brain differences

A biological hypothesis proposed to explain sex differences in information processing concerns brain differences. Researchers have explored the differences between the female and male brain and tried to apply them to an explanation of sex-related cognitive differences. This is an extremely controversial area, especially in the field of communication. The conclusions reviewed here are tentative and not universally accepted. They operate from an assumption of difference, which many people find objectionable, and they are often based on questionable procedures (Halpern, 1986). There are essentially no anatomical differences between the brains of males and females (Halpern, 1986), although there are some sex-related differences that are irrelevant to cognitive functioning. For example, menstruation in women begins as a brain event.

Table 2.1 Hemispheric processes

Left Hemisphere	Right Hemisphere
Analytical	Analogical
Abstract	Appositional
Convergent	Artistic
Causal	Coincidental
Deductive	Divergent
Exclusive	Depressive
Linear	Holistic
Logical	Idealistic
Manic	Imaginative
Mathematical	Inclusive
Propositional	Inductive
Rational	Intuitive
Realistic	Multiple
Sequential	Simultaneous
Singular	Synthetic
Symbolic	Temporally cyclic
Temporally linear	Visually imaginative
Verbal	Visual-spatial

However, some differences have been discovered with regard to brain development. Brain growth in children, as measured by head circumference, occurs in spurts rather than at a regular, steady rate. (cf. Eichorn & Bayley, 1962; Epstein, 1978; Telzrow, 1981). Sometimes periods of rapid growth are followed by periods of slow growth, and occasionally by plateau periods. It appears that male and female children experience different patterns of brain growth. For example, between the ages of ten and twelve, girls' head growth is about twice that of boys, but the situation is reversed at around fifteen years of age (Epstein, 1978). These developmental differences have proven to be highly useful to persons in speech pathology, language development, and educational curricular decision making (cf. Telzrow, 1981; Sonnier, 1982).

However, except for this developmental difference, male and female brains do not differ significantly. Males and females have brains of approximately the same complexity. Male brains are slightly larger and heavier than female brains because brain size is positively correlated with body size and men, on the average, tend to be larger than women.

However, the area that has been of interest to brain researchers concerns differentiating the functions of the right- and left-brain hemispheres of the cerebral cortex. Since the mid-nineteenth century when language was found to be localized in the left hemisphere of the brain (Walsh, 1978), attempts have been made to identify brain areas which serve specific functions. Until recently, the implications of such research were relatively unexplored.

The two sides of the cerebral cortex (the left brain and the right brain or the left side and the right side), are connected by a large set of neural fibers known as the corpus callosum. It has been hypothesized that each side of the brain serves different functions, so that the two hemispheres contribute differently to the perception of information organization. The purpose of hemispheric specialization is thought to be an improvement in the efficiency of the human organism since information may be processed more expediently due to the brain's "division of labor" (Dimond, 1978).

What are the two sets of functions of the brain? The left side of the brain processes information in a logical, sequential, analytic way, which is particularly well suited to language-related functions (Wittrock, 1978). Thus, the left hemisphere is known as the "verbal" hemisphere. Consistent with this explanation, persons who experience stroke, tumor, or other left-hemisphere trauma frequently lose their ability to comprehend or produce language, to read or interpret written symbols (Lesak, 1976).

The right side of the brain interprets information in a holistic, gestalt manner, frequently involving a visual-spatial organizational structure. Persons who experience right-hemisphere damage have difficulty perceiving wholes, locating their position in space (as in map reading), copying figures accurately, and also have difficulty appreciating or understanding aesthetics, including art and music (Lesak, 1976). A summary of the processes of the left and right hemispheres appears in Table 2.1.

Approximately 95 percent of all right-handed people control verbal and analytic functions from the left hemisphere of the brain and spatial, holistic, and nonverbal functions from the right hemisphere. The percentage is somewhat smaller for left-handed people (Halpern, 1986; Reeves, Lang, Thorson & Rothschild, 1988).

In some people the two hemispheres of the brain do not develop to the same extent. Some persons have larger left hemispheres while others have larger right hemispheres. Investigations of elementary-school children demonstrate that some are "left-hemisphere learners" who demonstrate an above-average verbal proficiency, but who also have poorer visual-spatial skills, and experience some difficulty in generating images. At the same time, "right-hemisphere learners" have delayed language development, may demonstrate reading and spelling problems, but have average or superior visual-spatial skills (Hartlage 1980). In research on dyslexia and other brain-related disorders, evidence has appeared which seems to indicate that the larger hemisphere of the brain frequently takes over and minimizes the contribution of the other hemisphere (Witelson, 1977).

Table 2.2 Modes of information processing

Analytic	Holistic	Gestalt
1. Predominantly left brain	1. Combined left and right brain	1. Predominantly right brain
2. Data are processed sequentially	2. Data are processed sequentially and simultaneously	2. Data are processed simultaneously
3. Process is within awareness	3. Process is out of awareness	3. Process may be in or out of awareness
4. Process is symbolic, partial, and quantitative	4. Process combines symbolic and signal functions	4. Process is nonsymbolic and nonquantitative
5. Data are processed systematically	5. Products of random right-brain activity are systematized	5. Data are processed randomly

One writer, explaining brain functions in information processing, has stated.

it is hypothesized that three modes of data processing are possible within the brain. One mode is analytical processing which is essentially left hemisphere, one mode is Gestalt processing which is essentially right hemisphere, and a third mode is holistic which involves an interaction between the two hemispheres (Powers-Ross, 1978).

The three modes of information processing are summarized in Table 2.2 (Howell, 1982).

Gender differences in brain lateralization

Since the specialties of the two hemispheres roughly conform to the sex differences found in cognitive processing and verbal and spatial skills, psychologists have suggested that the sexes may differ in the way their hemispheres process information (Kimura, 1985).

Initially, two competing theories were proposed to explain how these differences operated. One theory (Buffery & Gray, 1972) suggested that men were more bilateral, allowing better development of spatial skills. The second theory (Levy, 1976) argued just the opposite.

Specifically, Levy (1976) argued that women excel in verbal skills because they are more bilateral than men. This means they better integrate their left and right hemispheres in learning and thinking. Men are more strongly lateralized than women, possibly because of high levels of fetal hormones (Levy & Gur, 1980). Strong lateralization is associated with high spatial performance (Levy & Reid, 1978). Of the two theories, Levy's has been favored by the majority of research (i.e., Restak, 1979; Tan-William, 1981).

However, Levy's ideas have been quite controversial and have not received unqualified support from the empirical evidence. For example, Mc-Keever and Van Deventer (1977) failed to find the expected effects for verbal and spatial tasks. Some research (e.g., Harshman, Hampson & Berenbaum 1983) has indicated that reasoning or intellectual ability is an important mediating variable Levy neglected to examine. Further, Kimura (1985) suggests that how bilateral women's brains are might depend on the type of task being considered.

Basow (1986) points to a political aspect of this research. Although science is supposed to be value-free, we conduct science in a political and cultural context. This context may determine the questions asked and the interpretation of the answers.

Since we live in a culture where men dominate, this may affect our understanding of brain-difference research. When

> the frontal lobes of the brain were regarded as the main area of intellectual functioning, research studies found men had larger frontal lobes, relative to the parietal lobes, than did women. When parietal lobes were regarded as more important, the findings themselves changed. Men now were 'found' to have relatively larger parietal lobes, relative to their frontal lobes than did women. Today, there is no firm evidence of sex differences in brain structures or proportions, so interest has turned to sex differences in brain organization, following a predictable pattern. When men were thought to be less lateralized than women, that was thought to be superior. When men were thought to have more brain lateralization than women, that then was thought to be superior (Basow, 1986, p. 22).

As a result of these issues associated with brain-difference research, we turn to other explanations for sex differences in information processing.

Social and psychological differences

Some evidence exists that support the explanation that the cognitive differences between women and men are due to psychosocial pressures to conform to sex-role stereotypes. First of all, some studies have shown that differences in spatial abilities between the sexes can be removed or diminished by training.

Sprafkin, Serbin, and Connor (1983) found, with preschoolers, that children who received special training with typical "boys' toys" (blocks, dominoes, tinker toys, and paper cut in geometric shapes) scored higher on a test of visual-spatial ability than children who did not receive the training. Connor, Serbin, and Schackman (1978) found that sex differences in spatial abilities in first graders disappeared after training. Brinkmann (1966) reported similar findings using eighth graders.

Bradshaw and Nettleton (1983) reviewed the literature on cognitive sex differences and concluded that verbal abilities are even more subject to social influences than spatial abilities. Girls may channel their achievement needs into the verbal area when they find that math and science courses are closed to them.

Halpern (1986) observes that girls' dominance in verbal skills and boys' dominance in spatial abilities may simply be the result of early strategies boys and girls have learned which have become dominant in their repertoires. Girls may be less successful at spatial tasks because they have not developed spatial strategies and rely, instead, on verbal strategies to accomplish spatial tasks. The opposite would be the case for boys and verbal skills. Thus, cognitive sex differences are not biologically determined but are the result of socially reinforced strategy choices.

Finally, the findings that psychological gender is a more precise predicator of empathy skills than biological sex argues for a "nurture" explanation of differences. Psychological gender, you will remember, is the result of internalizing socially accepted traits for masculinity and femininity. As Hoffman (1977) notes, the messages imposed by our culture advise that empathy is appropriate feminine behavior. Basow (1986) comments that females report more empathy than males on self-report measures, but do not show more empathy than males when observational measures are used. Since self-reports can be biased by the respondent's desire to answer in a socially appropriate fashion, this result is best explained by social expectations, not biological differences.

Conclusions

In this chapter we examined the role of information processing in the communication of women and men. We discussed the two substantiated cognitive differences between the sexes: verbal ability and spatial ability. We examined the information processing skill of perception, which includes the selection, organization, and interpretation of stimuli. We selectively attend to, recall, and expose ourselves to stimuli in our environment. We organize that stimuli in a variety of ways, and in doing so, are influenced by such processes as figure and ground, closure, perceptual constancy, proximity, and similarity. Interpretation frequently relies upon context and comparison. We may make errors at any of these stages in the perceptual process. Perceptions vary as a result of physiological factors, including gender, past experiences, present feelings, and circumstances. However, the documented gender differences in perception are relatively slight.

Next we turned our attention to the listening process and discovered that listening is a complex area of perception. Studies which have considered listening differences between women and men have been impaired or invalidated by questionable definitions of the concept and by even more doubtful ways of measuring performance. It appears that women and men listen differently, but no conclusions can be drawn as to whether one gender or the other listens better.

We considered empathy, an area in which women are believed to excel. Traditional female occupations, such as nursing, teaching, and parenting, require high levels of empathy. However, empathy can be learned, and the research does not show that women are actually better at empathy than men. Feminine- and androgynous-typed individuals may be most empathic.

Finally, we looked at competing explanations for the differences we found in male/female information processing. Both biologically and sociologically based explanations have some support in the literature. However, neither alone does a satisfactory job of explaining all of the findings. It would be more profitable for researchers to construct new frameworks and ask slightly different questions in the future. For example, instead of asking whether sex differences are best explained by nature or nurture, we might try to explore sex differences more closely. Perception, listening, and empathy are all composed of component parts. Perhaps women and men differ in some parts but not in others. As we gain more insight into the precise nature of cognitive sex differences, we should be better able to explain them. We need to keep in mind that in our review of the literature, men and women do not differ as much as conventional wisdom would have us believe. In many instances, she thinks like a man, and he thinks like a woman because they both think alike.

3 The self-perceptions of women and men

III. Developing self-esteem
  A. Effects on men's and women's self-esteem
  B. Other variables affecting self-esteem

C. Making changes
  1. Nontraditional social learning can affect self-views

IV. Conclusions

Introduction

In the first chapter we said that communication occurs simultaneously between self and others. The views we hold of ourselves and others hold of us are fundamental to the communication process. These views serve as benchmarks from which to gauge the appropriateness and probable success of our communication efforts. Accordingly, it is important to understand how our self-views as women and men develop. Our **self-concept** involves an evaluation of all we think we have been, are, and aspire to be. Our self-concept includes tangible features, including physical measurements and descriptions of our body size and type, as well as our judgments of the appropriateness of our values and desires. In brief, our self-concept is the sum total of our assessment of the "I" that represents individuality. To a very significant degree the self-concept is determined by the interactions others have with us, as it is in the reactions that others have to us that we gauge something about who we are. In a very real sense it is impossible to think of our self-concept apart from the interactions others have with us (Mead, 1977).

The self-concept is sometimes discussed in terms of two components: self-image and self-esteem. **Self-image** consists of all those aspects of self described physically or which pertain to the roles we play in our lives. Naturally, when describing our self-image we tend to describe those features we think are particularly important at the time. For instance, a well-known author on a television interview might mention that he or she has written four new books, graduated from a Midwestern university, and has received a coveted award. She or he might not mention other aspects of her or his image, which they judge to be less relevant to the context of the interview, such as being married, being a grandparent, liking pets, and so forth.

Self-esteem concerns the value we place on the images we have of ourselves. If we add to our self-description that we feel pleased about the way we have juggled our career and family responsibilities, disappointed in not being able to deal well with criticism, or comment about the difficulty we have had in withstanding job pressures, then we are referring to self-esteem. Directly or indirectly, all the above comments reflect some evaluation we have of our self with reference to goals we value. To a significant degree, self-esteem is influenced by evaluative information received from others. We may receive this information directly, i.e., your boss says you are doing a great job at work, or indirectly, i.e., you contrast the beautifully kept home of a working woman on a television drama with your own. It is a problem of contemporary society that many women maintaining full-time jobs and assuming responsibility for rearing children are distressed and depressed when they evaluate their role performance. The myth of the "super mom" exerts much negative influence on many women's self-esteem.

"You don't realize how eighteen years with that large, impersonal corporation has changed you, Fred."

COCHRAN.

Reprinted courtesy Penthouse Magazine © 1990.

Interestingly, self-image and self-esteem seem not to be correlated. A physically attractive and accomplished physician may have low self-esteem, despite the fact that in this culture she or he would be evaluated positively. You may remember reading the poem "Richard Corey." This poem is about a man who was the envy of his neighbors and who seemed to "have it all"— wealth, looks, status—yet committed suicide, illustrating the lack of correlation between self-image and self-esteem.

We will examine both self-image and self-esteem in some detail below, as we try to understand how women and men develop and maintain self-perceptions.

The development of self-images

We have two sources of information contributing to our self-images as men and women, one based on biology, the other based on how we are socialized into a culture which prescribes normative definitions of masculinity and femininity for us.

cathy®

by Cathy Guisewite

Biological information

For most of us, how we initially develop images of ourselves as women or men seems to be fairly straightforward. We determine by comparing our bodies with others that we are more like one biological sex than the other and quickly come to understand that, biologically speaking, we are either male or female. Because of issues discussed in Chapters 1 and 2, most scholars reject the idea that self-image is directly biologically programmed. Instead, we turn to socialization to understand the development of the self.

Socialization

From birth it is clear that male and female babies are treated differently, not only in our culture, but also in others as well (Williams & Best, 1982). In our own culture we dress male and female babies in different-colored clothing and parents treat them quite differently (Bell & Carver, 1980; Moss, 1970). We even describe them differently. Male infants are more likely than female infants to be described as "strong," "solid," or "independent." Female infants, on the other hand, are often described as "loving," "cute," and "sweet" (Condry & Condry, 1976). That gender typing occurs at such an early stage in our development is ample evidence of the importance placed on gender as an "interaction marker," i.e., a message that influences how we orient ourselves toward interaction with others and how we anticipate others will react to us.

Since gender prescriptions are so pervasive, it is surprising that children do not develop specific gender-role orientations any earlier than they do. It appears that before three years of age children are still extremely flexible in their gender orientation. Little boys have not yet learned to do only "little boy" things; little girls have not yet learned to do only "little girl" things (Seegmiller 1980). Between the ages of five and seven, gender constancy (the tendency to see oneself consistently as male or female) appears to develop in most

Table 3.1 Masculine and feminine scale items (Heilbrun, 1976)

Masculine Items		Feminine Items	
Aggressive	Hard-headed	Appreciative	Helpful
Arrogant	Industrious	Considerate	Jolly
Assertive	Ingenious	Contented	Modest
Autocratic	Inventive	Cooperative	Praising
Conceited	Masculine	Dependent	Sensitive
Confident	Opportunistic	Emotional	Sentimental
Cynical	Outspoken	Excitable	Sincere
Deliberate	Self-confident	Fearful	Submissive
Dominant	Sharp-witted	Feminine	Sympathetic
Enterprising	Shrewd	Fickle	Talkative
Forceful	Stern	Forgiving	Timid
Foresighted	Strong	Friendly	Warm
Frank	Tough	Frivolous	Worrying
Handsome	Vindictive		

children (Tibbetts, 1975). From this time on girls and boys begin to develop different communication behaviors, including differences in language usage, although these differences are not attributed to differences in innate development or maturation (Price & Graves, 1980). Martin and Craig (1983) as well as Fishman (1978) argue that these differences are learned by children acting in accordance with others' expectations. The implication, of course, is that parents, teachers, and other caretakers guide our development of gender orientation. It is so important that the "proper" orientation be learned that we do not leave things to chance. We guide our young ones every step of the way.

However, males tend to be more rigid in their sex-typing than are females. For example, when told before they actually performed a task that "girls do this task better," boys then went on to do the task less well than little girls doing tasks described to them as ones in which boys excelled (Gold & Berger, 1978; Lane, 1983). The intensity with which little boys reject female-typed behavior is thought to be associated with the considerable effort boys make in differentiating themselves from their mothers, who have been, and still are, the primary caretakers of children.

Little boys are in a precarious circumstance. They are dependent upon their mothers, whom they are instructed not to be like. To be not like their primary caretaker requires their behaving in ways clearly indicative of masculinity. This masculine behavior serves as evidence to themselves and to others that they are not being overly influenced by their mother's femininity. Girls have no such difficulty in developing an appropriate gender orientation. Unlike boys, girls are expected to model their mothers. Since there is no conflict in

What stereotypes do people in our culture hold? Listed below are a group of adjectives used to describe people. Place an "M" for male and an "F" for female next to each item to designate it as part of the male stereotype or part of the female stereotype in our culture.

_____ 1. Appreciative
_____ 2. Aggressive
_____ 3. Considerate
_____ 4. Arrogant
_____ 5. Contented
_____ 6. Assertive
_____ 7. Cooperative
_____ 8. Autocratic
_____ 9. Dependent
_____ 10. Conceited

_____ 11. Excitable
_____ 12. Cynical
_____ 13. Fearful
_____ 14. Deliberate
_____ 15. Fickle
_____ 16. Frank
_____ 17. Friendly
_____ 18. Industrious
_____ 19. Sentimental
_____ 20. Outspoken

After you have completed this exercise, compare your response with the reactions of your classmates. Do you agree on most items? On which items do you disagree? How do you account for the disagreement?

---

their behaving like their caretaker, they are generally more secure in their development. This increased security is associated with an ability to take risks, including doing "boy things," hence, their ability to do tasks ascribed to the other sex.

The socialization model we have been discussing is called the social-learning model. This model explains that children learn the appropriate sex-typed behavior through observation, imitation of role models, and rewards and punishments for good or poor imitations. After a time, children find that modeling the appropriate sex-typed behavior (e.g., girls copying their mothers and boys their fathers) is rewarding in and of itself. Social learning takes place in many environments, the first of which is the family.

The family

Richardson (1988) notes that parents have strong gender role expectations for their children, thus, they decorate their rooms, choose their clothing and toys accordingly. Parents, especially fathers, treat their daughters and sons differently. Fathers generally interact more with sons than daughters (Rossi, 1984) and handle them more roughly (Culp, Cook & Housley, 1983).

Although fathers may engage in more child rearing functions today than in the past, they may interact differently with their children than do mothers.

Additionally, mothers and fathers may model different behaviors. Even if both parents work, the mother is usually more involved with home and child-care activities. The father may do the outdoor chores, while the mother performs the indoor work. Fathers may play more with their children, while mothers are more associated with maintenance activities (Bronstein, 1984). However, some evidence indicates that working mothers tend to have children whose gender stereotypes are much less rigid than children of nonworking women (Basow, 1986). One logical explanation for this is that since working mothers are obviously assuming another role, children cannot help but notice their mothers' flexibility. Inasmuch as working mothers are also quite often single mothers, children must often assist with home chores. By undertaking these additional responsibilities, children demonstrate to themselves through their own behavior that they are capable of performing both "masculine" and "feminine" tasks. A broadened understanding of what constitutes permissible behaviors for men and women accompanies the realization that they are rewarded for performing multiple tasks.

Educational institutions

Educational institutions provide clear messages about gender roles (Sadker and Sadker, 1985). Children who are enrolled in nursery schools and day care centers appear to develop stereotypical beliefs earlier than other children. Two- and three-year-old children enrolled in nursery school demonstrated substantial knowledge of prevalent gender-role stereotypes (Kuhn, Nash & Brucken, 1978). Children in school settings are not only knowledgeable about sex-role stereotypes, but they are also often reinforced for enacting them. In observing more than one hundred fourth-, sixth-, and eighth-graders over a three-year period, Sadker and Sadker (1985) concluded that boys are reinforced for assertive, active learning behavior, while girls are reinforced for passive, quiet learning behavior.

Several researchers have found that boys generally receive more attention and more favorable attention in school than girls. However, this finding may be restricted to a white population since Taylor (1979) found that black males received the most unfavorable teacher treatment compared to females of both races and white males. Race may interact with sex in affecting teacher behavior, but few studies have looked at this interaction, so we cannot be certain.

Some people believe schools have changed radically in keeping with the sweeping social changes of the 70s. Thus, sexism in schools is thought to be a thing of the past. Unfortunately, Sadker, Sadker, and Klein (1986) have observed recently that many of the gains in equality made in the 1970s have been eroded, and schools are becoming more sex-role stereotyped again.

Finally, with reference to the social-learning model, let us examine the pattern of staffing in most schools. This pattern reinforces sex stereotypes by occupation and, thus, often fails to provide alternative role models for children at a formative period. In elementary schools, for example, most custodians are male; nurses, teachers, lunchroom workers are female; and principals are male. Although 80 percent of elementary-school teachers are women, fewer than one-fourth of the principals are women. In high schools, fewer than 10 percent of the principals are women (Sadker et al., 1986).

While traditional educational environments can encourage stereotyping, non-sexist schools may have the opposite effect. A comparison of traditional schools which emphasize gender-role socialization and open schools, which stress the individual development of each child, revealed that children in traditional settings tended to have more stereotyped notions of gender roles than children in open schools (Bianchi & Bakeman, 1978; Koblinsky & Sugawara, 1984).

Examine the following jobs and professions. Place an "M" by those jobs you would prefer to be performed by a man if you were the consumer and a "W" by those jobs you would prefer to be handled by a woman if you were the consumer. If you have no preference, place an "N" in the blank provided.

_N_ 1. Bartender —

_N_ 2. Hair stylist ——

_W_ 3. Physician +

_N_ 4. Professor +

_W_ 5. Lawyer +

_N_ 6. Accountant +

_N_ 7. Elementary-school — teacher

_N_ 8. Airline pilot +

_W_ 9. Nurse —

_W_ 10. Housekeeper/cleaning — person

_W_ 11. Babysitter —

_N_ 12. Restaurant serving person —

_N_ 13. Cook —

_M_ 14. Automobile mechanic +

Examine your responses. How many of the positions could be filled by either sex for you? Do you prefer women in traditional roles, such as nursing, elementary-school teaching, and babysitting and men in such roles as airline piloting, automobile mechanics, and bartending? What conclusions can you draw about your own responses? Compare your feelings with those of your classmates.

Which of the positions that are listed above generally earn a great deal of money and which generally result in small incomes? Place a "+" after each job that generally results in a salary that is above average and a "−" behind each that is generally below average. Now examine those jobs predominately held by women and those predominately held by men. Are men or women associated with occupations that are lower paying? How do you account for this difference?

Games and toys

Just as the family and educational institutions affect sex-role socialization, children's games and toys encourage notions of gender differences. Very young children do not show any preferences for toys based on gender appropriateness; but, as they move through the lower elementary grades, they begin increasingly to avoid non-traditional play objects (Vieira & Miller, 1978). Thus, boys prefer trucks, scientific kits, and robots, while girls play with dolls and stuffed toys (Basow, 1986). This preference for the appropriate toy is, no doubt, encouraged by parents, peers, and advertisers. Advertisers rarely show girls playing with toys marketed for boys or vice versa (Schwartz & Markham, 1985).

Differences in the play behavior of children include boys playing outdoors more than girls and engaging in more team sports and fantasy games. Girls tend to play indoors with dolls and board games. Whereas, girls often play alone or in small groups, boys tend to play with lots of others. Boys also tend to play in groups of children of different ages with the youngest child playing on the same level as the oldest child in the group. Girls rarely play in groups of varying ages; but, when they do, the oldest girls play on the level of the youngest in the group.

Children's literature

In addition to the games children play, other influences encourage the development of traditional masculine and feminine self-views. Perhaps one of the most pervasive influences is the kind of literature children read, and that others read to them. Children's books have been discussed as important influences in the development of self-concepts (Heintz, 1987), and some evidence exists that sexism in children's literature influences adult sexist behavior, especially for males (Cooper, 1986). Many surveys of children's literature and textbooks have been conducted. They tend to confirm that many (if not most) of these materials provide only limited roles for females, a preponderance of male characters, limited occupational goals for women, and traditional gender stereotyping. In brief, these materials advance less than a full range of human interests, traits, and capabilities for either gender (cf. Heintz, 1987; Schulwitz, 1976; Stewig & Knipfel, 1975).

Girls and boys are frequently depicted differently in children's literature. Girls are pictured as kind, attentive, and serving, while boys are pictured as adventuresome and strong (Oliver, 1974). Boys are referred to by the functions they perform or the activities in which they engage, while girls are known in terms of their appearance or the way they look to others. Accordingly, children's literature imparts the distinct impression that "boys do," but that "girls are" (Rachlin & Vogt, 1974).

What other differences between males and females appear in children's literature? Broverman, Broverman, Clarkson, Rosenkrantz, and Vogel (1970) listed male-valued descriptors in children's literature as "aggressive, independent[,] and adventurous", and female-valued traits as "very gentle, very interested in own appearance, and very strong need for security." In an examination of the pictures in selected children's books, boys were shown in three primary male activities: fishing, building, and camping. The girls were shown swinging, jumping rope, and playing in the sand. Women's leisure activities were shown as sedate, structured, and confining, while men's were characterized by physical action, aggression, and adventure. Girls were encouraged to be domestic; boys were encouraged not to engage in domestic activities (Liebert, McCall & Hanratty, 1971). Given these findings, it may not be surprising that boys prefer to read about boys, while girls have no preference for stories about boys or girls (Connor & Serbin, 1978). Boys may prefer stories about boys since they are both more exciting and about their own gender. Girls, on the other hand, may have a difficult time choosing between a more exciting story or a story about people of the same sex.

Bottigheimer (1987) argues that *Grimms' Tales* present a silencing of women. In the *Tales,* according to her reading, speech is taken away from women and given to men. For example, she notes the absence or early death of the mothers of Snow White, Cinderella, and Hansel and Gretel. Further, she observes that the mother in "The Twelve Brothers" speaks only once, then disappears from the tale completely. This pattern also recurs in "The Goose-Girl."

Some efforts have been made to alter the way girls and boys are depicted in children's literature. A comparison of stories from the decade of the 1930s with stories written between 1964 and 1974 revealed that, although males were still more prevalent than females and the range of occupations for males was much broader than for females in both eras, three changes were evident from the early period to the later. These changes included: 1) a broadening of gender role standards, 2) women becoming more masculine rather than men becoming more feminine, and 3) differences between men and women were most apparent in the area of occupational choice (Hillman, 1974).

Let us summarize how women and men gain images of themselves. We have observed in this chapter's section that a number of factors account for our views of "maleness" and "femaleness." Biological differences may not be directly responsible for our behavior, but they are used from birth to determine how we will be socialized. Socialization processes, which occur through social learning in the family, at school, in toys and play activities, and in children's

To what extent do you believe our attitudes about women and men have changed? Arrange to interview at least two men and two women who are at least 60 years of age. Prepare a set of interview questions in which you inquire about the roles of women and men 40 years ago, 20 years ago, and today, from their perspective. Consider asking similar questions about each 20-year interval. For instance, you may want to ask what percentage of women worked outside the home at each point in time, how women who worked outside the home were viewed, how many children were raised in each family, how much day care and other child care was available, how frequently a family would hire an evening babysitter, how a woman would spend a typical day, how a man made a living, how many hours a day a man worked, what kind of work was typical for a man, how much time men spent with their children, and how men were viewed who spent a lot of time with their families and less time engaged in their job or occupation. Be certain to include questions about the attitudes of the person you interview toward any changes she or he perceives. Does this person believe people were happier? Were people able to achieve their goals? Why? Write a short report on your findings and draw some conclusions from your investigation.

---

literature, affect the way individuals perceive themselves. We shift our attention now from the way we learn to perceive ourselves as women or men to the specific effects this learning has on women's and men's self-concepts.

Effects on women's and men's self-concepts

The various factors discussed previously no doubt contribute to the differences researchers have observed in the self-views of men and women. We will review these differences in three categories: character attributions; aspirations and goals; and comparisons between the sexes.

Vollmer (1986) observes that "as a result of sex roles in our society, men generally conceive of themselves as more active, independent, superior, and self-confident than women. Women describe themselves as more gentle, helpful, understanding, and warm than men do" (p. 351).

Richardson (1988) argues that boys' school-and-leisure experiences propel them toward a competitive outlook and a propensity to see themselves as go-getters. She states that team sports encourage boys to incorporate into their personalities the following traits: competitive spirit, achievement orientation, courage, aggression, and endurance. Girls' games provide training for

While girls are increasingly enrolling in traditionally male courses, they continue to have more limited perception of their future options.

the development of more delicate socioemotional skills (Lever, 1976). Thus, males and females make different attributions about the types of people they are (i.e., competitive or nurturing) based upon their different social learning.

Moreover, females and males have different aspirations and expectations for themselves. Richardson (1988) notes that young girls have limited perceptions of their life options. In a survey of upper-elementary-school children she reports that nearly all the girls chose one of the following for a future occupation: teacher, nurse, secretary, or mother. Boys' choices, however, were much more varied and imaginative.

Occupational aspirations are related to the study courses students pursue. Traditionally, girls have perceived math and science as male specialties, while boys have seen English and other courses with an emphasis on reading as female areas. When females avoid math and science courses, they are excluding themselves from many occupations, i.e., engineering, medicine, etc. When males forego English and reading activities, they are cut off from occupational opportunities as well, i.e., teaching, writing, etc. Girls are less likely to perceive themselves as college material than boys, are less likely to do well on their SATs, and less likely to plan to go to college (Cano, Solomon & Holmes, 1984; Cordes, 1986).

Occupational aspirations are also tied to educational background. This sense of what is appropriate for future occupations has been shown to be related to the social learning children obtain from literature. Girls who read nontraditional stories rated traditionally male jobs as more appropriate for females than girls who read traditional stories (Ashby & Wittmaier, 1978). Similarly, when women were placed in nontraditional roles in stories, children's perceptions of the appropriateness of these activities for girls increased significantly (Scott & Summers, 1979).

Finally, socialization influences comparisons between girls and boys. A clear message males and females receive is that the two sexes are in opposition to one another since such strong distinctions are drawn between them (Basow, 1986). Scher's (1984) work supports this contention by observing that the ideal self for men and women differs. The "typical man" and "typical woman" are described by both sexes as different in sex-typed ways (Basow, 1986).

Developing self-esteem

Self-esteem is developed in women and men through their experiences, interactions with others, and cultural messages. Men and women may learn how valuable they are through their relative visibility in language, a topic we will examine in detail in Chapter 4. As we shall see, women are somewhat invisible in a language that relies on "he" to stand for both he and she. Much language also assumes a male audience or standard without using the word "he" at all.

Johnson (1984) recalls conversations she participated in where a male university administrator called the university deans "eunuchs," a male biochemist said he had "a blow in the groin" when he saw the new curriculum, and a male dean said of a colleague, "if he were on fire, I wouldn't piss on him." As Johnson points out, the examples presume that all deans are male, that impact is measured by male pain, and that disgust is metaphorically male.

Table 3.2   Differences in self-esteem

Summary

* Men rate higher on personal self, social self, and self-criticism; no differences occur on physical self, moral-ethical self, family self, identity, or self-satisfaction.

* Fourth- and fifth-grade boys rate themselves higher on self-esteem than fourth- and fifth-grade girls; female teachers rate their female students higher, while male teachers rate their male students higher.

* Men have a higher expected success rate on non-social skills than do women; even when men do not perform better, people perceive that they do.

* Individuals from the middle class score higher on self-esteem than do individuals from the lower class.

* Individuals from Euro-American backgrounds score higher on self-esteem than do individuals from Mexican-American backgrounds.

* Older children score higher on self-esteem than do younger children.

* Children whose caretakers were someone other than their parents score higher on self-esteem than do children who were cared for by their own parents.

* Low self-esteem is related to depression.

* Traditional and liberated women base their self-esteem on different factors.

* Single women have higher self-esteem than do married women.

* Similarity in self-esteem appears to be a factor in selecting someone to date or have a relationship.

In a language where women are invisible, they may be demeaned. An advertisement for Knights of Columbus Insurance reads, "Priceless Possessions . . . Your Wife and Children." An advertisement in a golf magazine states, "A great golf course is like a good woman. Beautiful . . . and a little bit Bitchy" (reprinted in Basow, 1986).

Additionally, self-esteem is affected by the differential treatment males and females receive. The differences in boys' and girls' school experiences provide an interesting example. Although boys do not succeed as well in school as girls, especially in reading (Lipmen-Blumen, 1984), their academic problems are taken seriously by teachers (Greenberg, 1985). Sadker et al. (1986) state that boys are the center of attention in American classrooms; girls play a secondary role. Although the boys' central role is often an uncomfortable one involving discipline and negative feedback, as time goes on this changes for boys and they are less likely than girls to be underachievers beyond elementary school (Sadker et al., 1986).

These researchers also speculate that the increased attention boys have received throughout their schooling, even the negative attention, adds to their sense of self-worth.

For girls, the experience is different. The school environment is more suited to a girl's socialization than a boy's, so girls are generally more comfortable and successful in the early grades. However, the rewards for neatness and docility come at the expense of developing some of the interaction and academic skills boys are forced to acquire. When girls reach puberty, they are more likely than boys to become underachievers (Greenberg, 1985).

Men's and women's self-esteem may also be affected by others' perceptions of their worth. Goldberg's (1968) work is instructive on this point. When persons were asked to judge the quality of two essays, one attributed to a male author and the other to a female, they judged the male's as better. In another study (Paludi & Bauer, 1983) when individuals were provided with essays written by a male author, a female author, and an author whose gender was unknown (merely identified by initials), they selected the male's essay as best, followed by the author whose gender was unknown, followed by the female's essay. Similarly, when rating speeches, audiences rate female speakers as less competent than male speakers, even when there are no differences in content or delivery (Miller & McReynolds, 1973).

Effects on men's and women's self-esteem

Given all the preceding information that indicates society values men more than women, we would expect to find dramatic differences in males' and females' self-esteem. However, this is not the case. Although the tendency is for males to have a stronger sense of self-worth, the difference is slight and the findings are mixed.

Some studies have found no difference in the levels of self-esteem between men and women (Drummond, McIntire & Ryan, 1977; Seidner, 1978; Zuckerman, 1980), while some have determined men are higher in esteem (Gold, Brush & Sprotzer, 1980; Loeb & Horst, 1978; Smith & Self, 1978; Stoner & Kaiser, 1978).

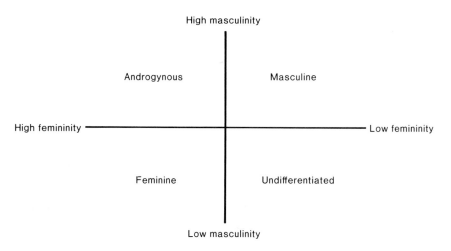

This rather surprising finding may be explained in several ways: developmental differences; different standards; psychological gender; and different types of self-esteem. It is possible that studies using respondents of different ages may not be comparable. Thus, conclusions may be impaired because of age differences. Schmich (1984; cited in Basow, 1986) found that while boys and girls initially score similarly in self-esteem, by adolescence males score higher than females.

A second reason for finding relatively small differences between males' and females' self-esteem levels may be that males and females view different elements as central to their self-concept and, thus, judge themselves differently. If males compare themselves to a typical male and females to a typical female, there is evidence they would be employing different standards of evaluation (Scher, 1984). Additionally, females seem more self-accepting than males evidenced by a better match between their self and ideal descriptions (Basow, 1986).

The relationship between psychological gender roles and self-esteem has been examined. The highest levels of self-esteem are found among people high in masculinity and low in femininity (Cate & Sugawara, 1986; Gauthier & Kjervik, 1982; Stericker & Johnson, 1977) or both high in masculinity and high in femininity (androgynous) (Zeldow, Clark & Daugherty, 1985). The strong relationship between psychological gender and self-esteem may override sex differences in this area and explain why men and women do not seem to differ dramatically on this variable.

Finally, discussions of esteem-level differences between men and women may be clearer if we consider differences among specific types of self-esteem. Men tend to score higher on personal self (how they view themselves as a person apart from others), social self (how they view themselves as a person

interacting with others), and self-criticism (ability to identify problems in their behavior). There appear, however, to be no differences between men and women with respect to esteem related to physical selves, moral-ethical systems, interaction with families, self-satisfaction with accomplishments, or a general understanding of self (Stoner & Kaiser, 1978).

There are also interesting differences between men's and women's esteem insofar as decision making is concerned. Most of these differences speak to differences in focus; i.e., men esteem their ability to do certain things, women others. Specifically, men pride themselves in their ability to be task-oriented and bring a given project to completion in a timely way, while women are more concerned about being open-minded (Stake & Stake, 1979).

Table 3.3   Changes in self-esteem

Summary

* Women who possess instrumental skills tend to display high self-esteem.

* Females who have internal locus of control have higher self-esteem than do females who have external locus of control.

* Individuals who score high in masculinity score high in self-esteem.

* Consciousness-raising groups, discussion groups, and classes can assist individuals to alter their self-esteem.

Other variables affecting self-esteem

Do factors other than gender affect people's self-esteem? Yes, a number of other variables have been identified. For example, a child's caretaker affects his or her self-esteem. Children whose fathers were their major caretakers had the lowest self-esteem scores; children whose parents both served as caretakers ranked next; and the highest self-esteem scores were reported for children whose parents cite others as major caretakers (Burge, 1980). These results may serve to alleviate the guilt working women feel when they place pre-school-age children in the care of others.

Depression is correlated with low self-esteem for both women and men (Wilson & Krane, 1980). However, women tend to report depression more than men (Hammen & Padesky, 1977). Dawson-Bailey (1989) reports that eating disorders, associated with both low self-esteem and depression, are more often found in women than men.

Traditional and liberated sex-role attitudes seem to make a difference in self-esteem, especially for women. Traditional women tend to base their self-esteem more on friendship and social involvements and less on interests and abilities, while it is just the reverse for liberated women. Marital status also appears to affect women's standards for measuring self-esteem. We might hypothesize that the roles of wife and mother are so important in our society that a woman who fulfilled neither of these roles would suffer from a lowered self-esteem. However, this does not appear to be the case. Single women value personal growth and achievement, stating that they are self-determined, whereas, married women value personal relationships and describe themselves with reference to kinship roles and household activities. Single women have a different level of self-esteem than married women; but, since they evaluate themselves on different standards, it is not in a negative direction (Gigy, 1980).

All of us have a view of our "ideal" self, the self we aspire to be. Consider your favorite childhood storybook character, a sports figure, a politician, a musical star, a television celebrity, a dancer, a musician, a movie star, a political activist, or another well-known person with whom you identify. Write a short essay on the qualities of this character that are important to you, explain the influence he or she has had on your life (if any), and tell how this person is different from you. In your essay, consider some of the stereotypical characteristics of women, including expressive, reactive, emotional, warm, caring, and dependent, as well as the stereotypical characteristics of men, including task-oriented, aggressive, egocentric, strong, silent, responsible, and competitive. To what extent does the person you select exhibit either set of characteristics? To what extent do you endorse or reject the stereotypical characteristics of your gender? Consider the material in this chapter describing how we gain images of ourselves as women or men through biology and socialization, how women and men are characterized, and how women and men differ in their self-concepts. What conclusions can you draw?

Making changes

Our feelings about ourselves are always in process. We do not view ourselves in the same way all the time with all the people and all the situations we encounter. We know that our self-concept changes in the course of time. You may have felt more negative or more positive about yourself when you were in elementary school than you did when you were in high school. You may feel better about yourself now than you ever have before. You may have radically changed your goals or your assessment about the type of person you are and the things you can accomplish.

Nontraditional social learning can affect self-views

If traditional game-playing encourages different self-views for boys and girls, nontraditional game-playing may encourage alternatives. Fourth-through-sixth-grade children were first given the freedom to select any toy they wished from a group of stereotypical feminine toys (dolls and doll furniture) and masculine toys (vehicles). Only girls demonstrated stereotyped responses; that is, they consistently chose dolls and doll furniture. In a second situation, the children, rather than being free to select their own choices, were provided with either feminine or masculine toys. In both situations, the play construction varied with the toy rather than the child's gender. In other words, a boy playing with a doll would create a feminine story, while a girl playing with a vehicle would construct a masculine story (Karpoe & Olney, 1983).

An internal locus of control allows women to perceive themselves as favorably as men. Sixth-grade girls with a high internal locus of control (who perceived themselves rather than outside forces to be responsible for the events in their lives) viewed themselves as favorably as did sixth-grade boys. Sixth-grade females with a strong external locus of control (who perceived people and events outside of themselves to be controlling their lives) viewed themselves significantly lower on measures of self-esteem (Seidner, 1978). Girls who have an external locus of control may be more susceptible to the debilitating effects of our sex-biased culture than girls who look within for control of their lives. However, cultural reality demands a woman recognize that sometimes her success is out of her control. Discrimination against women should not be seen as women's failure to exert control.

Finally, women can raise their self-esteem by participating in consciousness-raising groups. Women who participated in such groups tended to overcome low self-esteem, reduce depression in their lives, decrease their tendency to blame others, and feel that they were more in control of their own lives (Weitz, 1982).

Conclusions

In this chapter we considered the self-perceptions of women and men. We determined that people acquire or develop images of themselves, partly because of biological differences, and largely through social learning. Our family experiences, education process, the toys we play with and the games we play, as well as the children's literature we have read, all contribute to our notions of being women or men. These notions affect our self-attributions, our goals and aspirations, and our assessment of the differences between women and men. The evidence indicates that females in general have more limited self-images than men and tend to have lower self-esteem than men. Men and women are not altogether different in terms of self-esteem; women, however, tend to be more self-accepting than men. In addition, some factors in addition to sex influence our self-concepts. Although we are observing changing conceptions of women and men at this time in history, we also have elements of resistance to that change. Abundant evidence exists indicating that people are often disparaged for violating our stereotypic expectations. When we interact, for instance, with a woman who behaves shrewdly, aggressively, and with confidence, there is a tendency to evaluate her more negatively than if she were a man.

It is not that we "like' such behavior in men, but rather that such behavior in men is expected. Changes in self-concept may result in changes in other behaviors, including our communicative behavior. Changes in self-concept may also be dependent on changes in society's sex-role expectations which restrict roles and choices for both women and men.

Communication begins with self and with others. The way we have learned about ourselves as women or as men affects how we communicate with others. This, in turn, affects others' perceptions of us and communication with us. How others see and communicate with us spirals back and influences our self-concept. The material presented in this chapter will be useful to you as a foundation for understanding how women and men strive to negotiate meaning with each other in a variety of contexts.

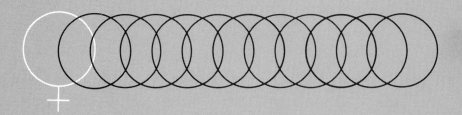

Section 2

This section examines the verbal and nonverbal codes that we use in order to make messages. Chapter 4 analyzes verbal language patterns. We argue that the English language itself contains messages about women and men. Many language practices including naming, honorifics, and the use of generics give us ideas and shape our thoughts about women and men. In chapter 5 we discuss how women and men are

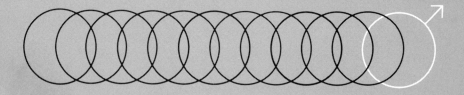

Codes

believed to use verbal codes. We compare the perceptions of great difference to the research findings. In general, studies have not found that men and women talk as differently from one another as they are believed to. Chapter 6 surveys the large body of research on gender and nonverbal communication. Finally, in chapter 7 we investigate two specific applications of verbal and nonverbal codes: self-disclosure and self-assertion.

4 Images of women and men

Introduction

This chapter investigates images—the pictures we conjure up in our minds to represent men and women. We are helped in forming these mental pictures by the language we use. Consequently, the chapter surveys aspects of our language practices that affect how we view women and men. We observe that our language often reflects the sexist nature of society and serves to perpetuate the status quo. However, we note some changes in these reflections as society shifts and evolves. We suggest further changes in the hope they will have continued impact on contemporary culture.

During the past 25 years people have expressed concern about language which discriminates between women and men, excludes women, and encourages the subordination of women. Harrigan and Lucic (1988) characterize the gender and language research of the 1970s as analyses of the ways in which language characterized women as less powerful, less visible, and less important than men.

Language about women and men

Language which refers to women and men deserves our consideration because language has a significant influence on the way we perceive the world. The reciprocal relationship between our perceptions and the language we use to express them is known as the Sapir-Whorf hypothesis. Benjamin Whorf, a fire-insurance expert, and Edward Sapir, a linguist, advanced the idea that language both limits and expands perception. Their hypothesis contends that if you have a large vocabulary for colors, for instance, you will be able to perceive a wider range of colors than someone with a smaller color vocabulary. Similarly, if you live in Southern California, you may know names for different types of surf and be able to "see" the surf differently than someone would from the Midwest who lacks your extensive surf vocabulary. Thus, Sapir and Whorf asserted that language is not merely a reflection of the speaker's thoughts, but instead, actually helps shape them by naming certain things and letting others go nameless. This idea has direct implications for our next topics: "man-linked" words, "generic man," and "generic" pronouns.

Man-linked words and generic "man"

Man-linked words include the suffix, "-man." For example: "post*man*," "service*man*," "fire*man*," "milk*man*," "sales*man*," "telephone line*man*," and "crafts*man*." Generic "man" refers to the practice of using the word "man" to symbolize the category of all human beings. According to Smith (1985), in the English language prior to A.D. 1000, *"mann"* was a true generic. The term

Sometimes people argue that the names we are called are irrelevant to the way we perceive ourselves. For instance, being called a "girl," a "lady," or a "woman" are synonymous, they argue, and women who object are being picayune. As we demonstrated in this section of the text, words have appreciable impact on people's perceptions of themselves and of others. Complete the following sentences to determine your own meanings for these words.

1. A bitch is _____
2. A witch is _____
3. A lady is _____
4. A gentleman is _____
5. A man is _____
6. A girl is _____
7. A bastard is _____
8. A wizard is _____
9. A woman is _____
10. A boy is _____

You may be interested to know that #2 and #8 are female and male equivalents just as are the pairs #3 and #4, #5 and #9, #6 and #10. Consider the relationship between #1 and #7. What conclusions can you draw based on this exercise? Attempt to identify other pairs that are female/male equivalents. Do these words have negative or positive meanings for most people? Can any of the pairs be interpreted so that the male term is positive and the female term is negative or vice versa? Why do you think this occurs?

"wif" denoted a female and "wer" a male. However, through a gradual process man subsumed "wer" and "wif" changed to woman. In this process, the generic meaning of "man" was lost, although the practice of using it generically was retained. A number of research studies have systematically investigated the meaning people ascribe to man-linked words and the generic "man" (Todd-Mancillas, 1981). With some exceptions, these studies indicate that when the word "man" is used, women feel excluded or are uncertain as to whether or not they are included.

One study considered job advertisements (Bem & Bem, 1973). High-school seniors read 12 job advertisements for positions such as appliance salesman, photographer, telephone frameman, taxicab driver, assistant buyer, telephone lineman, and others. Some of the jobs were labeled in man-linked terms (e.g., telephone lineman, telephone frameman) and some of them were neutral (e.g., photographer, taxicab driver). Jobs traditionally associated with men—the man-linked jobs—were described as "men" working with other "men." Similarly, jobs stereotypically held by women, e.g., telephone operator, dental assistant, etc. were described as an opportunity for a "woman" to work with other "women" or "girls." Other neutral jobs were described either without a gender referent or with both gender referents. Traditionally male and female jobs were described for "people" or for "men and women." Some of the jobs were gender reversed: jobs traditionally held by men were described as opportunities for women; positions traditionally held by women were described as positions for men.

The study found that in the ads specifying a gender bias only 5 percent of the women and 30 percent of the men were interested in applying for "opposite-sex" jobs. In the neutral job ads, 25 percent of the women and 75 percent of the men were interested in applying for "opposite-sex" jobs. Finally, in the sex-reversed ads, 45 percent of the women and 65 percent of the men were willing to consider "opposite-sex" jobs. These findings indicate how gender-biased language can influence men's and women's pursuit of employment options.

A second study by the same authors obtained similar results. Female college students rated the advertisements in *The Pittsburgh Press*. Some students read job advertisements listed under "Jobs—Male Interest" or "Jobs—Female Interest" columns. Other students read ads where the jobs were not segregated by sex. In the first case, when the jobs were divided on the basis of sex, only 46 percent of the students were as likely to apply for the male-interest jobs as the female-interest jobs. However, 86 percent of the students preferred the male-interest jobs when they were not designated by a sex label. (Bem & Bem, 1973). Thus, placement of the jobs under the male or female label influenced selections made by female students.

Another study featured sentences which included the word "man" or a man-linked word such as, "The potentialities of man are infinitely varied and exciting." In nine cases, students were asked open-ended questions in which they would describe in their own words the sex of the persons discussed in the sentences. The remaining nine sentences were followed by forced-choice options in which students were required to identify the person's sex. In the open-choices, the person was described as a male 66 percent of the time, as a female 5 percent of the time, and as neither male nor female 29 percent of the time. In the forced-choices, the person was identified as a man 86 percent of the time and as a female 9 percent of the time (Kidd, 1971). Both the forced-choice and the open-choice options resulted in persons interpreting "man" more frequently as masculine than as neutral, referring with equal likelihood to men and women.

In another study college students were asked to submit photographs from newspapers and magazines that would be appropriate for illustrating chapters in an introductory college sociology book. Half the participants received the table of contents with generic "man" chapter titles, such as "Social Man," "Urban Man," "Political Man," "Industrial Man," and "Economic Man." The other participants received a similar table of contents, but the chapter titles were neutral, including "Culture," "Population," "Race and Minority Groups," "Families," "Crime and Delinquency," and "Ecology." Those students who received generic "man" titles supplied photographs of men at the rate of 64 percent. With neutral titles, only 50 percent of the photographs were of men only (Schneider & Hacker, 1973).

More recently, Pincus and Pincus (1980) surveyed children in grades three, seven, and ten, as well as adults, to determine their interpretations of sentences using the word "man" or man-linked words. They determined that children had difficulty understanding "man" as a generic, and even adults found the use of the word "man" to be ambiguous.

Finally, Wolfe, Struckman-Johnson, and Flanagin (1986) examined children's and adults' perceptions of the use of "man" as a generic. Their results suggest that understanding the use of generic "man" comes relatively late in the process of learning language. Ninety-one percent of the adults tested indicated an understanding of "man" as a referent for the entire species. However, the eleven-year olds who responded to their questionnaire interpreted "man" as referring to a male individual 47 percent of the time, "the man" 84 percent, and "a man" 76.5 percent. All instances of "man" in the singular were perceived by the sixth graders as sex-specific (i.e., not generic) most of the time. "Man" and man-linked terminology remain a problem.

Although the studies reviewed here are not conclusive, they tend to support the idea that man-linked words and the generic "man" are not viewed as referring with equal likelihood to women and men. Additionally, their use is troublesome since it narrows the perception of what is appropriate for women. Finally, the usage of such terms tends to imply that women are a substandard or deviant form. Women are viewed, at best, as afterthoughts or as second-class citizens. The authors of one article state that using man-linked terms is reminiscent of a time when women were viewed as the possessions of their husbands and fathers (Burr, Dunn & Farquhar, 1972).

Man-linked words are exclusionary since they exclude women in the same way woman-linked words (e.g., chairwoman, saleswomen) exclude men. Inclusive words, such as "chair," "people," "mail carrier," and "salesperson," include both men and women.

Generic pronouns

A second area of concern are words known as generic pronouns. **Generic pronouns** are those pronouns such as "he," "him," "his," and "himself" which are supposed to refer with equal likelihood to women and to men. As early as 1970, the generic nature of such terminology was questioned. One author charged that this language was androcentric, or male-centered, sexist, and used to limit the behavioral options of women (Densmore, 1970). Another author sarcastically stated that it appeared all persons were male, until proven otherwise (Murray, 1973). In addition, traditional generics were criticized on the grounds they were confusing (Murray, 1973), ambiguous, exclusive, and unequal (Martyna, 1978), and defined women as secondary or deviant (Farwell, 1973). Strainchamps (1971) maintained that the use of generic pronouns is evidence our language retains more of an outdated sexism than any other civilized language.

Given these criticisms of generic pronouns, several empirical investigations have considered whether traditional generics actually refer to women and men equally or whether their use encourages a male bias. For the most part, the findings indicate that a male bias exists. Soto, Forslund, and Cole (1975) found that people are more likely to perceive the word "he" as referring to men than to women. Similarly, MacKay and Fulkerson (1979) found that when college students interpreted the generic "he," they assumed in 87 percent of the cases the word referred exclusively to men. In another study one year later, MacKay also found that students who read textbook paragraphs containing the traditional generic pronouns used to refer to neutral antecedents assumed the terms referred to men 40 percent of the time (MacKay, 1980).

In another study, subjects read a one-sentence statement, then wrote brief narratives about the person in the statement. Some subjects read, "In a large coeducational institution, the average student will feel isolated in his introductory courses." Or, "Most people are concerned with appearance; each person knows when his appearance is unattractive." Other subjects read the same sentences, but the generic "his" was deleted and the pronouns "his or her" were inserted. In a third group, the word "their" was inserted for "his." This study indicated a significantly greater tendency for people to write essays describing males in the traditional generic situation than in either of the alternative conditions (Moulton, Robinson & Elias, 1978).

Wilson and Ng (1988) found that generic pronouns invoked sex-specific images that exerted an influence on how their subjects saw visual images. In this study, students viewed four pictures (two males and two females) through a tachistoscope which was set 2msec below a viewer's threshold value, thus making the pictures somewhat ambiguous and difficult to discern. Prior to viewing each picture, students were shown a sentence that had either a masculine or a feminine generic in it. Then they were asked to identify the picture as a male or female face. Male faces were over-reported when students saw the sentence with a masculine generic and under-reported when the sentence had a feminine generic.

In the previous five studies, the researchers were interested in the effects of hearing or reading generic pronouns. Hamilton (1988) examined the effects of people using masculine generics themselves. Hamilton found that "one's own use of masculine generics can bias one's cognitions . . . [leading to] more male-biased imagery in the mind of the user" (p. 795). As Hamilton notes, this study provides clear support for the Sapir-Whorf hypothesis that the language one *uses* (as opposed to hears) shapes one's thoughts and perceptions. The results of these studies indicate how improbable it is that generic pronouns act, in fact, as genuine generics.

A second area of investigation concerning generics involves how women and men use them differently. Martyna (1978) examined the extent to which people used alternative rather than traditional generics in their writing. She asked students to complete six male-related statements, six neutral statements, and six female-related statements. An example of a male-related statement follows: "Before a judge can offer a final ruling . . ." An example of a neutral statement would be, "When a person loses money . . ." Finally, a female-related statement would be, "After a nurse has completed training . . ." Martyna found that men were more likely than women to use "he" in the completion of male-related and neutral sentence fragments; that women were more likely than men to use alternative generic forms such as "she," "he or she," and "they" for the neutral sentences; and that both men and women demonstrated a preference for gender-specific pronouns when they completed the male-related and female-related sentences.

In contrast, Wheeless, Berryman-Fink, and Serafini (1982) found that men and women both used similar pronouns, and women were not more likely than men to use significantly more alternatives to the generic "he." This may be the case because pronoun usage is the area that presents the most confusion to people, even if they are sensitive to the existence of gender-biased language (Harrigan & Lucic, 1988). In the face of this confusion, we may see inconsistent results across studies.

A third area of research in generics concerns their association with stereotypes. Studies indicate both that people respond stereotypically to generics and that altering the generics has a mediating influence on stereotypic responses.

When college students were asked to complete sentence fragments referring to traditional male roles, traditional female roles, and gender-neutral roles, their responses conformed to stereotypes. The overwhelming response to the completion of sentences that included male roles was to use "he"; the overwhelming response to the completion of sentences that include female roles was to use "she," and "he" or "they" was used in the neutral condition (Wheeless, Berryman-Fink & Serafini, 1982).

Just as earlier researchers examined man-linked words in job descriptions, Stericker (1981) investigated the impact of pronouns on job attitudes. She used job descriptions perceived as feminine, such as interior decorator and clerk typist, as masculine, such as lawyer and taxi-driver, and as neutral, such as child psychologist and high-school teacher. Stericker used three conditions: one which used "he," one which used "he" or "she," and one which used "they." Although the males' interest did not alter under the different conditions, she found that the use of "he or she" encouraged female interest in the jobs.

Further research examines the developmental differences in generic usage. Switzer (1989) surveyed first graders and seventh graders in an attempt to replicate Moulton, Robinson, and Elias' (1978) study. Moulton et al., you will remember, had adults write brief narratives about a person after reading a one-sentence statement about that person. The sentence contained either "his," "his or her," or "their." Switzer modified this design so that the children heard the beginning of a story about a new student, then were asked to write out the ending. The story was adapted to the two age groups in her study. One group of children in each age group heard the story with "he," one with "he or she," one with "they," and one with "the student." Switzer's results were consistent with most previous studies in that the child tended to respond to "he" as sex-specific (not generic) and that girls used inclusive terms more than boys. However, she also found an interesting age difference. The first graders reported much less inclusive language than did the adolescents. Switzer comments that early adolescents may be combining their more advanced linguistic awareness with their social awareness of the changing roles for women and men.

In a different context, Hughes and Casey (1986) found no significant developmental differences among third-grade, eighth-grade, and college students in their pronoun choices for words such as "person," "student," "baby," "doctor," and "criminal." They found the masculine pronouns were the predominant choice for most of the words across all age groups. They explain their findings by saying that "language users conform to the traditional prescriptive grammar rule dictating the use of generic *he* when pronoun antecedents are not gender-specific" (p. 65). Given many of the previous studies' findings that masculine generics are not truly inclusive, these students' reliance on the prescriptive grammar rule that calls for them is disturbing.

Finally, some research looks at how susceptible to change is people's use of masculine generics.

Teachers may be able to alter the pronoun usage of their students. One instructor taught two sections of a child psychology course and substituted the feminine forms, "she" and "her" for the traditional generic pronouns. At the end of the course student papers were examined for the students' usage of pronouns. The results showed that students tended to use "she" in their papers significantly more than did a control group (Adamsky, 1981).

Flanagan and Todd-Mancillas (1982) examined the effects of two approaches to teaching inclusive generics. In one approach, the students' decision to use inclusive generics was forced on them by an instructor telling them they would be required to use them in all future assignments. In the second approach, material on inclusive pronouns was presented for the students' information only. Flanagan and Todd-Mancillas found both approaches encouraged the use of inclusive generics, but the authority model produced more change in pronoun use.

The studies allow us to draw a number of conclusions concerning pronoun choices. First, just as man-linked words are not perceived to refer with equal likelihood to men and women, traditional generic pronouns are not perceived to refer equally to men and women. Second, males and females use generics somewhat differently, with females generally employing more alternatives. Third, masculine generics are often associated with masculine stereotypes, such as jobs perceived to be men's work, with the feminine generics often associated with feminine stereotypes. However, changing the generic form can affect the stereotype, allowing women to consider "men's" work. Fourth, there may be some developmental differences in the ways people use generics, but these differences may be tempered by the prescriptive grammar rule advising the use of the generic "he." Finally, students will alter their pronoun use when alternatives are modeled by instructors, especially when such change is mandated. The potential change that can occur is encouraging in the light of the possible damage that occurs to women when traditional forms are used.

Alternatives to traditional man-linked words and generic pronouns

What kinds of alternatives exist for man-linked words and pronoun usage? One author suggests that we may categorize alternative forms into three possibilities (Todd-Mancillas, 1984). First, we can use currently existing words and phrases to include both men and women. For instance, we can pluralize sentence subjects rather than relying on singular forms. An example of this usage would be, "Writers should consider their audiences," instead of "A writer should consider . . ." It is also possible to use the *nonstandard,* ungrammatical plural generic "their," as in "Everyone should open their books." Slater,

Weider-Hatfield, and Rubin (1983) found that speakers could use non-standard generics in speeches without a concomitant loss in their credibility. In fact, by women's use of the generic they actually enhanced their perceived competence.

We can substitute words such as "people" for "man," "citizens" for "mankind," and "handmade" for "manmade." We can also use the indefinite "one," as in the sentence, "One can always find tutorial service available at this university." In addition, man-linked words can be eliminated in favor of neutral words: "firefighter" for "fireman," "mail carrier" for "mailman," and "chair" for "chairman."

A second category of alterations includes those changes requiring some relatively new forms of words. Forms such as "s/he," "wo/men," "chair-person," and "personkind" are relatively new forms that can be used. Parallel constructions might be considered: Whenever "he" is used, it is followed by (or preceded by) "she." We then use "women and men," "her or his," and "him and her." Alternating the usage of the masculine and feminine third person, singular form may also alleviate the sexism which appears inherent in the

Table 4.1 Neologisms for traditional third person, singular pronouns

Miller and Swift	Densmore	Cole	Traditional
tay	she	se	she/he
ter	heris	hes	her/his
tem	herm	hir	her/him

constant use and order of traditional pronouns. It may be particularly useful to employ these forms to avoid stereotyping by occupation so that a person would use "he" in referring to a nurse, an elementary-school teacher, or a homemaker, and would use "she" in referring to a medical doctor, a bank president, or a U.S. Senator. It may be useful to alter pronouns from paragraph to paragraph rather than from sentence to sentence to maintain continuity. In either case, the use of the word "she" in these instances refers, just as does the use of the word "he," to men and women equally.

A third category of alteration includes *neologisms,* or new words, which are more difficult to interpret. Three sets of neologisms have been suggested. Miller and Swift (1972) suggest "tay" for "he and she," "ter" for "her and him," and "tem" for "his or her." Densmore (1970) recommends "she" for "she or he," "herm" for "him or her," and "heris" for "her or his." Last, Cole offers "se" for "he or she," "hes" for "her or his," and "hir" for "him or her." (Soto, Forslund & Cole, 1975). All these proposals are for alterations in third person, singular pronouns and are summarized in Table 4.1.

While none of these neologisms have become accepted in our language, some research indicates it is not impossible to expect they might. Nontraditional generics are neither more difficult to understand nor perceived as less pleasant than traditional generics. A large number of students read different forms of an essay in which one form used the traditional generics, one form used the alternative form "s/he," and the third form used the neologism "tey" for "she and he." Subjects read one of the three forms, then completed a comprehension test, and also rated the essay's aesthetic quality. Neither the comprehension scores nor the aesthetic ratings of the essays were significantly different from each other in the three forms (Todd-Mancillas, 1984).

In another study, subjects read essays in which five kinds of pronouns were used. In the first condition, the essay included the traditional generic forms (he, him, his). In the second condition, the alternative generic forms were the feminine form (she, her). The third condition used the alternative generics "he/she," "she/he," "him/her," "her/his," etc. Another alternative generic form was used in the fourth condition which included "tay" for "he or she," "ter" for "her or his," and "tem" for "him or her." In the last condition the alternative generics were "se" for "she or he," "hes" for "his or her," and "hir" for "her or him." Subjects were asked about the perceived quality of the essay and the comprehensibility of the essay. This investigation demonstrated that none of the alternatives were perceived as significantly affecting the quality or the comprehensibility of the essay (Soto, Forslund & Cole, 1975).

The 1970s and 1980s were an exciting time of change in the elimination of "sexist" expressions and in "neutralizing" our language. Publishers such as Scott Foresman & Company, McGraw-Hill Book Company, and Macmillan Publishing Company issued statements that assisted authors in eliminating sexist expressions in their writing. Publishers of research journals, including the American Psychological Association, the Speech Communication Association, and the International Communication Association, issued statements concerning the use of nonsexist language in journals and other publications. English teachers began to accept and encourage alternatives.

One specific example of change was the new edition of *Roget's Thesaurus,* the book of synonyms and antonyms. The new edition eliminated sexist categories. For example, "mankind" was replaced with "humankind," and "rich man" was replaced with "rich person." Susan Lloyd, editor of the 1980s edition, stated that the sourcebook makes much more explicit the existence of women.

Snyder (1986) observes that the *Chronicle of Higher Education* has recently become sensitive to the issue of sexist language. Snyder cites several recent articles in the *Chronicle* to support her observation. First, the *Chronicle* reported on the Canadian Social Science and Humanities Research Council's guidelines for the elimination of sexist language in grant proposals and research reports. Second, the *Chronicle* reported on the Speech Communication Association's guidelines for eliminating language bias in the classroom. Third, an article appeared in a recent *Chronicle* reporting that "the official motto of the California State University system *vir veritas vox* (man, truth, voice) had been changed to *vita veritas vox* (life, truth, voice) to avoid gender specificity." (p. 49) However, Synder goes on to say that the change was "reported by a 'spokes*man*' for the board of trustees (sigh!)" (p. 49).

Thus we see both progress and stagnation. Completely inclusive language has been slow to catch on. In Bodine's (1975) examination of 33 senior- and junior-high grammar books, she found that 28 condemned the use of "he or she" and the singular use of "they." Instead, these texts encouraged students to use the pronoun "he" in their writing. Purnell (1978) examined political speeches to determine the extent to which women were included. She examined generic terms used for groups of both genders or individuals of either gender, the gender typically ascribed to working people, and the specific references to women and men. She found women were not regularly included, and when women were included, they were sometimes referred to as "housewives." Interestingly, when the speakers listed "Americans," they excluded the

It is frequently easier to eliminate sexist language than we realize. A childrens' book, *Mother Goose and Father Gander: Equal Rhymes for Girls and Boys* (Larche, 1979), includes popular nursery rhymes which have been rewritten without a sexist bias. Some examples follow:

Jill and Jack Be Nimble

Jack be nimble, Jack be Quick,
Jack, jump over the candlestick.
Jill be nimble, jump it too,
If Jack can do it, so can you!

Bo Peep and Joe Peep

Little Bo Peep has lost her sheep
And doesn't know where to find them.
Leave them alone, and they'll come home,
Wagging their tails behind them.

Little Joe Peep has lost his sheep
And doesn't know where to find them.
Let them be, and let them run free,
They're sowing wild oats behind them.

Rub-A-Dub-Dub

Rub-a-dub-dub, three folks in a tub,
And who do you think they be?
The butcher, the baker, the candlestick maker,
They've all gone off on a spree.

These children's nursery rhymes demonstrate how simply we can change sexist terminology and forms to nonsexist alternatives. Copy a poem, a piece of prose, or another literary form that includes sexist language or man-linked words. Rewrite the piece to eliminate possible sexist references.

---

category of housewives. Purnell found a few nonsexist references and a decrease in obvious sexist forms such as "fellow" Americans; nonetheless, women appear infrequently in the language of politics.

Changing sexist forms may be particularly important for educators. We have already observed that teachers can model nonsexist forms and that students often alter their language based on these models. A number of communication educators have called for sensitivity to sexism and modification in usage (cf. Karre, 1976; Pincus & Pincus, 1980; Sorrels, 1983; Sprague, 1975; Todd-Mancillas, 1981; Trenholm & Todd-Mancillas, 1978). Among the changes called for are attention to the selection of textbooks and other materials to insure they are nonsexist, modelling nonsexist behavior, encouraging individuality, assisting students in constructively surmounting the constraints of gender roles, including discussions on sexism in communication, the avoidance of sexist forms, and the use of inclusive language forms.

Why have language changes been so slow and sometimes apparently regressing to older, more sexist forms? Part of the reason for this phenomenon may lie in the disparament of these language changes. For instance, we hear people sarcastically ask if they should use forms such as "Portuguese person-of-war" for "Portuguese man-of-war," "personhole cover" for "manhole cover," and name changes such as "Forman" to "Forperson" and "Pearson" to "Pearperson."

As noted in *Women and Language* (1986), one of the most used techniques for arguing against changing sexist language is ridicule and trivialization. However, as Blaubergs (1980) points out, "for a 'trivial concern' sexist language has received an inexplicable amount of attention in both academia and the media, and an inordinate degree of resistance to change" (p. 139). As Shear (1985) argues, "readers tempted to dismiss the topic as insignificant are invited to reflect on similar telling details that have affected the course of American history, like 'colored' signs for water fountains and waiting rooms" (p. 40).

However, feminists have been divided over the issue of the relative importance of language changes, given the nature of other forms of inequality (Lakoff, 1973; Nilsen, 1973). Some suggest that pronouns may occur too frequently in sentences, making it difficult to monitor them for the average speaker or writer (Lakoff, 1975).

Bate (1978) contends that in writing, people hesitate to adopt terms they have difficulty expressing, such as "s/he," "Ms.," and "chairperson." She also reminds the reader that language changes occur slowly and people are more likely to adopt more important changes first and only later adopt lesser important forms. For instance, you might alter "men" and "man" quite early, but not change "freshman" to "first-year college students" until later.

Other sexist practices

When we examine the language about women and men on the basis of man-linked words, generic "man," and generic pronouns, we find that women tend to be excluded in a great deal of the language we hear and allocated to a secondary, subordinate role. In addition to these systematic methods of excluding or subordinating women, other practices exist which tend to differentiate between women and men. We will consider some of those differences here.

Names and the use of honorifics

For centuries people in our culture have changed their names when they married. Most typically, the female member of the couple assumed her husband's surname. However, this practice is no longer legally mandated. In changing her name, and in a variety of other ways, the woman became a member of her husband's family. Both linguistically and in reality the woman changed, or lost, her identity. Miss Manners recently received a letter from a reader who complained about the absence of the mother's identity in a birth announcement she had received (Martin, 1988). The announcement stated that "Mr. and Mrs. Joseph Allen Jones are delighted to announce the birth of their daughter." The reader commented that a woman's name, not just her roles (wife and mother) belongs on a birth announcement. Miss Manners agreed.

At various points in history women have rejected this alteration in their names. In 1915 Charlotte Perkins Gilman envisioned *Herland,* a Utopia populated by women. When three men stumble upon Herland, they discuss naming practices with the women. One of the men mentions that men give women their names upon marriage:

> 'Do your women have no name before they are married?' Celis suddenly demanded. 'Why yes,' Jeff explained. 'They have their maiden names—their father's names, that is.' 'And what becomes of them?' asked Alima. 'They change them for their husbands,' my dear,' Terry answered her. 'Change them? Do the husbands then take the wives' maiden name?' 'Oh, no,' he laughed. 'The man keeps his own and gives it to her, too.' 'Then she just loses hers and takes a new one—how unpleasant! We won't do that!' Alima said decidedly (Gilman, 1979, p. 118).

Most recently, with the current women's movement, a number of women have elected to maintain their original names, to use their former last names as a middle name which is written out in full, or to hyphenate the former last names with the new last names. Cheris Kramarae, who is quoted frequently in this text and has made a significant contribution to the understanding of gender and communication, creatively solved the problem of a married name. Kramarae was married in the state of Ohio at a time when the state did not allow women to retain their own names. Her name, upon marriage, became Cheris Rae Kramer. When the state laws were liberalized, she restructured the name and became Cheris Kramarae. William R. Todd-Mancillas, was born William R. Todd. His last name was that of his father. As an adult, with increased sensitivity to the influence of naming, he changed his name to reflect his mother's family name as well. Others, such as artist Judy Chicago, assumed the name of their home cities.

Foss and Edson (1988) investigated the communication implications of women's choices for married names by examining the accounts women gave about their choices. They identified three groups of women: (1) those who take their husbands' surnames; (2) those who retain their birth names; and (3) those who use hyphenated or new names after marriage. They discovered three explanations for name choices: (1) concerns about self; (2) concerns about relationships; and (3) concerns about cultural or societal expectations. These explanations were prioritized differently for the three groups of women. Women who took their husbands' name placed the highest priority on relationships. For women who kept their birth names, concern for self was the highest priority. Women who hyphenated or created new names gave equal weight to concerns about self and relationships.

Occasionally, people become concerned about the next generation and the possibility of people having four hyphenated last names. They maintain that name changes avoid this problem. Our own point of view is that such problems are not without solution and that some changes will be necessary to reflect the emerging equality of women.

The first author and her husband decided to retain their surnames when they married. Their children received both last names without a hyphen. However, they soon discovered that people were only using the final last name, their father's name. To reinforce both names, they hyphenated the children's last names. The parents will not be surprised or alarmed if the children decide to use only one of their last two names, or to combine them in some more creative way.

In addition to the choice of married names, given names also differentiate between the sexes. As Smith (1985) comments, first names are chosen above all other considerations to reflect the child's sex. If you know someone who is expecting a baby and you ask what names are being contemplated, you will hear two lists—one for girls and one for boys. Most of the given names in our culture clearly carry feminine or masculine connotations. There are unisex names (i.e., Chris, Dana, Dale, or Lee), but they are rare. Smith insists that "Given names . . . with which we become enduringly associated within a few days of birth, efficiently reinforce the male-female dichotomy within our society" (Smith, 1985, 39).

An examination of the use of honorifics (i.e., *Miss, Ms., Mr., Mrs.,* etc.) reveals inequality between women and men. Smith (1985) notes that *Mrs.* and *Miss* distinguish married from unmarried women, while no similar contrast is applied to men. He also observes that the contrast between women is a relatively recent innovation. Prior to the early nineteenth century, *Mrs.* as an abbreviation for Mistress applied to all adult women, while *Miss* referred to all female children.

The term *Ms.* was conceived as a parallel term to *Mr.*, a form of address which gives no indication of marital status. However, Atkinson (1987) found in a survey of 325 people that few understood the term *Ms.*, many even believed it should be used only for divorced or widowed women. This notion led Atkinson to conclude that women are identified by three categories: "AVAILABLE (Miss), TAKEN (Mrs.), and USED BUT AVAILABLE AGAIN (Ms.)" (p. 37).

However, *Women and Language* (1986) notes that the *Writer's Rhetoric and Handbook* pronounced *Ms.* "accepted by most and preferred by many" (p. 48). Further, the same issue of *Women and Language* excerpts an article from *Ms.* magazine celebrating that in 1986 The New York *Times* finally accepted *Ms.* as an honorific in news articles. Other newspapers (i.e., the Minneapolis *Star and Tribune* and the *Milwaukee Journal*) have stopped using honorifics in general and identify people by their full names first and by their surname alone in subsequent mentions.

The language of the deaf

Even American Sign Language (Ameslan), the language of the deaf, reflects sex stereotypes. The head, in signing is divided into two areas; above the center of the ear is used to indicate "he," "him," "his," "man," "father," and "son," while below the ear are the signs for "she," "her," "women," "mother," and "daughter." The area closest to the brain is used to designate the masculine referents, while the area closest to the mouth is used to designate the feminine referents. To compliment a woman, a sign is used that begins above the ear and then comes down to the traditional feminine area on the head which suggests a woman is like a man ("she thinks like a man," "she acts like a man"). Masculine features are used to compliment women. Professions are sex typed in Ameslan. The word for "secretary" is a combination of "girl" and "writes" or "a girl who writes." The term "president" is formed by signing the word "man" with a rising flare or a salute from the forehead which suggests "a respected man." Intellectual terms, in Ameslan, are either masculine or neutral. Emotional terms, words for appearance, and words for talking are feminine.

A very interesting example is the word for "love," which is expressed differently for women and for men. For women, the term is signed by open palms gently crossed over a woman's breasts. For men, the sign is made by crossing the arms at the wrist, with closed fists over the heart. Love appears to be a positive state for women, but one of entrapment for men (Jolly & O'Kelly, 1980).

Religious languages

All Western religions originated in patriarchal societies, therefore, the language and metaphors used to express their insights are overwhelmingly male-oriented. Nearly always, masculine pronouns are used in reference to God and to humanity. Typically, in Western religions women are perceived to be less Godlike and less perfect than their male counterparts. In addition, masculine language is frequently used to maintain the position of males as the heads of the church. The Aztec Indians, who believed the origin of human beings was from one single principle with a dual nature, used one pronoun in their religious writings which referred to a neutral he/she/it being (Miller & Swift 1976). Religion reflects society's attitudes.

Table 4.2   Terms for women and men

Women		Men	
Chick	Broad	Man	Stud
Girl	Woman	Guy	Hunk
Old lady	Honey	Male	Bastard
Piece	Madam	Boy	
Female	Whore		
Old maid	Dog		
Bitch	Cow		
Lady			

Many religious people are seeking changes in the language of worship to make it more inclusive. As Henry (1985) reports, the women attending a weekend program in Ohio called Feminists at Prayer: A Jewish-Christian Exchange, believe that God transcends sex. The Unitarian Universalist Women's Federation (1986) recently published a document for leading workshops on inclusive language, stating that language is a social-justice issue and adopting inclusive language furthers religious goals.

Definitions and descriptions of women and men

If you were asked to list all the terms for women and men you could name, what conclusions would you draw? In one study of elementary-school children, high-school students, and junior-college students, the author found that a much longer list was provided for women than for men and that words for women were generally much less favorable than words for men (Kleinke, 1974). We appear to have far more names for women than men, and many have a more negative connotation than the male terms. In Table 4.2 some of the terms regularly offered by college students are listed. The differences between the two lists in length and positive/negative connotation reflect attitudes. Unfortunately, it is not only in the area of connotation where definitions for men and women differ.

One author examined the differences in definition for "woman" and "man" in the *Oxford English Dictionary* and found discriminatory treatment. The definition offered for "woman" was (1) an adult female being, (2) a female servant, (3) a lady-love or mistress, and (4) a wife. For men: (1) a human being, (2) the human creature regarded abstractly, (3) an adult male endowed with manly qualities, and (4) a person of importance or position (O'Donnell, 1973). The definitions place men in a more positive light and women in a subordinate position. The connotation and the denotation for "men" and "women" are decidedly different.

"Dear Abby" included this letter in her syndicated column on February 11, 1982:

DEAR ABBY: I found this in the "AORN Journal"—a publication put out by the Association of Operating Nurses:

"The Chickenization of Women"

"Women are frequently referred to as poultry. We cluck at hen parties. When we aren't henpecking men, we are egging them on. In youth we are chicks. Mothers watch over their broods. Later we are old biddies with an empty-nest syndrome. Is it just a coincidence that so many women's wages are chicken feed?"

ANN D'ARCY, OKLAHOMA NURSE

DEAR ANN: No. And ain't it fowl?

Men and women are referred to by a number of slang terms. Sometimes women are referred to as "chicks" and men as "cocks." List some other terms you and others use to refer to men and women in addition to those provided in Table 4.2. After you have listed these terms independently, discuss the terms with your classmates. What similarities and differences occurred among the lists? Which of the terms are negative and which are positive? Determine if your classmates agree about the positive or negative nature of each word. If you disagree on the evaluation of a term, discuss your rationale.

Terms for Men	Positive or Negative?	Terms for Women	Positive or Negative?

"When a lady never marries, she's an *old maid.*"
"Then when a man never marries, is he an old butler?''

DENNIS THE MENACE® used by permission of Hank Ketcham and © by North America Syndicate.

The longer list of names for women and their more negative nature can be attributed to a variety of reasons. First, the group in power typically does the naming or labeling. In our culture men tend to name people, places, and things. How many dictionaries have been written by women compared to the number written by men? In a recent brochure advertising a new book, *The Story of English* by Robert McCrum, William Cran, and Robert MacNeil, the copy suggests that many new words came from the experience of the American pioneers. However, the examples given are all from male pioneers: cowboys, gamblers, and railroad workers.

Second, women are observed and men are the observers. As we will note in the later chapter on nonverbal communication, women tend to be the objects of observation as they dress in more unusual, provocative, and colorful ways. More names are needed for the objects of observation than for the observer. Third, women are viewed as subordinate to men and, consequently, have more negative terms applied to them. Last, women have a wider range of behaviors than do men, so that a larger vocabulary might be necessary to encompass a variety of roles.

Let us examine some specific generalizations we can make about the differences in labeling women and men. First, names for women are sometimes created by adding another word or a diminutive to a name for men. Women's professions are sometimes indicated by adding the suffixes "-ess" or "-ette," as in changing waiter to waitress, drum major to drum majorette, or actor to actress. Also, women serving in traditional male professions are sometimes referred to by adding the word "female" or "lady" before the profession, as in, "She is a female doctor"; "She's a lady attorney"; or "She is a female senator." In each of these cases, women appear to be subordinate, less important, and their work more trivial.

Second, names for women are frequently more sexual than names for men. In one study, about ten times more sexual terms cited were associated with women than with men (Stanley, 1972). Our culture often views women as sex objects or as objects of conquest. Some of the less vulgar sexual terms for women include "broad," "slut," "cherry," "slit," and "whore." Few comparable names exist for men. Those that do are often positively associated with sexual prowess (e.g., "hunks"). Ethnic women are especially likely to be labeled in a derogatory, sexual fashion (Allen, 1984).

Third, different metaphors are used for women and men. Women are frequently depersonalized as some form of food, e.g., honey, sugar, cookie, piece of cake, pudding, tomato, cupcake, suggesting, as one author wrote, that women appear to be "laid out on a buffet" (Nilsen, 1972). Men are sometimes referred to as a "hunk" or a "big cheese," but these terms are far less common than the many terms for women. Many flower names are applied to women, e.g., "rose," "clinging vine," "sweet pea," "petunia," while the names of flowers, when applied to men, suggest that they are effeminate, for example, "pansy." Women are referred to by undesirable animal names—"cow," "pig," "sow," "heifer," and "dog," or by baby animal names—"bunny," "kitty," "chick," or "lamb." Men are named aggressive animal names—"stud," "buck," "wolf," and "tomcat."

Fourth, polar opposites are used to describe women and men. The same term used to describe women is often considered negative, whereas, when applied to men is positive. Consider the lists of words offered in Table 4.3. A "governor" is viewed as someone who is the head of a state or in charge of land, while a "governess" is in charge of other people's children. Most people would rather be a "bachelor" than an "old maid," or a "Don Juan" than a "whore." As you examine the list of female terms, you might observe that a number of the words have become associated with sexuality, e.g., "whore," "madam," "mistress," and "lady," or are used to suggest gay men, e.g., "queen."

One study examined the different connotations people have for the terms "bitch" and "bastard." Men associated "cold," "untrustworthy," and "deceitful" with "bastard," and "insincere," "tactless," and "dominant" with "bitch." Women described "bastard" as "loud," "narrow-minded," and "untrustworthy," and described "bitch" as "cold," "tactless," and "phony." The authors conclude that when a woman is called a "bitch" it suggests she is being moved from a stereotypically feminine role to a masculine role; whereas, men who are called "bastard" are only viewed as an exaggeration of their masculine identity (Coyne, Sherman & O'Brien, 1978).

Table 4.3 "Parallel" terms for women and men

Women	Men
Whore	Stud
Old maid	Bachelor
Madam	Sir
Mistress	Master
Lady	Gentleman
Governess	Governor
Queen	King
Majorette	Major

Fifth, more familiar terms are used for women than for men. Women are frequently addressed by their first names, even when they have professional status, while men are more often addressed by their formal titles with an honorific. In addition, few people would call a man "honey," "baby," "sweetie," "hon," or "sugar," but most females have been addressed by these terms, even by people whom they have not previously met.

Sixth, women are identified by their associations with others far more frequently than are men. As we stated previously, many women are known as "Mrs. husband's name." How frequently are men known as "Mr. Barbara Jones"? Similarly, countless obituary columns, marriage announcements, and other similar personal news stories have been gathered to demonstrate how frequently a woman will be identified as someone's wife, mother, daughter, or sister.

Seventh, women are more likely to be referred to by euphemisms than men. **Euphemisms** are seemingly inoffensive words substituted for more offensive terms. The two most common euphemisms for women are "lady" and "girl." The word "lady" has positive connotations for some, but many women can still recall the images of a white-gloved, soft-spoken, pretty, polite, and always proper woman the term tended to create. In the military, the term "lady" is reserved for the wives of officers (or as a degrading term applied to male recruits), while the word "wife" is used for the wives of the enlisted men. To many people, the term "lady" suggests a class struggle in which only some can hope to become "ladies," while others must be satisfied to be "wives."

"Girl" is problematic, too. The term "girl" refers to a young woman, typically one who has not yet pubesced. However, adult women refer to themselves as "girls" both in self-praise (good girl) and self-blame (bad girl) situations (Slama & Slowey, 1988). Adult males, however, use "boy" only in self-blame situations. The authors explain this difference by suggesting that our culture tends to "infantize" females throughout their life span while disapproving of immaturity for males.

The essay reprinted below appeared in *The Chronicle of Higher Education.* The author offers a unique perspective on sexist language. After you have had an opportunity to read the essay, write a response as though you were writing a letter to the editor of the *Chronicle.* Share your letter with your classmates and listen to their letters. Discuss differences in your perceptions of this complicated issue.

If the 'Miss' Fits, Use it—Sexist Language Is Appropriate to Describe Sexist People
By Robin Barratt

EVER SINCE HIGH SCHOOL, I have been ready at only a few moments' notice to address my creditors as "Dear Friends," or, in a more formal or possibly more impecunious mood, as "Dear Sales Representatives." I recently found myself balking, however, at the prospect of using a nonsexist salutation in a letter to a "feminist" anti-abortion group.

I finally decided on "Dear Sirs"—an opening that did not credit the organization with any political concerns I did not feel it represented. My reluctance to use nonsexist language in this case made me reconsider much of the rhetoric I have routinely used.

Obviously, form is important—without nonsexist language, for example, a child is presented with a world of sex-segregated occupations (fire*men*, sales*women*). It is no wonder that it was considered an insult when, following the publication of *Burger's Daughter,* the South African government referred to Nadine Gordimer as an "authoress." It is also considered insulting to call my fellow Barnard College students "girls"; we are women, thank you.

Still, there are contexts in which the use of feminist-sounding language would be a separation of form from content. Particularly given the current conservative climate, there are meetings women are not likely to be chairing in the immediate future; it would be more misleading than nonsexist to refer to the men who do as "chairpersons."

The *American Heritage Dictionary* defines feminism as "militant advocacy of equal rights and status for women." If a female chairperson is dedicated, rather, to the eradication of women's social/political rights, surely her intent is not reflected by her politically correct title. *Ms.* Schlafly?

Nonsexist language is as much a question of application as of gender. In the interest of accuracy, possibly movements and people who ignore women's rights should be discussed in terms echoing this lack of concern. Simply changing the pronouns in a textbook isn't enough if women are not thought of as part of the audience—and, in history and other courses, as part of the subject as well.

I once took a summer course on the religious experience of *man*kind, which was an accurate description of its content. Granted, female prophets were few and far between, but the role of women within a religion is at least half the religious experience of *human*kind.

Of course, everything's relative, and it is a matter of choice whether one finds the campus eating establishment's advertisement for "waitpersons" to be offensive, humorous, asinine, or a real breakthrough.

Linguistic change is important when it reflects or causes social change; however, acceptance of feminist rhetoric does not guarantee acceptance of women's rights. It only helps when you mean what you say.

Robin Barratt began her senior year at Barnard College in January.

Some empirical evidence shows that "girl" and "lady" have more negative connotations than the word "woman" when referring to an adult female (McCarthy, Hamilton, Leaper, Pader, Rushbrook & Henley, 1985). Brannon (cited in Slama & Slowey, 1988) found job applicants described as "girls" were rated less favorably than those described as "women."

In addition to terms used as synonyms for "woman" and "man," there are also differences in the denotation and connotation of words used to describe men and women and their behaviors. As Tannen (cited in *Women and Language* 1986) eloquently states, the descriptions are "drenched with gender" (p. 48).

Tannen cites an article in *Newsweek* during the 1984 presidential campaign. The article quotes a Reagan aide who describes Geraldine Ferraro as a "nasty woman" who would "claw Reagan's eyes out." Tannen points out that "nasty" would be a tame adjective to apply to a man, and that men would punch or sock rather than claw, with more effective results. The *Newsweek* article goes on to praise Ferraro for "a striking gift for tart political rhetoric, needling Ronald Reagan on the fairness issue[,] and twitting the Reagan-Bush campaign for its reluctance to let Bush debate her." Tannen observes that "needling" and "twitting" would not sound like praise for a man's verbal abilities. Tannen concludes, "intended to describe her behavior, the words bend back and portray Ferraro as trifling. When we think we're using metaphors, the metaphors are using us" (p. 48).

Conclusions

In this chapter we considered the images of women and men in language. We learned that while man-linked words and traditional generics are widely used, they do not refer with equal likelihood to women and men. They may, in fact, be limiting the behavioral options of people. However, alternatives to these traditional generics exist that can include men and women both linguistically and conceptually. We also observed that many of our language practices are discriminatory to women. Our labels for men and women and our descriptions of them have systematically different connotations that are negative for women. Awareness of these differences can lead to more sensitivity and less negativity. We considered the importance of this area by discussing the effect that language has on thought and behavior. In the following chapter we will turn our attention to the ways in which women and men use language in interactions with others.

5 Language usage of women and men

Introduction

Thus far we have looked at the communication process and the ways gender relates to it. In the last chapter we considered how language creates images of women and men and shapes our perceptions. In this chapter we consider first, how our perceptions affect expectations of difference between women's and men's language production and, second, actual differences between the sexes. We suggest explanations for the findings reviewed and conclude with some strategies for changing the status quo. We want to emphasize from the outset that while some research points to differences in men's and women's language behaviors, this does not imply absolute differences between women and men. In addition, we note that cultural norms are changing so rapidly it is entirely possible that differences noted today will be inaccurate in the future. Insofar as communication codes reflect differential statuses of code users and inasmuch as women have achieved greater socioeconomic equality in recent years, some dramatic changes should be inevitable. In fact, this chapter might be viewed as language stereotypes and behaviors in transition.

Stereotyped perceptions of language differences

Nearly everyone has an opinion about how women and men differ as communicators. Stereotypes about men and women abound. In 1977 Kramer found that teenagers had significantly different perceptions of male and female speakers. Thirty-six items differentiated between female and male stereotypes in Kramer's study. Giles, Scholes, and Young (1983) replicated Kramer's (1977) study in Britain over six years later to determine cross-national validity and to test for change over time. They concluded that despite much social change in sex roles in the intervening years, the "speech stereotypes accorded the sexes appear not to have abated" (p. 255) as their findings were quite similar to Kramer's.

In an influential and controversial book, Lakoff (1975) suggested that women and men speak differently from each other. Lakoff argued that women's language keeps women in their (inferior) place by denying them the means of strong self-expression and providing them expressions that suggest triviality and uncertainty. Lakoff's work has been important in focusing attention on the subject of women and language, but it takes a position that some researchers find offensive (Spender, 1980).

Let us examine some of the specific ways we stereotype the language of women and men, keeping in mind some of Lakoff's early ideas, although Lakoff advanced her opinions, as *descriptions* of women's speech, not of people's *perceptions* of it.

Before you begin to examine the material in this chapter, compile a list of language differences you believe exist between women and men. Include such features as which sex uses assertive language, which sex is more "proper" in language usage, which words are used by men and which by women, what topics are typically discussed by men and which are generally reserved for women, and which sex uses more expressiveness or feeling communication as contrasted with goal-oriented communication. After you have compiled your list, read the chapter. Then, mark those statements which are consistent with other people's stereotyped notions of female/male differences in language usage. Finally, write a short response to each of your statements in which you identify it as true, false, or limited in some manner by the research which has been completed.

A common perception is that women use empty talk, that they seldom say anything of importance, that they deal in the trivial and the unimportant. Lakoff (1975) speculated that women use adjectives such as "adorable," "sweet," and "divine" more than men do. People believe that more emotional speech and more extensive use of details characterize women's speech (Kramer, 1977; Shimanoff, 1987). Men's speech, however, is viewed as bold and straightforward, focusing on important subjects (Fillmer & Haswell, 1977).

In addition, women's speech is viewed as unassertive and lacking in power (Siegler & Siegler, 1976). Lakoff (1975) believed that women had a tentative register that indicated they lacked full confidence in the truth of their claims. Male language is viewed as aggressive, contrasting with female language, which is seen as passive (Fillmer & Haswell, 1977; Fitzpatrick & Bochner, 1981). Women are characterized as more submissive, more susceptible to social pressure, more responsive to the needs of others in their language, while the opposite traits are ascribed to men (Kramer, 1974, 1975; Markel, Long & Saine, 1976; Shuy, 1969; Strainchamps, 1971).

Men are believed to be more likely than women to use hostile language and profanity. In 1975, Lakoff speculated that women were less likely to use profanity than men. Staley (1978) found evidence that this perception persists. Staley asked students between the ages of 18 and 47 to respond to a questionnaire listing a series of emotional situations. For each situation the respondents reported the expletive they would use, the expletive they thought a typical member of the other sex would use, and their opinion of the strength of the expletives identified. The results were most interesting. Women overpredicted the number of expletives used by men, while men underpredicted

By permission of Johnny Hart and NAS, Inc.

the number of expletives used by women. Even when identical expletives were ascribed both to men and women, the strength of these expletives was judged to be stronger when men used them rather than when women did. In general, women are perceived as more "proper" and polite than men (Quina, Wingard & Bates 1987), and are expected by both sexes to adopt a more polite way of speaking than men, regardless of topic (Kemper, 1984).

Another stereotype about men and women is that they use different words and discuss different topics. This is closely related to the idea of women and men differing in the "politeness" of their speech, although it actually goes beyond this notion. For example, men are perceived to use more jargon and also tend to claim authority in areas such as business, politics, baseball, and women's speech. Women, on the other hand, in addition to avoiding harsh language, are viewed as discussing social life, books, food and drinks, caring for their husbands, and social work (Kramer, 1978).

As we shall see in the following sections, the clichés about the language of women and men appear to be stronger than are the actual differences (Kramer, Thorne & Henley, 1978). We perceive men and women to be more different than alike. But we have not always demonstrated these differences in behavioral studies. The reasons for this stem, in large part, from several factors inherent in the research. First, much of our information about male/female language differences is based on introspection (Eakins & Eakins, 1978; Lakoff, 1972, 1973, 1974, 1975, 1978) and personal observation (Lakoff, 1975; Parlee, 1979). Second, distinctions among self-reports, reports of others' perceptions, and observations of behaviors are not always clearly drawn. For these reasons, as well as because of the influence of subcultural differences on our perception, and the influence of living in a society which stresses differences between women and men rather than similarities, we tend to perceive exaggerated differences in the verbalizations of women and men. In an attempt to separate stereotypic beliefs from actual behavior, we will now consider actual differences found in women's and men's language behavior. As we do this, we keep in mind the difficulties associated with this task.

Some evidence indicates that women engage in communication for social and affiliative reasons more than men (Wheeless & Duran, 1982). For instance, in mock jury deliberations, two researchers found that females scored significantly higher than males in positive reactions, i.e., utterances which exhibited solidarity, released tension, or expressed agreement. Men scored higher than women in the aggressive category of attempted answers, i.e., utterances that expressed a suggestion, an opinion, or an orientation (Strodtbeck & Mann, 1956).

Similarly, in small-group settings women initiate more verbal acts; men provide more suggestions, opinions, or information; and women offer more reactions including agreements or disagreements (Aries, 1982). In a study which sought to determine behaviors predicting male and female democratic leadership, females contributed a significantly greater percentage of positive socioemotional communication acts than male democratic leaders (Fowler & Rosenfeld, 1979).

In an investigation of preschoolers which indicates that girls develop language strategies earlier than boys, Haslett (1983) observes that "Females are reinforced more than males for being other-directed and nurturant" (p. 128). Also in examining preschoolers, Cook, Fritz, McCornack, and Visperas (1985) found support for differences between boys' and girls' functional use of language. Specifically, Cook et al. found boys using speech to initiate activity, direct others, and assert themselves more than girls.

Women are more supportive conversationalists (Thorne & Henley, 1977). In a study which used male-male dyads and female-female dyads, it was determined that female dyads were more affiliative and socially expressive than were male dyads. Specifically, women were much more positive in affect and laughed more than males (Ickes, Schermer & Steeno, 1979).

An interesting investigation examined the communication behaviors of adolescents on a co-ed three-week bicycle trip. In this study, females were more likely than males to offer verbal support and comfort; however, males were more responsive when the situation required physical assistance. Although it was not observed that males and females actually differed in their camping abilities, males were perceived as the more competent campers. The researchers concluded that in tasks requiring physical assistance, males may have taken the initiative and females may have deferred because they shared the perception that males were more competent (Zeldin, Small & Savin-Williams, 1982).

These observed functional differences may contribute to our stereotypes of women as emotional speakers and men as rational speakers.

Differences in women's and men's vocabularies

Distinct differences have been noted in the working vocabularies of men and women (Crosby & Nyquist, 1977; Lakoff, 1975). Among other differences, men have been found to use more colloquial (nonstandard) linguistic forms than women (Price & Graves, 1980).

Color language

Men and women are also known to differ considerably in language used to describe colors, with women generally having a far more expansive and precise range of options to choose from than men. Before reading further, ask a friend of the other sex to name the colors of ten items in the room. At the same time, write down your own descriptors for those same items. Compare your lists. You may find that they conform to the research findings in this area.

Lakoff (1975) noticed that women have a far more discriminating set of names for colors than men. Words such as "puce," "chartreuse," "mauve," "ecru," and "teal" are more likely to show up in women's discourse than men's. We want to note, however, that while women generally have more expansive and more precise color vocabularies, there are many exceptions to this rule. For instance, people—both men and women—employed as interior designers, painters, hair stylists, and artists are aware of color nuances far more so than the norm. We also may be witnessing a change in the sensitivity to color learned by young people. Rich's (1977) research suggests that younger men's color vocabularies, while not equally as expansive as women's are, nonetheless, more sophisticated than their fathers's.

Sexual language

Men and women do not discuss genitalia and sexual functions in similar language. Sanders and Robinson (1979) asked male and female research participants to identify the terms they would use to describe intercourse and male and female genitalia. They were also asked to identify their use of these terms in four different contexts: (1) informal conversation in a mixed-sex group, (2) informal conversation in a same-sex group, (3) private conversation with their parents, and (4) private conversation with their lover.

Context obviously affected language use, with the most clinical terminology used by both males and females when conversing with parents. However, there was a sex difference also, since females used language more conservative and clinical in all contexts than reported by males, and both males and females were more hesitant to name female than male genitalia. That both male and female participants were more reluctant to label female genitalia is interesting because no such similar hesitation confronts men when referring to their own genitalia. In fact, men often use a form of "power slang" such as "my weapon" and "my pistol." The language used by women in discussing their own genitalia was sometimes so vague as to be unclear, which, Sanders and Robinson argue, may contribute to difficulties between men and women in discussing their sexuality.

Simkins (1982) asked undergraduate students the terms they would use to describe female genitalia, male genitalia, and sexual intercourse in the same four settings of Sanders and Robinson. Simkins found that men and women tended to use formal terminology in mixed company and with parents. With same-sex friends, males used colloquial terms for all three concepts, while females retained more formal terminology. In discussion with a spouse or lover, both males and females used formal terminology for the female genitalia; females retained a preference for formal terminology for male genitalia, while men used more colloquial terms. Both males and females used colloquial terminology for sexual intercourse.

Profane language

We noted previously that women and men are expected to use profanity and hostile language at different rates. Selnow's (1985) results tend to confirm that expectation, while Staley's (1978) findings indicate that men and women swear at about the same rate, but that their similar behaviors are perceived differently. A methodological difference might account for these different results. Selnow asked his respondents to estimate on a four-point scale (1 = never, 2 = rarely, 3 = occasionally, 4 = frequently) their own use of profanity in everyday conversations. Staley asked people to respond to a series of emotional situations with the expletive they would use in those situations. Thus, Staley probably got closer to actual communication behavior than Selnow. As previously discussed, Staley noticed that an expletive used by a man was perceived as stronger than the same expletive used by a woman. This type of perceptual artifact might have affected Selnow's results.

Qualifying language

Research indicates that women use more intensifiers than men. *Intensifiers* are adjectives and adverbs that, as the word implies, intensify the noun or verb being described. For instance, the words "so," "such," "quite," and "awfully" are all examples of intensifiers. Research dating back to the 1920s (Jespersen, 1922) indicates that women use more intensifiers than men. More recent research confirms those earlier beliefs (Key, 1975; Lakoff, 1975; Mulac, Wiemann, Widenmann & Gibson, 1988; Schultz, Briere & Sandler, 1984). When

McMillan, Clifton, McGrath, and Gale (1977) contrasted men's and women's speech in same and mixed-gender groups, women were found to use five to six times more intensifiers than men. However, as Mulac and Lundell (1986) caution, we might be wise to look at intensifiers in the context of other language behaviors to separate male from female speakers. Mulac and Lundell found that intensive adverbs were used more by women than men. However, it was only in combination with several other language behaviors that intensifiers were accurate in predicting a speaker's sex.

Hedges convey just the opposite meaning from intensifiers. Rather than exaggerate meaning, *hedges* are used to soften or weaken other words or phrases. As such, their use may indicate the tentative, or seemingly tentative commitment one makes to the thought being expressed. Examples of hedges include "maybe," "perhaps," "somewhat," "you know," "in my opinion," and "it seems to me." All of these expressions indicate something less than assurance or conviction about what is being expressed. *Disclaimers*, a special class of hedges, are words or phrases which weaken or disparage the speaker's subsequent request or statement. The disclaimer suggests the speaker is not serious, sincere, or very interested in his or her request. For instance, a person might say: "If you don't mind, could we . . ."; "I know this will sound unreasonable, but would you . . ."; "Of course, I don't know anything about politics, but I think . . ."

Research on hedges is somewhat mixed, with some findings indicating that adult women use more hedges than adult men (Crosby & Nyquist, 1977), but other research indicates nonsignificant differences (Staley, 1982). Inasmuch as Staley's work was done with children and adolescents (ranging in age from 4 to 16), the results of these two studies are not clearly comparable. It could be that Staley's work demonstrates that linguistic behaviors are changing as a function of increased attention given to men's and women's communication behavior. Another interpretation is that skill in using hedges is something acquired as one grows older.

In another study examining the use of hedges, Sayers and Sherblom (1987) found that in mixed-sex dyads males and females used about the same number of hedges. Sayers and Sherblom varied the sex and age of the conversational partners in their study, and they conclude that hedges are a weak predictor of speaker's sex and are strongly influenced by situational factors such as age and sex of the conversational partner.

Verbal fillers

Verbal fillers frequently occur in our communication with others. *Verbal fillers* are those words or phrases we use to fill in silences, such as "like," "right," "okay," "well," and "you know." We are sometimes afraid of allowing a silence to occur when we are talking, so we fill in the blanks with meaningless words.

Research by Hirschman (1975) and Mulac, Lundell, and Bradac (1986) found that women use more fillers than men. On the other hand, Mulac and Lundell (1986) found that verbal fillers were more indicative of men's speech than women's. Mulac and Lundell believe that men used fillers as a "floor holding" device, i.e., something to say so they would not lose their speaking turn. These different findings suggest the wisdom of examining the function of language behaviors rather than simply looking for the behaviors.

Grammatical language

Related to men's and women's differences in vocabulary is the greater tendency of women to engage in hypercorrection. *Hypercorrection* is reminding others of the correct (proper) form of language usage when they have made an error (e.g., "You mean 'lie' instead of 'lay' don't you"? or "Do you mean 'set' the glass on the table"?). Crosby and Nyquist's (1977) work indicates that women do tend to engage in hypercorrection more than men.

In general, then, men's and women's vocabularies differ in some interesting ways. In some instances women and men differ in the extensiveness of vocabularies used to describe certain phenomena (e.g., colors). Men and women talk about sexuality differently. They may use the same number of expletives, although women are perceived to use fewer. Women use more intensifiers, although alone they may not be a precise predictor of speaker's sex. While it is not certain whether women use more hedges or verbal fillers, it is the case that they hypercorrect more than men. Taken together, these differences indicate that women use words and expressions more polite and reserved, but also less direct and assertive than men. However, it is advisable to remember Spender's (1980) argument about differences in the area of vocabulary. Spender writes that "individuals generally acquire and use more words associated with their daily tasks—so a schoolteacher for example would probably use a different repertoire from a truck driver—and in a society which practices a sexual division of labor—and of interests—it would not be surprising to find that women have a different vocabulary from men" (pp. 33–34). Male and female vocabulary differences may be primarily the result of different spheres of activity and, thus, subject to change as activities change.

Differences in women's and men's questions and assertions

In addition to differences in men's and women's vocabularies, there are also interesting differences in the types of questions they ask and the assertions they make. Understanding these differences further enables us to understand the orientations men and women bring to their conversational interactions.

Boys make more requests than girls in seeking help.

Compound requests vs. direct requests

When we make a request of another person, we may do so in a direct manner or we may add qualifiers and other terms to soften the requests. If you wish to have someone come closer to you, you may simply say, "Come here." On the other hand, you may say, "Please come here," or "Would you please come here," or "If you don't mind, would you please come here." If you use the command, "Come here," you are making a direct request or giving a direct order; if you use any of the other longer forms, you are making a compound request. Apparently women use compound requests more frequently than do men (Thorne & Henley 1975; Zimmerman & West 1975). Women are more likely to ask others to do things for them with more words than men.

In two studies examining the request patterns of preschool children, boys made more direct requests than girls. Pellegrini (1982) found boys made more requests for help in completing a puzzle than girls. Another investigation demonstrated that boys who were 4, 8, and 12 years of age all made more direct requests than did girls of the same ages (Haas, 1981). In general, girls try to solve problems themselves rather than request help when presented with a problem.

Tag questions

Tag questions occur when we make a declarative statement, then follow it with a question relating to the same statement. For example, "It's really hot in here, isn't it?" or "This is a good movie, don't you think?" and "They are all going out to dinner, aren't they?" are all tag questions.

We sometimes use tag questions when we are not certain of information. If someone has told you something you did not hear completely, or if you have reason to believe a situation has changed, you might inquire, "You're going to attend U.S.C. this fall, aren't you?"

We also use tag questions when we try to elicit information from another person, when we attempt to obtain an answer to a question, or when we try to strike up a conversation. For instance, we might ask, "Texas is really lovely at this time of the year, isn't it?"; "The game between Michigan State and Iowa was interesting, wasn't it?"; "This party is pretty dull, don't you think?"

Finally, we use tag questions when we are attempting to persuade someone to share our belief or opinion. You might suggest to your spouse, "Playing cards with the Millers tonight sounds like fun, doesn't it?" You might say to your parents, "The tuition at Georgetown is really expensive compared to Purdue where I want to go, isn't it?" To a friend you might say, "I can borrow your brown suit for my job interview tomorrow, can't I?"

Early research in this area is conflicting. Zimmerman and West (1975) found that women make more frequent use of tag questions in conversations than do men. In fact, women participants in Zimmerman and West's study used twice as many tag questions as men. In mixed-sex groups, women used three times as many tag questions as women in all female groups (McMillan, Clifton, McGrath & Gale, 1977). However, men in a professional meeting used far more tag questions than the women in attendance (Dubois & Crouch, 1975). Recent research (Mulac & Lundell, 1986) has indicated that tag questions are more common in women's language than men's.

In light of these somewhat mixed findings, it may be wise to examine the context (informal conversation, business meeting, etc.) and the function of tag questions (i.e., whether the purpose is to draw out conversational partners, to request agreement or confirmation, to forestall opposition, etc.), rather than simply searching for their presence.

Number of questions

Do women or men ask more questions? In a study of interaction among male-male dyads and female-female dyads, a greater proportion of the women's comments consisted of answers to questions than did the men's comments (Rosenfeld, 1966). However, in an analysis of the conversations of three middle-class couples between the ages of twenty-five and thirty-five, the women posed three times as many questions as the men (Fishman, 1978). Thus, it is not clear which sex asks more questions.

To give you the opportunity to develop alternatives to some of the linguistic forms discussed in this section, complete the following exercise. Enter the requested response in each of the spaces provided:

1. Imagine that another person has entered the room and left the door open rather than shutting it (as it was before he or she entered). You wish to have the door closed.
    DIRECT REQUEST: _____

    COMPOUND REQUEST: _____

2. You are seated at dinner and no one has passed the salt and pepper. You would like to season your food.
    DIRECT REQUEST: _____

    COMPOUND REQUEST: _____

3. You are attempting to maintain a conversation with another person who is quiet. You know that the other person attends an out-of-state college and you decide to discuss college life.
    TAG QUESTION: _____

    DECLARATIVE STATEMENT: _____

    DECLARATIVE STATEMENT FOLLOWED BY A DIRECT QUESTION: _____

4. The person with whom you are speaking has made a very negative statement about people with your ancestry. She or he does not know that you are a member of the group and you do not wish to disclose the information. However, you do want to indicate to this person that his or her perceptions may be incorrect.
    TAG QUESTION: _____

    DECLARATIVE STATEMENT: _____

    DECLARATIVE STATEMENT FOLLOWED BY A DIRECT QUESTION: _____

5. The other person in a conversation has asked you a highly personal question which you feel uncomfortable answering. Provide a response which would allow you to refuse to answer the question without offending the other person:
DIRECT STATEMENT: _____

DIRECT STATEMENT PREFACED BY A QUESTION OR QUESTION FORM SUCH AS "DID YOU KNOW?" _____

6. You are attempting to talk to a new acquaintance about a matter of importance to you, but he or she is not responding to you. Your desire is to continue the conversation.
DIRECT QUESTION: _____

DECLARATIVE STATEMENT FOLLOWED BY A DIRECT QUESTION: _____

DIRECT STATEMENT PREFACED BY A QUESTION OR QUESTION FORM SUCH AS "DID YOU KNOW?" "DID YOU HEAR?" OR "GUESS WHAT?" _____

7. You are interviewing a potential employee. You need to ask this person about his or her experience.
DIRECT QUESTION: _____

TAG QUESTION: _____

DECLARATIVE STATEMENT FOLLOWED BY A DIRECT QUESTION: _____

8. You are talking with someone you recently met and she or he tells you about something that is unfamiliar to you, but which you would like to learn about.
DIRECT QUESTION: _____

TAG QUESTION: _____

Perhaps more useful than determining whether questions are asked more frequently by one sex or the other is considering the rationale for question asking. Eakins and Eakins (1978) state that asking questions and interrogating people is associated with the behavior of a superior, while acquiescing or replying is often considered to be the behavior of a subordinate.

Fishman (1978) offers a quite different reason for asking questions. Fishman theories that women ask questions to elicit verbal responses from men. Frequently women preface their comments with phrases such as "Do you know what?" In these instances, they may be attempting to gain a "What?" or similar response which serves to give them the floor and grant them permission to speak.

Tannen (1986) agrees that questions, as other conversational devices, can be used to show interest or power. We are familiar with questions as genuine requests for information. Tannen illustrates how questions may also be used for criticizing or giving orders: "Instead of saying 'Don't do that!' people ask 'What are you doing?' or 'Why are you doing that?' " (p. 57).

In general, women and men may differ in their use of assertions and question asking. Most research shows that women make more compound requests than men and ask more tag-end questions. However, some studies that have tried to examine tag-end questions abandoned the variable because neither men nor women used many of them (i.e., Martin & Craig, 1983). It is not clear which sex asks more questions, although several researchers have observed that trying to answer this question is not a worthwhile endeavor. Instead, we might focus on the types of questions men and women ask and the functions these questions serve in context.

Generally, it is worth noting that none of the language differences reviewed in this chapter are immutable. While some of the findings support the stereotypes discussed previously, many do not. In sum, the findings suggest a much more complex situation than the stereotypes provide.

Some studies indicate (Martin & Craig, 1983; Mulac et al., 1988; Sayers and Sherblom, 1987) that sex differences in language behavior are sensitive to context, such as the sex of the conversational partner, and as such, are moderated and changed. Specifically, Mulac et al. (1988) found that in mixed-sex dyads, both men and women changed their verbal style to emulate their partner's. However, despite this capacity for change, as we noted previously, stereotypes of difference persist. These stereotypes, coupled with the actual differences we have discussed, lead to attributions made about speakers. We will now turn our attention to these attributions.

Attributions made about speakers based on language cues

Some people have written about the effects of using specific language behaviors on judgments about the speaker. For example, Bock, Butler, and Bock (1984) found that using profanity in a classroom speech results in negative evaluations from the student audience for both men and women. Women received more negative comments for using excretory profanity and men for sexual profanity, although speeches by both sexes using any profanity were more negatively rated than speeches without profanity.

Some research indicates that behaviors used by women are devalued by listeners. Compound requests are viewed as less assertive than direct requests or orders and are seen as feminine behavior (Newcombe & Armkoff, 1979).

An examination of the effects of tag questions and hedges yielded some disturbing results. In this investigation, these behaviors were detrimental only when they were used by women. In small groups, women using tag questions and hedges were perceived to have little knowledge, little intelligence, and little influence. These same negative effects were not produced by men using tag question and hedges (Bradley, 1981). In fact, men who used these devices were perceived as polite and other-directed. These findings imply that the linguistic devices which women have traditionally used may not be the significant elements in the devaluation of women's language; rather, women's lower status may be the relevant factor. Women may be underestimated because of their biological sex rather than their linguistic style.

However, in a simulated courtroom setting, Wright and Hosman (1983) discovered that the use of hedges decreased attractiveness ratings for both male and female witnesses. The difference between Wright and Hosman's and Bradley's findings on the variable of hedges may be due to the different contexts in which they were studied. Certainty may be more attractive in a witness than in a discussion partner.

As Hosman (1989) explains, hedges may signal two types of uncertainty which are related differently to attributions:

> One type of uncertainty is lack of control in a context. Speakers who are uncertain may hesitate or hedge, which, in turn, causes them to be perceived as nonauthoritative. The other type of uncertainty is due either to understanding that the world is probablistic, requiring qualification of comments, or to planning one's comments. This could be labeled "rhetorical uncertainty" and would be a more positive form attributionally than the other type (p. 402).

In Hosman's work, sex was not a relevant factor in making these attributions.

Some researchers have examined general communication style to see if different styles receive different attributions. Quina et al. (1987) wrote 12 sentence pairs to represent 12 examples of "feminine-style language" and "nonfeminine style language." Quina et al. used Lakoff's (1975) observations to form the "feminine sentences." Non-feminine language in this study was constructed in opposition to the feminine (i.e., feminine: "Have you tried the other desk?" Non-feminine: "Try the other desk").

As we have seen, not all of Lakoff's speculations are true of women's language behavior. Given this methodology, the findings of Quina et al. are not unexpected. They found that the feminine-style sentences as a group defined styles corresponding to sex-role stereotypes. The feminine style was seen as less competent than the non-feminine style.

However, the feminine style did convey some positive qualities not recognized by Lakoff (1975). Sensitivity, friendliness, and sincerity were some valued qualities conveyed by the feminine style in this study.

Mulac and his colleagues (Mulac, Incontro & James, 1985; Mulac & Lundell, 1986) have demonstrated what they call a "gender-linked language effect." In this effect, raters do respond differently to the audiotaped speech of women and men. As in the work of Quina et al., the difference is not completely in favor of males. Males are rated as more dynamic speakers than females, while females receive higher evaluations of aesthetic quality. Mulac and his associates see this gender-linked effect as separate from sex-role stereotypes since pretesting reveals respondents are unable to guess accurately the speaker's sex from listening to the tape.

Finally, Zahn (1989) found some differences in evaluations of contributions attributed to males and females in transcripts of informal conversations, but "both male and female speakers were responded to with considerable variability from conversation to conversation" (p. 69). Zahn's conclusion is that evaluators looked at more than speakers' sex when making judgments about them. The optimistic interpretation of these recent findings includes the notion that while stereotyped descriptors still exist, they may not interfere with evaluations if raters are not directed to take sex into consideration. Thus, males and females may not be judged differently for using the same behaviors, and females may not be devalued for using different linguistic devices than males. However, such an optimistic outlook needs the support of continued study.

Explaining differences in language usage of women and men

In our previous discussion, we have looked at the perceptions we hold about men's and women's language. We have then examined the evidence to see how many of these perceptions have been supported. Finally, we have looked at how perceptions interact with speakers' behaviors to create attributions about those speakers. In this section we will look at several explanations for the findings we have just reviewed.

Dominance and control by men

One of the most important questions to ask while reading through the various conflicting findings in this area is, "Why?" Why are differences found? Why are similarities found? Why are men and women behaving in these ways?

One of the most common answers to these questions is the notion that men dominate and are in control in our culture. You observed in chapter 4 that the language used to discuss women and men illustrates this point very well. Researchers in other fields have observed the importance of learning about dominance and submission from our symbolic systems. Sociologist Hugh Duncan (1968) states it is axiomatic that "Hierarchy is expressed through the symbolization of superiority, inferiority, and equality, and of passage from one to another" (p. 52). He explains that individuals learn the role behaviors associated with being a superior, an inferior, and an equal. He proposes as well that individuals move in and out of these roles throughout their lifetimes.

Although women and men do not play static inferior and superior roles, a great deal of verbalization fits the model of submission and dominance. Well-known and respected writers on sex differences, such as Thorne and Henley (1975), Lakoff (1973), and Kramarae (1981), have argued that the language used by women and men demonstrates and perpetrates a superior-subordinate relationship. Specifically, Lakoff writes that "women's language" stems from the idea that women are marginal to the serious concerns of life. She hypothesizes that variations in language patterns reflect and support the different and unequal roles of males and females in our culture. Thorne and Henley (1975) write that there is an assumption that male speech is the norm, adding that male dominance is apparent in the content of the words each sex is expected to use. Jesperson (1922) observes that men are the "chief renovators" of language.

Spender (1980) argues eloquently that even the research reports we read are affected by male control and dominance. She notes that "the way a question is formed determines in part the answer that can be given; in language/sex research there are numerous questions which have been formulated in terms of the inadequacy of women's language, with the result that many of the 'answers' are confined to measurements of that inadequacy" (p. 7).

For example, Spender points to the research process on the subject of tag-end questions, discussed earlier in this chapter. Three distortions are apparent when conflicting results were found, Spender says. First, we cannot really know how many studies found nonsignificant differences between men's and women's use of tag-end questions because journals do not regularly publish unconfirmed hypotheses (and the prediction in sex-*difference* literature is always for difference). Second, Spender believes it is possible that tag-end questions may only be labeled as such when women use them and are called something else (confirmatory questions?) when men use them.

Finally, and most provocatively, Spender observes that Dubois and Crouch's (1975) finding that men use more tag-end questions than women was not "accompanied by a single suggestion that it is *men* who might lack confidence in their language" (p. 9). Thus, Spender concludes, the belief that women's language is deficient to men's can be maintained regardless of research outcome.

Interruptions, overlaps, silence, and other structural differences that we discussed in this section are difficult to deal with in conversations. To gain some practice in dealing with these strategies, complete the following exercise.

1. You have been talking to another person, but he or she has interrupted you three or four times. You begin again, but she or he interrupts once more. After he or she has completed his or her thought, you state:

    _____

    What do you think the other person's response would be if you made this statement: _____

    _____

2. You are disclosing some very exciting news to a friend who is uncharacteristically quiet. Each time you express excitement or enthusiasm, the friend is silent. You try once more, but again he or she is silent. You say:

    _____

    What do you think your friend would say or do in response?

    _____

3. You have met a new person and you are engaged in your first extended conversation with him or her. During the conversation, the

Masculine and feminine behaviors

In chapter 1, we considered the different notions of masculinity and femininity identified in our culture. Men are viewed as instrumental, task-oriented, aggressive, assertive, ambitious, and achievement-oriented. Women, on the other hand, are viewed as relational, socioemotional, caring, nurturing, affiliative, and expressive. As we reviewed the literature on male/female differences in language, we noted that women tend to be more affiliative in their language usage (Ickes, Schermer & Steeno, 1979), more accommodative (Brenner & Vinacke, 1979), more expressive (Balswick & Avertti, 1977), more receptive to subordinates, more encouraging, more willing to provide information, and more concerned with pleasant interpersonal relationships (Baird & Bradley 1979).

other person regularly overlaps you. How do you feel about his or her overlaps? _____

What would you say or do in this situation? _____

4. In a conversation with someone you are dating, you observe that your level of enthusiasm has caused you to overlap or interrupt the other person several times. The other person finally responds by stating that she or he does not believe how rudely you are acting. How do you feel?

What do you say to him or her? _____

5. You are feeling very upset by a personal problem, and your employer initiates a conversation with you. During the conversation, you tend to be unresponsive because you are focusing on your problem. After a period of time, she or he begins to use tag questions, direct questions, and questioning prefaces to her or his direct statements. How do you respond to these questions? _____

After you observed that you were falling into silence rather than responding, would you explain your situation? _____
Why or why not? _____

A number of studies have shown that these are pervasive societal expectancies for females and males (Bem, 1974; Hilgard & Atkinson, 1967; Spence, Helmreich & Stapp, 1975; Tyler, 1965). Berryman and Wilcox (1980) remind us that societal expectations and stereotypical beliefs are relevant because of their potential prescriptive nature in determining sex-role-related communication behavior. Broverman, Vogel, Broverman, Clarkson, and Rosenkrantz (1972) posited that gender-role standards exert real influence which induce people to behave in specific ways. Ruble and Higgins (1976) maintain that sex-role norms are so pervasive in our interactions with others, that we are disposed to behave in sex-appropriate ways. These researchers imply that our beliefs and mythology about sex-role differences in language are as important as actual differences since the beliefs may *cause* female/male differences in behavior.

Keeping these two explanations in mind, we must be cautious in our labels for male and female behavior. For example, what appears as "supportive" behavior may, in fact, be "acquiescence." After all, inasmuch as women generally occupy lower status positions in this culture, it would be anticipated that they would behave supportively. By definition, lower-status people fulfill their cultural roles by supporting higher-status persons. Thus, it may not be a matter of choice when women are generally more attentive to the people they communicate with and when they concentrate more on complimenting contributions of others rather than venturing their own solutions. All of this might just be a form of "gender shucking." Nor might it do any good to ask women whether such behavior is executed as a consequence of their adjusting to inequitable circumstances since, victims of discrimination often learn to adapt to their situation without an awareness of having made such adaptations. The writings of Brouwer, Gerritsen, and DeHaan (1979) lend some plausibility to this line of thought.

Biological causes

Other explanations have been offered to account for differences between women and men in their language use. Several studies have considered physical development, biology and genetic differences; they have postulated that "nature, not nurture" causes the differences that emerge (Dibble, 1976; Jonas & Jonas, 1975). Certain theorists have even implied that women may be biologically more suited for performing tasks which involve understanding and producing language (Maccoby & Jacklin, 1974). Still other theorists posit women as having innate tendencies toward lower self-esteem which, in turn, encourages men to assume a more dominant role in their interactions with one another (Stake & Stake, 1979).

While one cannot rule out biologically based explanations for gender differences, prudence should suggest our heeding Hirst's (1982) advice in this matter:

> It is important that researchers keep in mind the social implications of sex difference research; experiments that could needlessly produce results open to popular misinterpretation should be avoided. For example, a finding that less physically androgynous females had superior verbal ability could have easily been distorted in the press as, say, breast size determines a female's verbal ability, or worse yet, her secretarial abilities. Scientific research is not done in a social vacuum (p. 111).

Neer and Hudson (1982) demonstrate behaviorally that sex differences are not consistently evident in the communication role preferences of women and men, a conclusion which provides further evidence against biology offering a parsimonious explanation for linguistic differences.

Understanding and conforming to communication rules

As an alternative to biological explanations for sex differences in communication behavior, contemporary theorists often explore "rules-based" explanations. Shimanoff (1980) proposes that communication can best be understood as consisting of rules. She explains that some communication rules are explicitly stated, while others are unstated and implicit. The implicit rules are identified by observing communicative behavior. For a person to behave in accordance with a communicative rule, she or he must know the rule, that is, be able to distinguish between behavior conforming to it and behavior inconsistent with it; moreover, she or he must be willing to comply with it.

The appeal of rules theory lies in its potential for explaining many of the previously discussed differences in men's and women's language behavior. Perhaps, for instance, what we normally perceive as less assertive and more compliant behavior in women may, in fact, be greater sensitivity and respect for prescribed rules for interaction. The rules approach also offers some explanation for why we may not always find differences between men's and women's language behaviors. Along these lines Natale (1975) argues that, in an effort to gain approval, women are hypersensitive to other's speech behaviors and will often forego their own idiosyncratic speech styles to emulate their partner's speech style.

Making changes

In this chapter we have determined that women are disadvantaged by the language style identified with them. However, it is important to note that differing language systems are detrimental to both men and women since they limit behavioral options. In addition, the divergent language systems are conducive to misunderstandings between men and women. Given these problems, this section suggests strategies for changing the status quo.

Should women adopt a male style? Some authors have argued that women should adopt the language behaviors associated with men (Lakoff, 1975). Some research findings support this suggestion. For instance, Wright and Hosman (1983) determined that female witnesses in a courtroom setting were perceived as more credible when they used fewer hedges.

However, not all of the research indicates that women benefit from adopting men's language behaviors. In the same study Wright and Hosman also found that women were perceived to be more attractive when they used numerous intensifiers, a traditional form for women.

A related study (Bradac, Hemphill & Tardy, 1981) examined the effects of "powerful" and "powerless" speech on the attribution of blame to a defendant and a plaintiff in an artificial courtroom situation. The "powerless" style was comparable to the female style as it included hedges, intensifiers, polite forms, and hesitations. The "powerful" style included short or one-word replies. In one instance, respondents attributed greater fault to the individual who used the "powerful" style. These results imply that the "powerless" female style may be advantageous in eliciting less attribution of blame.

The above might indicate that women are better off not emulating men's language styles. Such a conclusion is further supported by research indicating that female speech is often rated as more attractive (Mulac & Lundell, 1986) and more closely approximating ideal speech (Kramer, 1978) than male speech. Even when women emulate men's verbal assertiveness, they are often viewed as less credible than men (Bradley, 1980). Rather than encouraging women to change completely their verbal behavior, another strategy might be to reinvest women's language with the positive values that research shows it does have.

A second approach is to consider how both men's and women's language styles might be modified to meet the needs of individual interactants. Women and men who wish to communicate with each other with minimal misunderstanding and with maximal effectiveness should consider a wide range of language options. A woman who is dealing with a man attempting to control the conversation through interruptions, overlaps, and delayed responses might adopt a similarly aggressive stance rather than submit to domination. On the other hand, a man conversing with a woman who is unusually silent, might consider patient probing and active listening. This more flexible and varied approach appears to hold the most promise for constructive alteration of our language styles. To the extent we can adopt new behaviors as necessary, we can modify the stereotypes harmful to all of us. Our language, as a symbol system, can be used to move us from a situation where discrimination is the norm to a more egalitarian social order in which both men and women are afforded opportunities for self-actualization.

Conclusions

In this chapter, we have considered men's and women's language behavior. We found that a number of stereotypes exist influencing our thinking about the language of women and men and that many of these beliefs have been questioned by research findings. This literature also indicates, however, some real differences in language behavior, which affect attributions made about women and men. There are a number of explanations for these findings. These include explanations based on cultural influences as well as explanations based on biological (innate) dispositions for developing various linguistic styles. Perhaps the most promising of these theories are those which draw from "rules-based" orientations, which suggest that men and women behave in accordance with prescribed rules for structuring and enacting sex-specific behaviors. In any event, both men and women will need to understand and appropriately challenge these rules to construct a more liberating repertoire of language behaviors.

6 Nonverbal communication and gender

Introduction

In this chapter, we consider the major nonverbal codes that women and men use: proxemics, kinesics, tactile communication, paralinguistics, and artifactual communication. These codes do not include all possible nonverbal cues. Knapp (1980) mentions the environment, Burgoon, Buller, and Woodall (1989) include chronemics or time considerations, and Malandro, Barker, and Barker (1989) include both of these plus taste and smell. However, in the interest of brevity, we will limit our consideration to those cues we can see (proxemics, kinesics, and artifactual communication), hear (paralinguistics), or feel (tactile communication), recognizing that other cues which involve taste, smell, or an overlap of several senses are also part of the nonverbal codes. We observe that women and men use some nonverbal codes differently and that they also differ in their ability to decode the meaning expressed in the nonverbal medium. Our observations will necessarily be brief since they constitute only one part of this text. A more thorough discussion can be found in Mayo and Henley's (1981) comprehensive treatment of gender differences in nonverbal behavior, Hall's (1984) work, or one of the nonverbal texts referenced above.

Nonverbal communication is clearly as important, if not more important, than verbal communication. The research results in this area demonstrate the significance of these cues (cf. Hegstrom, 1979). *How* we say something is at least as important, perhaps more important, than the content of our message, or *what* we say. Mehrabian (1981), for example, estimates that 93 percent of the social meaning of a face-to-face transaction comes from the nonverbal cues emitted in that transaction. You probably have had the experience of asking someone "What's wrong?" based only on the nonverbal cues the person communicated. If someone is frowning, has slumped shoulders, downcast eyes, and sighs, most of us would believe that person is in a bad mood, even if verbally she or he says, "I'm fine."

It is through nonverbal cues that a great deal of information about gender is communicated. As Hall (1984) notes, "The idea that we display our role, or present ourselves, via nonverbal behavior has long been accepted. . . . It has also been suggested that 'male' and 'female' are roles, each with its set of prescribed behaviors. To the extent that people display their sex role, nonverbal behavior takes on great importance as a vehicle for such display" (p. 3).

Hall observes that nonverbal behaviors are important cues for observers as well. She states that deciding whether a person is male or female is one of the most basic of everyday distinctions. We are able to make this distinction on the basis of many nonverbal cues (i.e., jewelry, gaze behavior, gestures, voice pitch, etc.). Hall additionally states that if there are not enough cues present for us to know the sex of someone or if the cues appear to be mixed, we feel uncomfortable and confused.

Specific differences in various codes

Proxemic differences

Proxemics, the human use of space, was recognized as important as early as 1966 by Hall in her book, *The Hidden Dimension;* it was further examined in 1969 by Sommer in *Personal Space: The Behavioral Basis of Design.* These and other writers analyzed the relevance of space considerations to communication. Burgoon and Jones (1976) clarified the complex set of factors that govern proxemic usage. In the past decade, researchers have paid particular attention to the ways in which women and men use space. In this section we will examine the relationship between gender and proxemics.

Personal space
Two subtopics are basic to our examination of proxemics. **Personal space** is the area one maintains between herself or himself and others. Although you may rarely consider your own personal-space needs, you are likely to be very conscious of them when someone invades your space. Clear norms exist concerning physical distance in social interactions, and individuals frequently experience discomfort when others violate these norms. In general, individuals become more disturbed when others stand too close rather than when they stand too far away (Goldman, 1980).

Women tend to need smaller personal-space zones than men (Hall, 1984). However, one study (Berman & Smith, 1984) indicates that situation plays a large role in determining appropriate interpersonal distance. Berman and Smith had same-sex pairs pose for a picture depicting one of two situations. Half the pairs were asked to wear athletic jerseys and told to pose for a victory picture right after a hard-fought game. The other half were simply asked to pose together for a picture. There were no significant differences between male and female pairs generally in terms of distance. Yet, both female and male pairs stood significantly closer to one another when they were part of the winning-team picture than when they were simply having their picture taken.

Further differences in personal space include the facts that women tend to react more negatively when their space is violated by side-by-side, indirect intrusions, while men tend to react more negatively to frontal, face-to-face intrusions (Fisher & Byrne, 1975), and that females are approached more closely than males (Hall, 1984).

Territoriality
Territoriality is defined as our need to establish and maintain certain spaces of our own. This subject has been investigated more with animals than with people, although it actually represents a common need for both people and animals. While personal space is the area that surrounds us and moves with

Table 6.1 Proxemic differences of women and men

Female Behavior	Male Behavior
Women are approached more closely (cf. Leventhal & Matturro, 1980; Barios, Corbitt, Estes & Topping, 1976; Juhnke, Golman & Buchanan, 1976).	Men are approached less closely.
Women approach others more closely (cf. Fisher, 1973; Sommer, 1959; DeJulio, 1977; Giesen & McClaren, 1976; Snyder & Endelman, 1979; Argyle & Dean, 1965).	Men approach others less closely.
Women discriminate more about whom they approach (Dosey & Meisels, 1969).	Men discriminate less about whom they approach.
Women's approach creates less anxiety.	Men's approach creates more anxiety (Bleda & Bleda, 1978).
Women prefer to interact side-by-side (Leventhal, Lipshultz & Chiodo, 1978).	Men prefer to interact face-to-face.
Women are least comfortable with side-by-side invasions (Patterson, 1971; Ahmed, Mullens & Romano, Krail & Leventhal, 1976).	Men are least comfortable with frontal invasions (Fisher & Byrne, 1975).
Women are more likely to be placed on the side of a rectangular table (Roger & Reid, 1978).	Men are more likely to be placed at the head of a rectangular table (Lott & Sommer, 1967).
High-self-concept women approach others more closely than do low-self-concept women, and more than men of high or low self-concepts (Stralton, Tekippe & Flick, 1973).	High-self-concept men approach others more closely than low-self-concept men, but not as closely as high-self-concept women.
Sociability and status of females has no effect on the amount of space they are given (Wittig & Skolnick, 1978).	Unsociable, low-status males are given more room than sociable, high-status males, and more room than all women.
Women stand farther away from people who are speaking loudly (Ford, Cramer & Owens, 1977).	Men maintain the same distance away from people who are speaking loudly or softly.
Women respond as easily in close quarters as in larger spaces.	Men respond less in crowded conditions than in larger spaces (Prerost, 1980).
Women flee more quickly when invasion is accompanied by talk (Polit & LaFrance, 1977; Sundstrom & Sundstrom, 1977).	Men flee more quickly when invasion is not accompanied by talk.
Women have less territory (Frieze, 1974).	Men have more territory.

us as we move, territoriality refers to an unmoving area or set of areas. We establish our territoriality in a variety of ways: by fencing our yards, by moving furniture so that certain spaces are not easily accessible to others, and by leaving personal items on desks, chairs, or tables to indicate the territory is occupied.

Territoriality serves at least two functions. We communicate or transfer our personal identity—including our personalities, values, and beliefs—to the physical environment, and we regulate social interaction by establishing barriers or bridges to communication through the communication setting.

Women, in general, are allowed less territory than men. For instance, few women have a particular and unviolated room in their homes, while many men have dens, studies, or work areas often off-limits to others (Frieze, 1974). Similarly, it appears that more men than women have particular chairs reserved for their use. Women's rooms, such as the kitchen or sewing room, and their chairs, are typically not reserved exclusively for their use.

These and other differences between men's and women's use of personal space and territory appear in Table 6.1.

Kinesic differences

While proxemics refers to our use of space, **kinesics** is the term used to refer to bodily movement, facial expressions, and gestures. The importance of kinesics was underlined by two researchers who demonstrated that, while our facial expressions convey the basic type of emotion we are experiencing (anger, happiness, sadness, etc.), our body movement and positions convey how intensely we feel these emotions (Ekman & Friesen, 1967). As we shall determine, normative behavior in this area of communication is different for women and men in our culture.

Eye contact

Eye contact serves a variety of functions. It most commonly signals interest or attention. However, it can indicate either positive affect and liking or anger and threat, depending on the context and other nonverbal cues accompanying it. Additionally, eye contact may reveal status or dominance.

Generally, more dominant individuals receive more eye contact than less dominant ones (Weitz, 1976). More specifically, more dominant people gaze less while listening and more while speaking, while the opposite pattern obtains for less dominant individuals (Hall, 1984). Finally, gaze patterns serve as a regulator of conversation since they help people in turn-taking behavior.

In terms of gender differences in eye contact, the general pattern of research suggests that females of all ages have more frequent eye contact during conversations than males do (e.g., Cegala & Sillars, 1989; Hall, 1984). Females are gazed at more than males (Hall, 1984) and have more tolerance for and favorable reactions to receiving gazes from others than males (McAndrew & Warner, 1986). Female-female dyads engage in more mutual gaze than male-male dyads (Mulac, Studley, Wiemann & Bradac, 1987), while male-male dyads are more characterized by mutual aversion of gaze than pairs of females. Women appear to modify their eye-gaze behavior to adopt the behavior of men when talking to them (Mulac et al., 1987). The reverse is not true; men do not converge to female behavior when talking with women. See Table 6.2 for a summary of the differences in this area.

Facial expressions

Facial expressions also serve a number of different purposes. They provide corrective feedback to speakers, they express emotions, and they demonstrate responsiveness or involvement (Mehrabian, 1971). Smiling is one specific facial expression that has been studied. People attribute many positive characteristics to others who smile. These include intelligence, a good personality, and being a pleasant person. It should also be noted, however, that men who smile receive higher evaluations on such characteristics than do women (Lau, 1982).

Smiling may have a social motivation. For example, bowlers in a bowling alley smiled frequently when socially engaged, but significantly less so after having scored a spare or a strike (Kraut & Johnston, 1979).

Table 6.2 Kinesic (eye contact) differences of women and men

Female Behavior	Male Behavior
Women establish more eye contact than do men (cf. Ellsworth, Carlsmith & Henson, 1972; Ellsworth & Ludwig, 1972; Rubin, 1970; Russ, 1975; Thayer & Schiff, 1975).	Men establish less eye contact than women.
Women engage in a higher percentage of mutual looking than do men. (Exline, Gray & Scuette, 1965).	Males engage in more mutual eye gazing as they age (Muirhead & Goldman, 1979).
Women avert their gaze more than do men (Dierks-Stewart, 1979).	Men engage in staring behavior rather than in gaze aversion.
Women appear to value eye contact more than do men. (Kleinke, Busto, Meeker & Staneski, 1973; Argyle, Lalljee & Cook, 1968).	Men do not appear to be disturbed by people who do not watch them.

Social motivations are affected by class and culture. Mothers in lower-class families were shown to smile considerably less than their middle-class counterparts. The larger number of smiles by the middle-class mothers may be motivated by class expectations of being a "good mother" (Bugental, Love & Gianetto, 1971). Pairs of black women do not smile more than pairs of black men (Smith, 1983).

However, adult women smile more than adult men (Berman & Smith, 1984), especially when discussing positive topics compared to negative topics (Halberstadt, Hayes, & Pike, 1988). Deutsch, LeBaron, and Fryer (1987) found that women are expected to smile more than men. If they fail to do so, they are evaluated more harshly than men. In their study, Deutsch and her colleagues had students rate the characteristics of men and women both verbally described and shown either smiling or not smiling in photographs. The results showed that nonsmiling women were perceived as less happy, less care-free, and less relaxed than nonsmiling men.

Burgoon, Buller, and Woodall (1989) argue that for a woman, a smile is an interactional device. Women are more likely than men to respond to a smile with a smile of their own to keep the interaction flowing smoothly. This may have something to do with the finding that women smile more since some research indicates that women are smiled at more than men (Hall, 1984).

Nonverbal Communication and Gender   135

Who Can Resist Smiling at a Baby?

By Dick Pothier

HAVERFORD, PA.—Who could resist smiling at cute babies and puppies?

Most men, apparently, if there is another man around.

A majority of male subjects in a Haverford College research project apparently thought that smiling at a baby or a puppy somehow made them less masculine.

The research, carried out by two Haverford College students under the guidance of psychology professor Sidney Perloe, found that male students smiled much less often and less noticeably at babies and puppies presented in a videotape if there was another man—an experimenter—present in the viewing room.

But if there were no other men present, most male subjects smiled "to beat the band," Perloe said.

Women Smile Regardless

Women tested under the same conditions and with the same videotape of cute babies or puppies smiled a lot regardless of whether a male experimenter was around during the test, Perloe said.

"We think there are certain cultural rules among men that inhibit some emotional responses in men," Perloe said, "especially a response of tenderness or affection. This may all sound theoretical and academic, but I think there is some practical significance to this finding.

"For one thing, it seems to indicate that you can change the behavior of males in all-male groups—which is often boorish, crude and insensitive—by adding the presence of a woman."

In addition, Perloe said, the human smile is the evolutionary result of facial actions among non-human primates, such as apes and monkeys, "and as such, study of smiles is an important part of studying evolutionary behavior."

"Besides, I just think it's good for people to know about this kind of thing," he said. "If, for cultural and social reasons, many males are showing an inability to express tenderness toward a baby in the presence of another male, it's just useful to know about."

The finding does not include male parents, who probably are as affectionate as they can be toward their children, he said.

Senior Research Project

Perloe, who presented the smile-research project at a meeting of the International Primatological Association in Atlanta a few weeks ago, said that two Haverford students who have since graduated—Gregg Solomon and Samuel Blumberg—designed the experiment as their senior research project.

Men smiled more often before female experimenter

The concept of "toughness" or "masculinity" or "macho" behavior is almost entirely something that concerns men only in relation to other men, not in relation to women, Perloe said, which is why the presence of a female experimenter did not lead to the suppression of smiles. Indeed, nearly all the male subjects—all students at Haverford—smiled more broadly and more often when there was a female experimenter in the room.

During the experiments, while the test subjects—20 males and 20 females— watched a 12-minute videotape of babies and puppies, an unseen camera recorded their facial expressions, Perloe said.

Then a second group of 50 volunteers was shown films of the first group and was asked to guess what kind of response the test subjects were showing. The second group, which did not know the purpose of the test, found that some men smiled a lot and other men not much at all.

Later the experimenters compared the findings and found that men who were in the presence of another man suppressed their smiles far more often than men who knew they were alone.

Judging Degree of Smiling

The experimenters also measured the smiles of both groups using a research method called the "facial action scoring system," a method of judging and scoring the degree of smiling and its frequency.

"Smiles are really a very basic kind of signal," Perloe said. "In fact, most parents report that the first time their baby smiled at them was an ecstatic moment, and we believe smiles are the most communicative facial expression there is."

Women tend to smile more than men do, and, as a consequence, their smiles are more difficult to interpret. A smiling woman may be attempting to convey that she is genuinely happy, that she is behaving in a socially approved way, or that she is nervous and smiling to cover her feelings. Because men smile less frequently, their smiles are easier to interpret; they generally communicate positive feelings. Women's smiles suggest more affiliation and friendliness, while men's inexpressive faces tend to make them seem less approachable.

During the next few days, experiment with facial expression. If you are a woman, purposely try to smile less and show less facial expressiveness; if you are a man, try to smile more frequently than normal and to indicate your feelings through your face. Try to note sensitively the responses of others. Do you perceive any differences in how other people respond to you? For instance, did anyone ask if you were feeling differently than normal? Did people approach you less or more? Did people try to communicate with you more or less frequently? How do you explain these differences? What implications does smiling behavior have for communication? What inferences can you draw about the differences in communicative behaviors between women and men? For example, do you believe that women have more opportunities to communicate with others because of their facial expression?

Young children are aware of the differences in the frequency of smiling behavior in women and men. When children were asked to determine whether their parents were expressing positive or negative sentiment, the children used the facial cue of the smile to decide their fathers were offering positive comments. The children were, however, unable to determine whether their mothers were making positive or negative comments, regardless of whether their mothers were smiling or not. The authors explained that mothers smile so often that their mood cannot be determined by their smile alone (Bugental, Love & Gianetto, 1971).

Facial expressions are a fairly fine-tuned means of communicating nonverbally; yet, people may observe facial expressions more than they do other nonverbal cues. Women tend to reveal more of their emotions in their facial expressions than men (Hickson & Stacks, 1989; Mulac et al., 1987). This finding occurs consistently among adults, but less so among children (Basow, 1986), indicating that boys learn to suppress their nonverbal cues as they get older and learn their appropriate sex-role behavior. See Table 6.3.

Women and men do not move or carry themselves in the same way. You may sometimes make judgments about the biological sex of people ahead of you on the street simply on the basis of their posture and bearing. Perhaps you rarely discuss kinesic differences between women and men and seldom consciously alter your own behavior to reflect your biological sex. At the same time, definite kinesic differences exist between women and men.

In this exercise, you will have an opportunity to experiment with masculine and feminine posture and bearing. In a group of about six people, discuss feminine kinesic behavior. Consider arm and leg placement, the position of the pelvis, and the way people move when they walk. Assume these positions and experiment with walking around the room. Have the other members of the group evaluate the success you have in depicting feminine kinesics. After each of you has had the opportunity to display feminine postures and bearing, discuss masculine kinesic behavior. Each person should attempt to enact these movements and placement of their limbs. Again, respond to how successfully each person is able to assume the kinesic behaviors of masculine people.

When every person in the group has enacted both feminine and masculine kinesics, discuss the experience. How did you feel when you were behaving as a woman? How did this contrast with how you felt when you were behaving as a man? What attitudes or values seem to be associated with feminine kinesics? How do these perspectives differ from those which seem consistent with masculine kinesic behavior? For instance, you may find that the way women place their legs together contrasted with the way men place theirs farther apart is suggestive of different attitudes about sexuality. People with their legs pressed tightly together may seem more restrained than people with their legs open. How does kinesic behavior relate to differences in female and male socialization? What other reactions do you have to this exercise?

Posture and bearing

Posture and bearing comprise another area of investigation in kinesics. The research indicates that postural information can be used to determine relational messages between communicators. Head cues appear to communicate information indicative of pleasantness/unpleasantness, while body cues communicate information indicative of relaxation/tension (Mehrabian, 1965). Let us consider some of the specific differences in the posture and bearing of women and men in our culture.

Table 6.3   Kinesic (facial expression) differences of women and men

Female Behavior	Male Behavior
Women use more facial expression and are more expressive than men (cf. Buck, Miller & Caul, 1974; Mehrabian, 1972).	Men use less facial expression and are less expressive than women.
Women are better at conveying emotions than men (Schiffenbauer & Babineau, 1976).	Men do not convey their emotions through their faces.
Women demonstrate superior recognition memory of their own expressions (Yarmey, 1979).	Men do not recall their own facial expressions.
Women smile more than men (cf. Argyle, 1975; Dierks-Stewart, 1976; Frances, 1979; Parlee, 1979).	Men smile less than women.
Women are more apt to return smiles when someone smiles at them (Henley, 1977).	Men are less likely to return a smile than women.
Women are more attracted to others who smile (Lau, 1982).	Men are not more attracted to others who smile.

In general, we may conclude that men's posture and bearing are closely related to male proxemic behavior. Basically, men take up more space. Men tend to establish more trunk relaxation, greater backward lean and open-leg positioning. Women, too, reflect their proxemic behavior as they tend to sit and stand in a more closed position and demonstrate more trunk rigidity (Hall, 1984; Peterson, 1976). Women appear to show more sensitivity to the other person and flexibility in their behavior than men. Men maintain their more relaxed postures, regardless of the sex of the other person to whom they are talking. A summary of these posture and bearing differences appear in Table 6.4.

Gestures
The differences between the use of gestures by women and men are so evident that masculinity and femininity can be distinguished on the basis of gestures alone. One study determined that "naive" judges, i.e., individuals with no training or background in nonverbal communication or in psychology, could identify masculinity and femininity on the basis of expressive cues (Lippa, 1978). Table 6.5 gives a summary of these differences in men's and women's use of gestures.

Nonverbal Communication and Gender   139

Table 6.4 Kinesic (posture and bearing) differences of women and men

Female Behavior	Male Behavior
Women tend to hold their legs more closely together.	Men tend to have their legs apart at a 10-to-15-degree angle.
Women maintain their arms close to their body.	Men hold their arms about 5-to-10-degrees away from their bodies.
Women rely on more closed body positions.	Men rely on more open body positions (Aries, 1982).
Women tend to engage in less body lean.	Men tend to engage in more backward lean (Aries, 1982).
Women walk with their pelvis rolled slightly forward.	Men walk with their entire pelvis rolled slightly back.
Women present their entire body from their neck to their ankles as a moving entity when they walk (Birdwhistell, 1970).	Men move their arms independently and exhibit a slight twist of their rib cage.

Table 6.5 Kinesic (gestural) differences in women and men

Female Behavior	Male Behavior
Women use fewer gestures than men. Women discriminate in their use of gestures and use fewer gestures with other women and more with men (Peterson, 1976).	Men use more gestures than women. Men do not discriminate between male and female partners in their use of gestures.
Women tend to keep their hands down on the arms of a chair more than do men (Peterson, 1976).	Men rarely keep their hands down on the arms of a chair.
Women use fewer one-handed gestures and arm movements (Shuter, 1979).	Men use more one-handed gestures and arm movements.
Women play with their hair or clothing, place their hands in their lap, and tap their hands more frequently than men (Peterson, 1976).	Men use sweeping hand gestures, stretching the hands, cracking the knuckles, pointing, and using arms to lift the body from a chair or table more frequently.
Women tend to cross their legs at the knees or cross their ankles with their knees slightly apart (Peterson, 1976).	Men tend to sit with their legs apart or with their legs stretched out in front of them and their ankles crossed.
Women tap their hands.	Men exhibit greater leg and foot movement, including tapping their feet (Peterson, 1976).

Haptic differences

Tactile communication or **haptics** is the use of touch in human communication. Touching may be positive or negative. On the positive side, we know that touch is essential to the growth and development of persons from birth onward. A variety of studies have demonstrated that persons who receive insufficient touching may develop such disorders as speech problems, allergies, eczema, and delayed symbolic recognition. Research conducted at times when care for infants was severely limited (during major world wars), indicates that when babies' physical needs are met but not their need to be held and touched, they become ill and die (Adler & Towne, 1978; Bowlby, 1952; Montague, 1971).

Touch is interpreted positively when it occurs within an intimate context. Some writers equate touching with sexual interest (Jourard & Rubin, 1968). Others equate touching with social and psychological intimacy (Burgoon, Buller, Hale & deTurck, 1981). In this context, touch will be used reciprocally. In general, if touch is used reciprocally, it indicates solidarity among equals (Henley, 1973). In relationships between equals, touch is perceived as a reinforcer of the bonds of friendship or love (Summerhayes & Suchner, 1978). Research indicates that women are more prone to reciprocal touching than are men (Stier & Hall, 1984), possibly indicating greater solidarity among female than male same-sex friendships.

Touch may be viewed negatively when it is used unilaterally. When one person has access to another person's body, but the first person is not allowed the same privilege in return, touch becomes an indicator of status rather than of solidarity. In this light, touch may be viewed as the ultimate invasion of personal space. When we consider the variety of contexts in which unilateral touching occurs, e.g., doctors touching nurses, customers touching waitresses, teachers touching students, managers touching subordinates, police officers touching accused persons, counselors touching clients, and ministers touching parishioners, it becomes evident that unilateral touch demonstrates differential power or status. In the animal world unilateral touch occurs also between dominant and subordinate animals as a sign of superiority of status (Lawick-Goodall, 1971).

Some evidence indicates that women tend to touch and be touched more frequently than men (Willis, Rinck & Dean, 1978). Recent studies, however, have arrived at slightly different findings. Willis and Rinck (1983) found women more likely to initiate touch than men. Jones (1986) asked 20 female and 20 male college students to keep accurate records of their touch behavior over a three-day period. Results indicated that men initiated touch less frequently than women, but, contrary to earlier research, were touched more often than women, and that women tended to exert greater control through touch than men. The results of this study support an earlier perspective that

Table 6.6 Tactile differences between women and men

Female Behavior	Male Behavior
Women touch others less than men do.	Men touch others more than women do (Henley, 1973a, 1973b, 1977; Heslin & Boss, 1975).
Women are touched more by others (Austin, 1973; Henley, 1973a, 1973b).	Men are touched less than women.
Women value touching more than men do (Fisher, Rytting & Heslin, 1976).	Men do not value touch as much as women do.
Women distinguish between touching behavior which indicates warmth and touching behavior which suggests sexual intent.	Men do not make distinctions between various kinds of touch (Druley, Casriel & Hollender, 1980).
Women view touch as an expressive behavior which demonstrates warmth and affiliation.	Men generally view touch as an instrumental behavior leading to sexual activity or as childish behavior, indicative of dependency and a lack of manliness (Druley, Casriel & Hollender, 1980).

"touching" is generally perceived as a "feminine-appropriate behavior" (Maier & Ernest, 1978, 577). Males in this study were also less likely to reciprocate touching, indicating that touching may be seen as a "masculine-inappropriate behavior."

Jones alternatively suggests that differences in touching behavior may be reflective of women's greater communication competence. Jones also found some evidence that male-male dyads touch the least of any dyad combination; this finding was in accord with other, earlier research (i.e., Andersen & Laeibowitz, 1978; Stier & Hall, 1984).

However, Berman and Smith (1984) found that the male-male pairs did not differ from female-female pairs in the tendency to touch, although girl dyads generally engaged in more mutual touch than the boy dyads. Berman and Smith's unusual result may be due to their methodology. They observed their respondents in two situations (celebrating a winning team or just having a photograph taken). Other researchers have asked people to recall how much they touch one another. Due to social sanctions against male touch in our culture, this may have affected respondents' reports. A summary of female-male haptic differences is presented in Table 6.6.

Table 6.7 Paralinguistic differences between women and men

Female Behavior	Male Behavior
Speak at a higher pitch than men do.	Speak at a lower pitch.
Speak more softly.	Speak louder than women (Markel, Prebor & Brandt, 1972).
Speak with more expressive intonation patterns (O'Neill, 1969).	Speak with less expression.
Intonation patterns are characterized by a sense of uncertainty, questioning, and helplessness.	When making a statement, do not use the rising intonation associated with asking a question (Rosegrant & McCroskey, 1975).
More likely to pronounce the complete "ing" ending on words.	Likely to substitute "in" for "ing" ending (cf. Shuy, Wolfram & Riley, 1967).
Come closest to standard speech norms (Levine & Crockett, 1966).	Use a greater number of nonstandard and stigmatized words (Labov, 1972).

Paralinguistic differences

Paralanguage literally means that which accompanies language and consists of all the vocal cues individuals use to communicate. Our vocal cues can be categorized into (1) **pitch**—the highness or lowness of our voices; (2) **rate**—how rapidly or slowly we speak; (3) **inflection**—the change or lack of change in pitch we incorporate; (4) volume—the loudness or softness of our voices; (5) **quality**—the pleasant or unpleasant characteristics of our voices, including such characteristics as breathiness, harshness, nasality, or whininess; and (6) **enunciation**—our pronunciation and articulation. In addition to these vocal cues, paralanguage includes much conversational maintenance and regulatory behavior, such as the silences we include in our speech, interruptions, and the non-word sounds such as "mmmh," "ooh," and "uh."

Studies have demonstrated that paralanguage conveys a great deal (Mehrabian & Ferris, 1967) and that listeners can usually identify both the race and gender of a speaker from paralinguistic cues (Lass, Mertz & Kimmel, 1978).

Pitch, volume, and quality

Eakins and Eakins (1978) explain why it is we are generally able to detect one's gender on the basis of vocal quality alone. The male larynx is usually larger and thicker than the female's. The larger larynx vibrates less quickly and produces a lower pitch. Also, the size of the upper body cavity and diaphragm affects the amount and control of air to produce volume. Males and females can be trained to use breath control to produce adequate volume, but males naturally produce a little bit more loudness without training.

However, Henley (1977) and Pfeiffer (1985) dismiss this explanation. They argue that the higher pitch and softer volume of women's speech is not attributable solely to anatomical differences. While they admit there are some differences in anatomy, they assert that much of the difference in men's and women's voices is learned and constitutes a requirement of their different social roles.

An interesting sidenote to the discussion of paralinguistic differences between women and men is the impact of gender differences on the interpretation of certain vocal qualities (Addington, 1968). Two vocal characteristics yield the same impressions regardless of whether they are associated with men or women. Both men and women with "flat" voices are perceived as sluggish, cold, withdrawn, and masculine. Those having nasal voices are perceived as having a number of other undesirable characteristics. Other vocal characteristics, however, yield different impressions, depending on the speaker's sex. A female speaker with a breathy voice is perceived as pretty, petite, feminine, highstrung, and shallow; a male speaker with a breathy voice is perceived as young and artistic. Women with "thin" voices tend to be perceived as sensitive and having a good sense of humor, but also immature; it is unclear how men with thin voices are perceived. Tenseness in vocal quality causes women to be seen as younger, more feminine, more emotional, more highstrung, and less intelligent; tenseness among men results in perceptions of being older, less yielding, and more difficult. Women with "throaty" voices are perceived as more masculine, lazier, less intelligent, less emotional, less attractive, more careless, less artistic, more naive, more neurotic, less interesting, more apathetic, and quieter. On the other hand, throatiness in men resulted in their being perceived as older, more mature, more sophisticated, and better adjusted. Finally, orotundity (fullness) is associated with liveliness, gregariousness, pride, and humorlessness among women, but when characteristic of men's voices seems to imply energy, health, artistry, sophistication, pride, interest, enthusiasm, hardiness, and artistic inclination.

Conversational management

Talk time
One of the most prevalent notions about women's and men's conversation is that women talk more than men. People of both sexes perceive women, rather than men, to gossip, to "gab," and "to cackle like a group of old hens." People who talk a great deal are described as sounding like a "bunch of old women."

To begin with, we note that contrary to this prevailing stereotype, men may talk more than women (Eakins & Eakins, 1976; Swacker, 1975; Wood, 1966). In a relatively recent comprehensive review of the subject, Thorne (1981) reports that there has not been a single study indicating that women talk more than men. In a metaanalysis across 37 studies, Smythe and Schlueter (1986) found no difference in men's and women's talkativeness. That we would persist in the belief that women talk more than men is another instance of cultural stereotypes prevailing over demonstrable evidence to the contrary.

Control of the topic

Certainly one of the most obvious ways of regulating conversation is by controlling the topic under discussion.

In *Through the Looking Glass,* this conversation between Alice and Humpty Dumpty occurs:

> "I don't know what you mean by 'glory,' " Alice said. Humpty Dumpty smiled contemptuously. "Of course you don't—till I tell you. I meant there's a nice knockdown argument for you!"
>
> "But 'glory' doesn't mean a nice knockdown argument," Alice objected.
>
> "When I use a word," Humpty Dumpty said, in a rather scornful tone, "it means just what I choose it to mean—neither more nor less."
>
> "The question is," said Humpty Dumpty, "which is to be master—that's all" (Carroll, 1965).

Although Humpty Dumpty was referring to the definition of words, his point is also useful when we consider topic selection in conversations. In a very real sense controlling conversational topics is nearly synonymous with controlling our interpersonal realities (Thorne, 1981).

Male-male, female-female, and male-female dyads have been investigated to determine patterns of topic change. Males, in male-female conversations, appear to assert their claim to control topics (Fishman, 1977, 1978; Zimmerman & West, 1975). Male-female dyads in developing relationships do not talk as long about a topic as do two people of the same sex. In addition, male-female dyads use different strategies to change the topic. They tend to use more abrupt and direct methods, which may indicate they are attempting to avoid over-commitment. In male-male dyads men tend to use more indirect and gradual methods of topic change, that is, procedures which could be associated with a relational control process. Men may wish to avoid confronting the issue of who is to control the change of topics within conversation in male-male dyads (Ayres, 1980).

Associated with topic changes are the topics to which the conversation is changed. Male 4-, 8-, and 12-year olds make more references to sports and specific locations, while females of the same ages make more references to school, items they wish for, their needs, and their identity (Haas 1981). Kelly, Wildman, and Urey (1962) contend that the use of stereotypically male topics may inhibit females from participating in conversations. Thus, both the content and the structure of the interaction encourage male control of the conversation.

Topic control is accomplished in a variety of ways. Among the more common are minimal responses to the other person's comments, silence, and interruptions. Delayed responses are also used to bring a topic to its conclusion. Keep in mind that for another person to control the topic, you must be willing to "relinquish the floor." The other person cannot control the subject of conversation unless you allow him or her to do so.

Interruptions

Interruptions occur when the listener begins speaking before the speaker utters her/his last word. For instance, if one person were to state, "I can't wait to tell you what my mother said," and the second person began his or her comment, "Did you talk to Professor Fisher?" on the third word of the first person's statement ("wait"), we would call the second person's question an interruption.

Why do people interrupt each other? Some persons may interrupt because they are unaware of the implicit conversational rules implying that one person does not respond to another's comment or question until it is clear the speaker has finished. Few people, however, are genuinely unaware of this rule. More often, individuals interrupt because they are enthusiastic about something they have to share and are impatient about "waiting their turn." In this instance, interruptions indicate conversational involvement. Kennedy and Camden (1983) found that some interruptions function to confirm the previous speaker. However, some individuals may presume that what they have to offer is more important than the first person's message or believe that they are of higher status than the speaker and are, therefore, entitled to interrupt them.

Research on interruptions and gender has been mixed. Some findings indicate that men interrupt others more than women do, and women are more frequently interrupted than men (Baird, 1976; Eakins & Eakins, 1978; Hall, 1984; Kramer, 1974; Thorne & Henley, 1975; Zimmerman & West, 1975).

However, more recent research refutes these findings. Smythe and Schlueter (1986) found no differences in male and female interruption behavior. Conger and Dindia (1985) also found that the interruption behavior of men and women did not differ; although interruptions were asymmetrically distributed in dyads, the asymmetry was not related to the sex of the interrupter. Finally, Dindia (1987) reached the same conclusions—men did not interrupt more than women, and women were not interrupted more than men. Again, she found in all dyads regardless of sex composition, one person interrupts more than the other; but, who interrupts more is not predictable by sex.

These contradictory results may be explained by Dindia's methodology. She used a procedure to remove the correlation between dyadic partners from consideration. Previous studies ignored this correlation and treated the data from both partners as independent observations. Dindia points out that this is a faulty statistical analysis that can bias the results. Also, past research did not always test the effect of the partner's sex and the interaction between the speaker's sex and the partner's sex. Since Dindia tested for these effects, we can be more confident in her results.

Thus, there may be no actual difference between men and women in interrupting behavior. Yet Hawkins (1988) found that listeners expect men to interrupt more than women, although they do not expect women to be interrupted more and interrupting males were judged as behaving inappropriately, especially when they interrupted women. Research on interruptions needs more clarification, however, the current view holds that men and women behave similarly on this variable.

Overlaps

Another means of controlling conversation is through the use of overlaps. **Overlaps** occur when the individual who is listening makes a statement before the other person has finished speaking, but at about the same time as the speaker's last word is uttered, or a word which could be perceived as his or her last word. For example, if someone states, "I would like to go to the movie at the Varsity tonight," and the second person responds "Yes, me too!" while the first person is verbalizing "tonight," the respondent's act would be considered an overlap.

Overlaps can be more easily justified than can interruptions. Often, the second speaker senses that the first speaker has about finished expressing his or her thought and has simply begun talking a moment too soon. On the other hand, the person who overlaps may be attempting to shorten the first person's statement or may be competing for a turn as speaker. Whatever the rationale, men overlap women more than women overlap men (Zimmerman & West, 1975).

Silence

Another means of controlling conversation is through the use of silence. Zimmerman and West (1975) examined the use of silence in female-female, male-male, and male-female dyads. They found that females in female-male conversations were silent more than any other person in the various combinations. In male-male and female-female conversations, the silences were scattered among the comments in a relatively equal manner. These researchers explained their findings by noting that most often the females who fell silent in the female-male dyads did so after one of three occurrences; a delayed minimal response by the male, an overlap by the male, or an interruption by the male. In these instances the female may have been uncertain about her partner's reaction to her comment or about the other person's feelings concerning the conversation.

As Ragan and Aarons (1986) point out, silence can also function as a powerful communication strategy whereby refusing to respond verbally to someone's objections may elicit his or her compliance. Fishman (1983) states that men were more likely than women to use silence in this strategic manner to control conversations. Other paralinguistic differences between men and women appear in Table 6.7.

Artifactual communication

Artifactual communication, or exchange of messages by means of objects or object language, refers to our display of material things, including our hair styles, clothing, jewelry, cosmetics, and other adornments. Artifactual communication allows others to determine our age, status, role, values, lifestyle, occupation, nationality, socioeconomic class, group memberships, personality, as well as our gender (Rosenfeld & Plax, 1977).

Our clothing serves to clarify for each of us the sort of person we believe we are (Fisher, 1975); it allows us individualistic and personal expression (Procter, 1978). Clothes satisfy our need for creative self-expression (Horn, 1975), thus, interest in clothing indicates a high level of self-actualization (Perry, Schutz & Rucher, 1983). Clothes also allow us to identify ourselves with a particular social culture or subculture (Procter, 1978; Hillestad, 1974).

While we usually dress for warmth and comfort, we may also use clothing to express particular levels of modesty or immodesty, inasmuch as clothing can accentuate erogenous zones (Procter, 1978). We may attempt to attract others through our clothing choices. Some evidence indicates that women are rated more sexually than males for wearing revealing clothes (Abbey, Cozzarelli, McLaughlin & Harnish, 1987). Clothing satisfies sensual needs as it touches the surface of our bodies, while at the same time allowing us to display publicly our physical economic resources and status (Rosencranz, 1972).

A number of studies and books have considered the evolution of clothing fashions for women and men (cf. Brain, 1979; Polhemus & Procter, 1978). Such features as restrictiveness, restraints, comfort, and utility have been examined in connection with specific clothing styles. Modesty appears to be a more frequent characteristic of women's clothing than of men's throughout history (Flugel, 1930; Lurie, 1981). Such modesty may be associated with the

Table 6.8 Artifactual differences between women and men

Female Behavior	Male Behavior
More sensitive to artifactual cues of others (Robertson, 1978).	Less sensitive to artifactual cues (Haley & Hendrickson, 1974).
More concerned about wearing normative clothing (Kelley, Daigle, LaFleur & Wilson, 1974).	Less concerned about normative clothing.
More likely to be observed or watched (Argyle & Williams, 1969).	Less likely to be observed or watched.
Dress to win approval (Fisher, 1975).	Dress to avoid disapproval.

various taboos which affect women, including childbirth, menstruation, and other physical features. Differences in disrobing behavior also imply the greater modesty imposed on women:

> A woman is required by convention to retain her hat and outer garments until asked to remove them. A man may immediately do so. Here again the removal of garments is a sign of male respect. Men's garments are treated as though they were used for purposes of display, women's garments as though they were used for purposes of modesty (Flugel, 1930).

One researcher postulates that differences between men's and women's clothing arose from the male's desire to assert superiority over the female and to hold her to his service (Langer, 1959). He contends that men were able to accomplish this goal by providing women with clothing that hampered or impeded their movements and activities. For example, a study examined the effects of clothing worn by Victorian women. The lack of comfort and restraining nature of the clothing created an image of submissiveness (Roberts, 1977). Roberts further explains that men's clothing during the same period provided them with an image of seriousness, strength, and activity.

Other historians have demonstrated a correlation between women's clothing styles and the sexual mores of the time. Before the 1920s women wore long skirts, high heels, and had well-defined waist lines. During the liberating era of the 1920s, women adopted the loose flapper dress which was considerably shorter and fitted loosely around a woman's waist. Following the Second World War when women turned from industrial positions to the traditional nurturing role in the home, their clothes again became more restrictive (O'Neill, 1969).

Men and women dress in different costumes for different events. Both men and women alter their clothing as they move from classroom settings to dating situations to job interviews. However, the changes may be less pronounced for one sex than for the other. Moreover, the costumes which a woman might wear in one of these situations may be very different from that of her male counterpart. Select three situations in which you would wear quite different clothing. Draw pictures, or explain in careful detail, exactly what you would wear. Then, draw or explain exactly what you think you would wear if you were of the other sex.

Situation	Male Outfit	Female Outfit

Compare your responses with others. How do males and females differ in each of the situations you have selected? What generalizations can you draw? Do you believe that women and men are changing their clothing styles to become more similar to each other than they have historically? How? What changes would you predict in clothing styles of the future for men and women? How do you believe men and women should dress?

You will recall that we discussed how women and men feel about themselves in chapter 3. Women and men have different body images. For instance, at least as many adult men as women are overweight. Nonetheless, most diets and exercise programs are geared toward women. Weight problems appear to be more salient to women than to men. Consider the physical configurations of men and women and discuss how clothing is used to conceal, emphasize, or alter particular physical characteristics. For example, why do men wear tight pants? Why do women wear low-cut tops? As you envision an ideal mode of dress for women and men, which bodily parts would you emphasize or de-emphasize? How would women's and men's bodily parts be covered or exposed differently? Why? Discuss your reactions with your classmates.

Women's roles and their clothing needs have, as indicated in the following passage, dictated changes in styles. Changes were required as women moved between home and the workplace:

> Until recent years, changes in women's fashions have not been necessitated by changes in life conditions in the same manner as have been true of men. Their duties for the most part have been restricted to the home. But with the entrance of women into the world of business this has been changed. Short skirts and the discarding of corsets came about as the result of the modern girl's interest in athletics. High-heeled shoes and heavy skirts went out when the business world opened its doors to women. The busy life of the woman of today leaves little time for the afternoon affairs that our grandmothers so much enjoyed, and with their disappearance has come the disappearance from the wardrobe of the modern woman of dressy afternoon clothing (Hurlock, 1929, 81–82).

Were Hurlock alive today she might well be impressed (if not shocked) by current changes in fashion.

The trend toward "unisex" clothing which originated in the 1960s constitutes an interesting chapter in the history of fashion. Women and men have been encouraged to wear similar, if not identical, outfits in a variety of colors, textures, and designs. In many instances, women have simply adopted the more comfortable, practical, and durable clothing men have already been wearing for some time. In addition to practicality and comfort, women may have been making the statement that they wanted equal rights or the same privileges afforded men in our culture. At any rate, the unisex styles have had a tendency to reduce rather than accent the differences between women and men. As one author notes, "Whatever reduces the false separations between men and women is bound to reduce their suspicions and hostilities and thus permit them a fuller expression of their human potentiality" (Hurlock, 1972).

As a sidenote, unisex clothing styles have not appeared to affect children's perceptions of appropriate dress, their parents' classification of the same clothing, or their parents' attitudes toward sex roles. Instead, the results of one study (Wenige, 1977) indicate that differentiation rather than similarity of sex-appropriate clothing is still accepted by many adults and transmitted to children. The ambiguity evidenced by adult fashions and parental mode of dress evidently has little influence on pre-school children's perception of clothing (Wenige, 1977).

The multiple roles played by women and men require fine distinctions in appropriate clothing. Morganosky and Creekmore (1981) determined that clothing attractiveness and clothing awareness were related to leadership traits for females and males. Women who wore form-fitted outfits rather than loose-fitting outfits, the layered look rather than an unlayered look, and high neck-

Table 6.9   Nonverbal sensitivity differences between women and men

Female Behavior	Male Behavior
Better judges of nonverbal behavior (Hall 1978). More accurate decoders of nonverbal communication (Zuckerman, DeFrank, Hall & Rosenthal, 1976; Kestenbau, 1977; Henley, 1977).	Men who have occupations such as acting, art, and mental health are equal to, or superior to, females in decoding nonverbal cues (Rosenthal, Archer, DiMatteo, Koivumaki & Rogers, 1974).
More sensitive to verbal-nonverbal cue conflicts in the perception of sincerity (Friedman, 1979). Not superior to men in decoding brief, unintended, uncontrolled, or "leaked" nonverbal cues (Rosenthal & DePaulo, 1979).	More accurate in judging deception (Siegal, 1980).
Use gestures in making assessments of the relationships between people.	Use actions in making assessments of the relationships between people.

lines rather than low or moderate necklines made a more positive first impression in applying for a job (Rucker, Taber & Harrison, 1981). In another study Gordon, Tengler, and Infante (1982) found that women who were more clothing conscious dressed more conservatively on the job and had higher levels of job satisfaction.

Differences that appear to occur in the clothing choices and the artifactual communication of women and men are summarized in Table 6.8.

Nonverbal decoding differences

Women and men are different in their sensitivity to nonverbal communication. These decoding differences are summarized in Table 6.9.

In general, women are more sensitive to nonverbal cues than men (Berman & Smith, 1984; Henley, 1977; Kirouc & Dore, 1983). However, this finding is complicated by the fact that this advantage for women is most apparent for vocal cues (Hall, 1984).

Explaining gender differences in nonverbal communication

Let us consider some reasons or explanations for the gender differences in nonverbal communication. The explanations for nonverbal differences fit into the same categories as those advanced for the verbal behaviors discussed in chapter 5.

Dominance and control by men

When nonverbal cues are used in a reciprocal manner, they indicate interpersonal solidarity. When they are used unilaterally, they indicate status. In other words, if one person touches another person on the arm, and the other person responds by touching the first in a similar way, we infer that the two are of similar status levels and are expressing interpersonal solidarity. However, if the touch of one person results in the second person yielding to the touch but not responding with reciprocal touching, we may surmise that this is a display of status awareness. As early as 1956, the status meanings of asymmetrical behavior were discussed. One theorist speculated that, "Between superordinate and subordinate, we may expect to find asymmetrical relations, the superordinate having the right to exercise certain familiarities which the subordinate is not allowed to reciprocate" (Goffman, 1956).

Proxemic differences have been accounted for by using the dominance/submission explanation. Anthropologists and others have observed that the dominant being is generally not approached as closely as the weaker (Henley, 1977; Sommer, 1959, 1969). Women, then, may be approached more closely than men because they occupy the more subordinate status.

The dominance/submission hypothesis has also been used to explain differences in eye contact between the genders. Women's traditionally subordinate position in our culture may necessitate more eye contact and an averted gaze. Because women are not part of the dominant group, they are required to monitor the members of the dominant group to check the appropriateness of their behavior (Rubin, 1970). For instance, we often gaze at strangers for pronounced periods to learn about them and better predict appropriate responses to them (Cohen, 1979). Interestingly, when women maintain a prolonged gaze, they frequently do so with a slight tilt of their heads which appears to reduce the threat in the act (Henley, 1977). The dominance of men and the submissiveness of women appear to help explain the increased watchfulness of women as well as their averted gaze.

Differences in kinesic behavior may also indicate differences in dominance-submissiveness. When persons of differing statuses communicate, those with higher status typically manifest more relaxed positions and postures. For instance, a study done in a hospital setting demonstrated that nurses and attendants showed far more circumspection in their kinesic behavior than did the physicians with whom they worked (Goffman, 1956).

Differences in men's and women's gesturing behavior has also been attributed to differences in their degree of dominance or submission. (Frieze & Ramsey, 1976; Henley, 1977; Key, 1975). One writer theorizes that since men are known to dominate conversations, interrupt conversations, initiate conversations, speak more than women, and control the topic of conversations, that women are forced to express themselves in more dramatic ways; hence, they rely on gestures (Scheinfeld, 1944). Women may also be viewed as using more gestures when talking to men than when talking to women because increased gesturing is likely to elicit greater attention and heighten the probability of their being noticed and receiving approval (Rosenfeld, 1966).

Differences in men's and women's pronunciation have also been explained as manifestations of dominance and submissiveness. It has been hypothesized that as the subservient group, women are required to be more concerned about their speech than are men (Eakins & Eakins, 1978). In other ways, too, persons with lesser status are required to be more concerned about behaving properly and appropriately so as not to incur the disapproval of more dominant others. This vigilance must also be maintained until one's status increases significantly. High-status persons, on the other hand, are allowed the luxury of informality and lack of concern for the proprieties since they have already achieved success.

Spender (1989) argues that men's dominance results in a perception of women's talkativeness even when it cannot be documented empirically. When she tape records conversations, she will often ask the participants afterwards if they had their fair share of the conversation. She reports that men often say no, that women spoke more than they. On the other hand, women usually say they had their fair share. Spender says this is the case even when, by analyzing the tapes, she knows that men spoke ninety percent of the time and women spoke ten percent. She concludes, if women are not supposed to talk in the presence of men, even talking ten percent of the time may be more than their fair share.

However, as Hall (1984) points out, the dominance explanation has some problems in explaining the data involving nonverbal behaviors of women and men. Women have been compared to blacks on the grounds that both are oppressed groups and, thus, should behave similarly. Yet the evidence does not show this to be the case because

> actual sex differences have not consistently shown patterns that suggest a role for oppression. Asymmetry in touch between men and women has not been definitely demonstrated. Women's preference to approach others more closely than men do can even be interpreted as *assertive* behavior; an oppressed or intimidated person might linger on the fringes of socially appropriate distance rather than approaching closely (Hall, 1984, 150).

Masculine and feminine behaviors

Perhaps the simplest and most robust explanation for male/female differences in nonverbal behavior is that they are taught or socialized to behave differently (La France & Mayo, 1976). Let us consider how differences in men's and women's socialization might explain some of the findings presented thus far. We will begin by explaining differences in their proxemic behavior. We know that women are expected to be more affiliative and interpersonally sensitive.

How, proxemically, might these tendencies be communicated? By "increasing" distance between self and others? Of course not. Logically, we would expect "decreased" distancing between self and others to communicate heightened affiliation and sensitivity (Rosenfeld, 1965). And this decreased distancing is precisely what is taught young girls, further reinforced by touching norms promoting the more frequent touching of girls than boys. Conversely, boys are encouraged to distance themselves from others and to prepare to expect occasional, although unpredictable, confrontation with others. This, of course, disposes men negatively to evaluate close proximity with others (Leventhal & Matturro, 1980). Since men are encouraged negatively to evaluate close proximity with others, and, moreover, since their vigilance disposes them to maintain a safe distance from others, we might expect men to make fewer proxemic distinctions when interacting with others. In fact, this is precisely what occurs. Women are much more sensitive to and conscious of the distances they maintain from others (Rosegrant & McCroskey, 1975).

How else might women be socialized to be more affiliative and interpersonally sensitive? Gender differences in gaze behavior provide another possibility (Rubin, 1970). Not only does gaze indicate to others an interest in and appreciation for the person being observed, but it also avails the gazer opportunity to collect valuable information about the people being observed. The research indicates that women more closely monitor others to an extent considerably greater than men's (Exline & Winters, 1965). Additional research indicates that this additional feedback does, in fact, result in greater social approval from others (Efran & Broughton, 1966; Henley, 1977). This greater social approval is precisely the type of interpersonal feedback needed to promote gender-related socialization patterns establishing and continuing the nonverbal communication differences discussed in this chapter. Hence, we can see that the socialization hypothesis finds considerable support in fact.

Gender differences in smiling behavior have also been explained on the basis of differential socialization. As discussed in a previous section, women smile more often than men. In fact, women smile so often that their own children may upon occasion have difficulty interpreting a given smile's meaning since the gesture may be associated with so many different, sometimes conflicting, emotional states that it loses communicative meaning. Even so, the everpresent women's smile is seldom taken as a threat and is generally interpreted as affiliative, an interpretation in keeping with the proxemic and gaze findings discussed above. A recent Chicago *Tribune* article (deCourcy, 1988) suggests that women smile to reassure others about their own worth, to be polite. Men, on the other hand, tend to internalize rather than externalize emotion (Caul, 1974). This is evidenced by their smiling less often, usually either to express solidarity with others or to threaten others, as in a sneer (Beekman 1973). Interestingly, both men and women report as intimidating a woman who smiles infrequently (Chesler, 1972). This latter finding is borne out in the complaints of many aspiring female executives whose serious attitudes and task-oriented work ethic often allow them to advance to modest positions of authority, but whose serious mein also prevents (because of its incompatibility with cultural expectations) further advance.

Biological causes

The traditional response to nonverbal gender differences contends that primary and secondary sex characteristics are responsible. In other words, men stand with their legs wide apart as a means of accommodating their genitalia, female students carry their books in front of them rather than on their hips as do males because of their distinctive arm-bone structure, and men have longer strides than women because they are physically larger. While perhaps true, these explanations do not help us understand the more profound differences in nonverbal communication between men and women discussed above.

Closely related to physiologically based explanations is the assertion that women and men are innately or "naturally" different. Consistent with this position is the anecdote of the woman who explains that she is "more comfortable" when she crosses her legs rather than when she sits with both feet on the floor, or the one about the man who states that it is not "natural" for men to hug or kiss one another (although abundant cross-cultural evidence indicates that such behavior is normative in many cultures), or the story of the individual who discusses the propriety of nonverbal behavior on the basis of "the way I have always behaved." In adopting this perspective, one is implying than men and women must behave differently, and that these differences are best explained on the basis of innate grounds rather than on the basis of any socio-cultural influences.

Although widely accepted, theories of nonverbal sex differences in communication which rely upon physiological differences or innate factors are without sufficient scientific support. Interestingly, research in this area seems to indicate that it is actually the absence of innate physiological differences that may account for nonverbal differences. Theorists argue that when examined on the basis of secondary sex characteristics, humans, like many other species, are overwhelmingly more similar (unimorphic) than different (dimorphic). If we were rated on a spectrum on the basis of our secondary sex characteristics (or our anatomy), we would tend to cluster together rather than be clearly differentiated into two distinct groups (Birdwhistell, 1970). Because we are actually more alike than different, we establish elaborate codes allowing others to determine our sex. The parent who feels compelled to dress a new baby in appropriate sex-typed clothing exhibits this behavior. It is difficult to distinguish between male and female children on any basis other than artifacts—the color, cut, and texture of their clothing; the presence of jewelry; and the presence of gender-appropriate toys. It is not much easier to distinguish between male and female adults, except on the basis of nonverbal cues.

If, as Birdwhistell and others suggest, we are more alike than different, why have we established such extensive nonverbal codes for distinguishing between women and men? Theorists speculate that originally such distinctions might have been useful to protect the species or have more easily allowed men and women to identify one another for the purposes of procreation. Inasmuch as fostering population growth no longer appears to be an appropriate objective for humankind, and, further, since distinguishing between men and women is no longer nearly as important as other types of distinctions we need to make to enrich and insure our survival, we need to consider other reasons for enacting sex differences through nonverbal behavior.

Understanding and conforming to communication rules

Differences in nonverbal communication behaviors might be due to differences in adhering to communication rules and the different roles men and women play in interaction. For instance, differences in gaze behavior may be attributed to the fact that women simply listen more and talk less than men (Argyle, Lalljee & Cook, 1968). Since we know that listeners—whether they be women or men—observe more than speakers (Duncan, 1969), it may be that women gaze more than men because of their role in the conversation.

Conclusions

In this chapter we have presented and discussed research findings contrasting men's and women's nonverbal communication behaviors. Specifically, we have discussed differences in their use of space and territory, with men tending to be more territorial and women tending to have smaller personal-space zones; differences in their smiling behavior, with women tending to smile more often and seemingly indiscriminately, as contrasted with men who tend to smile judiciously; differences in their postures, with men assuming more relaxed and expansive postures; differences in their gestures, with women tending to gesture more often but less authoritatively; differences in their touching behavior, with women tending to engage in more reciprocal touch than men; differences in their paralanguage leading to differences in conversational management; differences in their artifacts, especially clothing, with recent changes in fashion tending to establish masculine apparel as "generic" and appropriate for both sexes.

While some attempt has been made to explain these differences on the basis of innate or physiological differences between men and women, more promising explanations are found when considering differences in the ways men and women are taught to be men and women.

Differences in socialization account for men's dominant nonverbal behavior and women's affiliative or subservient nonverbal behavior. Inasmuch as socialization is a learned phenomenon, there is every reason to believe in our ability to modify it, so that in the future we will be less bound by sex-related norms for our nonverbal behavior.

7 Self-disclosure, self-assertion, and gender

Introduction

In the previous sections of this text, we have considered how gender and communication are intertwined on both perceptual and behavioral levels. This chapter is concerned with two specific communication behaviors: **self-disclosure,** the intentional sharing of intimate information about one's self with others; and **self-assertiveness,** the communication of one's needs and wants in an effort to gain another's volitional understanding and/or compliance. Self-disclosure is practiced in an effort to make oneself known honestly to another, whereas, self-assertiveness is practiced in an effort to convince others to comply with, or at least appreciate, one's needs. Both processes are self-presentational and instrumental in the management of interpersonal relationships.

We embark on this discussion with the clear understanding that men and women are generally more similar than different in their self-presentational styles, and that individual differences in these two communication behaviors are far more extreme when contrasting individual personalities—regardless of sex—than when contrasting men as a group with women as a group. We need to consider these considerable similarities to offset the possible impression that men and women are so different in their communication behaviors that meaningful communication between them is impossible.

That there are meaningful differences in the communication behaviors of men and women has been clearly established. Otherwise, there would be no point in writing a book on gender and communication. However, to recognize there are meaningful differences is not to suggest that those differences overwhelm all the real similarities between men's and women's communication behaviors.

Self-disclosure

When researchers study self-disclosure, they characterize it in many different ways. Three of the more common ways to understand self-disclosure are as an aspect of the personality, or an individual trait; as an individual behavior; or as a result of dyadic interaction. Consequently, we will review the gender literature on self-disclosure from each of these three perspectives.

The trait approach

The research using a **trait approach** has focused on other personality traits associated with disclosive behavior. These findings have been relatively consistent for both men and women. For instance, people who score high in social poise and extroversion tend to score high in self-disclosure (Ashworth, Furman, Chaikin & Derlega, 1976). This finding is not surprising. It simply means that people who are poised in social settings and who enjoy talking tend to talk about themselves.

Self-esteem is also positively correlated with self-disclosure; i.e., people with high self-esteem tend to disclose more than people with low self-esteem (Fitzgerald, 1963). In addition, people with high self-esteem are attracted to other highly disclosive people, and, in fact, tend to perceive others as having low self-esteem if they do not match their own level of self-disclosure (Gilbert, 1977). We can presume that if people are high in self-esteem and disclose a lot, they perceive their disclosures as positive and stimulating. Accordingly, they may be attracted to other high self-disclosers because they seek reciprocity for the positive stimulation they think they bring to their interpersonal transactions. This interpretation is compatible with findings indicating people tend to disclose to others perceived as similar to self (Skol & Kaionzky, 1985).

People who are high in self-disclosure also tend to be high in self-actualization (Lombardo & Fantasia, 1976). They report their having fulfilled their potential to be a higher degree than people who disclose less and also appear to be higher in self-satisfaction. In what is probably one of the most interesting self-perception measures developed in recent years, Prisbell and Andersen (1980) have also demonstrated high correlations between self-disclosure and "feeling good."

Other personality factors have an inverse relationship to self-disclosure. For example, intimate self-disclosure is inversely related to a person's need for approval (Brundage, Derlega & Cash, 1977). Similarly, anxiety seems to be inversely related to self-disclosure (Post, Wittmaier & Radin, 1978). These relationships might be explained by the considerable body of evidence demonstrating that communication apprehension (fear of communicating with others) is also inversely related to self-disclosure (McCroskey & Richmond, 1977). It appears, then, that although anxious people need (like all the rest of us) others to communicate with and build relationships with, they have difficulty doing so because their anxiety disposes them to anticipate the worst outcomes of self-disclosure. It is as though they were saying to themselves: "Things are bad enough as they are. Why make them worse by disclosing information that might make them want to avoid me even more?"

This information on the relationships between personality factors and self-disclosure serves to illustrate just a few of the interesting correlations or systematic associations between self-disclosure and various personality dispositions. These relationships are true for both men and women. As stated before, however, the differences between men's and women's disclosure behaviors are also quite interesting. From a trait perspective, the main difference between women and men that researchers have discovered involves the discloser's attractiveness.

Men perceiving themselves as attractive tend to disclose more than men perceiving themselves as less attractive, while women perceiving themselves as attractive disclose less than women perceiving themselves as less attractive (Cash & Soloway, 1975). These differences may be due to the tendency of men to dominate, or engineer disclosure interactions, by their disclosure of information followed usually by their partner's disclosure of information (Derlega, Winstead, Wong & Hunter, 1985). Another possibility is that men who perceive themselves as attractive feel compelled to capitalize on this advantage by drawing increased attention to self to heighten the possibility of others noticing their attractiveness.

Women might not behave similarly because of a learned inclination to de-emphasize their strengths or because of the expectation that their role is to react to the disclosures of others. In addition, women who perceive themselves as attractive may not feel the need to draw further attention to themselves. Their appearance per se may be deemed sufficient as a way to attract others. This idea may be reinforced by the pervasive cultural messages (e.g., advertisements) which commonly depict attractive women, but which much less often illustrate their active involvement in anything.

The behavioral approach

When we approach self-disclosure from a **behavioral perspective,** we note many differences between women and men. To begin with, a preponderance of evidence indicates that although men report greater intention to disclose (Gilbert & Whiteneck, 1976; Sermat & Smyth, 1973), they tend not to follow up on these intentions (Wiebe & Scott, 1976); and women actually disclose more than men do (Cline & Musolf, 1985; DeForest & Stone, 1980; Dooley, Whalen & Flowers, 1978; Greenblatt, Hasenauer & Freimuth, 1980; LeVine & Franco, 1981; Littlefield, 1974). Fewer studies suggest no differences in the amount of disclosure made by men and women (Brooks, 1974; Kohen, 1975; Montgomery & Norton, 1981). And even fewer studies suggest that men disclose more than women (Gilbert & Whiteneck, 1976; Sermat & Smyth, 1973). For the most part, it is now believed that in general women disclose more than men. But because the research has been mixed in its findings, additional investigations have been undertaken to determine under what circumstances men and women disclose differently. Consideration of these studies suggests quite interesting differences in men's and women's communication behavior.

Positive versus negative disclosures

With consistency, research has indicated that disclosure of positive information about self results in greater personal satisfaction than does the disclosure of negative information (Hecht, Shepard & Hall, 1979). Not surprisingly, the receipt of positive information results in the discloser being perceived as more attractive (Dalto, Ajzen & Kaplan, 1979). It is, therefore, somewhat disturbing to note that women appear to disclose more negative information about themselves than do men (Critelli & Neumann, 1978). Men are especially prone to avoid disclosing negative information about themselves when communicating with women (Cash, 1975). Men, therefore, appear to be somewhat more conscientious about how their disclosure of negative information might affect their development of a romantic relationship than women are.

The net effect of disclosing negative information about self is to make oneself more vulnerable. In some circumstances doing so may elicit empathy and willingness to help the discloser, but it may also register the lesser status of the discloser, which, of course, would clearly be compatible with generalized cultural images of women. However, Shimanoff (1988) recently found that while women did report disclosing emotions more fully than men, both men and women reported a similar preferential hierarchy for disclosing emotions. Negative or "face-threatening" emotions are reportedly disclosed less fully than mixed disclosures, which are reportedly disclosed less fully than those which imply approval or are "non-face-threatening." This three part hierarchy was largely similar in Shimanoff's data, regardless of gender.

Disclosure of cognitive versus affective information

Disclosures may entail the sharing of information about how one thinks about certain issues or how one feels about those issues. The differences are important in that disclosure of cognitions would indicate **task orientation** (a preoccupation with getting work done), while disclosure of affective information would speak to one's **emotional experiences** (how one is experiencing his/her life and relationships with others), regardless of whether work per se is getting done. In general, men appear to be more inclined to disclose cognitive information, while women are more inclined to disclose affective information (Highlen & Gillis, 1978; Janofsky, 1971). Moreover, women are especially inclined to disclose affective information to other women. These findings suggest that women are more concerned with monitoring the emotional climates of their relationships, and since they sense greater affinity with other women similarly oriented, they, of course, are even more inclined to disclose such information to women. Men, however, are more inclined to disclose information concerning the work tasks confronting them, and this would reflect a greater preoccupation with achievement.

These findings are, of course, compatible with some of the cultural stereotypes concerning men's and women's communication behavior. They remind us that while cultural stereotypes are to be viewed with suspicion, they are often partially correct and deserve consideration when developing a more accurate, data-based understanding of human communication. However, unlike stereotypes, knowledge derived from empirical investigations does not imply that the status quo needs to be perpetuated. It is entirely possible, for instance, that men can learn to be more affectively expressive and that women can learn to be more instrumentally oriented. However, as Bate (1988) points out, understanding the difference between an affective and an instrumental approach may itself be complicated by gender if the sexes have different ways of thinking about "self." If a man's selfhood and identity is tied to his job, then disclosing information about work may be an affective expression, although a woman listener may not perceive it as such. Further, a male listener may hear a woman's statement about her inner feelings as a task disclosure since it may sound to him as if it is a problem that can be solved with some advice.

Disclosure of intimate versus nonintimate information

In addition to information being either positive or negative, cognitive or affective, it can also vary in intimacy. Usually when intimate information is disclosed, it is done so for the purpose of allowing another to know more clearly and deeply something of the discloser's personality and unique self, and inevitably allows the reduction of psychological distance between self and others. To become intimate with another means to get closer either psychologically or physically. When considering intimacy of information disclosed, we find some curious differences between men's and women's communication behaviors, although it is not entirely clear whether these differences are real or artifacts of the particular research methodologies employed to obtain this information. On the basis of self-report data (data obtained by administering questionnaires and simply asking people how they would behave under certain circumstances), it appears that women have greater intention to disclose more intimate information than men (Gitter & Black, 1976; Morgan, 1976), and that neither men nor women appear more intent in controlling the manner in which this information is disclosed (Tardy, Hosman & Bradac, 1981) (i.e., neither men nor women report greater intention to manipulate the other in the disclosure of intimate information).

However, when actually engaging in acquaintance exercises, it appears that men are, in fact, more manipulative, i.e., they attempt to exercise greater control in eliciting and negotiating the intimate information disclosed (Davis, 1978). Accordingly, it may well be that while men do not intend to manipulate others, they do so more than female communicators. Alternatively, men may, indeed, intend this behavior, but reporting that one engages in manipulation—even if one is aware of it in the first place—is something not done.

It is because of the above inconsistencies in research that Bochner (1982) and Winstead, Derlega, and Wong (1984) argue that the findings of self-report studies should be considered separately from the finding of behavioral studies. The differences in methodologies, they argue, may themselves seriously affect the nature of the information obtained. While both types of information are important, reasonable interpretation of their significance is best obtained when not confusing the manner of knowledge collection with the knowledge itself. This is good advice to follow in any area of research.

Perhaps you have not thought as much about sex roles in our society as you have while you were reading this text. Sex roles are sometimes so integral to people that they do not think about them. In this exercise, you will have an opportunity to think about your own sex roles and to share that information with others. Spend about thirty minutes reflecting upon reasons that you are pleased you are a woman (or man), and reasons that you are not pleased to be a woman (or man). After you have compiled your lists, spend about one hour with a group of people of the same sex and share your feelings. After each person in your group has had an opportunity to share his or her feelings, put the two groups together so the men and women can hear the perceptions of other-sex people.

After you have engaged in this interaction with others of the same sex, write a short essay on the experience. In your essay, consider how much you were willing to self-disclose about your feelings in the two groups. You are more likely to have disclosed more with people of the same sex than with people of the other sex. Was this true for you? Why or why not? Did you write down some feelings you were unwilling to share in either group? Why or why not? Does this exercise demonstrate any of the research findings reported above on self-disclosure? Explain. What have you learned about sex roles in this exercise?

Intimacy of topic under discussion

When the discussion topic is controlled, i.e., neither the male nor female research participants are allowed to discuss anything other than the particular topic assigned by the researchers, it is found that men and women do not differ in the amount of information disclosed concerning relatively nonintimate topics (politics), but that when more intimate topics are discussed (sex), women are inclined to disclose more than men (Lombardo & Berzonsky, 1979). This finding is compatible with previously discussed findings concerning women's greater orientation toward socioemotional issues.

The dyadic approach

The **dyadic approach** to self-disclosure is similar to the transactional approach to communication discussed in chapter 1. From this perspective, self-disclosure is seen as emerging from the dyadic context. Self-disclosure, thus, is not the property of the individual; it is affected by many dyadic factors.

The basic characteristic of self-disclosure as an interaction is that it occurs in a dyad, or a two-person group, and that both people send and receive disclosures. The earliest literature on self-disclosure discusses its "dyadic effect." This reference by Jourard suggests that self-disclosure occurs only in the dyad and a large number of studies have investigated it in this setting (cf. Burke, Weir & Harrison, 1976; Casciani, 1978).

Self-disclosure may occur in a larger group than the dyad, however, Jourard (1971) believes that the presence of a "third party" may inhibit disclosure. People appear to manage an appropriate level of self-disclosure in the dyad rather than in a larger group (Davis, 1977; Derlega & Chaikin, 1977). Individuals are more willing to disclose personal information in a dyad than in a triad. The necessary level of confidentiality, which appears to be more attainable in a dyad than in a triad, may be responsible for the difference (Taylor, DeSoto & Lieb, 1979). Although disclosure may occur in larger groups, the dyad appears to be the optimum group in which it can occur, at least for men.

Gender differences in the dyad and triad have been examined. Men self-disclose more in dyads than they do in small groups of three or more; females not only self-disclose significantly more in a small-group setting than do men, they also self-disclose more in small groups than they do in the dyad (Pearson, 1981). The people in the dyads and small groups included individuals who were known to the disclosers as well as persons who were previously unknown to them.

Researchers who have studied self-disclosure within the dyad have concluded that self-disclosure is generally reciprocal, that is, as the disclosure of one person increases, so does that of the other person (Feigenbaum, 1977). In addition, when individuals do not reciprocate, they are generally viewed as incompetent (Bradac, Tardy & Hosman, 1980; Hosman & Tardy, 1980). Patterns of reciprocity appear to occur within the first five minutes of interaction in cross-gender dyads (Kohen, 1975). It appears that a person may be well advised to offer disclosures similar to those which she or he is receiving.

The only limitation on reciprocity which has emerged occurs with men in high-self-disclosure situations. In a laboratory situation, experimenters moved from low through moderate to high self-disclosure. In each case, women reciprocated the level of disclosure; men reciprocated in the low and moderate conditions, but did not reciprocate in the high-disclosure situation (Archer & Berg, 1978). Men may feel discomfort in offering high self-disclosure in an experimental setting, or they may be unaware of any demands that disclosure by the other person places on them. In any case, they did not offer reciprocally high levels of self-disclosure.

Closely related to the reciprocal nature of self-disclosure is the relationship between self-disclosure and trust (McAllister, 1980). Individuals who trust each other are more likely to self-disclose than are individuals who do not. Similarly, self-disclosure frequently results in trust among persons (Wheeless & Grotz, 1977; Ellison & Firestone, 1974). Trust exerts a strong influence on the willingness of both persons to disclose in a dyad. Moreover, trust is an important factor in developing a sense of interpersonal solidarity or "oneness" between the members of the dyad (Wheeless, 1978). This feeling of trust may have roots in early childhood. People who felt that their parents were nurturing or high in affection tend to be more trusting and higher in self-disclosure (Pedersen & Higbee, 1969; Snoek & Rothblum, 1979).

Gender of the listener

The gender composition of the dyad makes a difference in self-disclosure behavior. Whether one is discussing adolescents (Mulcahy, 1973) or adults (Littlefield, 1974), women have been found to disclose more information when communicating with other women than when communicating with men. Men, however, do not demonstrate a similar inclination to disclose more when communicating with men than women, i.e., same-sex composition affects more dramatically the amount and level of intimacy of information disclosed by women than men. Furthermore, both men and women disclose more to women than men (Derlega, Hunter, Winstead & Wong, 1985). Women tend more than men to be the recipients of self-disclosure regardless of the discloser's gender. As Winstead (1986) observes, "the presence of a female has a powerful effect on the social behavior of another; it makes him or her more self-disclosing, more open, and less lonely" (p. 93).

Hacker (1981) notes that when men disclose to women they tend to confide their weaknesses while enhancing their strengths, to give a balanced view of strengths and weaknesses. When women disclose to men, they tend to conceal their strengths while confiding their weaknesses. In this disclosure pattern, men and women reinforce traditional sex-role stereotypes where men are in a dominant position compared to women.

Gender and attractiveness of listener

In general, both men and women tend to disclose more to attractive others, regardless of their gender, than they do to less attractive others (Young, 1980). This, of course, would make intuitive sense since disclosure is a vehicle for achieving intimacy; therefore, one would be inclined to develop intimacy with attractive others. The factor of the attractiveness of the person being disclosed to appears to be somewhat more important for women than men (Kohen, 1975; Robison, 1976; Sote & Good, 1974).

Table 7.1 Gender differences in self-disclosure are dependent upon a variety of factors

Positive or negative nature	*Both sexes are equally likely to offer negative information. *Men are less likely to disclose positive information than women. *Women offer more negative than positive information.
Cognitive or affective information	*Women offer more affective information than men.
Intimate or nonintimate information	*Women report that they disclose more intimate information than men. *In interactions, men set the pace of intimacies and women match the pace set by men.
Topics under discussion	*Men and women do not differ on the amount they self-disclose on nonintimate topics, such as politics. *Women self-disclose more on intimate topics such as sex and religion.
Gender of the target person	*Females prefer other females to whom to self-disclose. *In mixed-sex dyads, females and males do not self-disclose to a different extent.
Attractiveness of the target person	*In general, both women and men self-disclose more to an attractive person than to an unattractive person. *Attractiveness may be a more relevant variable for women than for men.
Interaction of attractiveness and the gender of the target person Attractiveness of the discloser	*Both women and men self-disclose more to attractive individuals of the same sex. *Both women and men provide less negative self-disclosure to attractive persons of the opposite sex. *Men who perceive themselves as attractive self-disclose more than men who perceive themselves as unattractive.

However, men appear to be more sensitive than women to the attractiveness of the other in male-female communication transactions, and demonstrate more discrimination in the amount and type of information disclosed to an attractive woman versus a less attractive woman. Specifically, men are inclined to disclose more positive and less negative information to an attractive than an unattractive woman (Harrel, 1978). Women show much less inclination to exercise similar discrimination in their disclosure with attractive versus less attractive males. In part, these differences in disclosure behavior lend further support to the suggestion that men tend to be more discriminating and manipulative in controlling disclosure norms than women, particularly in male/female transactions.

Table 7.1— *Continued*

	*Women who perceive themselves as attractive self-disclose less than women who perceive themselves as unattractive.
Age of the discloser	*In general, women self-disclose more than men of all ages. *For both women and men, self-disclosure increases as they mature and become older.
Nonverbal behaviors	*Increased eye contact encourages self-disclosure in women, but inhibits self-disclosure in men. *As the amount of personal space decreases among interactants, women self-disclose more while men self-disclose less. *For both women and men, increased touch is associated with increased self-disclosure. *Increased movement on the part of a male target of disclosure and decreased movement on the part of a female target of disclosure resulted in increased self-disclosure on the part of clients in a counseling setting.
Influence of sex-related variables	*For men, increasing levels of femininity and decreasing levels of masculinity are associated with an increasing level of self-disclosure. *For women, increasing levels of masculinity coupled with decreasing levels of femininity are associated with increasing levels of self-disclosure; however, the addition of masculinity to stationary levels of femininity is not associated with increased self-disclosure. *Homosexual men and heterosexual women are similar in self-disclosive behavior, while homosexual women and heterosexual men are not.

Other listener and sender attributes

Petronio, Martin, and Littlefield (1984) discovered that women find several receiver-and-sender characteristics more important as prerequisites for self-disclosure than men. Specifically, women are more concerned than men that a potential recipient of their disclosures be discreet, trustworthy, sincere, liked, respected, attentive, warm, and open. For themselves as senders it is more important to women than men that they be accepted, willing to disclose, honest, and relaxed. Related to this finding that sender and receiver qualities are more important to women than men is the fact that men are often more willing to self-disclose to total strangers than they are to good friends. Women generally prefer to self-disclose in the context of friendships where, perhaps, they can be more certain of the listener's characteristics.

Self-disclosure and nonverbal behaviors

Another area of research has considered the impact of nonverbal behaviors on self-disclosure between women and men. The research in this area suggests that self-disclosure is significantly affected by eye contact, personal space, touch, and bodily movement. Eye contact has a different effect on self-disclosure for women and men. Direct gazing appears to promote the intimacy of self-disclosure between women, while it decreases the self-disclosure between males (Ellsworth & Ross, 1975). This finding was confirmed in a more recent study in which high verbal intimacy in male dyads was associated with low eye contact, and low verbal intimacy was accompanied by high eye contact (Amerikaner, 1980). These findings indicate that self-disclosure and eye contact are positively correlated for women, but negatively correlated for men.

Personal space appears to affect self-disclosure. Most studies demonstrate that women self-disclose more as the amount of personal space decreases and men self-disclose less (cf. Stotko & Langmeyer, 1977; Sundstrom, 1975). Only one exception occurs in the literature—a situation in which no correlations were found among the amount of self-disclosure, the gender of the discloser, and the amount of personal space available (Johnson, 1973). Most of the studies confirm a positive correlation between self-disclosure and physical closeness for women, but demonstrate a negative correlation between self-disclosure and physical closeness for men. This finding is consistent with the research on eye contact. Women appear to establish closeness with eye contact, physical space, and self-disclosure behavior. Men appear to distance themselves from others through lack of eye contact and increased physical space as they self-disclose.

Touch intervenes in the self-disclosure of women and men; moreover, touch is viewed as a positive indicator of self-disclosure for both women and men. As touch increases, so does self-disclosure (Lomranz & Shapira, 1974). Touch, unlike eye contact or physical space, appears to be positively related to increased intimacy and self-disclosure for both men and women.

Bodily movement also plays a role in self-disclosure. For example, when male counselors move more, self-disclosure by clients tends to increase; conversely, when female counselors move less, the self-disclosure of the clients increases (Gardner, 1973).

Self-disclosure development

Relationship stage
The stage of the communicators' relationship also affects self-disclosure. Early acquaintanceship, friendship, or intimacy all affect the levels of self-disclosure likely to occur. One area of particular interest is self-disclosure between strangers who never expect to see each other again. In these situations, which may take place on public transportation, in public places, or under disastrous conditions, self-disclosure frequently happens quickly. In these instances, people may feel more freedom to offer high levels of self-disclosure since they are unlikely to interact on any future occasion. Unlike other situations, self-disclosure in these situations is relatively risk-free. Long-term difficulties are generally not possible. As mentioned previously, men tend to prefer this risk-free situation for disclosing.

Developing relationships
In relationships between nonstrangers, a pattern in self-disclosure seems to emerge. First, a relatively high level of nonintimate information is disclosed; then, intimate information is disclosed at a gradually increasing rate (Taylor, 1965). The least amount of self-disclosure may occur between acquaintances who do not know each other very well, but between whom future interactions are likely to occur (Pearce & Sharp, 1973).

Self-disclosure between relative strangers who expect to see each other again is generally not preferred. People who are barely acquainted have indicated a preference for those who disclose very little rather than for those who disclose a great deal (Archer & Burleson, 1980; Culbert, 1968). When intimate disclosures are inappropriately timed, that is, when they occur too early, the other may perceive the person disclosing as suffering from maladjustment or inappropriate socialization (Kiesler, Kiesler & Pallak, 1967).

Table 7.2   Self-disclosure in relationships

In developing relationships	• A high level of non-intimate information is disclosed early, followed by intimate information which is disclosed at a gradually increasing rate.
Among friends	• Women prefer to self-disclose to female best friends. • Men self-disclose least to female friends. • Men who are emotionally unstable or meditative disclose more to male best friends than do men who are emotionally stable or not meditative.
In the family	• In general, children of both sexes self-disclose more to their mothers than to their fathers. • Women who are emotionally stable self-disclose more to their fathers than to their mothers.
In courtship	• In dating, a couple's self-disclosure is associated with self-report statements of loving. • Self-disclosure is associated with egalitarian ideals in couples. • Women self-disclose more discriminately than do men in their relationships.
In marriage	• Frequently, married couples who disclose more also express greater marital satisfaction; however, the history of the relationship, the nature of the disclosure, and the intent of the disclosure may intervene.
In deteriorating relationships	• Deteriorating relationships are marked by decreased levels of self-disclosure.

More specific information has been gleaned concerning the effect of a relationship's length on self-disclosure. Persons in the early stages of a relationship appear first to disclose nonintimate information in the order of positive statements, neutral statements, and negative statements. Then, in later stages, they disclose intimate information beginning with negative statements, followed by positive, and concluding with neutral statements (Gilbert & Whiteneck, 1976). However, Shimanoff's (1988) results indicate that even best friends prefer to avoid "face-threatening" disclosures.

Timing appears to interact with the gender of the discloser. A number of studies have demonstrated that men generally disclose information earlier in the development of a relationship than women do (Berger, Gardner, Clatterbuck & Schulman, 1976; Gilbert & Whiteneck, 1976). Men self-disclose more to acquaintances (Stokes, Fuehrer & Childs, 1980) and to casual friends (Woodyard & Hines, 1973) than women do. Women, on the other hand, are more likely to self-disclose to close friends or intimates (Highlen, 1978; Littlefield, 1974; Rubin & Sheneker, 1978; Stokes, Fuehrer & Childs, 1980; Woodyard & Hines, 1973).

Courtship

The dating relationship provides an interesting context in which to study self-disclosure, a behavior related to the self-report statements of loving for dating couples (Critelli & Dupre, 1978). People who report that they love each other also enjoy high levels of self-disclosure. This finding is not surprising and is probably related to the idea that we self-disclose more when we trust the other person.

The attitudes that couples express appear to be related to their levels of self-disclosure. Those who express egalitarian ideals (i.e., both persons should be involved in decision making, both persons should have opportunities for making money and spending it, either person can initiate sexual activity, etc.), rather than traditional ideals (i.e., the male initiates sexual activity, earns the living for the couple, is the primary decision maker, while the female is primarily a homemaker, etc.), appear to be more disclosive (Hill, Peplau & Dunkel-Schetter, 1980).

In developing heterosexual relationships men and women tend to disclose differently. Men appear more likely to define their relationship in a romantic-dating-sexual framework, regardless of the cues offered, to anticipate more sexual activity, to be less selective in making disclosures, and less likely to be selective in making sexual decisions. Females, on the other hand, are more likely to make distinctions between friendly and romantic relationships and more discriminating in their self-disclosure and sexual behavior (Rytting, 1976). Cline and Musolf (1985) found that women in long-term dating relationships were the most intimate in their disclosures, while men in long-term relationships had almost the lowest intimacy level of all the study groups. They speculate that this "mismatch" in intimacy level may be the cause of problems for dating couples.

Marriage

Marital couples show similar trends. Just as dating couples who disclose more report higher levels of love, marital couples with high levels of disclosure report greater marital satisfaction (Burke, Weir, & Harrison, 1976; Fiore & Swenson, 1977; Jorgensen & Gaudy, 1980).

While marital couples who self-disclose report generally higher levels of marital satisfaction, other factors may intervene. For instance, Philips and Goodall (1983) found that marital satisfaction was not always a function of self-disclosure. They maintain that the contribution of self-disclosure to marital satisfaction lies in the history of the relationship and the goals for the self-disclosing talk. For example, the spouse who overhears some negative information about his or her partner's occupational performance may find that marital satisfaction is enhanced by keeping the information confidential rather than by sharing it. Or, if a couple has never shared minute, day-to-day problems at work when at home, initiating such an activity may actually interfere with marital satisfaction.

Other studies report similar findings. Levinger and Senn (1967) and Voss (1969) demonstrate that marital satisfaction may be more affected by the communicator's favorable attitudes toward the information disclosed than by the amount of self-disclosure. In addition, they found that only two of seventeen topics were important in predicting marital satisfaction. These two topics were identified as "shared activities" and "children and careers." In other words, the couples may disclose about a variety of other topics, but the levels and amount of disclosure do not affect the amount of marital satisfaction they report.

The topics of self-disclosure were also examined with regard to differences in attitudes between men and women and in connection to the topics people need to disclose. The most significant areas for women were identified as "body" and "personality"; for men the most significant areas were "attitudes," "opinions," and "money" (Farber, 1979). These differences may modify the findings on the relationship between self-disclosure and marital satisfaction. For instance, if two people disclose their feelings on money and economic matters, the male may feel greater satisfaction than the female. Or if they discuss their perceptions of their own or other's bodies or personalities, the woman may feel satisfied, but the man may not.

Family

Family relationships have also been examined for patterns of self-disclosure. The findings in this context are fairly consistent. In general, children of either gender tend to self-disclose more to their mothers than to their fathers (Balswick & Balkwell 1977; Jourard & Lasakow, 1958; Littlefield, 1974; Morgan, 1976; Pederson & Higbee, 1969; Ryckman, Sherman & Burgess, 1973). However, fathers appear to be the recipients of more accurate disclosures (Woodyard & Hines, 1973).

Does any group disclose more to fathers than to mothers? Women who are emotionally more stable select their fathers rather than their mothers for their disclosures (Pedersen & Higbee, 1969); they may also have a closer relationship to their fathers, may be "androgynous" or "masculine," or may view their fathers as role models for their own behavior.

Deteriorating relationships

What happens to levels of self-disclosure when couples are in the process of terminating their relationship? Since higher levels of self-disclosure are related to higher levels of marital satisfaction, we would expect that couples separating, divorcing, or ending their relationship in other ways, would disclose less. Indeed, this is the conclusion of a study which considered relationship termination. People are less willing to disclose when they are attempting to disengage themselves from a relationship (Baxter, 1979).

Explaining gender differences in self-disclosure

In examining various aspects of self-disclosure in this chapter, we have observed a general pattern of women self-disclosing more, being disclosed to more, being more aware of cues that affect their self-disclosure, and of women and men disclosing on different topics and in different ways. Let us consider some explanations for their differences in disclosure. First, women may self-disclose more because they are socialized to be open and expressive, i.e., our culture promotes self-disclosure among women, yet restricts this behavior among men. Certainly there is much available cultural evidence compatible with such an explanation.

However, as Winstead (1986) states, self-disclosure behavior may be the result of a type of cultural self-fulfilling prophecy. People come to relationships with stereotypes in mind. A woman is expected to be relatively interested in listening to emotional disclosures. Both men and women affected by this stereotype are more likely to behave somewhat differently when interacting with a female than with a male, that is, "self-presentation depends on our assumptions (our stereotypes) about others" (p. 93). In addition, given the norm of reciprocity, women will respond to the disclosures they receive with disclosures of their own, further confirming the expectation of the emotionally disclosive female.

Second, a quite different explanation is that self-disclosure is simply more important to women than men. By implication, one would also conclude that relationships are more important to women than men. Why this would be the case we do not yet know, but it is, nonetheless, a possibility worth considering. A third explanation may be that our economic system has evolved in such a way as essentially to force women to assume subservient communication postures, i.e., women disclose more because lesser status people always disclose more to high-status persons than vice versa.

It may also be that gender differences in disclosure are more satisfactorily explained when focusing on male socialization patterns. Stereotypically, successful men are expected to compete and win, and competitiveness is not conducive to intimacy (Stokes, Fuehrer & Childs, 1980). Disclosing intimate information about self is incompatible with exploiting another person's weakness. Hence, men may disclose less than women because doing so would make them vulnerable. Having learned to disclose less in work and work-type settings, men may also restrict their self-disclosure in interpersonal settings (Rosenfeld, 1979).

The differences in men's and women's disclosure behaviors may be explained by developmental differences between females and males. When first learning to speak, girls and boys do not appear to differ significantly in their disclosure behaviors. However, between the ages of 6 to 12, girls appear to disclose more as well as more intimate information than boys (O'Neill, Fein, Velit & Frank, 1976). Among 14-year olds, girls still appear to disclose more than boys; they also appear to be more selective about the targets of their disclosures (generally preferring to disclose to confidantes, usually other females) (Klos & Loomis, 1978; Littlefield, 1974).

In general, then, adolescent girls appear to self-disclose more than boys (Rivenbark 1971), although boys appear to learn to disclose more as they grow older. For example, in comparing ninth graders with twelfth graders, it appears that when men grow older they appear to self-disclose more and are especially inclined to disclose more when communicating with females. A similar, though less pronounced, pattern emerged for females: both ninth and twelfth graders disclose more when communicating with other females than with males. Also, ninth-grade females tend to disclose more generally than ninth-grade males. Thus, high-school females tend to change less in their disclosure behavior than males, and when entering high school are already more inclined to self-disclose.

Snoek and Rothblum's (1979) research also seems to indicate that as people mature they tend to self-disclose more. These researchers found that college students disclose more than high-school students. Mark (1976) found that college students also disclose more intimate information than do high-school students. The findings of both of these studies are compatible with Rivenbark's (1971) previous finding that as people mature they tend to learn to disclose more, although it also appears that girls are inclined to self-disclose at an earlier age than boys. Perhaps this is because mothers traditionally have been (and continue to be) the primary caretakers of children, and rapport may be easier to develop between girls and mothers than between boys and mothers.

The self-disclosure of older adults, persons over sixty years of age, has been studied as well. In this age group, women self-disclose more than men, with over 75 percent of the disclosers—including both men and women—identifying women as their confidantes (Henkin, 1980). That women are identified more frequently as confidantes may be associated with the fact that there is a preponderance of older women largely because men die at younger ages than women. Henkin also reports a gradual decline in self-disclosure as people grow older, with people between the ages of 70 and 80 self-disclosing less than people between the ages of 60 and 70. Perhaps this decline is due to older people having increased health problems and fewer opportunities to disclose.

Finally, self-disclosure differences may be explained by examining psychological gender or sex-type rather than biological sex alone. Greenblatt, Hasenauer, and Freimuth (1980) demonstrated that masculine men have lower total disclosure scores than androgynous men, but that feminine females do not report higher total disclosure scores than androgynous women. Pearson (1980) demonstrated that masculine females disclosed more than feminine females, and feminine males disclosed more than masculine males. Somewhat compatible with all of these findings is recent research indicating a positive correlation between androgyny and disclosure (Sollie & Fischer, 1985; Wheeless, Zachai & Chan, 1988). In similar vein, Lavine and Lombardo

Older women self-disclose more than do older men and the person they disclose to is more likely to be another woman rather than a man.

(1984) found that undifferentiated individuals, both male and female, have depressed levels of disclosure relative to the other gender types (androgynous, masculine, or feminine).

We have examined a great deal of information on self-disclosure, learned about different patterns of self-disclosure for men and women, and have proposed some explanations for those differences. The question which remains is the extent to which we should attempt to include self-disclosive communication in our interactions with others. In other words, is self-disclosure a desirable behavior which we should encourage in ourselves and in others, or is it an undesirable behavior which should be discouraged?

The early writings of self-disclosure implied that this skill was related to a "healthy interpersonal relationship" in which people were willing and able to communicate all of their real selves to others (Jourard, 1958).

As a consequence of the positive attitude toward self-disclosure, practitioners have encouraged the communicative behavior in a variety of ways. Self-disclosure was identified as a dimension of interpersonal competence (Bochner & Kelly, 1974), as a component of dialogue (Johannesen, 1971), and was commonly taught in workshop settings (Lewis, 1978).

Today, researchers are less enthusiastic about prescribing self-disclosure for everyone in all interpersonal relationships. Jones and Brunner (1984) found, for example, that perception of communication competence is significantly affected by the discloser's sex. Female disclosers are perceived as more competent than male disclosers. Gilbert and Horenstein write, "the communication of intimacies is a behavior which has positive effects only in limited, appropriate circumstances" (Gilbert & Horenstein, 1975).

An examination of some of the outcomes of disclosure is helpful in presenting recommendations about self-disclosure since the theorists appear to disagree on the usefulness of this communicative behavior. While moderate self-disclosure generally results in positive outcomes, a great deal of self-disclosure is perceived as inappropriate (Lombardo & Wood, 1979), as unattractive (Gilbert, 1977), and as less competent (Jones & Brunner, 1984). More specifically, moderate disclosure appears to result in an increase in general satisfaction (Hecht, Shephard & Hall, 1979), loving (Critelli & Dupre, 1978), and personal solidarity (Wheeless, 1976). In addition, persons who offer positive self-disclosure are viewed as attractive (Gilbert & Horenstein, 1975).

Of particular interest to the reader may be the finding that disclosure tends to be reciprocated in similar amounts and intensities between/among satisfied interactants (Gelman & McGinley, 1978). When people like one another, they appear to search for common points of reference and then seek mutual disclosure of their ideas and feelings concerning those common frames of reference. We do this, in part, to determine whether we are sufficiently similar to another to want to develop a relationship with him or her. If we are attracted to the other, we will seek to match their disclosure amount and intimacy with our own, only increasing our disclosure when we feel and think the other feels comfortable with our doing so. This is a delicate and important interaction game played well by adept interpersonal communicators and one we should all strive to learn.

Self-assertion

Self-assertion is the ability to communicate your own feelings, beliefs, and desires honestly and directly while at the same time allowing others to communicate their own feelings, beliefs, and desires (Pearson & Spitzberg, 1990). Self-assertiveness is integral to successful interpersonal communication because without it one cannot successfully develop "mutually" satisfying relationships. It is for this reason that assertiveness training has become so widespread.

Andrew Salter conceived the idea of assertiveness training. In *Conditioned Reflex Therapy* (1949), Salter distinguished between nonassertiveness and assertiveness. Largely as a response to Salter's work, therapists began offering assertiveness training. In the late 1960s the concept became popularized and assertiveness training groups became widespread.

Distinguishing among assertiveness, nonassertiveness, and aggressiveness

Assertiveness is variously defined by different authors, but most specialists agree that the concept lies on a continuum somewhere between nonassertiveness, shyness, or passivity at one end and aggressiveness at the other. **Nonassertiveness** occurs when people are unable or unwilling to communicate their own feelings, beliefs, and desires to others. Suppose you ask a nonassertive person whether she or he would like to accompany you to a movie. Suppose, further, that this person has already seen the movie and did not enjoy it. While an assertive person is more likely to state that he or she had already seen it and did not enjoy it, the nonassertive person is less inclined to do so. Instead, he or she would say nothing, would stammer and stutter in an unclear way, or might offer a weak or oblique complaint only after viewing the movie a second time. Nonassertive people frequently choose to appease others rather than satisfy themselves. Although they may appease others, they rarely are personally satisfied. Because they are less satisfied, they often are resentful and unhappy.

Nonassertive people are often viewed sympathetically by others, or may be the victims of anger from others who feel they cannot enter into honest discussions with them. Nonassertive people are often depressed and anxious and rarely achieve their goals. Nonassertiveness in our culture appears to occur more frequently in women than it does in men. Though observational work does not reveal any tendency for women to be more timid than men, females report themselves to be less assertive (Chandler, Cook & Dugovics, 1978).

Aggressiveness has been more widely studied than nonassertion. It involves communicating your own feelings, beliefs, and desires honestly and directly without allowing others to communicate their own feelings, beliefs, and desires. An aggressive person disregards the rights of others in an effort to insure that his or her own rights are protected. The aggressive person frequently hurts others; people often feel defensive or humiliated when dealing with such a person. Aggressive people want to win, but they often "win the battle and lose the war." In other words, while they may be successful in coercing others into doing what they want to do in the short run, in the long run the aggressor tends to be avoided, or at least resented. Since healthy people prefer negotiated, collaborative relationships in which they have equal opportunity to be heard and to influence, they generally avoid others tending to be coercive and aggressive. Thus, even if aggressive communicators are successful in their battles with others, those victories are usually only short lived at best.

Sometimes it is easier to be assertive with people we hardly know than it is to behave assertively with our friends. Consider the following two situations and write down your response to each, how you felt during the time you were waiting in each case, and what you felt when your friend arrived. Imagine that you and a friend both enjoy a particular musical group. You learn that the group is on tour and will be performing in a nearby city. As a gift, you buy tickets for yourself and your friend, even though the price is quite high. You tell your friend, and she or he is very enthusiastic about the concert and agrees to drive to the concert as a way of thanking you for the tickets. The night of the concert arrives, but your friend does not. Finally, half an hour late, he or she shows up, but offers no explanation. Provide answers to the following questions:

1. If your friend was the same sex as you,
   a. What would you say or do when he or she arrived?
   b. How would you feel while you were waiting?
   c. How would you feel when he or she finally showed up?

2. If your friend was the other sex,
   a. What would you say or do when he or she arrived?
   b. How would you feel while you were waiting?
   c. How would you feel when he or she finally showed up?

Do you have different responses to the situation depending on the sex of your friend? Why or why not? Would you characterize your response as nonassertive, assertive, or aggressive? Compare your answers with those of others to determine how most people would respond. What have you discovered about assertiveness in this exercise?

Gender differences in assertiveness, nonassertiveness, and aggressiveness

Men are more frequently aggressive than women. When people were asked to determine the level of physical shock to administer to an opponent in a study, male subjects facing a male opponent recommended the highest level of shock more often than any other combination of persons (female subject with a female opponent, female subject with a male opponent, or male subject with a female opponent). Males were far more aggressive with other males than they were with females; female subjects did not vary the amount of physical shock they recommended on the basis of the other's sex (Hoppe, 1979). This study suggests that men are generally more aggressive than women. Furthermore, men are particularly aggressive with other men rather than with women.

Gender differences in self-assertion were examined in a study which considered performance, self-esteem, and dominance behavior in mixed-gender dyads. Men are more assertive than women during the process of decision making, and people perceive men to be more assertive than women in these situations. Nonetheless, this study suggests that the differences in assertiveness are not the result of differences in general self-esteem, but rather the result of females' behavior being mediated by self-evaluations. When women have confidence in themselves, they assert themselves (Stake & Stake, 1979). In other words, women may be unassertive in problem solving because they do not have high regard for their own ability to perform or to contribute to the specific topic under discussion; however, when they have confidence in their ability to contribute or add to the discussion, they demonstrate assertiveness.

Another significant aspect of gender differences is other people's perceptions of assertiveness and aggressiveness. Stereotypically, men are perceived to be assertive while women are not. Any specific instance of assertive behavior on a woman's part is less likely to elicit the inference that she is assertive in general than is a particular instance of assertive behavior on a man's part. Since women are generally presumed to be unassertive, specific instances of assertiveness by women may simply be perceived as isolated, unique events rather than part of a general behavioral repertoire. For instance, if a woman sends back food in a restaurant, onlookers might not conclude she is an assertive person, but if her male partner sent back his food, they would probably conclude he was assertive. The woman's behavior would be viewed as unique or exceptional for her, while the man's conduct would be seen as compatible with an assertive (masculine) personality (Hess, Bridgewater, Bornstein & Sweeney, 1980).

Explaining gender differences in self-assertion

We have observed that assertiveness appears to be related to gender. Women tend to fall in the range from nonassertive to assertive, while men tend to fall in the range from assertive to aggressive. Interesting explanations for these gender differences have been offered.

One author suggests that a "threshold of assertiveness" may exist for people, especially for women, allowing them to behave in an assertive way up to a point, but then not allowing them to go any farther (Lange, 1981). Two other authors hint at this "threshold effect" when they explain that when a person's "polite restraint" is too well developed, he or she may eventually become incapable of making assertive responses (Alberti & Emmons, 1974). This possibility is consistent with the socialization processes we have discussed previously. The encouragement of women to be polite, quiet, and considerate of other people's feelings, while men are not so instructed, offers some explanation for the difference.

Men tend to err by behaving too aggressively at times, while women may err in behaving too nonassertively. Each of us has difficulty in saying "no" to unwanted requests. Five situations are listed below. If you are a man, provide a nonassertive response in which you attempt to say "no" to the other person; if you are a woman, provide an aggressive response in which you attempt to say "no" to the other person. Then, write an appropriate assertive response. How would you feel if you offered the aggressive or nonassertive response you suggested? How would the other person feel? How would you and the other person feel if the assertive response were provided? What would you be most likely to do in each of the situations: provide a nonassertive response, an assertive response, or an aggressive response? Why?

1. **Friend**   I've been studying all week and I need a break. Let's go barhopping tonight.
    NONASSERTIVE OR AGGRESSIVE RESPONSE: _____

    ASSERTIVE RESPONSE: _____

2. **Instructor**   I know that I forgot to tell you that your paper needed to be typed, but I would like to receive it in typed form. Would you take it home tonight and type it for me—it's only 20 pages.
    NONASSERTIVE OR AGGRESSIVE RESPONSE: _____

The desirability of self-assertion

Self-assertion appears to be a positive skill and is positively correlated with other positive attributes, including self-acceptance (Currant, Dickson, Anderson & Faulkender, 1979). Assertiveness is also related to a number of communication skills. Verbal intensity, talkativeness, and a good communicator style are all correlated with assertive behavior (Norton & Warnick, 1976). Among the verbal characteristics of assertive people is their tendency to talk more than others, to be more intense, and to have a direct, open style of communication. People who are assertive tend to be enthusiastic about communication and interactional opportunities.

Assertive people tend to have better interpersonal relationships. In the area of marital relationships, for example, assertiveness is related to satisfying marriages. Marital problems are frequently caused by one of the partners being dominant and aggressive, or by both of the partners behaving in a nonassertive manner (Alberti & Emmons, 1978). When one person is aggressive, the other

ASSERTIVE RESPONSE: _____

_____

3. **Roommate** I hope you don't mind—I have a big exam to study for and I've invited a few friends over to study in our room tonight. We'll probably stay up until 2 or 3.
NONASSERTIVE OR AGGRESSIVE RESPONSE: _____

_____

ASSERTIVE RESPONSE: _____

_____

4. **Parent** I hope you can come home early during final-exam week—your grandparents will be here.
NONASSERTIVE OR AGGRESSIVE RESPONSE: _____

_____

ASSERTIVE RESPONSE: _____

_____

5. **Friend of other sex** We've gone out three times—don't you think it's about time we slept together?
NONASSERTIVE OR AGGRESSIVE RESPONSE: _____

_____

ASSERTIVE RESPONSE: _____

_____

experiences fear and anger. If the second person is nonassertive, the marriage may remain intact, but be unsatisfying, especially to the nonassertive partner. If the second person is assertive, they may leave the marriage; if they are aggressive, open conflict may ensue. When both partners are nonassertive, a lack of understanding often occurs, with neither partner communicating openly and honestly with the other. Marriages with two nonassertive people may withstand the "test of time," but are frequently reported to be unsatisfying.

Assertive people also seem to fare better at their workplace. College recruiters were presented with videotapes of male and female applicants who either would display nonassertive or assertive self-presentation styles. Recruiters evaluated the nonassertive candidates as less suited for supervisory positions than the assertive candidates, regardless of the candidate's gender. The assertive candidates were more frequently invited for a second interview than were the nonassertive candidates, and the qualifications of the assertive candidates were viewed more positively (Dipboyle & Wiley, 1978).

Assertiveness is negatively related to anxiety. The large number of studies in this area demonstrate that high levels of anxiety are incompatible with assertive behavior (Ferrell, 1977; Warren, 1977; Wolpe & Lazarus, 1966).

Assertiveness is inversely related to trait anxiety, neuroticism, interpersonal anxiety (Orenstein, Orenstein & Carr, 1975), communication apprehension (Pearson, 1979), and the fear of social situations (Hollandsworth, 1979). Conversely, then, we can summarize by stating that assertive people tend to be low in anxiety, neuroticism, fear of interpersonal interaction, fear of speaking with others, and fear of interacting in social situations. People who are more assertive tend to be less impulsive (Green, Burkhart & Harrison, 1979). Impulsiveness may be related to anxiety or lack of clear and consistent planning. In general, then, assertiveness appears to be related to positive outcomes.

The above indicates that both men and women should strive to be assertive. However, we have observed that our culture imposes stereotypes on men's and women's assertive and aggressive communication behaviors. Men are expected to err on the side of communicating too aggressively, while women are expected to communicate nonassertively. Inasmuch as we recognize the advantages of behavioral flexibility, we might consider whether men and women suffer for violating cultural norms.

As Spender (1980) points out, the role played by sex may determine the evaluation of a behavior as much or more so than the behavior itself. As Spender insists, "Women will still be judged *as women* no matter how they speak, and no amount of talking the same as men will make them men, and subject to the same judgments" (p. 79). Warfel (1984) talks about the issue of assertiveness as a conflict between two competing hypotheses: the deficit hypothesis, which argues that "women lack power because their actions lack power" (p. 253) and the discrimination hypothesis, which states that "actions are perceived to be powerless due to the powerlessness of the source" (p. 253). Clearly, the deficit hypothesis points toward the validity of assertiveness training. Spender's position, the discrimination hypothesis, questions assertiveness training both on the grounds that it is not ultimately useful to women and that it buys into a male-defined order rather than attempting to deal with discrimination against women.

Evidence is mixed as to which hypothesis is more valid. Warfel's (1984) own study reveals that people do use biological sex as a way to process information (support for the discrimination hypothesis), yet the deficit hypothesis has also received partial support since "powerful" speakers, regardless of sex, were seen as more dominant than "powerless" speakers. In role-playing scenarios, women have been found to be evaluated more positively when communicating assertively (Sereno & Weathers, 1981). These results might imply that women can, to good effect, violate the culturally prescribed nonassertive role traditionally assigned them.

"I've been a housewife for twenty-five years now, and I've decided to retire next month."

However, other research seems to indicate that women may, in fact, be evaluated negatively when they communicate assertively (Hall & Black, 1979). In Hall and Black's study, either assertive or aggressive women presented pro-feminist arguments. Women raters rated both types of presentations negatively. On the basis of Sereno and Weather's (1981) findings these results are unexpected. Thus, we simply do not know yet how men and women will be perceived when they expand their communication styles. We do know, however, that in contrast with aggressive presentational styles, assertive women are rated as more attractive (Pendleton, 1982). We also know that assertiveness training has been successful in changing women's behaviors and attitudes, at least in the short run. Lewittes and Bem (1983) demonstrated the effectiveness of assertiveness training in increasing quiet women's participation in a small, mixed-sex, task-oriented discussion. Anderson, Schultz, and Staley (1987) found that training positively influenced people to change their attitudes toward argumentativeness. The change in the female participants, in particular, was dramatic. McVicar and Herman's (1983) research indicates that middle-aged female participants experienced significant increases in assertiveness and self-actualization both immediately after the program and when tested five months later. Thus, we are confident that through systematic training women (and probably men as well) can learn to be assertive.

Conclusions

In this chapter, we considered two self-presentational communication skills: self-disclosure and self-assertion. Self-disclosure, the process of offering personal information about ourselves to other people, has been examined extensively during the past thirty years. Self-disclosure can be examined from three perspectives, and in each approach it appears to be related to gender differences. The best advice on self-disclosure is to become aware of the findings in this area, to develop sensitivity to the other persons with whom you are communicating, and to respond to all the environmental cues as you determine the amount and level of self-disclosure in which to engage. Self-disclosure appears to be a generally positive communication skill when it is understood and used in moderation.

Self-assertion is an equally intriguing communicative behavior, but fewer studies of this skill have been conducted. Assertiveness, by definition, is behavior that can occur best in a negotiated transaction. Assertiveness requires that one be able to communicate openly and freely about their feelings, needs, and desires. Historically, women have tended toward nonassertive or passive communication styles, while men have tended toward overly aggressive communication styles. Both women and men can learn assertive communication styles. It remains to be seen how the adoption of assertive behavior will be perceived by others.

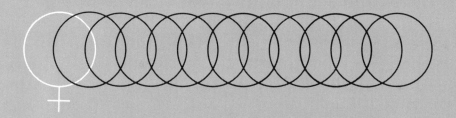

Section 3

In this section, we examine male and female communication behaviors in three contexts. In chapter 8 we address the intimate context, including friendship, romantic relationships, and family relationships. We observe that women and men often behave differently in these intimate settings. Chapter 9 deals with the public arena: task groups, public speaking, and the

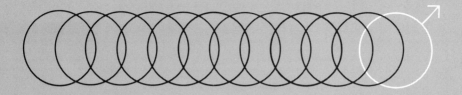

Contexts

business world. Finally, in chapter 10 we examine the media, observing the various images
of women and men presented in mediated
communication. In each context we note that
men and women are expected to behave
somewhat differently. These expectations are
often central to the production and reception
of actual communication enacted by men and
women.

8 Gender and communication in intimate contexts

Introduction

In this chapter we will discuss some of the intimate contexts in which men and women communicate. We will consider friendships between same-sex couples and mixed-sex couples. Romantic relationships, including dating, marriage, and in particular, dual-career marriages, will be discussed. This chapter will also consider family communication, including sex-role development, communication between parents and children, and communication in alternative family structures, including the single-parent family. Where possible, we will clarify research findings and offer some assistance to persons who wish to develop useful, nonsexist approaches to communication within intimate contexts.

First, however, we must define "intimate contexts," a term that is often used, but with various meanings for different people. **Intimate contexts** imply relationships that offer the partners a special kind of interpersonal sharing (Galvin & Brommel, 1986). Wheeless (1978) suggests that intimate relationships are identified by high solidarity, or closeness derived from similarity, between the partners.

In his work on marital intimacy, Feldman (1979) argues that intimacy in marriage involves the following three characteristics: "(1) a close, familiar, and usually affectionate or loving personal relationship; (2) detailed and deep knowledge and understanding arising from close personal connection; (3) sexual relations" (p. 70). With the exception of the third factor, sexual relations, Feldman's definition may be applied to all the contexts we are discussing in this chapter.

From a communication perspective, intimacy is often identified by **messages** of confirmation (acceptance and acknowledgment of the other), self-disclosure, sexual communication (Galvin & Brommel, 1986; Wheeless, Wheeless & Baus, 1984), and expressions of solidarity (Wheeless, 1978).

Conventional wisdom suggests that women are more skilled than men at these expressions of intimacy. Women are often believed to be more attuned to recognizing the feeling of intimacy than men. The film, *Dangerous Liaisons,* examined men's and women's approaches to intimacy, especially sexual intimacy. A character sums up the folk wisdom concerning the difference in these approaches by saying, "Men enjoy the happiness they feel. Women can only enjoy the happiness they give."

Gilligan (1982) argues that this is due to psychosocialization emphasizing caring and relational nurturance for females, while males are learning to focus on individuation and independence. In an empirical test of men's and women's responses to intimacy, McAdams, Lester, Brand, McNamara, and

Lensky (1988) used a series of pictures to stimulate college students to write scenarios. These stories were then scored for intimacy value. Although women scored higher than men on intimacy motivation, offering some support to Gilligan's perspective, men and women scored similarly low on fear of intimacy, indicating that a close, personal relationship is not anxiety producing for men.

As we explore friendship, courtship, marriage, and family relations, we shall continue to test conventional wisdom against the research findings.

Friendship

Friendships can range from casual to intimate. For purposes of our discussion, we are interested in close, intimate friendships. Many studies have examined friendship, both same-sex and male-female types. Let us consider first same-sex friendships and how they operate for women and men.

Same-sex friendships

Some evidence indicates that the process of forming friendships is different for the sexes. Female-female friendships may evolve from sharing self-disclosures, while male-male friendships are furthered by engaging in shared activities (Hays, 1985). Female-female friendships are promoted through "face-to-face" interaction; male same-sex friendships develop through the "side-by-side" model of doing activities together.

Barth and Kinder (1988) suggest these differences which cause people to become friends continue in the maintenance of friendships. Women like to have friends to whom they can relate in many different areas, while men tend to develop different relationships to meet different needs. Their results indicate that female-female relationships are more involved and deeper than male-male friendships.

Interestingly, in self-reports men and women say they have similar levels of intimacy with their same-sex friends, but in role-play situations, women were judged to display more intimate behaviors (Caldwell & Peplau, 1982). Some of those intimate behaviors displayed by women include engaging in more affectional touch than male-male friends (Davidson & Duberman, 1982) and engaging in more empathy and feedback after self-disclosures (Buhrke & Fuqua, 1987; Roger & Schumacher, 1983).

Kimmel (1987) argues that, by definition, masculinity is conceived of as being different from femininity. Herek (1987) adds that masculinity also includes homophobia, or fear of attitudes and behaviors related to homosexual relationships. Given these two constraints, it is not surprising that same-sex friendships are different for women and men.

Male-female friendships

Friendships between men and women are difficult to establish since activities are often sex segregated, sex stereotypes make men and women see each other as opposites, and sexual attraction may pose a problem for one or both friends or their respective romantic partners. The recent movie, *When Harry met Sally,* focused on the question of whether or not men and women can have platonic friendships. Although Harry and Sally illustrate a friendship between a man and a woman, ultimately they fall in love and have a sexual relationship, too. The film portrays male-female friendship as an important relationship, but one that serves as a precursor to a romantic relationship. Harry and Sally's romance is seen as stronger and better because they are friends first.

Can men and women be friends without moving into either sex or romance? It is possible, although difficult. One of the difficulties, demonstrated in research, is that women and men behave differently in friendship, yet expect their partner to mirror their own behaviors (Richmond, Gorham & Furio, 1987). Specifically, Richmond et al. (1987) found that men and women differ in affinity-seeking strategies to such an extent that women exhibit more empathy and sensitivity, while men try to associate themselves with rewards for the friend as well as complementing the other and engaging in helpful strategies. Both men and women predict incorrectly that their partner of the other sex will select the same strategies they prefer.

Finally, male-female friendships may be somewhat more beneficial for males than females. Males disclose more in cross-sex friendships, but females disclose less compared to their behavior with same-sex friends (Rose, 1985). However, even in disclosing males and females may still be constrained by role-playing since males disclose mainly their strengths and females disclose mainly their weaknesses in female-male friendships (Rose, 1985).

Romantic relationships—dating

Sexuality

Sexuality is an important component of romantic, intimate relationships, and a variety of male/female differences in sexuality have been demonstrated. Beginning in the late 1960s, sex among college women increased dramatically, although still falling short of men's activity levels (Kaats & Davis, 1970). More recent studies report that men remain the initiators in sexual activity even though the attitude of the woman in the couple determines whether or not the two will engage in intercourse (Peplau, Rubin & Hill, 1977). Men also tend to overestimate their partners' desire for sex (Peplau, Rubin & Hill, 1977), are inclined to be more sexually permissive than women, condone permissiveness for men but not for women (Gray, White & Libby, 1978), and tend to interpret behavioral cues as more sexual than do women (Bouchez, 1987).

Female sexual behavior is primarily related to being in love and going steady, while male sexuality is more indirectly and less exclusively associated with romanticism and intimacy in relationships. Men show a slightly higher frequency of coitus and a slightly higher number of coital partners than women do. Men report a significantly higher sexual urge than women do, while women are more tolerant of marrying a nonvirgin than men are (Mercer & Kohn, 1979).

The above differences in self-report data must be interpreted cautiously, however, since they may be an artifact or symbol of social acceptability. For instance, one study demonstrated that men reported their first coital experience to others sooner and told more people (almost exclusively male peers) than women did. Women told fewer persons, waited longer to self-disclose this information, and were more likely to disclose this information to a man than men were to disclose their sexual experience to a woman. Moreover, in response to this disclosure men were likely to receive approval, women disapproval (Carns, 1973).

When women and men are asked about the strategies used in "come-ons" and "put-offs," both sexes perceive a double standard. The majority of students felt that strategies of "come-ons" would be used by men and that the strategies of "put-offs" would be used by women. However, when men and women were asked about their own strategies, they were found to be remarkably similar. Both men and women used indirect strategies for facilitating sex (e.g., seduction), and both used more direct strategies for disallowing sex (e.g., simply saying "no") (McCormick, 1979).

Issues in dating

Testing the relationship
Baxter and Wilmot (1984) found that females were more likely than males to engage in what the researchers called "secret tests." **Secret tests** are strategies for gathering information about the state of the relationship and the partner's commitment to it without directly broaching these "taboo topics" (Baxter & Wilmot, 1985b). This finding is congruent with the researchers' contention that females are more active monitors of relationships than men (Baxter & Wilmot, 1985a; Rubin, Peplau & Hill, 1981).

Saying "I love you"
Although women are often believed to be more relationally attuned than men, Owen (1987) found that men were more often the initiators of a declaration of love, a critical communication event in the relationship. Owen's data suggests several possible reasons why this is the case: (1) it is a way to coerce commitment from women; (2) men are less able than women to withhold their

cathy®

by Cathy Guisewite

expressions of love when they feel love; (3) women are more capable of discriminating between love and other related emotions; and (4) women wait until they hear the phrase from men because they interpret their role as reactive rather than proactive.

Breaking up

Baxter (1986) examined the language in the accounts of 157 respondents' essays on "Why We Broke Up." Nine categories of reasons emerged from these essays. Females and males differed in both the number of reasons and the main reasons cited. Females provided more reasons than males. The main reasons given by females were desire for autonomy and lack of openness and equity. The main reason provided by males was the need for more romance. Thus, a picture emerges of men and women desiring different things from the dating relationship.

Romantic relationships—marriage

Marrying was once thought to be the logical conclusion of courtship. However, at the present time a variety of alternatives are possible. Yet despite the wide range of choices, marriage still remains a popular relationship. Between 90 and 95 percent of all Americans will marry at least once, and if they divorce, they are likely to remarry within five years (Fitzpatrick, 1988). Perhaps this is because marriage seems to be good for one's health, especially for men. Single women and men are more likely to report stress, to use drugs, and to contemplate suicide than married people of either sex. Divorced men demonstrate the most stress and drink the heaviest of any group (Cargan & Melko, 1981). Moreover, married people are rated as happier, more secure, and more reliable than single people (Etaugh & Malstrom, 1981). However, married females often report stress related to role conflict and work overload (Gerson, 1985).

Conflict in marriage

Power

Many communication variables have been examined within the context of marriage. Communication that relates to power is a well researched topic.

One area where conflict may occur in marriages is disagreement concerning which of the two partners has control. Traditionally, men dominated in most marriages and exhibited the most power. Kidd (1975) reviews some of the recommendations offered in popular magazines noting, for instance, an article in the *Ladies Home Journal* in 1956, which recommended that women and men behave according to traditional patterns. The article implied that when women and men did not behave in traditional ways, their sexuality was at fault (Kidd, 1975). Similarly, an article published in a 1957 issue of *Reader's Digest* recommended that women deceive their husbands deliberately during sexual intercourse. Marion Hillard, the author, wrote:

> A man can feel kinship with the gods if his wife can make him believe he can cause the flowering within her. If she doesn't feel it, she must make every effort to pretend (Kidd, 1975).

In 1967, 48 percent of all spouses expected husbands to have the greater share of influence, 10 percent expected wives to have most or somewhat more influence, and 42 percent responded that they thought each of the mates would have about the same amount of influence. In actual interaction, husbands were more likely to have a high degree of influence on their wives. Role differentiation was also stressed in the reports of this study, too, since 80 percent of the wives reported contributing most or more of the social-emotional support (Smith, 1967).

Beginning slowly in the 1960s and increasing steadily thereafter, a new notion of appropriate interpersonal relations evolved, challenging the dominant positions of husbands. As the "self" increased in importance, social roles were subordinated and their power to define relationships diminished (Kidd, 1975). However, as recently as 1985 Barnes and Buss found support for the rational, logical approach to conflict on the husband's part and the wives' emotional, critical approach. White (1985) found that wives are more accurate judges of their husband's position in disagreements than the reverse. White suggests that this may be the case because of power differentials in marriage making it important for persons with less power to understand those with greater power.

Competence

Does the greater power of one partner occur as a result of his or her greater competence? Control by husbands is greatest when the husband is more competent and when the cultural norms are patriarchal; that is, when expectations are that men should be in charge. Patriarchal norms become unimportant when the husband is not perceived as competent. Egalitarian, or shared marital control, occurs when the norms are egalitarian and when the husband's levels of competence is perceived to be the same as the wife's (Nye, 1982). Competence, then, appears to mediate in decision making and conflict behavior.

Education and salary levels
Education and salary levels also affect power in the family. The more educated both spouses are, the more egalitarian the authority between them. The husband's authority increases with his salary. The working wife makes 25 percent of the financial decisions by herself, 53 percent with her husband, and does not participate at all in 22 percent of the decisions. Non-working wives make about 14 percent of the financial decisions by themselves, 44 percent with their husbands, and do not participate at all in 43 percent of the decisions (Gottman, Markman & Notarius, 1970). Working mothers participate in household tasks less than non-working mothers, although their husbands participate more. Working mothers make fewer decisions about routine household matters than non-working mothers, yet their husbands participate more. At the same time no differences occur between husbands and wives in comparisons involving working- and non-working-wife situations. Regardless of whether women work or do not work, husbands tend to make more decisions for the family (Hoffman, 1970).

Communication behaviors
Communication in marriage has been studied both in conflict situations and in nonconflictual discussions. Although many researchers believe that all communication has a control dimension even where there is no overt conflict involved (Watzlawick et al., 1967). Subtle differences occur in the communication behavior of persons who have control in a relationship. Partners who perceive themselves to have power in a marital dyad tend to use more bilateral strategies, those in which persuasion is used as opposed to the person simply doing what she or he desires. Direct strategies are those in which persons state what they want outright rather than trying to manipulate the other person through hinting, making subtle suggestions, or using other forms of manipulation. In heterosexual relationships men are more likely to use direct and bilateral strategies than women, possibly because they expect compliance. Women perceive themselves as influencing their partners from a subordinate position, while men perceive themselves in a position of relative power (Falbo & Peplaue, 1980).

Millar and Rogers (see, for example, Courtright, Millar, & Rogers, 1979; Rogers & Millar, 1979) and their colleagues have completed a great deal of research on marital interaction. Fundamental to their research is the distinction between dominance and domineeringness. **Domineeringness** is the extent to which one attempts to control interactions and relationships through "one-up" statements, statements asserting one's rights or intentions (e.g., a wife might assert, "I really enjoy my night class this quarter; I think I'll plan on enrolling in night classes every quarter").

Dominance differs from domineeringness in that it is a condition resulting from the interactions between two people rather than the assertions of one over the other. **Dominance** is said to occur when one interactant's one-up statement is followed by the other interactant's making a "one-down" statement, or statement affirming or acquiescing to the assertion made in the immediately preceding one-up statement. In the example of the wife asserting her feelings about night classes and her plans to enroll in more night courses, dominance would be exhibited if her husband responded, "I know what you mean—you should go right ahead and sign up for another class."

Millar and Rogers-Millar posit that while domineeringness may or may not increase one's own dominance, it does decrease the likelihood of the other person's dominance. Thus, to avoid being dominated, a person could increase his or her own domineeringness. They also found that a relationship exists between domineeringness and marital satisfaction. The higher the wife's domineeringness score, the less communication satisfaction she reports. Although the husband's domineeringness score is also inversely related to marital and communication satisfaction, the relationship is not as well-established as it is for wives. Further, there tends to be a moderately positive correlation between husbands' dominance scores and marital satisfaction (Courtright, Millar & Rogers, 1979; Rogers-Millar, 1979).

Burggraf and Sillars (1987) argue that sex differences are barely apparent in marital conflict. Instead, they found that conflict styles were highly reciprocal rather than differentiated according to stereotypic sex roles. Dillard and Fitzpatrick (1985) also found little difference in the compliance-gaining behavior of husbands and wives in conflict. In situations of uncertainty, Turner (in press) found that husbands and wives reported similar emotions and similar communication strategies for dealing with the uncertainty.

Fitzpatrick (1988) suggests that couple type, rather than sex, is a more accurate predictor of many communication behaviors in marriage. Couple type is defined as adherence to one of three prototypic ideologies of marriage: traditional, independent, or separate. Traditional couples believe in a high level of interdependence, are willing to engage in conflict, and espouse a conventional belief in marriage. Independents reject the traditional ideology of marriage, emphasize both autonomy and sharing, and as traditionals, are willing to engage in conflict. Separates express a need for autonomy and differentiated space. They do not report a willingness to engage in conflict. From this perspective, it would be more important to know whether a person is in a separate, independent, or traditional marriage than to know their sex to predict their communication behavior.

Researchers have also examined self-disclosure in marriage. Rubin (1984) reports that in her practice she repeatedly hears women complain that their husbands do not tell them what they are feeling. In a study investigating self-disclosure patterns in marriage, Shimanoff (1985) found that wives report disclosing more and valuing disclosure more than their husbands. However, observation revealed that women and men did not differ in their actual patterns of disclosure.

Rubin (1984) offers a possible explanation for this discrepancy. Women may fail to recognize their husbands' comments as self-disclosures. Men may also have learned to repress their feelings so well that they may not be fully aware of them and, thus, may not be able to disclose them. Rubin says men complain, " 'I tell her, but she's never satisfied. . . . No matter how much I say, it's never enough' " (p. 71).

In the area of nonverbal behavior, however, some differences have been noted between husbands and wives. Noller and Gallois (1988) report that wives show more nonverbal behaviors (i.e., smiles, eye widens, head movement to partner, etc.) than husbands, both as speakers and listeners. Noller (1986) found that wives are more accurate than husbands at encoding nonverbal messages, although husbands and wives do not differ significantly in decoding each other's nonverbal messages.

In reviewing the results of these studies, we face a seeming paradox. Much research claims that marriage is an idiosyncratic relationship, governed by norms of reciprocity rather than conformity to stereotypic sex roles (Burggraf & Sillars, 1987). As such, husbands and wives are more alike than different in their marital interaction.

However, another body of research (Rubin, 1984) suggests that wives and husbands are "intimate strangers" and behave very differently in marriage since they come from two different cultures. To reconcile this apparent contradiction, we suggest that in many behaviors, women and men do not differ; but, in their interpretation of behavior and the underlying rule structure that motivates behavior, husbands and wives may be very different.

Ritter (1989) reports research that concludes husbands often argue to win, while wives argue to get approval from the other. Thus, they argue based on different goals. In a related observation, Ritter notes that men commonly focus on outcomes, yet women care more about process. Rubin (1984) observes that women need talk to feel intimate, but men feel intimacy just being in physical proximity with their wives.

Dual-career marriages

Despite differences between men and women, spouses are often highly similar to one another in a variety of ways. Married couples typically have similar ethnic origins, similar socio-economic backgrounds, and frequently attain approximately the same educational levels (Chronkite, 1977). Couples frequently have similar vocabularies and reasoning abilities. Couples are typically similar in age, with husbands being about two or three years older than their wives, and similar in size, with husbands being slightly larger in height and weight (Detroit Free Press, 1981). Research on married couples also indicates that wives are especially prone to perceive similarity between themselves and their husbands on a variety of marriage-related issues (White, 1985).

One area where women and men have differed in the past but are now similar, is the area of work. Most couples in the past had single-career marriages, i.e., only the husband worked. Today, many couples are involved in dual-career marriages. Let us consider the nature of these marriages.

Most marriages are dual-earner marriages since two-thirds of all married women now work outside the home (Basow, 1986; Thornton & Freedman, 1983). From an economic standpoint, many couples find it necessary for both partners to work outside the home to reach or approximate their desired standard of living. However, dual-earner marriages are often conventional, and the wife's job is seen as secondary to, or less important than, her husband's. Dual-career marriages, where both spouses are equally committed to their jobs and their families, are somewhat rarer. Parker, Peltier, and Wolleat (1981) estimate that dual-earner marriages outnumber dual-career marriages by ten to one. Dual-career marriages represent a life style strikingly different from traditional marriages (Aldous, 1982).

In general, dual-career marriages are relatively prosperous. As might be expected, these couples use family planning to insure that they have only one or two children. Moreover, women are especially likely to use birth control effectively if they are genuinely committed to their jobs (Safilios-Rothschild, 1970).

Contrasting traditional and dual-career marriages

Russell (1975) compared traditional couples (the wife did not work and did not plan to work), neo-traditional couples (the wife did not work, but planned to work), and pioneer couples (the wife worked). The study found that the husbands with wives with a greater need for personal achievement, perceive this need and want their wives to participate in career-related and socioeconomic decisions more than husbands with wives needing only average achievement. Husbands with wives who have a high need for achievement are also more willing to perform more household tasks than husbands of wives needing only average achievement. Pioneer husbands perceive their wives participating more in financial decisions and socioeconomic decisions. These husbands also perform more child-care-related activities than the traditional husbands, although their wives think they should do even more. Conversely, traditional wives are usually satisfied with the amount of domestic work performed by their husbands.

Marital satisfaction

What effects do two careers have on marital satisfaction? Will dual-career marriages last longer or not as long as traditional marriages? It is not clear whether dual-career marriages are happier or less happy than traditional marriages. The level of satisfaction is influenced by the attitudes and behavior of each spouse. Job involvement is one influencing factor. Happiness tends to be higher if both spouses are equally involved in their work. When only one spouse becomes highly involved in a job, marital adjustment seems to suffer (Ridley, 1973). In general, women with high work commitment demonstrate higher marital satisfaction than women not working outside the home (Safilios-Rothschild, 1970).

Yogev (1987) has shown that despite the non-traditional behavior of dual-career couples, marital satisfaction in these relationships is related to perceptions that spouses fit sex-role stereotypes. Both husbands and wives report more satisfaction if the husband is seen as more intelligent, competent, and of higher professional status than his wife.

Difficulties in the dual-career relationship

What are the special problems of the dual-career marriage? Perhaps the most outstanding problem in such marriages is managing the high stress level. Leslie (1977) states that couples maintain they frequently lack the energy or the time to complete all of their many tasks. Couples point out that in two full-time careers, management of a home and family, and other responsibilities place enormous demands on both partners. Relationship stress also occurs as a result of differential personal growth and role changes, generally on the part of the woman (Rice, 1979).

In dual-career couples it is the wives who assume the larger share of home and childrearing responsibilities, while simultaneously meeting the demands of a full-time job. Both husbands and wives, however, report greater marital satisfaction when they equally share home and childrearing responsibilities (Yogev & Brett, 1985). Wives, more than husbands, feel distress when the relationship is inequitable (Ragolin & Hansen, 1985). In addition, and what can make the lives of working wives and mothers even more difficult, is the fact that husbands tend to be deficiently expressive and nurturing (Fitzpatrick & Indvik, 1982). Thus, not only do wives do more than their husbands, but they are also insufficiently acknowledged and supported for doing so.

Unfortunately, many women do not understand that it is unrealistic for them to fulfill all the traditional responsibilities while simultaneously working full time. Accordingly, they often feel anxious, depressed, and incompetent. In addition, and not surprisingly, they often become physically ill. Thus, in their quest to be "superwomen," they often end up feeling "subhuman."

Not only do women face problems within their family units, but managers and executives may not respond flexibly to the women's many roles. Women may perceive themselves primarily in terms of their careers, while their superiors may limit their options by viewing them as wives and mothers. Conversely, women may request leaves, flex time—working an eight-hour day, but beginning and ending earlier or later than the typical 9-to-5 job—or seek other adjustments to help them in their roles as wives and mothers. However, these options may be denied them because they are perceived by their superiors as workers who should put their jobs first.

Dual-career marriages from a communication perspective

There has been scant research examining the dual-career relationship from a communication perspective (Heacock & Spicer, 1986). A number of articles focus on the outcomes of communication, but few examine the communication process itself. For example, decisions about family life, such as whether to have children, to move, or to take out a loan, have been analyzed without a study of the communication processes involved in negotiating these decisions.

Krueger's (1982, 1985, 1986) work is a notable exception to the above generalization. Krueger has examined decision-making strategies and patterns in satisfied dual-career couples. Her results tend to cluster in four areas. First, although the couples demonstrated many commonalities in communication behavior, the men tended to direct the conversations more through the use of such strategies as proposal making and disagreement. Furthermore, these strategies were accepted and supported by the wives.

Second, although women asked 60 percent of the questions during the process, the questions they asked were equally divided between those that put them in a subordinate position and drew on their husbands' expertise ("What should we do?") and those that put them in a dominant position and directed the discussion ("Why do you think that is a good idea?").

Krueger also found that women tended to overreport the degree of equality they perceived in the process when compared to both her objective assessment of their participation and their husbands' assessments. She suggests several reasons for this, including the possibility that a female's expectation is to be subordinate, which may cause her to overvalue those times when she succeeds in controlling.

However, this observation may be related to a fourth idea reflected in the data. Krueger argues that there may be two arenas of control in decision making. Based on a very small sample, she suggests that women seem to guide the process, while men guide the content in decision making. If this is the case, women may see their control over process as equally important as men's content control.

One other study investigating communication behavior in the context of dual-career marriages is that of Rosenfeld and Welsh (1985). These two researchers were concerned with differences in self-disclosures in dual-career couples as compared to single-career marriages. They found, as expected, that dual-career spouses had more nearly equal self-disclosure patterns than single-career partners. Single-career wives report more breadth, depth, and amount of self-disclosure than their husbands. Dual-career spouses only differed in depth of self-disclosure, with wives reporting more than husbands. In general, dual-career spouses seem more likely to reciprocate self-disclosure than single-career spouses (Chelune, Rosenfeld & Waring, 1986).

Summary

Although dual-career marriages are difficult, they can be managed in a highly satisfactory manner. Couples who share the household duties seem to face fewer problems than couples who do not (Ragolin & Hansen, 1985). Maples (1981) found that flexibility tends to provide a feeling of deep satisfaction for couples. Among the flexible methods of solving household problems are sharing the work between the spouses and involving the children as soon as possible; hiring household help; planning carefully; and foregoing many of the routine social activities engaged in by couples with more time.

Couples experimenting with new modes of communication and willing to go beyond stereotyped ways of relating provide stability for each other. Dual-career couples have to work particularly hard at remaining close to each other. Schedules, deadlines, children, and other obligations may contribute to a sense of distance, alienation, or isolation. Open communication, touching, and sexual contact can alleviate the distance sometimes experienced (Shaevitz & Shaevitz, 1980).

Husbands and wives can each contribute to the success of the dual-career marriage. Husbands who identify with their wives' career goals, who derive satisfaction from their accomplishments, and who do not feel threatened by their wives, contribute to more successful marriages. Wives can contribute to the success of their relationships by defining their own notion of "the full life" rather than accepting societal expectations and norms (Pogrebin, 1978).

Finally, no evidence exists to indicate there are any disadvantages for the children in dual-career families (St. John-Parsons, 1978). Children in dual-career families are less likely to hold traditional sex-role attitudes than children of single-career families (Schaninger & Buss, 1986).

Improving marital satisfaction

In general, marital satisfaction is difficult to achieve. Changing conceptions of women and men as well as different relational styles contribute to the problem. Many men have difficulty dealing with women who are ambitious and independent, while many women have difficulty accepting men who manifest either too little or too much emotion.

Women and men have different perceptions, use different verbal and nonverbal symbols, and differ in their abilities to self-disclose, be empathic, listen, and be assertive. The frustrations which occur when others do not reciprocate our behaviors mitigate against successful and satisfying marriages. Men tend to show a greater investment in a relationship during its early, premarital stages than during the marriage itself (Dawkins, 1976). Conversely, women tend to adopt a more distanced stance toward their partners in earlier than later phases of their relationship.

The changes occurring in our culture make it increasingly important for people to rely upon communication to negotiate role expectations and definitions. While Rawlins (1983) details the dilemmas associated with achieving relational satisfaction through communication, we can point to some communication practices which encourage relational satisfaction.

Communicator style
Happily married couples report that they alter their communication styles with their spouses more than when they are communicating with others. These couples also tend to communicate in a relaxed, friendly, open, dramatic, and attentive style (Honeycutt, Wilson & Parker, 1982).

Self-disclosure
Happily married couples also tend to disclose to one another. However, more important than the amount of information disclosed to one another is the sense of reciprocity and balance in the disclosures. Highly disclosive spouses tend to be happier when married to spouses who are themselves highly disclosive (Davidson, Balswick & Halverson, 1983; Hendrick, 1981).

Trust
Trust is also related to marital satisfaction. Persons who are married for a long time appear to score high on measures of mutual trust, and also appear to reciprocate trust more than they do love or self-disclosure. Failure to reciprocate trust appears to be a strong predictor of failing relationships. Couples who dissolved their relationships showed the highest discrepancy in levels of trust of the other person.

Parental identification and self-concept
At the beginning of the contemporary women's movement in 1960, parental identification was shown to affect personal reports of marital satisfaction. Luckey (1960) found that men who identified with their fathers were more often in satisfactory marriages than unsatisfactory ones, but that women who

identified with their mothers were not necessarily more satisfied in their marriages. At that time women's marital satisfaction tended to be more closely associated with the extent they perceived their husbands as similar to their fathers. Current research leads us to conclude that people of either gender who have strong self-concepts generally report more satisfactory marriages.

The elements of our self-concept—**self-image** (our sense of the roles we play) and **self-esteem** (evaluation of our role performance)—are both related to marital satisfaction. We know that the communication of role expectations affects marital satisfaction. Women and men are provided with a wider range of roles than those couples participating in the 1960s research. Marital satisfaction, at least for women today, is related to their ability to meet, and exceed, the role expectations expressed to them by their spouses (Petronio, 1982).

Communication skills
Montgomery (1981) finds that effective marital communication requires four things: "openness," which is made possible by mutual self-disclosure; "confirmation and acceptance" of self and others; "transactional management," which requires the ability to control the communication situation; and "situational adaptability," which is the ability to change appropriately in a particular situation.

Pearson & Spitzberg (1990) state that four stages are especially relevant in the development of intimate relationships, each stage requiring a particular communication skill. The stages are: (1) sharing the self, (2) affirming the other, (3) becoming "one," and (4) transcending "one." Sharing the self is similar to self-disclosure. Affirming the other person may be considered as similar to empathy.

When we become "one" with another person, we experience a kind of bonding. It is generally true in this process that couples develop special ways of communicating unique to their relationship. Special words, pet names, and code words for shared experiences all contribute to the "us" that is created from a "you" and a "me."

Transcending "oneness" in intimate relationships resembles self-actualization in personal development. When we feel truly secure in our intimate relationships, we are able to gain and offer independence and equality. Each partner has the security of a loving, understanding relationship and the freedom to develop as an independent person, too. She or he is able to put "we" and "me" together in a harmonious way.

Assistance for troubled marriages
When marriages need assistance, communication training (Epstein & Jackson, 1978) and other skill development (Warmbrod, 1982) have been useful. A variety of agencies and groups offer support systems and training sessions for marital improvement. Many of these organizations focus on communication skills such as listening, empathy, openness, self-disclosure, assertiveness, and

clarity. Both women and men can become successful marital partners and develop more effective and mutually satisfying interaction patterns. Couples probably realize greater growth by attending workshops and seminars together rather than separately. As we observed in chapter 1, communication is a negotiated process, and successful communication in marriage is dependent upon both persons interacting in positive, useful ways.

Family communication

Sex-role development

As we discussed in chapter 3, the family is an important institution for social learning. Our communication in families is the means by which much sex-role information is transmitted. Lavine and Lombardo (1984) found that fathers play an important part in the development of androgyny in their children. They found extensive interaction between father and child was associated with the development of androgyny.

Arntson and Turner (1987) found that even at the age of five and six children have differing role expectations for their mothers' and fathers' communication behavior. Although these boys and girls did not speak differently themselves, when they role-played their mothers and fathers, they did reflect differences. Specifically, they role-played mothers as having more praising communication and fathers as having longer punishing communication.

Parent-child interaction

Researchers have become increasingly interested in interaction patterns between parents and their children (Nye, 1982), with studies largely focusing on mother-child interaction. These studies demonstrate that mothers adjust their speech when interacting with children to gain the child's attention, to probe the child's language ability, to provide the child with experience in conversational turn-taking, and to teach grammatical structure (Sachs, 1977; Snow, 1977). These maternal speech adjustments have been labeled "motherese" (Newport, 1976). Motherese includes reduced sentence length and complexity, higher pitch, and exaggerated-intonation patterns. It frequently includes many questions and imperatives, few subordinate clauses, few past tenses, and longer pauses between utterances.

Fathers and mothers do not speak the same way to their children (Bellinger & Gleason, 1982; Malone, 1982), they do not speak about the same topics (Buerkel-Rothfuss, Covert, Keith & Nelson, 1986), nor do parents speak the same way to their daughters as to their sons (Snow, Jacklin & Maccoby, 1983). However, mothers and fathers may be similar in terms of general frequency of communication, particularly during the child's adolescence (Buerkel-Rothfuss et al., 1986).

We learn about sex roles as we grow and mature; similarly, we learn about family roles. We learn that the role of mother may be different from the role of father or child. To understand some of these roles better, complete the following exercise. Provide as many descriptive terms as you wish for each of the following categories.

1. The characteristics that best describe a father are

   _____

   _____

   _____

2. The characteristics that best describe a mother are

   _____

   _____

   _____

3. The characteristics that best describe a son are _____

   _____

   _____

   _____

4. The characteristics that best describe a daughter are

   _____

   _____

   _____

The communication between parents and infants was examined in a laboratory playroom. Researchers found that fathers spoke less and took fewer conversational turns, but their speech to their children was similar to the mothers' in the average length of the conversational turns, average length of the utterances, average number of verbs, and relative proportion of questions, declaratives, and imperatives. Depending on the child's sex, fathers and mothers responded differently to the children. Both mothers and fathers took more conversational turns with sons than with daughters and had longer conversations with daughters (Golinkoff & Ames, 1979).

Rondal (1980) studied the speech of five French-speaking couples with their male children (ages 18 to 36 months). He identified differences between paternal and maternal speech, and he described those differences as fulfilling

5. If I become a mother/father, I would like to be described as

_____

_____

_____

6. As a son/daughter, I could be described as

_____

_____

_____

7. I would like my daughters, if I have any, to be described as

_____

_____

_____

8. I would like my sons, if I have any, to be described as

_____

_____

_____

After you have completed the sentences individually, discuss your responses with the other members in your class. What similarities occur among your lists? What differences? How do family roles relate to sex roles? How can family roles be separated from traditional sex roles? To what extent do you envision a family similar to the family in which you grew up? To what extent do you envision your family to be different from the family in which you grew up?

complementary functions. Mothers used longer average lengths of utterances compared to fathers. They also corrected the incorrect speech of their children to a greater extent than did fathers. The longest utterances to children, however, were from fathers, which related to a larger number of requests from the children for clarification.

Differing conversational patterns occur more often when parents are talking individually with their infants than if both parents are conversing with the child. While the lengths of the dialogues increase in the dyadic setting, the non-reciprocal dialogues are proportionately less likely to occur. This conclusion suggests that the dyad consisting of parent and child is the ideal context for parent-child interaction rather than the triadic context including both parents and the child (Killarney & McCluskey, 1981).

Parents engage in more touching with their infants and small children than with their older children since our culture does not encourage touching among family members to the same extent as some other cultures. Some researchers have pointed out that lack of body contact with the mother and prolonged social isolation results in abnormal adult behaviors (Harlow & Haesen, 1963). Yet fathers seem to engage in more physical play with their young children and infants than the mothers (MacDonald & Parke, 1986).

In addition to examining infant-parent interactions, research has also been conducted on adolescent-parent interactions. Oliveri and Reiss (1987) found that adolescents feel more consonant with their mothers, particularly in the area of kinship relations. Fathers' distinctive contributions to adolescents were in the area of friendships and the affective aspects of relationships. The authors note that interpersonal interaction between parents and children is affected by sex-role differences. Mothers are perceived as authorities in the area of family affairs, whereas, fathers seem important in developing children's sensitivity to affective cues.

Single parenting and other family structures

Single parenting is a topic of increasing currency. Our contemporary social reality forecasts that one adult in every four will become a single parent. Half of the women in our society are likely to be single mothers. Single-parent families, those families which include only one parent and at least one dependent child living in the same household, may occur as a result of divorce, separation, widowhood, non-marriage, or adoption. The childbearing decision, once left to chance, has become an act of choice in many cases.

These new choices alter the complexion of the family unit and result in larger numbers of single-parent families. In 1979 the estimate was that one out of every six children, or eleven-million children, were living in single-parent families (Mandes, 1979).

Although single-parent families are prevalent in our society, single parenting is not yet a routinized form of family functioning. The role expectations of the single parent are ambiguous with the behaviors she or he should exhibit unclear. The kind of communication that exists in a single-parent family is reflective of the family's ability to adjust to their situation (i.e., death, divorce, etc.).

Family communication is changing. The traditional nuclear family is being replaced by a variety of different kinds of families, including the single-parent family. However, these changes probably do not signal the death of the American family as much as its reformulation.

Interaction between parents and children is also changing. Fathers may be spending more time interacting with their children and mothers and fathers may not be dramatically different in the ways they speak to their children. The changing nature of the talk which occurs within the family challenges us to be flexible in our interactions with our own family members and with other families. As we readjust, we must be careful to demonstrate our respect for others and our willingness to adapt to new circumstances.

Conclusions

In this chapter we explored communication which occurs in intimate contexts. Intimacy is difficult to define, although most agree it involves closeness and interpersonal sharing. We learned in this chapter that women and men differ in several ways affecting their intimate relationships. Differences in sexuality, self-disclosure, empathy, and relational goals imply differences in both platonic and romantic relationships for women and men.

Communication in marriage is not always different for women and men. In general, men and women often behave in reciprocal fashion in marriage. However, the underlying rule structures, enabling them to interpret each other's behavior may be very different. Intimacy, dating, marriage, and family life may have different meanings for men and women.

The dual-career marriage has increased in recent years. New and complex problems occur within dual-career marriages. Generally, both traditional and dual-career marriages are likely to prosper to the extent that partners respect one another's integrity and adapt to one another's career and personal ambitions.

Fundamental to achieving these objectives is the ability to be flexible, open-minded, and patient, both with one's self and partner. Pursuant to these recommendations, we have examined the impact of a variety of factors, including conflict, power, dominance, and communication. We have proposed methods for improving marital satisfaction and have discussed the importance of interaction patterns, communicator style, self-disclosure, trust, parental identification, and self-concept.

In addition to studying marital communication, current efforts are being made to understand family communication better. Research indicates that parents and children communicate in predictable ways, and that mothers and fathers differ somewhat in the amount, especially in the type, of communication they have with their children. Single-parent families have become more prevalent and present special problems for individuals within such families. While family structures are going through shifts and changes, family communication can be highly satisfying and improved for both men and women.

9 Gender and communication in public contexts

III. Communication in the business world
   A. Occupational choices
      1. Perceptions of children
      2. Perceptions of adolescents and young adults
      3. Fear of success in adults
      4. Summary
   B. Employment interviews
   C. Discrimination in hiring practices
   D. Women as managers
      1. Self-perception of female and male managers
      2. Others' perceptions of male and female managers
      3. Differences in management style between women and men
      4. Effective managers
IV. Conclusions

Introduction

In the last chapter, we considered the communicative behaviors of women and men in intimate settings; in this chapter, we will examine communication in public contexts. In dividing the material between chapters 9 and 10, we are aware of following the pervasive model of Western thought that dichotomizes the public and private spheres. In this dichotomy women are usually associated with the private sphere, while men control the public arena. Although our material is divided into two separate chapters, we are aware of the many linkages between the private and public domains. As Kramarae (1988) observes, "domestic interaction or women's informal associations [are social activity which] needs to be understood in order to make communication theory have potential for adequate and beneficial explanation and planning [of national policies]" (p. 46).

Keeping these links in mind, we will now examine women's and men's communication behavior in small groups, leadership situations, and public-speaking contexts. Communication in the business setting will be highlighted as we consider occupational choices, employment interviews, management, discrimination, and sexual harassment. We will observe that women and men not only communicate somewhat differently, but they are also treated very differently in public contexts. As we explore these differences, think about whether men's and women's differing patterns are a cause or an effect of their differential treatment in public life.

Specific communication behaviors

Small-group interaction

When women and men are studied in small groups, the findings are consistent with the conclusions drawn in earlier chapters: men are more instrumental; women are more expressive; and men tend to talk more than women. In the context of a group, men tend to initiate more verbal activity than women and demonstrate more task-related behavior than women. Women tend to offer more positive responses than men, but are more opinionated. Men tend to be more informative, objective, and goal-oriented than women in small groups (cf. Gouran 1968; Heiss 1962; *Women and Language,* 1986).

One of the more common purposes for small-group communication is problem solving. Early research in this area implied that women were superior at tasks which were personally interesting, while men were superior at abstract multiple-choice problems (South, 1927). Men may be superior to women in problem-solving ability, but this difference is reduced when mixed-gender groups are examined, and when women are highly motivated to solve problems (Hoffman, Maier, & Norman, 1961).

Women are often perceived as less competent in small-group problem solving or decision making (Meeker & Weitzel-O'Neill, 1977). Women may be able to overcome these perceptions by increasing their demonstrated competence. Bradley (1980) found that women who demonstrated high task-related competence were treated with friendliness, reason, and relatively few displays of dominance from male interactants. She also found, however, that these women were not particularly well liked. Thus, perceived competence appears to carry a price tag for women in the small-group setting.

Risk taking

Small groups are prone to risky decision making; however, women's groups are far less prone to risky decisions than are men's (Bauer & Turner, 1974; Maier & Burke, 1967; Minton & Miller, 1970). Why this may be we are not certain. But some explanation may lie in the fact that women's greater sensitivity toward others makes them generally less likely than men to act out of defensive impulse, yet more likely to make serious effort to work with—not against—others. Women tend to be more cooperative than men; similarly, they seem to be more willing to share resources with their opponents than men (Benton, 1973; Leventhal & Lane, 1970). Some theorists have conjectured that men play to win, while women play to avoid losing. Women appear to be more interested in fair outcomes than in winning (Hattes & Kahn, 1974; Phillips & Cole, 1970). This emphasis on acceptance and affiliation may reduce women's risky decision making in small groups.

Coalition formation

Coalitions often form in the small-group setting. Both women and men tend to join the majority coalition. Women, however, are more likely to do so when they are weak; men are more likely to do so when they are strong (Bond & Vinacke, 1961). When three men are placed together, they tend to engage in a dominance struggle in which the two strongest males form a coalition and exclude the weakest male (Uesugi & Vinacke, 1963). When triads (three-person groups) include two men and one woman, the men compete for the woman's attention (Amidjaja & Vinacke, 1965). Conversely, when women are in the majority, they tend to include any person who may be left out, regardless of gender (Amidjaja & Vinacke, 1965; Vinacke, 1959).

Gender composition of the group

Do men and women prefer to work in same-sex or mixed-sex groups? Women prefer to work only with women when the group is small, but prefer to include men when the group is large. Men, on the other hand, prefer to work with women both in small and large groups. Furthermore, cohesiveness within a small all-male group takes a longer time to materialize (Marshall & Heslin,

We explained above that in the small group setting men tend to initiate, while women tend to respond or react to the comments of others. This proactive behavior of men and reactive behavior of women is consistent with male/female differences in other spheres of life. To explore your own proactive or reactive style, complete the following exercise.

First, list five to eight events you expect or hope will occur. They might include places you wish to visit, conversations in which you wish to engage, relationships which you wish to establish or terminate, tasks you wish to begin or complete, or information you wish to learn. Then, list the person, event, or circumstance you believe is responsible for your reluctance to achieve your goal. For example, you might list a parent, friend, employer, instructor, or intimate; you might list an event such as your graduation from college, your accumulation of a certain amount of money, your "meeting the right person," or a certain point in time.

I Am Waiting for   **Because**

_____   _____
_____   _____
_____   _____
_____   _____
_____   _____
_____   _____

Now list some situations or circumstances where you have made the "first move." Consider recent events, conversations, difficult interactions, places you have visited, information you have learned, relationships you have initiated or ended, jobs you have been offered, or tasks you have accomplished. After you

---

1975). Women appear to perceive communication in the smaller group as more personal or more appropriate for same-sex persons, whereas, men do not discriminate between smaller and larger groups.

Do people communicate differently based on the gender composition of the small group? Fisher (1983) found that the gender composition of groups did not affect the interaction patterns they displayed, although the cooperative-competitive orientation influenced both the content and relationship patterns of interaction. Contradictory findings stem from Yamada, Tjosvold, and Draguns' (1983) research, which indicates that gender composition

have made your list, identify people or circumstances you could have used as an excuse for not accomplishing this particular goal.

Recently, I Initiated   **And I Did Not Wait for**

_____   _____
_____   _____
_____   _____
_____   _____
_____   _____
_____   _____

Examine your two lists and attempt to determine how they are distinct from each other. In what circumstances do you allow others to control your life? When do you proact? How can you account for these differences in your life? Discuss your lists with your classmates. Do you perceive any male/female differences? Why do they occur? How do these differences generalize to the small-group setting? For example, if you observe that men tend to react in personal relationships while they affirmatively proact in work-related situations, you might consider some differences between women and men in responding to their personal needs versus the goal-oriented needs of the members of the small-group discussion. What effects do these differences have on the outcome of a discussion in a small group? How can the situation be altered? To what extent do you believe it should be changed? As you consider alterations which can occur, do not overlook the relationship between other experiences which women and men have in the small-group setting. Consider the experiences of children in play situations, the relationships of men and women engaged in an intimate setting, and the roles of women and men in other situations.

---

affects interaction style more than cooperation. Presently, a number of researchers are undertaking investigations seeking to clarify and resolve these contradictory findings.

Ellis and McCallister (1980) hypothesized that we might better understand relational control patterns by considering psychological gender rather than biological sex. They found that masculine individuals are inclined to compete for control, feminine individuals seek equality and submissiveness, and androgynous individuals, while moderately competitive, seem to focus most of their attention on generating ideas. Patton, Giffin, and Patton (1989) observe that women seem more adept at learning instrumental skills to bring an androgynous orientation to small-group work than men are at developing socioemotional skills.

Finally, we might ask how sex composition affects the outcome of a small group's decision-making process. Lafferty and Pond (1985) studied five-person groups working on a survival task to be scored for accuracy of outcome. The most successful group in Lafferty and Pond's study was composed of all women. The all-male group was ranked fifth (out of six groups) in its accomplishment. The mixed-sex groups ranked as follows: three females, two males = second; four females, one male = third; four males, one female = fourth; three males, two females = sixth. In this study, having a majority of females in the group enhanced the outcome.

Summary

We may summarize the research on small-group interaction by observing that men tend to dominate, are goal-oriented, competitive, and aggressive. Women tend to be submissive, less inclined to make risky decisions, cooperative, more concerned with including all the group members, yet provide strong opinions. Both men and women can be seen as competent in small-group settings, although women may suffer a loss of liking to achieve this perception of competence. Mixed-gender groups are preferred by men, and by women if the group is large. Differences in small-group interaction may be more clearly and consistently explained on the basis of psychological gender than biological sex. Finally, sex composition may affect outcomes of small groups, with women's groups having an advantage. This advantage may be the result of women learning to blend instrumental behavior with socioemotional skills, while men have not adopted new skills as readily.

Leadership behaviors

Small-group leaders tend to be men more often than women (Craig & Sherif, 1986). Part of the explanation for this stems from the fact that men are generally more verbal than women. Men tend to initiate more verbal acts, make more suggestions, defend their ideas more strongly, yield less readily to interruptions, and, in general, to dominate (Hall, 1972; Kaess, Witryol & Nolan, 1961). Abundant research indicates that men are more likely than women to emerge as small-group leaders (Tindall, Boyler, Cline, Emberger, Powell & Wions, 1978).

However, Megargee (1969) found that dominance, as well as sex, influences leader emergence. When dominant and submissive men and women were paired, the following results occurred: (1) dominant males and females emerged as leaders over same-sex, submissive partners; (2) in mixed-sex groups, dominant males emerged over submissive females; (3) in mixed-sex groups, submissive males emerged over dominant females. Megaree explains that dominant females tend to yield to dominant males, implying conformity with cultural norms. However, in light of the fact that our culture has changed considerably during the past two decades, these findings may no longer accurately describe women's willingness to be subservient to men.

Women appear to be equally as capable as men to serve as leaders (Brown, 1979; Stitt, Schmidt, Price & Kipnis, 1983). For instance, when women are provided with a solution to a problem, they are as capable and careful in obtaining group acceptance as are men (Maier, 1970). Similarly, in high-task-clarity conditions, no differences between women and men as leaders can be ascertained (Ruch & Newton, 1977). However, two researchers found that, although men and women perform equally well as leaders, group members perceive men to be more successful than women in leadership roles (Jacobson & Effertz, 1974). Also, Offermann (1986) discovered that even when female leaders receive positive evaluations for their individual performance, group members fail to generalize those evaluations to future expectancies. Thus, a group member may perceive a particular female as a good leader, while still believing that female leaders do not do as well as male leaders.

Despite this negative perception of women leaders, Klein's (cited in the National Report on Human Resources, 1989) study indicates that adults actually learn more when women are in positions of authority. Klein surveyed 29 small-group exercises that were part of leadership-training conferences throughout the U.S. Of these groups, men led 16 and 13 had women leaders. Group members reported significantly more learning in the groups led by women. Klein believes the novelty of having a woman in a leadership position causes people to concentrate more on what is going on in the group, producing more learning.

The impact of sex-role stereotypes on leadership

A number of studies have examined the impact of sex roles on leadership behavior. Male leaders are expected to be independent, aggressive, analytical, competitive, self-disciplined, objective, and task-oriented, while female leaders are expected to be dependent, passive, non-aggressive, sensitive, subjective, and people-oriented. As a consequence of these expectations, it has been conjectured that leadership behavior is logically related to sex-role identification (Baird & Bradley, 1979; Bartol & Butterfield, 1976; Day & Stogdill, 1972; Fowler & Rosenfeld, 1979; Haccoun, Sallay & Haccoun, 1978; Welsh, 1979).

Cann and Siegfried (1987) observe that women are at a disadvantage in leadership evaluations since there is considerable overlap between the stereotypes of a good leader and a typical male. This overlap might imply that " 'maleness' equates with effective leadership while 'femaleness' may be seen as inappropriate" (p. 401). Thus, the researchers conclude women must be as concerned with overcoming this negative attitude as with performing leadership tasks.

However, Goktepe and Schneier (1988) found no significant difference in the evaluations of male and female small-group leaders.

Task-orientation and socioemotional orientation

Leadership in small groups has frequently been considered in terms of task-orientation and socioemotional orientation. A number of writers have indicated that both leadership functions must be present for effective group functioning. The task leader insures that the job is completed, and the socioemotional leader insures that the group members are satisfied with group process and outcome (cf. Hersey & Blanchard, 1977; Hill, 1973). Women are more likely to serve as social leaders and men as task leaders. Some studies have found that females are highly associated with **expressive behaviors,** such as concern and consideration, while males are linked to **instrumental activities,** such as initiating structure and giving direction (Baird & Bradley, 1979; Bartol & Butterfield, 1976).

However, more recently Winther and Green (1987) found that male leaders use more of a socially oriented style than female leaders. Winther and Green's finding may be the result of women's greater effort to become task oriented to gain recognition in the leadership role. This result may also signify a willingness on men's parts to be behaviorally flexible.

Psychological gender and leadership

Some researchers have sought to determine whether psychological gender better predicts effective leadership behavior than biological sex does. These studies have been consistent in their findings and have demonstrated that masculine individuals engage in more controlling behaviors than feminine or androgynous individuals. The findings of these studies have also demonstrated that androgynous individuals exhibit a more equal distribution of both dominant and submissive acts than do either of the other two gender-typed groups (Patton, Jasnoski & Skerchock, 1977; Porter, Geis, Cooper & Newman, 1984; Serafini & Pearson, 1983).

Summary

The communicative behaviors of men—including the initiation of more verbal acts, a greater number of suggestions, strong defense of their ideas, the tendency not to yield to interruptions, and dominance—account for their emerging as leaders more often than women. In addition, sexism mitigates against women serving as leaders. This is evident from findings indicating that even when women leaders perform by objective standards equally as well as men, they are, nonetheless, often perceived as less effective than men. We have also noted that this perceptual bias may be a result of associating leadership with an emphasis on task orientation. Both men and women can modify their orientations toward leadership and learn new behaviors allowing them to become more adept at achieving task and socioemotional objectives.

Public speaking

Public speaking differences between men and women have been examined, although several researchers have observed that women are often shut out of the public area. Women are not expected to engage in public speaking. In discussing informal communication networks among women in developing nations, Kramarae (1988) asserts that "women are discouraged or disbarred from public speaking in many places in the world" (p. 48).

Before we conclude that women only have this problem in third-world countries, Klemesrud (1983) reminds us in a *New York Times* article that public speaking is very difficult for American women since it conflicts with their traditional sex role. Friedley and Nadler (1983) argue that the field of speech communication sees debate, with its emphasis on public address, as a masculine activity. Logue (1985) buttresses that argument with the following statistics: national-level debate participation in 1984–85 was approximately 75 percent male and 25 percent female; and all male teams made up 55 percent of the teams at the national level.

Campbell (1986) reports that "a leading light" in the speech-communication field recently told her that there were no great women speakers, particularly in our contemporary age. Although Campbell has shown him to be poorly informed by her recent publication of two volumes of great women's oratory, she comments that his misconception is shared by many in the field.

Therefore, we begin the study of men and women in public address with the knowledge that women are assumed to be inferior and less visible in this endeavor. However, several studies exist which comment on the public-speaking behavior of women and men. Some of these studies have focused on the speaker (source of the message) and others have studied the influence of the listener (receiver of the message). Let us begin our review by examining the findings of studies which have considered gender and the speaker.

The source
In general, high-status speakers, including men and Anglo-Americans, have been perceived as more effective communicators than persons with low status, including women, Mexican-Americans, and blacks (De La Zerga & Hopper, 1979; Noel & Allen, 1976; Ramirez, 1977; Wheeler, Wilson & Tarantola, 1976). These findings have been obtained even when audiences have been asked to evaluate precisely the same speech. The only difference across experimental conditions was that in one instance the speech was attributed to a man, in the other, to a woman.

Credibility is an important component of speaker effectiveness. Specific dimensions of credibility have been examined for male/female comparisons. In one study investigating persuasive discourse, male sources of messages received higher competence ratings than did female sources (Miller & McReynolds, 1973). In another study, females received higher scores on three dimensions of credibility: trustworthiness, dynamism, and competence (Vigliano, 1974). Pearson's (1982) research indicates that women may be viewed as higher in trustworthiness and coorientation (or perceived similarity), whereas, men may be viewed as higher in competence and dynamism. In a related study (Mulac & Torborg, 1980), male speakers were given higher dynamism ratings than female speakers, while females were given higher aesthetic-quality ratings. No difference was determined between men and women in terms of sociointellectual status.

Several studies have focused on public speakers in the communication classroom. Females appear to receive higher grades than males on their classroom speeches (Barker, 1966; Pearson & Nelson, 1981). Moreover, female students receive proportionately more positive than negative comments than male students (Pearson & Nelson, 1975; Sprague, 1971). In apparent consequence of this positive feedback, women's self-confidence seems to improve slightly as a result of taking public-speaking courses, while men's does not (Judd & Smith, 1977). Other studies demonstrate no difference in the public speaking of men and women. One study showed that gender did not correlate significantly with public-speaking-ability ratings, but that women received higher grades in the basic speech-communication classroom (Hayes, 1977).

Another study examined the influence of psychological gender on grading in the classroom. The research showed that feminine individuals received higher grades than did masculine individuals (Pearson, 1981a). This study, added to the others we have reviewed, implies that women or people with feminine orientations may be ably suited for the public-speaking context. Stereotypical characteristics associated with women, such as sensitivity to the needs of others, understanding, compassion, and warmth, may assist them in the public-speaking setting. In addition, feminine personality traits, including compliance, yielding, and responsiveness, may help women in achieving higher grades in the classroom.

In addition to studies focusing on student speakers in communication classrooms, some studies have examined evaluations of college professors to determine if males and females are rated differently. Basow and Silberg (1986) found that male students gave female professors significantly poorer evaluations than they gave male professors and than female students gave female professors.

Jennings, Crone, Comisky, and Lillman (1980) discovered that students evaluate their professors differently based on an interaction between humor and gender. Any sort of humorous presentation is positively related to appeal, delivery, and teaching effectiveness for male professors. Only hostile humor had the same positive effects for female professors. Female professors who used nonhostile humor, lost appeal, received lower evaluations on competence, delivery factors, and on a measure of general teaching effectiveness. The authors conclude that students may expect humor from men while they do not from women. Hostile humor may be viewed positively for women since it exhibits a degree of aggressiveness which grants women the authority to be humorous (Jennings, Crane, Comisky & Zillman 1980). Apparently, women who demonstrate masculine characteristics are allowed the opportunity to behave in other stereotypical masculine ways without incurring negative judgment.

Communication apprehension (a feeling of anxiety associated with the avoidance of oral communication) has been found to be related both to biological sex and psychological gender. Women report slightly more public-speaking apprehension than do men (Infante & Fisher 1974; McCroskey, Simpson & Richmond 1982). Greenblatt, Hasenauer, and Freimuth (1980) found that feminine females report more communication apprehension than masculine males, that androgynous males and androgynous females do not report differences in communication apprehension, and that androgynous females report less communication apprehension than feminine females. This study implies that femininity, rather than femaleness, results in higher levels of communication apprehension.

The research on communication apprehension is intriguing in light of the findings that women and people with feminine orientations receive higher public-speaking grades. It appears that women and feminine individuals tend to be better public speakers than men despite the fact they are also more anxious about public speaking. While communication apprehension is generally discussed in negative terms, perhaps in this instance apprehension serves to heighten one's preparation for, and consequent success, in public speaking.

Finally, Campbell (1986) has examined women orators and determined that there is a feminine style of rhetoric. This rhetoric is inductive, dependent on examples, often drawn from personal experience. Feminine rhetoric uses figurative language and rhetorical questions in an effort to make the audience participate in the rhetorical situation. The feminine style employs a narrative or dramatic organization. Campbell suggests that this style is a strategic way to reconcile the femininity of the speaker with the masculine tradition of public address. Let us now turn our attention to gender differences as they relate to the receiver of public messages.

The receiver

Some of the earliest work in this area focused on persuasibility. Early research findings implied that women were more easily persuaded than were men (cf. Carmichael, 1970; Rosenfeld & Christie, 1974; Schiede, 1963; Tuthill & Forsythe, 1982). Subsequent findings indicated no differences between women and men in persuasibility (Miller & McReynolds, 1973). At present, researchers and theorists are still attempting to determine what relationships, if any, exist between gender and persuasibility.

Factors other than gender differences may have accounted for the early findings that suggested women are more persuasible than men. For instance, Montgomery and Burgoon (1977) assert that the results of prior studies may be due to the specific topics used. Many persuasibility studies have been conducted using "male-oriented topics." Consequently, women may have demonstrated more attitude change simply because they were not firmly committed to a position on the issue. This explanation is compatible with Saltiel and Woelfel's (1975) theory of accumulated information and attitude change. It argues that people are prone to attitude change to the extent they have not yet accumulated information about the topic at hand.

Psychological gender has replaced biological sex as the independent variable in some studies focusing on the receiver. Montgomery and Burgoon (1977) determined that feminine females change attitudes more than do masculine males, and that this difference is greater than that obtained between androgynous males and androgynous females. Thus, in at least one study psychological gender has been demonstrated to have more predictive value than biological sex.

Considerable research indicated that female evaluators are more lenient or give higher ratings than males. Female student evaluators rate both male and female speakers higher than do male student evaluators (Pfister, 1955). Women rated persuasive speeches higher for persuasiveness than did men, both immediately after a speech and after ten weeks (Sikkink, 1956). Miller and McReynolds (1973) showed that women tend to rate a male speaker higher than men do. In contrast with male evaluators, female evaluators tend to give higher trustworthiness and dynamism ratings (Vigliano, 1974).

Sprague (1971) found that female college speech instructors make significantly more delivery comments (as opposed to content comments), positive comments (as opposed to negative comments), and personal comments (as opposed to impersonal comments) than did male college instructors (Sprague, 1971).

Despite women's apparent leniency, their criticisms are usually perceived as more helpful than men's. As receivers, women tend to be more willing to listen to speakers and reflect their understanding in positive and constructive feedback to speakers. In general, then, women appear to be both better encoders and decoders of public messages than men, although the prevailing stereotypes and practices often keep women from being heard in public contexts.

Summary
Individuals of high status are generally perceived to be more effective speakers than those with low status. Men are consistently perceived to be of higher status than women and the traditional belief persists that public speaking is a masculine activity. This is despite many studies which demonstrate that women have better encoding and decoding skills in public speaking. Our perceptions may continue to be colored by the attitude expressed by Samuel Johnson's eighteenth-century comment about women preachers: "Sir, a woman preaching is like a dog walking on his hind legs. It is not done well; but you are very surprised to find it done at all."

Because most studies showing women's proficiency were performed in communication classrooms, the context may have affected the results. Hall and Sandler (1984) suggest that the classroom can be a somewhat more egalitarian setting than other contexts. Since classes usually are organized with overt rules and criteria, women have a better chance to excel in classes than in other, less organized, settings; therefore, these results may not generalize to business and other public contexts. Women receive higher grades on their speeches, but also report higher levels of communication apprehension.

Although some persuasion studies indicate that women are more easily persuaded than men, more recent research suggests that psychological gender may be a better predictor of persuasiveness than biological sex. Specifically, both feminine men and women have been found to be more persuasible than either masculine or androgynous men and women.

Communication in the business world
The world of business has changed radically since the 1950s as women in large numbers have entered traditionally male fields such as accounting and management, and have become business owners (Wojahn, 1986). Men in business have sometimes been so slow to respond to these changes that decisions about hiring, firing, retention, benefits, and other personnel matters have not kept pace with the changing times.

"Just such an example happened in 1919, [when] Senator Reed Smoot established a salary ceiling for the staff of the Women's Bureau. 'No woman is worth more than $2,000 a year,' he told Mary Anderson, the first director" (Bird 1970). Although the economy has changed since the Senator made his statement, the underlying attitude about employing women, particularly in managerial jobs, has not. Women make up a larger percentage of the work force today than in earlier times, rising from about 20 percent in 1920 to about 45 percent in 1987 (U.S. Dept. of Commerce, 1989). Nonetheless, women still make less money for the same work. During the 1970s women wore buttons that were inscribed "$0.59" to remind people that women typically made $0.59 for every dollar made by men. During the second fiscal year of the Reagan administration, that figure slipped from $0.59 to $0.57. Today, the figure has risen so that women earn, on average, 70 percent of men's salary. However, in some occupations, the percentage is much lower (i.e., sales = 53 percent) (Basow, 1986).

In addition to lower earning power, sexist attitudes still persist in the workplace. A recent survey (*The Secretary,* 1988) reports the good news that 71 percent of the respondents said they did not care whether their boss was a man or woman. Yet, the same survey also reported that 25 percent of those responding would prefer a male supervisor, while only four percent reported a preference for a female supervisor. Those preferring male supervision did so, by and large, due to a belief that men have more authority in the workplace.

Comments, such as that made by Harry E. Figgie, Jr., Chair of Figgie International ("You don't build a company like this with lace on your underwear."), are still being made in 1989. Goodman (1989) singled Figgie, Jr. out for "Entrepreneur with an Attitude" Award for his statement. However, it is an attitude women face repeatedly in public life.

Occupational choices

Most occupations are perceived as appropriate for either men or women, but not for both, with most men and women tending to agree on those distinctions (Bridges, 1987; Jackson, 1983; Keys, 1985; Krefting, 1979).

Butler (1981) provides the following two job descriptions and asks which advertisement best fits the marketplace:

Wanted: Insurance Executive
Affectionate, childlike person who does not use harsh language to head our Investment Division. We want someone who is cheerful and eager to soothe hurt feelings. The position requires gullibility. This is the perfect job for the tender, yielding individual.

Wanted: Insurance Executive
Competitive, ambitious person with leadership ability needed to head our Investment Division. We want someone who is self-sufficient and dominant. The position requires strong analytical ability. This is the perfect job for an independent, self-reliant person.

Butler created these job descriptions by selecting adjectives from the Bem Sex-role Inventory which we discussed previously. Her point is that stereotypical feminine qualities interfere with our perceiving certain jobs as equally appropriate for both women and men.

Further, Wojahn (1986) cites evidence that men and women go into business for different reasons and judge their success differently. Women place a higher value on mutual respect in the workplace, customer satisfaction, and balancing work life with a good home and family life. Bridges (1987) concurs that women go into the business world expecting to engage in multiple roles in both private and public life.

Perceptions of children

Children as young as three-years old recognize that jobs are gender-typed. When children between the ages of three and six were asked the traditional question—"What do you want to be when you grow up?"—the boys tended to choose adventuresome careers, including police work and athletics; the girls selected nurturing, people-related careers such as nursing. Seventy percent of the boys and 73 percent of the girls chose stereotypical careers for themselves. In addition, 14 percent of the children felt it was not proper for men to pour coffee for seated women; 49 percent felt it was not proper for women to be repair-people (Beuf, 1974). More recent research confirms that nursery-school children continue to select stereotyped occupations for themselves and that boys' personal aspirations are more stereotyped than girls' (O'Keefe & Hyde, 1983).

Children in fourth, fifth, and sixth grades have been surveyed regarding career choices (Coles, 1978). The children were Black, Hispanic, and Anglo-American. The responses were analyzed by ethnicity as well as by gender. Hispanic and Anglo-American girls chose more nontraditional, higher status occupations than the Black girls did. No interactions occurred between gender and ethnicity for boys. Both females and males in all ethnic groups preferred careers stereotyped for their own gender, although girls, particularly Anglo-American girls, showed a greater tendency to cross the lines. In general, the Black girls tended to hold the most stereotypic views of job appropriateness.

In an intriguing study of children's perceptions of occupational choices, five- and six-year-old children watched a series of four films. One film presented a male physician and a female nurse; in another this was reversed; a third showed two females; the fourth depicted two males. In each of the two-minute films, the physician examined a small boy and wrote a prescription for

Gender and Communication in Public Contexts

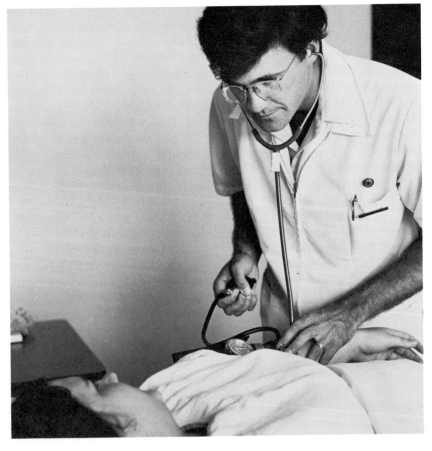

him, while a nurse took the boy's temperature. Of all the children shown the female physician/male nurse film, 53 percent said they had observed a movie about a male physician and female nurse. Of those shown the female physician/female nurse film, 91 percent identified the genders of the actors in each occupation correctly. All the children who viewed the male physician/female nurse were able accurately to identify the gender of the person in each occupation. The authors of this study contend that children see gender-role regularities as "lawful relationships," a perception which causes them to deny the fact that a female can be a physician or a male can be a nurse (Cordua, McGraw & Drabman, 1979).

Perceptions of adolescents and young adults

Another study sought to determine whether androgynous individuals were most flexible in their selection of potential occupations. Fifty-seven percent of college females identified as having androgynous gender orientations were enrolled in female-dominated majors, while 43 percent of them were enrolled in male-dominated majors. Curiously, males with feminine gender orientations did not appear to select nontraditional majors. Perhaps they were disinclined to enter female-dominated fields because of the greater social disapproval or because the occupations tend to be of low status and low pay (Stochton, 1980).

American adolescents were asked about educational and occupational expectations (Anashensel & Rosen, 1978). Men and women expressed similar educational expectations, but women's occupational expectations were lower than men's. The authors theorized that women frequently fear high occupational success, particularly in traditionally male jobs because their success can result in disapproval from males.

Fear of success in adults

Fear of success appears to be a dominant theme for women. A number of researchers have investigated the importance of this concept. In one study, career salience was examined in light of fear of success (Illfelder, 1980). Career salience is defined as the degree to which people are career-motivated, the degree to which occupations are important as a source of satisfaction. Illfelder's findings indicated a complicated relationship between fear of success and the extent a woman embraced a traditional sex-role orientation. Career salience was high among women having high fear of success, but who were also nontraditional in orientation. Career salience was also high among women not fearing success, regardless of how traditional their orientation.

Another study demonstrates that female fear of success may reflect a perception common to both men and women concerning the negative social consequences attending female success in competitive situations (Bremer, 1980). In other words, women do not experience fear of success in a vacuum. If they fear success, they do so because success may bring with it negative

Martha Friedman, psychotherapist and author of *Overcoming the Fear of Success* (1982), summarized some indicators of fear of success. She explains that people who fear success undermine their own efforts by doing such things as arriving late to work, not completing an assignment on time, selecting the wrong mate, sleeping through final exams, and behaving inappropriately in social situations. Though fear of failure frequently leads people to strive harder to achieve a goal, fear of success is often an unconscious impediment. Examples of fear of success include the single man who only dates married women; the female executive who quits her job to have a baby; the man who has 20 years of experience, but tells others he will lose his job because he has no college degree; the married woman who is involved in infidelity on a routine basis; the graduate student who drops courses and insults his or her professors; and the woman who desires a permanent relationship, but discourages relational development.

If you answer any of the following questions with a "yes," you may be afraid of doing too well according to Friedman:

(Place an "X" next to any item which is true for you.)

_____ 1. Do you think if people really knew you, they wouldn't like you?
_____ 2. Do you feel as if you are a fraud and that sooner or later you will be discovered?
_____ 3. Do you fear making a mistake?
_____ 4. Are you a perfectionist?
_____ 5. Do you procrastinate?
_____ 6. Are you overly critical of your own, or of others' work?
_____ 7. Do Sundays depress you?
_____ 8. Are you a workaholic?
_____ 9. Do you feel guilty when you are having a good time?
_____ 10. Do you fear exposure of something about yourself?

If you responded **yes** to any of these, Friedman contends that you may be afraid of doing too well. Many of us are to some degree afraid of success. When fear of success is pushed to an extreme, it may lead to tragedy. Among famous people, Richard Nixon, John Belushi, and Judy Garland are still cited as classic examples. Fear of success is an avoidance mechanism.

Since we believe success will have negative outcomes, such as disappointment, abandonment, rejection, and discouragement, we avoid it. We reason that when things are going well, they cannot continue; we believe that our luck cannot hold.

The fear of success may come from the mixed messages we receive. We are told to live up to our potential, to be all that we can be. On the other hand, we are informed with equal emphasis that the meek shall inherit the Earth, that money is not everything, and that it is lonely at the top. The fear of success is a special problem for women. They are susceptible because of socialization processes which suggest that successful women have jealous mothers, poor relationships with men, and are viewed as "castrating" inhuman beings. Friedman explains that people who combine low self-esteem with high guilt feelings are prime candidates for fear of success.

All psychologists do not agree that the phenomenon of "fear of success" exists. Betsy Brown, psychologist and director of the Center for Family Consultation in Mountainside, New Jersey, thinks fear of success is "nonsense." Brown concludes that both men and women have "achievement-related conflicts," and that some people may not wish to pay the price of success. Nonetheless, she argues that good reasons are frequently offered for refusing to strive for success, and that it is not at all an unconscious process. Harvey Ruben, psychiatrist and assistant clinical professor of psychiatry at Yale, believes that most people have a fear of failure. He states that success is a rare outcome and the phenomenon called "fear of success" is actually fear of failure.

Do you believe that a phenomenon such as "fear of success" exists? Do you believe that you, or others you know, have experienced this fear? Describe the condition as you understand it. Could "fear of success" be "fear of failure" with a different label? For instance, do people become so concerned with succeeding that they fail because of the pressure they place on themselves? Discuss differences between women and men in relation to the fear of success. Compare your responses on the ten questions listed above with those of your classmates. How can you account for differences? What can you and others do to avoid negative behavior which results in failure? What particular changes should occur that will help women? What changes would assist men in avoiding behaviors associated with "fear of success"?

social and personal consequences. Both men and women recognize that successful women may incur disapproval from others. This suggests that fear is not a characteristic of women, but rather an accurate perception of the state of affairs.

Moreover, the fear-of-success syndrome appears to be in a state of change. Garland, Hale, and Burnson (1982) report that men may predetermine women will fail, while women predetermine they will succeed. They found that when men had a positive attitude toward women in management, they believed success was based upon ability and efforts. When women responded to the failure of particular women in management, they explained it was due to the job itself rather than the woman's inabilities or deficiencies. Similarly, Jabes (1980) found that women managers were biased toward other women managers in positive ways.

Summary
Children from the age of three perceive occupations as gender-typed. Adolescents and young adults similarly concur that some jobs are for women and some are for men. Thus, it is not surprising that adults make occupational choices based on long-standing stereotypes. "Fear of success" may be a legitimate response to women's (and men's) recognition of gender-based barriers to particular career paths. Fortunately, both "fear of success" and the limited-gender appropriateness of particular jobs may be gradually diminishing.

Employment interviews

Prior convictions about sex-appropriate jobs, occupational goals which are different from men, and social attitudes which imply that women should not compete with men, all contribute to women's perception of their limited employability. What occurs in the employment interview? When women are interviewed for positions, they should not be surprised if they are asked illegal and sexist questions (Garrison, 1980). Women may be asked questions about their marital status, plans to have children, and other personal questions; they might even be sexually propositioned.

Employers who have been surveyed about women in the employment interview have identified some factors which impair women's chances of being hired. They report that women tend to look at a position in terms of short-run rather than long-term career goals, that marital status tends to hinder women in managerial roles (i.e., married women are less willing to spend extra hours on the job, are less willing to travel, and are less willing to engage in other unusual job requirements), and that women appear to be more nervous and less self-confident during interviews than men.

Wiley and Eskilson (1985) found in interviews simulated with college students that if men and women both use powerful language (see chapter 5), they will receive the same level of acceptance from the interviewer, all other

Women and men both participate in a variety of interviews. One of the most important interviews may be that to secure a job. One method of preparing for the employment interview is to write probable questions and to prepare responses you believe are appropriate. Try to write down the comments and questions an employer might state or ask in a legal employment interview. Then write the same interview again, this time including sexist comments and asking personal questions not relevant to the job. After you have written the two interview plans, compare them. What kind of questions do you believe are illegal? What comments should an employer avoid? What should you do if an employment interviewer asks you an inappropriate question? After you have considered some of these issues, practice the interviews. Interview at least one man and one woman with each of your two interviews. Exchange roles so you are interviewed in an appropriate and an inappropriate way. Discuss your findings in each of these situations. How did you feel when you were *asking* inappropriate questions? How did you feel when you were *asked* inappropriate questions? How much information was acquired in each situation? Discuss such issues as working for someone who regularly conducts inappropriate interviews; conflict in the interview setting; differences in perception of what constitutes an appropriate and an inappropriate set of questions; motivation for asking illegal questions; differences in power between the interviewer and interviewee; and non-verbal behaviors which might accompany illegal and legal questions.

---

relevant variables being equal. These researchers also found, however, that females more than males discriminated between applicants on the basis of speech style. Further, stereotypes are not completely overridden by speech style. Although applicants may be seen as equally competent (if both are using powerful speech), women are still perceived as possessing more warmth, for example.

Women who want to improve their opportunities for being hired can use the findings in these studies to assist them. They should consider before they occur how they will handle sexist questions and sexual suggestions. Women should familiarize themselves with the guidelines established by the EEOC (Equal Employment Opportunity Commission) regarding legal and illegal questions. If you are asked any illegal question, it is probably better for you to explain your concern about the question than to stall, offer a circumvented answer, or not answer at all. Consider methods of answering such questions which will not offend the interviewer, but will clarify your position.

Consider ways of demonstrating your confidence during the employment interview. Before you go to an employment interview, attempt to "second guess" the interviewer and write down some of the questions you will probably be asked. Then, prepare answers which are complete, honest, accurate, and specific. Avoid extra verbiage, euphemisms, platitudes, hesitant, or ambiguous language. Answer the question completely, but stick to the point of the question. Consider, too, your nonverbal communication in the employment interview. Do you appear nervous as you straighten your clothing, constantly move your glasses, or play with a piece of jewelry or a strand of hair? Show confidence through your nonverbal communication by using meaningful, clear, and confident gestures, sitting with both feet on the floor, establishing direct eye contact, and using responsive facial gestures rather than simply smiling throughout the interview. Nonverbal communication may make the difference between being hired or not.

Discrimination in hiring practices

Attempts to equalize the hiring situation for women have been met in certain quarters by charges of "reverse discrimination." Some writers have held that reverse discrimination is just as detrimental as is direct discrimination, and that women have not been denied opportunities as have other groups such as Blacks (Sher, 1977). Other authors counter that reverse discrimination may be justified to shift present practices and achieve equal opportunities for women (Jones, 1977). The problem of discrimination and reverse discrimination is very complex; it involves considerations such as persons losing self-respect because of special treatment, identifying individuals and groups who could and should benefit, and the extent to which such practices should extend.

Both primary and secondary sexism occurs in contemporary hiring practices. Primary sexism is unfair discrimination on the basis of one's biological sex; **secondary sexism** is found in differential hiring practices on the basis of gender-correlated factors. For instance, if a person is not hired because of pregnancy, she is a victim of secondary sexism. Similarly, anti-nepotism laws, last-hired-first-fired policies, promotion of full-time employees over part-time employees, previous salary establishing present rank, and preference for persons who have an uninterrupted work record, are examples of secondary sexism. Secondary sexism is more elusive and more complex than primary sexism; frequently people will point to a lack of primary sexism to prove that sexist practices do not occur. Warren (1977) argues that we should be particularly on guard against secondary sexism as it can easily undermine whatever progress we have already made in curtailing primary sexism.

Let us consider one of the examples of secondary sexism cited above to illustrate the complexity of this issue. Anti-nepotism laws are designed to prevent members of the same family from having administrative or managerial control over each other. For instance, if a man is a manager in a company, his wife cannot be a member of his unit. If a woman is a college president, her husband cannot be one of the deans. Who is more likely to hold the advanced position in a husband-and-wife team? To date, the husband is. It is more probable that the husband earns more money, has a more advanced position, and has proceeded through the ranks more quickly than his wife. This is because of a number of factors, including the likelihood that women are younger than their husbands, that they put aside career obligations for relational or personal concerns, and assume positions of support rather than leadership. Regardless of the cause, the result is the same: poorly designed or inappropriately enforced, anti-nepotism laws prevent women from working in positions from which they are prepared simply because their spouses might also be their supervisors.

In rigidly and mindlessly interpreting anti-nepotism laws, we seek to implement clear-cut solutions for one set of problems, only to incur another set of problems. Often we fail to realize that all decisions regarding personnel are ambiguous; that is, we rarely if ever are asked to choose between two equally qualified persons. Choices about hiring persons are based on unstated, ambiguous factors, as well as on the basis of specific job descriptions. In a sense, employers always run the risk of making errors in their judgments. If, for example, they decide to hire one candidate because of his or her superior educational background, they may be forced to lose the candidate who has years of reputable experience. Similarly, in the past employers have been determined to hire men rather than women because of some of the factors of secondary sexism mentioned above. Our tendency in these cases has been to lose women with unique capabilities and special experiences.

While no one can argue rationally that discrimination against one gender is more acceptable than discrimination against the other, it is bewildering that years of discrimination against women have not aroused the same outrage as the far fewer and more recent cases of reverse discrimination. Our goal should be to reject errors in judgment unfairly favoring either women or men. It is evident, moreover, that large institutions and businesses can do a great deal to reduce the adverse effects of sexual stereotyping in hiring practices (cf. Heilman, 1980).

As an example of the sorts of things business can do to at least decrease—if not eliminate entirely—discrimination against women, consider the amount of attention recently given to sexual harassment. Twenty years ago the term "sexual harassment" was rarely heard. Today, virtually every major corporation and industry has established elaborate procedures allowing alleged victims to file complaints. While not perfect, anti-harassment programs are certainly far more effective today than they were 20 years ago. In part, these policy changes stem from an understandable desire to avoid costly and embarrassing litigation. But, in addition to this motivation, business is also deeply concerned about their personnel. Before serious research was done on this subject, businesses had simply underestimated the pervasiveness and serious consequences of harassment which, for the victim, include nervousness, irritability, loss of motivation, sleeplessness, weight loss, inconvenient and costly transfers to other departments or programs, and stunted career advancement (Loy & Stewart, 1984). For the company, harassment can result in lower productivity levels (Hair, 1987). Mindful of these consequences and an obligation to safeguard the basic dignities of all employees, most reputable businesses now have elaborate and thorough procedures for preventing, detecting, and eliminating sexual harassment.

However, as Verbeeck (1986) points out, people's attitudes often make harassment policies difficult to enforce. Many men see harassment as an exaggerated issue, while many women fear their complaints will be ignored or, even worse, result in more on-the-job trouble. Blodgett (1986) reports that female attorneys have considerable difficulty when the harassment comes from a judge since that also compromises their client's interests. Thus, many women in law have chosen simply to ignore blatant sexual harassment in the belief that the harassers as older men will soon leave the profession taking their sexist ideas and behaviors with them.

Occasionally, however, even a sitting judge can be censured for sexually harassing comments. Blodgett cites the case of New York State Supreme Court Judge Anthony Jordan, Jr. who called a woman lawyer "little girl" and ruled against her after she objected to that form of address. Judge Jordan was censured by the Board of Judicial Standards for those and other demeaning comments directed at women attorneys.

Women as managers

One of the most widely studied issues in business settings concerning women and men is the role of women as managers. Bormann, Pratt, and Putnam (1978), for instance, conducted research demonstrating the importance of female dominance and male responses to that dominance. In their study they found that fantasies accompany perceptions of male and female leadership. One of the most common fantasies linked leadership with male potency. Men perceived female leadership as associated with their own loss of sexual potency. Their study indicates that women may have a powerful mythology to overcome if they are to succeed in management.

Fortunately, some very good research indicates that prior experience in working with female managers is often enough to change negative attitudes toward female managers (Wheeless & Berryman-Fink, 1985). Thus, if given opportunities for managerial employment, success on the job will probably in the long run be the single most important factor accounting for women's increased managerial responsibility. To facilitate the advance of women requires continued debunking of those various stereotypes and myths.

A number of myths have already been dispelled concerning women's abilities to manage. Some of these apparently unsupported stereotypes are that women are too emotional to make rational decisions (Biles & Pryatel, 1978; Dipboye, 1975); women have a lower commitment to work than men (Biles & Pryatel, 1978); women lack motivation to achieve (Biles & Pryatel, 1978); men are inherently more assertive than women (Dipboye, 1975); and men are intellectually superior to women (Dipboye, 1975). While such myths are being dispelled in the literature, women appear to remain at a disadvantage because of such stereotypes (Larwood, Wood & Inderlied, 1978; Colins, Waters & Waters, 1979) and because individuals prefer managers who possess masculines characteristics (Brenner & Bromer, 1981).

Self-perception of female and male managers

Both women and men may perceive themselves differently as managers. Women may perceive additional problems in their jobs that men do not. In self-evaluations, women and men provide significantly different responses. Male managers view themselves as performing better than women in comparable jobs, and as having more abilities and higher intelligence. Also, men rate their jobs as more difficult than the jobs women hold, an impression corroborated by their subordinates (Deaux, 1979). It is also true that men are more likely than women to view themselves as successful and to attribute their success to their own abilities.

Others' perceptions of male and female managers

Berryman-Fink and Wheeless (1987) found that women perceived greater communication competence for women managers than men. As they note, their study was based on the abstract notion of women managers, not on a specific manager, which might have affected its results. Supporting that explanation, Tsui and Gutek (1984) report that female managers were given higher performance evaluations than their male counterparts.

Subordinate evaluations indicate women are experiencing success as managers (White, Crino & De Sanctis, 1981). The evaluations of superiors provide mixed results for the woman manager (White et al., 1981). If evaluators hold sex-typed expectations, then women may receive poor evaluations.

In terms of specific communication behaviors, women managers considerate of subordinates are viewed more positively, (Petty & Lee, 1975; Petty & Miles, 1976), provided they do not overly attend to or monitor the subordinate's performance (Statham, 1987). Overattentiveness may be interpreted as lack of confidence in the subordinate's competencies. Statham reports that male subordinates are particularly prone to take offense at overattentiveness from female supervisors, and seem to prefer goal-oriented direction given by male managers. Statham, however, cautions that neither male nor female employees appreciate employers so focused on the tasks at hand that they fail to be supportive of subordinates. Statham's work also indicates that female subordinates are particularly resentful of lack of attentiveness and support.

Differences in management style between women and men

Are women and men different as managers? The jury is still out on that question. A number of studies have determined that women and men are not significantly different (Bartol, 1974, 1978; Bartol & Wortman, 1975, 1976; Inderlied & Powell, 1979; Marcum, 1976; Wexley & Hunt, 1974). Men and women do not appear to differ in motivation to manage (Miner, 1974); subordinates do not distinguish between male and female leaders in their use of positive and punitive rewards (Szilagyi, 1980); male and female supervisors have been perceived to exhibit similar patterns of leadership behavior and to be similar in terms of effectiveness (Day & Stodgill, 1972); and male and female leaders who exhibit similar behaviors are not judged differently by their subordinates (Alvares & Les, 1979).

However, other studies have reported differences between female and male managers. Several studies indicate that males exhibit stereotypic masculine characteristics, whereas, females exhibit stereotypic feminine characteristics in their management roles (Baird & Bradley, 1979; Bartol & Butterfield, 1976; Day & Stodgill, 1972; Haccoun, Sallay & Haccoun, 1978; Welsh, 1979).

Men may be more assertive or aggressive in their interactions with others and, thus, emerge more frequently as the leader, while women reveal more information about their feelings, beliefs, and concerns than men and are more person-oriented (Berryman-Fink, 1985; Hyman, 1980). Men generally dominate their conversations and interviews with employees and are more prone to use punitive approaches toward gaining compliance (Harper & Hirokawa, 1988). Conversely, women are more prone to use supportive strategies when seeking compliance (Todd-Mancillas & Rossi, 1985).

How do we account for the inconsistent findings concerning men and women? Some of the differences in the findings may be due to the procedures the researchers used. For instance, when students are asked to role-play managers, they may behave differently from persons who actually serve as managers. Women actually in the management field may behave similarly to men in the management field. Female managers may be self-selected, in other words, female managers may possess traditionally masculine characteristics. For example, male and female Master of Business Administration (M.B.A.) students do not differ considerably. Female M.B.A. students are creative, willing to initiate change in their own lives, and self-assured. It appears that the female M.B.A. student has little or no fear of sex-role inappropriateness (Foster & Kolinko, 1979). Similarly, male and female graduate students enrolled in introductory business courses at three American universities were found to have higher stereotypical masculine traits than individuals in the rest of the population (Powell & Butterfield, 1981). These findings suggest that women and men in management and business may be self-selected and hold masculine traits.

Two studies of female managers strengthened the contention that women in management may hold those characteristics, attitudes, and temperaments more commonly ascribed to men. Schein (1973, 1975) found that female middle managers are perceived to possess traditionally masculine characteristics. In addition, female corporate presidents are more task-oriented in their leadership style than males in the same positions, a finding implying that women in management may exhibit even more extreme traditionally masculine characteristics than their male counterparts (Helmich, 1974).

Another reason for the inconsistent findings in this area may be contextual, that is, the specific occupation or organization being investigated may account for differences. Some positions may be viewed as more appropriate for men or for women. For example, one study indicated that women have not actively pursued careers as school administrators because the strong norm still exists that this is a man's job (Schmuck, 1975). Another study contends that significant patterns of male-female differences in work attitudes are not evident when occupation and organization level are held constant (Brief & Oliver, 1976). It is clear that the organization's structure and culture are the most important factors regarding the presence of women (Vaden & Lynn, 1979). The willingness to accept women as managers may greatly reduce the perceived differences between them and their male counterparts. The situation in which a male or female manager finds himself or herself must be taken into consideration.

Effective managers

To the extent a woman or man can accurately perceive the organizational climate and adapt to it, she or he will probably be successful and be perceived as successful (Bedeian, Armenakis & Kemp, 1976). Geddes (1987) found that male and female managers are similar in terms of effectiveness.

Women and men are capable of assuming managerial roles. Female managers may provide some unique qualities and some special experiences men do not possess or have not developed. While male executives are commonly discharged because of their lack of sensitivity when dealing with others (McCall, 1983), women are frequently appreciated because of their ability to work effectively and courteously with others (Kushell & Newton, 1986). Moreover, women are often able to give clearer and more easily understood instructions than men (Wheeless, Hudson & Wheeless, 1987).

None of the above, however, suggests that women are easily assimilated into the managerial community. Problems abound. For one, difficult economic times cause managerial positions with their higher status and salaries to be more competitive. In addition, not all people are equally accepting of women in management roles. Women may find their subordinates do not accept their authority (Forgionne, 1977; Yerby, 1975). Also, women may have to learn styles of leadership distinct from their male counterparts. For example, one study demonstrated that female supervisors behaving in a directive, authoritarian style were viewed as less effective than female supervisors adopting a rational or friendly style (Haccoun, Sallay & Haccoun, 1978).

Another study has explored four potential power outcomes. A person could have a high need or desire to exert influence over others and a high degree of control of his or her interactions with others (high/high); a high need to exert influence, but a low degree of control (high/low); a low need and a low degree of control (low/low); or a low need and high degree of control (low/high). Since men have typically fallen into the high/high category, they have been very successful. When women adopt this posture, however, they are viewed negatively (Swanson & Wagner, 1979). It has been suggested that the high/high state may only have been successful because men used it, not because it was inherently better. Similarly, women who have adopted stereotypical-masculine interaction styles have not found they have been the recipients of less bias (Wiley & Eskilson, 1982). Thus, women should not strive to emulate men's managerial styles without considering whether those adaptations are compatible with their own personalities and objectives. On the other hand, neither would women want to adopt a stereotypic-feminine style for managing others as this is viewed even more disparagingly than the overly masculine styles (Arkkelin & Simmons, 1985).

Many people have attempted to assist women in learning effective managerial behaviors and skills. Much of this advice is in self-help books found in any community bookstore. Inasmuch as these materials reflect the dominant, however inaccurate, approaches toward achieving managerial success, it is instructive to consider their content and orientations. Bate and Self (1983) explain that women's self-help books fall into three different groups: (1) those that define success in terms of external indications such as money, power, and advancement to high-status positions (e.g., *Games Mother Never Taught You; Corporate Gamesmanship for Women; Beating Men at Their Own Game; The Woman's Selling Game; Is Networking for You?*); (2) those that present a mixed view of what constitutes success (e.g., *Women at Work; Networking; Skills for Success*) and (3) those that define success in terms of internal markers or the way a woman integrates her numerous roles according to her own priorities (e.g., *Having It All, Paths to Power,* and *Targeting the Top*). Bate and Self observe that the diversity of advice available to women implies that we are in a period of cultural transformation and that women's choices will have far-reaching significance.

Female Bosses Say Biggest Barriers Are Insecurity and 'Being a Woman'

By Jennifer Bingham Hull
Staff Reporter of THE WALL STREET JOURNAL

They are senior executives at large U.S. companies with average salaries of about $92,000. Their titles range from corporate secretary to president and chief executive officer, and while most are single, those who are married say they are both the main breadwinner and the main homemaker.

They attribute their successes to ambition, drive and a willingness to take risks, and they blame their failures on a male world and their lack of confidence in it. They were more often the first-born or only child in their families and favored their fathers.

This is part of a picture that emerges from a study of executive women recently completed by Korn/Ferry International, an executive search firm, and the University of California, Los Angeles, Graduate School of Management. The study is based on 300 responses to 600 questionnaires mailed to women at the level of vice president and above at Fortune magazine's lists of the top 1,000 industrial concerns and 300 of the largest companies in specialized areas. Most of the respondents are vice presidents. Their average age is 46.

While the study makes it clear that women are on the way up, it also shows that it has been a bit lonely being among the few women at the top.

Work-Place Problems

Asked whether "barriers to women have fallen at the senior management level," 63% of the women say no. And 70% say women don't receive equal pay for comparable jobs. Female executives most frequently mention "being a woman" as their major career obstacle, citing "the old-boy network," "insecure men," and the attitude that they're "too good looking to take seriously . . . will run off and get married" as work-place problems.

In comments on her questionnaire, a vice president of corporate finance says her biggest career obstacle has been her appearance. I "didn't look or sound the part—5'3½", female, with a Southern accent," she says. A vice president and director of manpower development complains of "lack of acceptance based on competence . . . the unwillingness of people to give me the toughest assignments." And a regional vice president says her biggest barrier to success has been her "tendency to unconsciously intimidate male superiors."

After "being a woman," lack of confidence was most frequently cited as the main obstacle to success. A senior vice president of marketing says she was forced to overcome "my own fears of not being as good or strong as the men I worked with because of lack of education and being the first woman." Asked to name her greatest career challenge, another woman simply responded, "myself."

These comments sound familiar to Barbara Franklin, a senior fellow of public management of the University of Pennsylvania's Wharton School. She serves on the boards of Dow Chemical Co., Westinghouse Electric Corp. and Aetna

Life & Casualty Co. Miss Franklin cites isolation and upbringing as reasons for insecurity. "Women aren't brought up with male egos. And . . . in the corporate scene nobody tells you when you've done a good job. There's just this deafening silence."

Lack of confidence, Miss Franklin says, comes from corporate women's inability to break into men's informal networks. "I see it now. Everybody I know plays golf. I don't play golf."

The study by Korn/Ferry and UCLA follows a similar survey done in 1979. Then, the researchers set out to analyze the characteristics of senior executives, surveying about 1,700 people in senior positions below the level of chief executive officer at Fortune's top 500 companies and the 300 more specialized concerns. When 99% of the respondents turned out to be men, the researchers decided to survey executive women and compare the two groups. Presidents, chief executive officers and chief operating officers were included in the female study in order to get a sufficient sample. The average age of the men surveyed was 53.

"I know men who say, 'I support your career. It's wonderful.' But that's not what they mean," says a woman who is a director of several companies.

Comparison shows the biggest difference between executive men and women to be marital and family status. Fifty-two percent of the women surveyed are single, compared with only 4% of the men. In addition, 61% of the women are childless, while 97% of the men were parents.

Executive women are far more likely to be divorced than their male counterparts. Of the women studied, 17% are divorced, compared with only 2.4% of the men. More than half of the executive women who are divorced say their career played a part in the separation.

A study recently completed by James Baron, assistant professor of organizational behavior at Stanford University and William Bielby, associate professor of sociology at the University of California, Santa Barbara, yields similar results.

Using data from the 1960s, the two men studied about 1,000 men and women in a cross-section of occupations. Some 86% of their male respondents were married, compared with only 61% of the women.

"As you move up the ladder, these pressures become even greater," Mr. Baron says. "Not only is being married a disadvantage to a woman in that position, but it's an asset for a man."

Paychecks and Housekeeping

In 1971, Miss Franklin was appointed to the Nixon White House to recruit women for high-level jobs in the federal government. "Many of them were either single or divorced," she recalls. "It's hard to find men in this age group willing to be supportive and understanding of the demands on a successful woman. I know men who say, 'I support your career. It's wonderful.' But that's not what they mean. They mean I support it as long as it doesn't interfere with someplace I want you to be."

Executive women who are married are generally running the home and bringing home more of the money. On the average these women provide 56% of their household income. Sixty-eight percent of the women say their careers have been more financially rewarding than their husbands', and 78% say their careers have progressed better. About half of the women say they're responsible for the housekeeping, and 29% say they share the work with their spouse. A majority of the women with children say they have the primary responsibility for their care.

"I'm out there writing notes to the housekeeper and arranging meals," says an executive search manager queried about the study. The woman is married to an executive at a large corporation and makes more money than her husband. She says she prefers to do the housework. "I find it easier in life to manage and administer that which I've been trained to do," she says, describing how they divide the work at home.

Refusing Transfers

Another difference between executive men and women is mobility. While 33% of the female respondents have been asked to relocate, only 21% have done so, compared with 81% of the men. Of the women who refused a transfer, the majority say their refusal hasn't hurt their careers.

While the survey portrays an executive woman who is still bumping into obstacles along the path to success, it also shows her making progress. Nearly half of the women over 52 years of age started in clerical positions, compared with only 23% of the younger female executives, who more often started in management. The younger women also have more earning power than their elders. Some 60% of the women earning more than $106,000 are between 38 and 52, compared with only 20% of those over 52.

Although executive women have more limited educational backgrounds than their male counterparts, more than in the past are graduating from college. Some 20% of the respondents don't have a college degree, compared with 8% of the men surveyed. But 34% of the younger women surveyed have advanced degrees, compared with only 14% of the older women.

Comparison of the two studies shows that female executives are also less conservative and less religious than male executives. Some 60% of the women say religion plays little or no role in their lives, while about the same percentage of men said religion was a significant or moderate influence on them. On economic issues, 49% of the respondents say they are conservative, compared with 74% of the men. On social issues, 21% of the women say they are conservative, compared with 42% of the men. Some 80% of the women favor passage of the Equal Rights Amendment and 90% favor a woman's right to abortion.

The studies also show a difference in family background between men and women in senior management. Sixty percent of the women surveyed say they were either the oldest or only child, compared with 49% of the men. In addition, 48% of the women say they were closer to their fathers while growing up, compared with 40% who were closer to their mothers. Fifty-four percent of these female executives say their mothers didn't work outside the home.

Koester (1982) also examined women's self-help books using fantasy-theme analysis. She writes that, according to the books, "Successful women managers operate as Machiavellian princesses controlling the impact of their gender in an organizational setting filled with intrigue and innuendo" (p. 165). Successful women, according to Koester's analysis, are those who balance the negative stereotypes of women, but retain their essential femininity. Koester, like Bate and Self, notes that the books present contradictory advice. She adds that their advice may be incomplete and debilitating as well since women can never completely balance the two stereotypes.

We conclude this section of the chapter with an extended excerpt from an article which appeared in the *Wall Street Journal*. The article is informative since it provides a descriptive picture of women as executives in contemporary culture. The views expressed may be more realistic than those espoused by the authors of the popular self-help books.

Conclusions

In this chapter we have considered gender differences in communication as they occur in public contexts. In earlier chapters we noted that women tend to be less assertive than men, that men tend to be less empathic than women, that women demonstrate more sensitivity to nonverbal cues, and that men are better able to focus on a single message in a multiple-message situation. In this chapter, we viewed some results of those differences in communication behaviors in public contexts.

We observed that women and men have different styles in the small-group setting. We noted that although people seem to prefer men in leadership positions, both men and women can be successful leaders. In public speaking women and men exhibit different skills, but in the speech-communication classroom women appear to excel. Although, traditionally the occupational choices of women and men have been different, we recognize that both men and women can now pursue careers previously reserved for the other gender. Specifically, while in the past women have rarely served as managers, today they are moving rapidly into managerial positions. Their success in these positions is not simply a matter of adopting and enacting male behaviors; instead, successful female managers may have developed unique styles responsive to the specific needs of their positions.

10 Gender and communication in mediated contexts

250   Contexts

Introduction

In chapter 4 we determined that the language we use teaches us how to perceive women and men. The media are other valuable learning sources for shaping our perceptions of women and men. Busby (1975) provides an extensive review of this topic concluding (1) that some aspects of sex roles are relatively unexplored; (2) that sex roles in the mass media are traditional and do not reflect alternatives; (3) that children model the behavior they perceive in various media; and (4) that men serve as gatekeepers, or controllers of information, in most media. Busby's conclusions are especially important if we accept Cathcart and Gumpert's (1986) argument concerning the centrality of mass media in our lives. Cathcart and Gumpert assert that the media are responsible for substantively changing interpersonal relationships and are instrumental in shaping an individual's self-image. We will keep these assertions in mind as we explore the literature in this area. Specifically, we will examine written media, such as magazines, newspapers, and print advertisements; media to which we listen, such as popular music; and media to which we listen and watch, such as television. Let us begin our investigation by considering the press.

Magazines and newspapers

Sex-role stereotypes

Magazines are written for many different groups of people. The target audience of the magazine appears to affect its stories, features, and kinds of advertisements. Kramarae (1981) notes that magazines for young children do not differentiate between the sexes (i.e., *Jack and Jill* and *Highlights*). These magazines are targeted to both boys and girls. However, at adolescence, magazines are very different for female and male audiences. Kramarae observes that girls' teen magazines emphasize improving one's appearance and personality, while in boys' magazines the emphasis is on gaining mechanical and physical skills. Kramarae notes that

> Clearly the interests of adolescent females and adolescent males are thought to be very different....How much the publishers establish the interest in separate journals and how much the journals reflect the interest established by other factors in the culture is clearly a very complex (and important) issue (Kramarae, 1981, 84–85).

This distinction between the interests of females and males is continued into adulthood as women and men both have some magazines written especially for them. Romance magazines, for instance, are written for women as escape literature. Adventure magazines, on the other hand, are written primarily for men. Romance magazines allow women to escape to fantasized relationships, while adventure magazines allow men to fantasize about being rugged individualists (Smith and Matre, 1975). Magazines in these categories tend to encourage traditional, stereotypical roles.

Another stereotype encouraged by men's magazines is woman-as-sex object. In an analysis of the image of women presented in *Playboy* magazine, Robards (1984) argues that the women presented in *Playboy's* centerfolds in the years 1980–1984 send a dual message. The model is sexually provocative and aggressive, yet at the same time, projects a demure, traditional persona. Robards concludes that the centerfold fits most of the feminine sex-role items generated by Broverman, Vogel, Broverman, Clarkson and Rosenkrantz in 1972.

However, Robards notes that there are some indications that the stereotype of women as sex objects may be changing in magazines, at least in *Playboy*. First of all, he observes that *Playboy's* circulation has declined in recent years and, in response, is attempting to market itself as a "lifestyle" magazine. In so doing, Robards argues, *Playboy* has to move toward a view of women that is acceptable to women. Some evidence (i.e., more mention of model's professions, the inclusion of older women, more women posed clothed, and more "independent" comments from the models) may indicate that *Playboy* is doing just that.

Because of their wide readership, magazines can effectively inform and persuade people on a variety of issues. Farley (1978) studied the coverage of the Equal Rights Amendment in women's magazines and found differences in coverage based on type of magazine, editorial policy, circulation, and social class of readership. However, she concluded that women's magazine editors appear to be attempting to change the status quo.

In another study examining changes in messages reflected in magazines, Ruggiers and Weston (1985) found that "new" women's magazines, such as *Working Women,* profile women to whom working for pay, often in non-traditional jobs, is an integral part of their self-images. Even more established magazines such as *Women's Day* and *Redbook* present women in a wide variety of work roles Ruggiers and Weston found. However, the established magazines often downplay the importance and power of the work role and focus instead on the traditional tasks these women still perform. Thus, we see that the status quo changes and yet continues to resist change.

Wojahn (1986) notes that thumbing through the pages of business magazines, *Inc., Forbes, Fortune,* or *Business Week,* gives the impression that "American business [is] still an all-male preserve" (p. 45). This is despite much evidence of women in corporate management, private companies, and entrepreneurial ventures, Wojahn observes.

Male-centered and female-centered news stories in newspapers have been studied. An equal number of male-centered and female-centered stories were selected. About 48 percent of the female-centered stories appeared in the first or second sections of the newspapers, while 78 percent of the male-centered stories were in the first or second sections. No significant differences were found in the stories' lengths or in the photo size used. The occupation of the woman or man in the story was provided as frequently for one sex as for the other. Personal appearance (excluding age) was mentioned in 38 percent of the stories about women and in 14 percent of the stories about men. Marital status (disregarding the title "Mrs.") was mentioned for 64 percent of the women and 12 percent of the men (Forfeit, Agor, Byers, Larue, Lokey, Palazzini, Patterson & Smith 1980). Some sexism appears evident. Stories about females are given less importance than stories about males; both personal appearance and marital status are more relevant when discussing women than men.

News photos were examined in another study. Men outnumbered women in photographs by a ratio of three to one in the *Washington Post* and about two to one in the *Los Angeles Times.* Men clearly dominated photo coverage on the first page of both papers. Half of the women's photos were on the lifestyle page, only 10–15 percent of the male photos were on those pages. Women's roles were mostly as spouse and fashion models, while men were pictured as politicians, entertainers, and in a variety of other roles (Miller, 1975). The relative proportion of women and men in these newspapers suggest that men are more newsworthy than women and that women's roles are more narrowly defined.

A more recent study showed that occupation, in addition to sex, played a role in photographs featured in the press. In this study, Sparks and Fehlner (1986) found that women in government were accorded as much facial prominence in photographs in *Time* and *Newsweek* as men in government. However, women entertainers and actors had significantly less facial prominence than their male counterparts. Facial prominence involved a ratio of how much the photo showed of the subject's face versus the body.

The women's pages of newspapers were studied in another investigation. High-circulation newspapers which were principally metropolitan had male editors for the women's pages 79 percent of the time. When men served as editors of the women's pages, more coverage was given to entertainment, recreation, and leisure. When women served as editors, more attention was given to club and social news as well as the women's movement (Merritt & Gross, 1978). It appears that the sex of the editor causes major differences in coverage on the women's pages.

As Gallagher (1984) points out, what the media do *not* say is equally as important as what they *do* say regarding the perpetuation of stereotypic, limited visions of women and men. Gallagher analyzes an editorial from the

Washington Post (January 1983). The editorial examined the plight of the unemployed and stated that minimum-wage levels are so low they are " 'women's pay' " (p. 4) and working for that threatens one's self-respect. As Gallagher states, although the subject is "ostensibly about unemployment, the editorial is actually about *male* unemployment" (p. 4).

Finally, Myers (1983) provides an interesting analysis of the press' treatment of Mary Cunningham and William Agee. Agee was the Chair of the Board of Bendix Corporation and Cunningham was a Bendix Vice-president in 1980. Initially, press coverage involved Cunningham's rapid rise in the Bendix Corporation variously attributed to her personal relationship with Agee and to her business acumen. Cunningham resigned from Bendix after the negative publicity. She and Agee were married in 1982. Later in 1982, the couple received more press attention when Cunningham served on Bendix's team of advisors during a takeover bid, although she was, by now, employed elsewhere.

Myers examines the press coverage that Cunningham and Agee received during 1980–1982 and comes to some revealing conclusions. First, she notes that more press attention was focused on Cunningham than Agee, but that Agee's press was more negative than Cunningham's. More importantly, she observes why each was criticized and praised. Agee's negative press seemed to come, Myers argues, from the perception that he was weaker or less "macho" than a board chair ought to be.

As Myers insists, "Quoted comments and sarcastic references to his 'wife's role as an adviser' and his seeming 'to take comfort' from her presence reinforce the conclusion that Agee was being criticized for not acting in a stereotypically masculine manner" (Myers, 1983, 81–82). Conversely, Cunningham was criticized for not adhering to the traditional feminine stereotype. She was described as "disruptive," "calculating," "manipulative," "intimidating," and "arrogant." When she was praised, it was often in terms indicating that, despite her situation, she had a regard for traditional feminine behavior. She was praised for resigning from Bendix and showing concern for Agee.

Finally, Myers demonstrates that Cunningham, more than Agee, was characterized by adjectives. Agee was described by adverbs to a greater extent than Cunningham. Myers accurately observes that "Mary Cunningham was praised or criticized for what she *was,* while William Agee was criticized, for the most part, for what he *did*" (p. 82). Thus, Myers concludes, the notions of woman-as-object and man-as-actor were perpetuated by the press. Obviously, this one case study is not conclusive proof of stereotypic press coverage in general. However, Myers demonstrates the value of careful analysis of the language practices of the press.

Advertisements

Early research

Advertisements in print media have been studied extensively. Research in the early 1970s suggested that women are largely portrayed in stereotypical roles. One study stated that although 33 percent of the work force was composed of females, only 12 percent of the workers pictured in advertisements were female. No women were depicted as professionals or in high-level managerial positions; however, they were portrayed as entertainers, clerks, airline flight attendants, assembly-line workers, airline employees engaged in food preparation, and school teachers. The researchers concluded that these ads did not portray the true range of women's roles in contemporary society (Courtney & Lockeretz, 1971).

Another study published in the mid–1970s considered the portrayal of women in advertisements. Among the findings were the following: (1) women are more concerned with their appearance and domestic duties than with complex decisions; (2) women are more often portrayed in domestic settings than men; (3) women are rarely portrayed in occupational settings; and (4) women wear pants or slacks in only a few ads (Culley and Bennett, 1976). Smith (1977) maintains that in the past two decades women have not moved very far from their limited roles; in the mid–1970s only 16 percent of the women portrayed in advertisements were in non-traditional situations.

Changes in the portrayal of women and men

Still other studies indicate change is occurring, albeit, slowly. One author concludes that women are being portrayed in more responsible roles (Levere, 1974), and that subsequent to the study by Courtney & Lockertz, women's appearance in working roles has more than doubled (Wagner & Banos, 1973). More encouraging news was recently available. Mitchell Siegel, research director of Alschiller, Reitzfeld, and Solvin, a New York ad agency, investigated the roles of women and men in current advertising. He determined that women are equally disapproving of the housewife who is in "endless" pursuit of dirt and the chauffeur-driven working woman. Judith Langer, a market researcher, states:

> What is evolving is a new kind of women who is active, alive and out in the world....She cares about her home but isn't obsessive about it. If she has a career, it isn't necessarily as a TV anchor woman. Advertisers are showing a softer woman who cares about relationships yet at the same time is strong (Bralove, 1982).

Gender and Communication in Mediated Contexts   257

Mediated sources affect the way people view themselves. Examine a set of print media, newspapers, magazines, and other periodicals to determine how women and men are portrayed. Some of these images are probably similar to you, but others are not at all like you. Create two collages—posters with multiple pictures—from the sources you have found. One collage should pictorially represent how you view yourself and how that image is portrayed in print media. The other collage should pictorially represent how persons of your gender are represented in the print media, but it is the antithesis of how you view yourself. For instance, an athletic woman might use pictures of strong women participating in a variety of sports as one set of representations. She might use weak or submissive female pictures for the collage which represents the antithesis. A nurturing man might choose pictures of men caring for children, feeding a newborn, or listening attentively to others to represent himself and select pictures of football players, beer drinkers, and macho men to epitomize his opposite.

After you have completed your collages, bring them to class and prepare a short talk on how you view yourself and how that self is represented in the media. You might discuss how you feel about yourself, how frequently pictures of "you" occur in the media, or how complex you feel you are compared to some of the stereotypical or simple representations of people. After each person has had an opportunity to share his or her perceptions, discuss similarities or differences in the collages. Are you surprised by some of your classmates views of themselves? How would their collages be different if you created one for them? How do others see you? To what extent do you feel that you are a "victim" of the images of women and men in the media?

Sullivan and O'Connor (1988) found that women's role portrayals in magazine advertisements have changed significantly, particularly between 1970 and 1983. Although, as in prior research, more men than women are shown in the advertisements, the women pictured represent a wide range of roles. Women are no longer portrayed as unable to make important decisions, dependent on men, or primarily sex objects. Advertisements are beginning to show multifaceted women and men who appear to be equally proficient at managing home and career.

In 1971 one writer suggested that advertised products appear to have a strong sexual cathexis (emotional appeal or connotation), which means that some products are viewed as masculine or feminine. For example, he cites automobiles as a masculine product (Stuteville, 1971). Nine years later, an article refuted that claim, stating that over 1/3 of the new cars purchased are bought by women for themselves, that life insurance purchased by women rose 100 percent in ten years, that women buy 2/3 of all wine, and that women control 80 percent of all spending, saving, and investing (*Advertising Age,* 1980).

In 1985 Bernstein reported in *Advertising Age* that across the country women led men as advertising majors by two to one. The article suggests that this dominance by women should have an effect on the industry and on future ads.

What do women prefer in advertisements? They are highly critical of traditional sex roles (Lundstrom & Sciglimpaglia, 1977; Witkowski, 1975). About 34 percent of women, as opposed to 22 percent of men, agree that advertisers use too much sex appeal in advertisements (Sexton & Haberman, 1974). Interestingly, pro-feminist, anti-feminist, and neutral-feminist women do not disagree about the portrayal of women in advertising (Duker & Tucker, 1977).

Men and women do not appear to disagree sharply on advertising either. Rossi and Rossi (1985) found that both men and women were aware of sexism in ads, although men rated the sexism in advertisements less than women. Both men and women prefer ad models who are attractive, although men appear to prefer the model to be female, while women prefer the model to be male (Baker & Churchill, 1977). The preference of a group of men in another study may provide a suggestion to advertisers. The researcher found that men preferred ads using a male and female rather than males only or females only (Kanungo & Johar, 1975). A man and a woman of similar status engaging in similar work on the job and at home might be most useful in minimizing sexism as well as in selling goods and services.

Popular music

Lyrics

Popular music is an important mass medium that has not received much attention from communication researchers. This is unfortunate since, as Stewart (1986) notes, popular music reaches an extremely large audience for extensive periods. For example, college students who monitor their recorded music exposure usually find they are exposed to music over one-half their waking hours.

Women have been stereotypically presented in the lyrics of popular music. Basically, women in pop music are idealized, presented as evil temptresses, or seen as victims (Butruille, 1983). However, one study of Cyndi Lauper's song, "Girls Just Want to Have Fun," indicates that women can break away from stereotypes to be active and in control. Peterson (1987) states that Lauper's song and video opens up previously male-defined public spheres for women's use. However, Peterson cautions against putting too much stock in one song since women are used and abused in much of rock music.

Stewart (1986) suggests that when women are in control of the material they record, we will hear different themes in rock music. Stewart cites Patti Smith, Chrissie Hynde, and Marianne Faithfull, among others, as examples of independent women rockers. Of course, none of these singers are mainstream artists.

Music videos

Some research on music videos indicates that women are depicted as sex objects and often the victims of violence (i.e., Hansen & Hansen, 1988; Sherman & Dominick 1986). However, in somewhat the same vein as Stewart (1986) and Peterson (1987), Lewis (1987) argues that some music videos produced for female singers are not sexist or violent, but rather, celebrate women. Lewis points to "Girls Just Want to Have Fun," "Love Is a Battlefield," and "What's Love Got to Do With It?" as examples of music videos that reject sexism and address a female audience "through forceful references to female experience and desire" (p. 356).

Television

Television is widely viewed by people of all ages. Young children may view as many as forty hours of television per week (Singer & Zuckerman, 1981).

Regrettably, television viewing is correlated with a belief in social stereotypes (Tan, 1982). That is, the more people view television, the more they tend to believe in social stereotypes (Zemach and Cohen, 1986). Similarly, television is capable of teaching sex-role stereotypes. One study which examined children in grades 1, 3, 5, and 7 studied the effects of light, moderate, and heavy television viewing. The television programs the children watched depicted male role models in greater numbers than female role models. To a greater extent, men were portrayed as members of the work force and had a larger diversity of occupations and higher job status than women. Women were rarely shown working outside the home. The light viewers' sterotypic responses increased with age (McGhee & Frueh, 1980). Sex-role stereotypes appear to be learned more easily by persons who watch television to a greater extent. Consistently, the study reveals people who are heavy viewers may be more conservative, homebound individuals.

Images of women and men in programming

What are some of the images of men and women presented on television? Women are generally portrayed in roles of diminishment and subjugation (Dohrmann, 1975; Lichter, Lichter & Rothman, 1986.) Men are portrayed as strong, assertive, and work-oriented; women are viewed as weak, passive, and family-oriented (Downs & Gowan, 1980). Men are depicted as possessing power and status and having a greater expectation of both rewards and punishment, (Downs & Gowan, 1980). It appears that situation comedies provide a more favorable image of women and blacks than do crime dramas (Lemon, 1977).

Men generally outnumber women on television by more than two to one. Seventy percent of the males shown on T.V. are portrayed as mature adults, while only a minority of the females are portrayed in this fashion. From 1975 to 1985 women portrayed 8 percent of all doctors, 18 percent of all executives, 25 percent of all lawyers, and 63 percent of all teachers seen on television (Lichter, Lichter & Rothmann, 1986).

In 1985 *Broadcasting* magazine criticized the current television season for its portrayal of women. *Broadcasting* noted that women on television were often invisible or victimized. "In this same article they stated that "When female characters aren't being drugged, kidnapped, tortured or murdered they are often reacting to threats against their safety or being portrayed as helpless and in need of protection" (p. 54). Lebino (1986) concurs and criticizes "Miami Vice" for its unsavory depiction of women as hookers and victims. Jarvis (1984) states that for every step forward women take in television portrayals, they take one or two steps backward.

In addition, Mulac, Bradac, and Mann (1985) found that characters on children's television shows speak in an exaggeratedly sex-stereotypic manner. Mulac et al. found that over 70 percent of the characters could be accurately labeled male or female by simply reading their dialogue. This, they observe, is very different from naturally occurring language. Mulac and his associates have found that untrained observers cannot successfully guess the sex of a speaker based on reading a transcript of "real-world" language.

In their study Mulac et al. found the following "gender-linked" differences to discriminate between male and female children's television characters:

> Female characters, in contrast to males, tended to use longer sentences, more verbs indicating a lack of certainty or assuredness ('I suppose,' 'It seems to me,'), more concrete (as opposed to abstract) nouns, more polite words or phrases ('please,' 'yes ma'am'), more verbs, more adverbial phrases beginning sentences ('In the summer, it rains a lot.'), and more adjectives showing judgment ('beautiful picture,' 'silly puppy').
>
> Male characters were distinguished by their greater use of vocalized pauses ('It's,' 'uhm,' 'ah'), verbs indicating action ('ran,' 'shouted'), justifications for behavior ('I ran because...'), verbs in the present tense ('He likes to count'), subordinating conjunctions ('there, next to the...'), and grammatical errors ('I don't have none') (pp. 500–501).

Furthermore, Mulac et al. found these differences, which you might remember from our discussion of verbal codes, were 200 percent greater for television characters than for real-world speakers.

However, not all researchers agree that the portrayal of women on T.V. is completely bleak. Many point to strides that have been made. Levine (1987) notes the strong women characters on "L.A. Law." *Glamour* (1986) declares that the 1986 T.V. season marks the end of the empty-headed female star. *Women and Language* (1986) cites a *New York Times* article observing that Tyne Daly and Terry Louise Fisher examine "Cagney and Lacey" scripts to eliminate what they call diminishing words, so that the character of "Mary Beth Lacey will say, 'Let's go' instead of 'Let's *just* go,' speaking to the women of America in the strongest voice possible" (p. 7).

Petersen-Perlman (1989) argues that the women in contemporary domestic sitcoms are portrayed as professional and independent. She asserts that these positive portrayals of women have also affected the portrayals of men. Men on sitcoms are now often assumed to be equal partners with their wives as part of a dual-career lifestyle. She cites "The Cosby Show," "Growing Pains," "Family Ties" and "Roseanne" as shows featuring a lot of husband-wife interaction and joint problem solving.

Soap operas present a view of reality and of men and women quite different from that shown on prime-time television. While the latter may focus on sexual themes (Greenberg, Graef & Atkin, 1980), there is more sexual activity and more sexual references in afternoon soap operas (Greenberg, Abelman & Neuendorf, 1981).

Women in soap operas tend to be much younger than the general population, and they are usually acted upon, raped, divorced, abandoned, misunderstood, given drugs, and/or attacked by unusual and mysterious diseases (Cassata, Skill & Boadu, 1979; Kinzer, 1973; Soares, 1978). Professional women are portrayed sympathetically, and women as well as men work outside the home at professional jobs (i.e., law and medicine). In general, women and men are presented as professional equals (Modleski, 1982). Women tend to be underrepresented in soap operas, just as they are underrepresented in prime-time television, although they appear more frequently in the afternoon (Downing, 1974). Women often provide advice and direction on "feminine" matters, and in soap operas they relate to each other as family members (Fine, 1981).

Men are portrayed in soap operas as more active and less tied to relationships than women. Most directives or orders of instruction are centered on "masculine" topics stated by men. Men maintain control of the action through the accentuation of the role of the medical doctor. The medical profession is by far the best-represented male occupation on these programs, followed by the legal profession (Downing, 1974).

Conversation for both women and men in soap operas tends to center on marriage, family, romantic relationships, professional relationships, personalities, health, deviant behavior, and routine business matters. Many of the conversations are "small talk." The topics tend to be conventional and stereotypic. However, the conversational styles in soap operas are similar to real conversational patterns. (Fine, 1981).

Soap operas appeal to many people because their stories never end. Modleski (1982) observes that the narrative of a soap opera "makes anticipation of an end an end in itself. Soap operas invest exquisite pleasure in the central condition of a woman's life: waiting" (p. 88). Despite the popularity of the soaps, social scientists have demonstrated little interest in soap-opera content. Downing (1974) made a content analysis of the soaps and concluded that because soap operas are directed toward women, they are not considered seriously by critics and individuals in the entertainment world. However, Press (1986) notes that with the recent publication of three scholarly books on soap operas, critics are perhaps beginning to take women's cultural forms more seriously.

Cartoons on television have also been examined. Both men and women are victims of sex-role stereotyping in cartoons. In general, women in most cartoons tend to be nonexistent or in need of help from men. The exclusion of women appears to be particularly pronounced in the chase-and-comic-fall type of cartoon, such as "Bugs Bunny." When females are depicted in cartoons, they are usually in need of male assistance. Some cartoons with teaching concepts as their purpose include active females, but the males still far outnumber the females (Streicher, 1974).

Television commercials

Television commercials have been as thoroughly examined as advertisements in print journalism. Some conclusions are consistent over time. First, commercial narrators are predominately male; the percentage of male voice-overs ranges from 87 percent (Courtner, 1974) to 91 percent (Bretl & Cantor, 1988) to 93 percent (O'Donnell, 1978).

Second, men have a wide variety of professions, while women are typically portrayed as housewives (Verna, 1975; Busby, 1975; Schneider & Schneider, 1976; Courtney, 1974) or without a known occupation (Bretl & Cantor, 1988). When both men and women have occupations, the men's are accorded higher status (Bretl & Cantor, 1988).

Third, men and women tend to sell different products on television commercials. Men in their roles as medical doctors prescribe medicine (Mant, 1975); they also sell automobiles, travel packages, alcoholic beverages (Busby, 1975), and gas and oil (Time, 1973). Women sell products for women (Marecek Piliavin, Fitzsimmons, Krogh, Leader & Trudell, 1978), hygiene products (Courtney 1974), female cosmetics (Time, 1973), and domestic products (O'Donnell & O'Donnell, 1978). To sell these goods, women demonstrate the product's use by performing domestic tasks. Men simply make claims about their products (Courtney, 1974). Generally speaking, men tend to advertise products used outside the home, while women sell products used inside the home.

Finally, males and females have different personality attributes in commercials. Women are portrayed as more dependent, passive, unauthoritative, emotionally unstable, less career-oriented, less knowledgeable (Verna, 1975) and ill more frequently (Mant, 1975). On the other hand, men are pictured as more ambitious, dominant, braver, and stronger (Busby, 1975). The National Organization for Women examined television advertisements and found that women were portrayed as "domestic adjuncts" (37.5%), "demeaned housewives" (22.7%), "dependent upon men" (33.9%), "submissive" (24.3%), "sex objects" (16.7%), "unintelligent" (17.1%), and "housegod functionaries" (42.6%) (Duker & Tucker, 1977).

Some changes are occurring in television commercials. For example, the age of the characters has changed. In the past, young adult characters were used to sell products. Today, there is a shift to persons of 50 years and older. At the same time, women continue to be depicted as younger than their male counterparts in commercials where they appear together (Schneider & Schneider, 1979).

Males and females now occur approximately as often as primary character in prime-time television commercials (Bretl & Cantor, 1988). This represents a gradual shift from earlier studies which showed that males were more often the main characters in commercials (McArthur & Resko, 1975). In addition to being present in relatively equal numbers, women and men are also presented in similar fashion in terms of the arguments they use to promote products (Bretl & Cantor, 1988).

As a result of these and other studies, it is obvious that changes should be made in the roles of women and men on television commercials. First, the roles should be altered due to their negative impact on children's understanding of sex-role behavior. As discussed above, children view a great deal of television, and this is one way they learn about sex roles. Young children believe that commercials are more real than older children do. When children were told that the commercials were real, they had attitude changes toward women, reflecting the traditional role models they viewed (Pingree, 1978). In other words, children who believe that commercials are real begin to accept the more traditional depictions of women and men as accurate.

Television commercials should change to give advertisers a larger market. Social changes are occurring that affect female and male behavior. Since people are becoming more open to new ideas, advertisers may be able to respond to the broadening of markets without excluding old-market segments (Scheibe, 1979). For instance, depicting men drinking tea or depicting women drinking beer will probably broaden the tea and beer markets without causing losses in their current patronage. As you observe television commercials that interrupt your favorite programs in the next few days, consider some of the study findings presented here.

Conclusions

In this chapter we considered the images of women and men in the media. We learned that the portrayal of women and men in newspapers, magazines, print advertisements, popular music, and on television is not always accurate. Women are generally under-represented, and both women and men are portrayed in narrow sex roles. However, these images are changing to depict real women and men in their complex, evolving roles. Bias toward or against either sex is injurious to both men and women. Stereotyping, or oversimplifying the roles women and men play, may have a variety of negative outcomes. Altering the sex-role stereotyping occurring in the media is a complex process. To the extent men dominate the media and media are viewed as ways of reflecting rather than changing society, the problems related to sex-role stereotyping will persist.

Epilogue

In this book we have tried to synthesize the research findings relevant to gender and communication issues. This has often been a difficult task because researchers have approached their questions from a variety of perspectives with a range of biases and unspoken assumptions. Researchers who believe they will find biologically based differences between men and women will probably produce different findings from researchers who have other expectations. Kramarae (1981) writes, "scientific statements about gender are made to fit the changing 'needs' and myths about society. . . . Social scientific research is not impersonal, apolitical, and factual, but interpretative (p. vi)." Therefore, you have observed some contradictions among the findings surveyed in this text. Despite these complicating factors, there are enough common findings for us to make some generalizations about the topics of gender and communication, at least from our perspective as researchers with our own set of assumptions about these issues.

First, the very presence of change indicates that gender and communication are inextricably entwined. The variety of findings and approaches illustrate that gender is not a biological given. Gender is socially constructed, often through communication behaviors. Most of our information and knowledge about ourselves and others comes from verbal and nonverbal cues. Further, much of our communication behavior is filtered through the lens of gender. We make decisions about what to say, how to interpret what we have heard, etc., based on our understanding of gender.

Second, we believe that communication is a process. Thus, gender can also be seen in a process fashion. Both are characterized by some change and movement. Certainly your parents and grandparents assumed different sex-role behaviors than the ones you may be enacting today. The change we see is not always linear, forward movement. For example, women in the 1930s had more political clout and visibility than women in the 1950s. Nonetheless, communication and gender are not static.

A third generalization that emerges from our examination of the literature is that men and women probably behave more similarly than differently. In terms of the aggregate, that is all men and all women, the average manner of communicating is very similar. In fact, there are more differences intragroup (among women alone or among men alone) than intergroup (between women and men). In terms of many of the communication behaviors discussed in the book, men and women are not radically different.

However, three areas of difference between women and men do emerge from our review. These differences are not behavioral, although they may affect people's behaviors. One factor that separates women and men is expectations. Several studies have made the point that people perceive differences between the sexes where, in point of fact, there are none. We often believe we see differences because we expect to see them, and even today, people still expect that men and women will behave differently from one another.

A second area of difference concerns the reasons and motivations men and women have for their behaviors. As Gilligan (1982) points out, though men and women may make the same decision, the moral reasoning supporting that decision may be quite different. In a similar vein, we have noted that while men and women may enact similar communication behaviors, the rules and reasons guiding those behaviors may differ. This can cause problems for both women and men, especially in intimate contexts.

Finally, we observed that the images we see in the media and hear in our language portray men and women very differently. Usually these differences put women at a disadvantage, especially in public contexts. If women are consistently portrayed as weaker, less intelligent, and more devious than men, they cannot be expected to behave professionally and competently in the workforce.

We have concluded that the differences we perceive, the different rules we have learned, and the different images we are exposed to are more damaging to men and women than any differences in our behavior. Throughout this book we have suggested that behavioral flexibility is one individual remedy for some of these problems. Behavioral flexibility suggests situational sensitivity and allows both women and men to focus on appropriateness rather than stereotypical consistency. As we try to adopt new behaviors and understand the complexities of the relationship between gender and communication, we should continue testing behavioral flexibility as a satisfying approach. Moreover, we must continue to explore the full spectrum of possibilities for change. We live in a time of choices, and our goal should be to make our own choices as informed as possible.

References

Abbey, A., C. Cozzarelli, K. McLaughlin, and R. Harnish. "The Effects of Clothing and Dyad Sex Composition on Perceptions of Sexual Intent: Do Women and Men Evaluate these Clues Differently?" *Journal of Applied Social Psychology,* 17 (1987): 108–126.

Adamsky, Cathryn. "Changes in Pronominal Usage in a Classroom Situation." *Psychology of Women Quarterly* 5 (1981): 773–779.

Addington, David W. "The Relationship of Selected Vocal Characteristics to Personality Perception." *Speech Monographs* 35 (1968): 492–503.

Adler, Ronald and Neil Towne. *Looking Out/Looking In.* New York: Holt, Rinehart, and Winston, 1978.

Alberti, Robert E., and Michael L. Emmons. *Your Perfect Right.* San Luis Obispo, California: Impact Publishers, Inc., 1974.

Albright, D. G., and A. F. Chang. "An Examination of How One's Attitudes Toward Women Are Reflected in One's Defensiveness and Self-Esteem." *Sex Roles* 2 (1976): 195–198.

Aldous, Joan, ed. *Two Paychecks: Life in Dual-Earner Families.* Beverly Hills, California: Sage Publications, 1982.

Allen, J. L. "Male Sex Roles and Epithets for Ethnic Women in American Slang." *Sex Roles* 11 (1984): 43–50.

Alvares, Kenneth M. and Dennis M. Lee. "Effects of Sex on Descriptions and Evaluations of Supervisory Behavior in a Simulated Industrial Setting." *Journal of Applied Psychology* 64 (1977): 405–410.

Ambert, A., and M. Ambert. *Sex Structure.* Don Mills: Longman, Canada, 1976.

Amerikaner, Martin. "Self-Disclosure: A Study of Verbal and Coverbal Intimacy." *The Journal of Psychology* 104 (1980): 221–229.

Amidjaja, Imat R., and W. Edgar Vinacke. "Achievement, Nurturance, and Competition in Male and Female Triads." *Journal of Personality and Social Psychology* 2 (1965): 447–451.

Anderson, Judith, Beatrice Schultz, and Constance C. Staley. "Training in Argumentativeness: New Hope for Nonassertive Women." *Women's Studies in Communication* 10 (1987): 58–66.

Anderson, P. A., and K. Liebowitz. "The Development and Nature of the Construct Touch Avoidance." *Environmental Psychology and Nonverbal Behavior* 3 (1978): 89–106.

Andrews, Patricia Hayes. "Upward Directed Persuasive Communication and Attribution of Success and Failure: Toward an Understanding of the Role of Gender." Paper presented at the annual conference of the Central States Speech Association, Indianapolis, Indiana, 1985.

Aneshensel, Carol S. and Bernard C. Rosen. "Sex Differences in the Educational-Occupational Expectation Process." *Journal of Social Forces* 57 (1978): 164–186.

Archer, Richard L., and John H. Berg. "Disclosure Reciprocity and Its Limits: A Reactance Analysis." *Journal of Experimental Social Psychology* 14 (1978): 527–540.

Archer, R. L., and J. A. Burleson. "The Effects of Timing of Self-Disclosure on Attraction and Reciprocity." *Journal of Personality and Social Psychology* 38 (1980): 120–130.

Argyle, Michael. *Bodily Communication.* New York: International Universities Press, 1975.

Argyle, Michael and Janet Dean. "Eye Contact, Distance and Affiliation. *Sociometry* 28 (1965): 289–304.

Argyle, Michael, Mansur Lalljee, and Mark Cook. "The Effects of Visibility on Interaction in a Dyad." *Human Relations* 21 (1968): 3–17.

Aries, Elizabeth. "Verbal and Nonverbal Behavior in Single-Sex and Mixed-Sex Groups." *Psychological Reports* 51 (1982): 127–134.

Arkkelin, Daniel, and Rosemary Simmons. "The 'Good Manager': Sex-typed, Androgynous, or Likable?" *Sex-Roles* 12 (1985): 1187–1197.

Arntson, Paul, and Lynn H. Turner. Sex Role Socialization: Children's Enactments of their Parents' Behaviors in a Regulative and Interpersonal Context. *Western Journal of Speech Communication,* 51 (1987): 304–316.

Ashby, Marylee Stull, and Bruce C. Wittmaier. "Attitude Changes in Children after Exposure to Stories about Women in Traditional or Nontraditional Occupations." *Journal of Educational Psychology* 70 (1978): 945–949.

Ashworth, Clark, Gail Furman, Alan Chaikin, and Valerian Derlega. "Physiological Responses to Self-Disclosure." *Journal of Humanistic Psychology* 16 (1976): 71–80.

Atkinson, Donna L. "Names and Titles: Maiden Name Retention and the Use of Ms." *Women and Language,* 10 (1987): 37.

Austin, David W. "Nonverbal Cues Influencing Client and Nonclient Perception of Counselors." Unpublished doctoral dissertation, University of Wyoming, 1973.

Ayres, Joe. "Relationship Stages and Sex as Factors in Topic Dwell Time." *Western Journal of Speech Communication* 44 (1980): 253–260.

Bailey, Roger C., and James P. Price. "Perceived Physical Attractiveness in Married Partners of Long and Short Duration." *The Journal of Psychology* 99 (1978): 155–161.

Baird, John E. "Sex Differences in Group Communication: A Review of Relevant Research." *The Quarterly Journal of Speech* 62 (1976): 179–192.

Baird, John E., and Patricia Hayes Bradley. "Styles of Management and Communication: A Comparative Study of Men and Women." *Communication Monographs* 46 (1979): 101–111.

Baker, Michael J., and Gilbert A. Churchill, Jr. "The Impact of Physically Attractive Models on Advertising Evaluations." *Journal of Marketing Research* 14 (1977): 538–555.

Ball, Joe M. "The Relationship between the Ability to Speak Effectively and the Primary Mental Abilities, Verbal Comprehension and General Reasoning." *Speech Monographs* 25 (1958): 285–290.

Balswick, Jack, and Christine Proctor Avertt. "Differences in Expressiveness: Gender, Interpersonal Orientation, and Perceived Parental Expressiveness as Contributing Factors." *Journal of Marriage and the Family* 39 (1977): 121–127.

Balswick, Jack O., and James W. Balkwell. "Self-Disclosure to Same- and Opposite-Sex Parents: An Empirical Test of Insights from Role Theory." *Sociometry* 40 (1977): 282–286.

Barker, Larry L. "Irrelevant Factors and Speech Evaluation." *Southern Speech Journal* 32 (1966): 10–18.

Barker, M., S. Peltier, and P. Wolleat. "Understanding Dual Career Couples." *The Personnel and Guidance Journal* (1981): 14–18.

Barnes, M. L., and D. M. Buss. "Sex Differences in the Interpersonal Behavior of Married Couples." *Journal of Personality and Social Psychology,* 48 (1985): 654–661.

Barnlund, Dean C. "A Transactional Model of Communication." In *Foundations of Communication Theory.* Ed. by Kenneth K. Sereno and C. David Mortensen. New York: Harper & Row, 1970.

Barrios, Billy A., L. Claire Corbitt, J. Philip Estes, and Jeff S. Topping. "Effect of a Social Stigma on Interpersonal Distance." *The Psychological Record* 26 (1976): 343–348.

Barth, Robert J., and Bill N. Kinder. "A Theoretical Analysis of Sex Differences in Same-sex Friendships." *Sex Roles* 19 (1988): 349–363.

Bartol, Kathryn M. "Male Versus Female Leaders: The Effect of Leader Need for Dominance on Follower Satisfaction." *Academy of Management Journal* 17 (1974): 225–232.

Bartol, Kathryn M. "The Sex Structuring of Organizations: A Search for Possible Causes." *Academy of Management Review* 3 (1978): 805–813.

Bartol, Kathryn M., and D. Anthony Butterfield. "Sex Effects in Evaluating Leaders." *Journal of Applied Psychology* 61 (1976): 446–454.

Bartol, Kathryn M., and Max S. Wortman, Jr. "Male Versus Female Leaders: Effects on Perceived Leader Behavior and Satisfaction in a Hospital." *Personnel Psychology* 28 (1975): 533–547.

Bartol, Kathryn M., and Max S. Wortman, Jr. "Sex Effects in Leader Behavior Self-Descriptions and Job Satisfaction." *Journal of Psychology* 94 (1976): 177–183.

Basow, Susan A. *Gender Stereotypes: Traditions and Alternatives.* Monterey, CA: Brooks/Cole Publishing Company, 1986.

Basow, Susan A., and Nancy T. Silberg. "Student Evaluation of College Professors: Are Female and Male Professors Rated Differently?" Paper presented to the Eastern Psychological Association Convention, Boston, 1986.

Bate, Barbara. *Communication and the Sexes.* New York: Harper and Row, Publishers, 1988.

Bate, Barbara. "Nonsexist Language in Transition." *Journal of Communication* 28 (Winter 1978): 139–149.

Bate, Barbara, and Lois S. Self. "The Rhetoric of Career Success Books for Women." *Journal of Communication* 33 (Spring 1983): 149–165.

Bauer, Richard, and James H. Turner. "Betting Behavior in Sexually Homogeneous and Heterogeneous Groups." *Psychological Reports* 34 (1974): 251–258.

Baxter, L. A. "Self-Disclosure as a Relationship Disengagement Strategy: An Exploratory Investigation." *Human Communication Research* 5 (1979): 215–222.

Baxter, L. A., and William W. Wilmot. "Taboo Topics in Close Relationships." *Journal of Social and Personal Relationships* 2 (1985a): 253–269.

Baxter, Leslie. "Gender Differences in the Heterosexual Relationship Rules Embedded in Brush-up Encounters." *Journal of Social and Personal Relationships* 3 (1986): 289–306.

Baxter, Leslie A., and William W. Wilmot. "Interaction Characteristics of Disengaging, Stable, and Growing Relationships." Edited by R. Gilmour and S. W. Duck. *The Emerging Field of Personal Relationships* Hillsdale, N.J.: Erlbaum, 1985b.

Baxter, Leslie A., and William W. Wilmot. " 'Secret Tests': Social Strategies for Acquiring Information about the State of the Relationship." *Human Communication Research* 11 (1984): 171–201.

Bedeian, Arthur G., Archilles A. Armenakis, and B. Wayne Kemp. "Relation of Sex to Perceived Legitimacy of Organizational Influence." *The Journal of Psychology* 94 (1976): 93–99.

Beekman, Susan J. "Sex Differences in Nonverbal Behavior." Paper, Michigan State University, 1973.

Bell, Nancy J., and William Carver. "A Reevaluation of Gender Label Effects: Expectant Mothers' Responses to Infants." *Child Development* 51 (1980): 925–927.

Bellinger, D. C., and J. B. Gleason. "Sex Differences in Parental Directives to Young Children." *Sex Roles* 8 (1982): 1123–1139.

Bem, Sandra. "The Measurement of Psychological Androgyny." *Journal of Consulting and Clinical Psychology* 42 (1974): 155–162.

Bem, Sandra. "Sex-role Adaptability: One Consequence of Psychological Androgyny." *Journal of Personality and Social Psychology* 31 (1975): 634–643.

Bem, Sandra L., and Daryl J. Bem. "Does Sex-biased Job Advertising 'Aid and Abet' Sex Discrimination?" *Journal of Applied Social Psychology* 3 (1973): 6–18.

Benton, Alan A. "Reactions to Demands to Win from an Opposite Sex Opponent." *Journal of Personality* 41 (1973): 430–442.

Berger, Charles, and R. Calabrese. "Some Explorations in Initial Interaction and Beyond: Toward a Developmental Theory of Interpersonal Communication." *Human Communication Research* 1 (1975): 98–112.

Berger, C. R., R. R. Gardner, G. W. Clatterbuck, and L. S. Schulman. "Perceptions of Information Sequencing in Relationship Development." *Human Communication Research* 3 (1976): 29–46.

Berman, Phyllis W., and Vicki L. Smith. "Gender and Situational Differences in Children's Smiles, Touch and Proxemics." *Sex Roles* 10 (1984): 347–356.

Bernstein, S. "Women Aim to Take Over." *Advertising Age*, 16 Sept. 1985, 18.

Berryman, Cynthia L., and James R. Wilcox. "Attitudes Toward Male and Female Speech: Experiments on the Effects of Sex-Typical Language." *The Western Journal of Speech Communication* 44 (1980): 50–59.

Berryman-Fink, Cynthia. "Male and Female Managers' Views of the Communication Skills and Training Needs of Women in Management." *Public Personnel Management* 14 (1985): 307–313.

Berryman-Fink, Cynthia, and Virginia E. Wheeless. "Male and Female Perceptions of Women as Managers." *Communication, Gender and Sex Roles in Diverse Interaction Contexts*. Edited by Lea Stewart and Stella Ting-Toomey. Norwood, N.J.: Ablex Publishers, 1987.

Berscheid, Ellen, and Elaine Hatfield Walster. *Interpersonal Attraction*. Reading, Mass.: Addison-Wesley, 1969.

Beuf, Ann. "Doctor, Lawyer, Household Drudge." *Journal of Communication* 24 (Spring 1974): 142–145.

Bianchi, B. D., and R. Bakeman. "Sex-typed Affiliation Preferences Observed in Pre-Schoolers: Traditional and Open School Differences." *Child Development* 49 (1978): 910–912.

Biles, George E., and Holly A. Pryatel. "Myths, Management and Women." *Personnel Journal* 57 (1978): 572–577.

Bird, Caroline, with Sara Welles Briller. *Born Female: The High Cost of Keeping Women Down*. Rev. ed. New York: McKay, 1970.

Birdwhistell, Ray L. "Masculinity and Femininity as Display." *Kinesics and Context*. Philadelphia: University of Pennsylvania Press, 1970.

Blaubergs, M. "An Analysis of Classic Arguments against Changing Sexist Language." *Women Studies International Quarterly* 3 (1980): 135–147.

Bleda, Paul R. and Sharon Estee Bleda. "Effects of Sex and Smoking on Reactions to Spatial Invasion at a Shopping Mall." *The Journal of Social Psychology* 104 1978): 311–312.

Blodgett, Nancy. "I Don't think That Ladies Should Be Lawyers." *ABA Journal* (Dec. 1, 1986): 48–53.

Bloom, L. Z., K. Coburn, and J. Pearlman. *The New Assertive Woman*. New York: Delacorte, 1975.

Bochner, Arthur. "On the Efficacy of Openness in Close Relationships." In *Communication Yearbook* 5. Ed. by Michael Burgoon. New Brunswick, New Jersey: Transaction Books, 1982.

Bochner, Arthur P., and Clifford W. Kelly. "Interpersonal Competence: Rationale, Philosophy, and Implementation of a Conceptual Framework." *Speech Teacher* 23 (1974): 279–301.

Bock, Douglas J., Jeri L. P. Butler, and E. Hope Bock. "The Impact of Sex of the Speaker, Sex of the Rater and Profanity Type of Language Trait Errors in Speech Evaluation: A Test of the Rating Error Paradigm." *The Southern Speech Communication Journal* 49 (1984): 177–186.

Bond, J., and W. Vinacke. "Coalition in Mixed Sex Triads." *Sociometry* 24 (1961): 61–75.

Bormann, Ernest G., Jerie Pratt, and Linda Putnam. "Power, Authority, and Sex: Male Response to Female Leadership." *Communication Monographs* 45 (1978): 119–155.

Bostrom, Robert N., and Carol L. Bryant. "Factors in the Retention of Information Presented Orally: The Role of Short-term Listening." *Western Journal of Speech Communication* 44 (1980): 137–145.

Bostrom, R. N., and A. P. Kemp. "Type of Speech, Sex of Speaker, and Sex of Subject as Factors Influencing Persuasion." *Central States Speech Journal* 20 (1969): 245–252.

Bostrom, Robert N., and Enid S. Waldhart. "Components in Listening Behavior: The Role of Short-term Memory." *Human Communication Research* 6 (1980): 221–227.

Bottigheimer, Ruth B. *Grimms' Bad Girls and Bold Boys: The Moral and Social Vision of the Tales*. New Haven, Conn.: Yale University Press, 1987.

Bouchez, Colette. "Male vs. Female." *Chicago Tribune*, 7 (Oct. 1987): 23–24, sec. 7.

Bowlby, John. *Maternal Care and Mental Health*. Geneva: World Health Organization, 1952.

Bradac, James J., Michael R. Hemphill, and Charles H. Tardy. "Language Style on Trial: Effects of 'Powerful' and 'Powerless' Speech on Judgments of Victims and Villains." *Western Journal of Speech Communication* 45 (1981): 327–341.

Bradac, J. J., C. H. Tardy, and L. A. Hosman. "Disclosure Styles and a Hint at Their Genesis." *Human Communication Research* 6 (1980): 228–238.

Bradley, Patricia Hayes. "The Folk-Linguistics of Women's Speech: An Empirical Examination." *Communication Monographs* 48 (1981): 73–90.

Bradley, Patricia Hayes. "Sex, Competence and Opinion Deviation: An Expectation States Approach." *Communication Monographs* 47 (1980): 101–110.

Bradshaw, J. L., and N. C. Nettleton. *Human Cerebral Asymmetry*. Englewood Cliffs, N.J.: Prentice-Hall, 1983.

Brain, Robert. *The Decorated Body*. New York: Harper & Row, 1979.

Bralowe, Mary. "Advertising World's Portrayal of Women is Starting to Shift." *The Wall Street Journal* (October 28, 1982): 33.

Brehm, S. S., L. Powell, and J. S. Coke. "The Effects of Empathic Instructions upon Donating Behavior: Sex Differences in Young Children." *Sex Roles* 10 (1984): 405–416.

Breisinger, Gary D. "Sex and Empathy, Reexamined." *Journal of Counseling Psychology* 23 (1976): 289–290.

Bremer, Teresa Hargrave, and Michelle Andrisin Wittig. "Fear of Success: A Personality Trait or a Response to Occupational Deviance and Role Overload?" *Sex Roles* 6 (1980): 27–46.

Brenner, O. C., and John A. Bromer. "Sex Stereotypes and Leader's Behavior as Measured by the Agreement Scale for Leadership Behavior." *Psychological Reports* 48 (1981): 960–962.

Brenner, Otto C., and W. Edgar Vinacke. "Accommodative and Exploitative Behavior of Males vs. Females and Managers versus Nonmanagers as Measured by the Test of Strategy." *Social Psychology Quarterly* 42 (1979): 289–293.

Bretl, Daniel J., and Joanne Cantor. "The Portrayal of Men and Women in U.S. Television Commercials: A Recent Content Analysis and Trends over 15 Years." *Sex Roles* 18 (1988): 595–609.

Bridges, Judith S. "College Females' Perceptions of Adult Roles and Occupational Fields for Women." *Sex Roles* 16 (1987): 591–604.

Brief, Arthur P., and Richard L. Oliver. "Male-Female Difference in Work Attitudes among Retail Sales Managers." *Journal of Applied Psychology* 61 (1976): 526–528.

Briles, J. *Woman to Woman: From Sabotage to Support*. Tak Hills, N.J.: New Horizon Press, 1987.

Brinkmann, E. H. "Programmed Instruction as a Technique for Improving Spatial Visualization." *Journal of Applied Psychology* 50 (1966): 179–184.

"Network TV's Treatment of Women Criticized." *Broadcasting* (1985): 54, 56.

Bronstein, P. "Differences in Mothers' and Fathers' Behaviors to Children: A Cross Cultural Comparison." *Developmental Psychology* 20 (1984): 995–1003.

Brooks, R. "The Relationship between Piagetian Cognitive Development and Cerebral Cognitive Asymmetry." Greeley, Colorado: University of Northern Colorado (1979): (ERIC Document Reproduction Service No. ED 160 224).

Brouwer, Dede, Marinel Gerritsen, and Dorian DeHaan. "Speech Differences between Women and Men: On the Wrong Track?" *Language in Society* 8 (1979): 33–49.

Broverman, Inge K., Donald M. Broverman, Frank E. Clarkson, Paul S. Rosenkrantz, and Susan R. Vogel. "Sex-Role Stereotypes and Clinical Judgements of Mental Health." *Journal of Consulting and Clinical Psychology* 34 (1970): 1–7.

Broverman, Inge K., Susan R. Vogel, Donald M. Broverman, Frank E. Clarkson, and Paul S. Rosenkrantz. "Sex-Role Stereotypes: A Current Appraisal." *Journal of Social Issues* 28 (1972): 59–78.

Brown, Stephen M. "Male versus Female Leaders: A Comparison of Empirical Studies." *Sex Roles* 5 (1979): 595–611.

Brundage, Toni E., Valerian J. Derlega, and Thomas F. Cash. "The Effects of Physical Attractiveness and Need for Approval on Self-Disclosure." *Personality and Social Psychology Bulletin* 3 (1977): 63–66.

Brunner, Claire C., and Lynn A. Phelps. "Interpersonal Communication Competence and Androgyny." Paper presented to the International Communication Association Convention, Acapulco, 1980.

Bryan, A. I., and W. H. Wilke. "Audience Tendencies in Rating Public Speakers." *Journal of Applied Psychology* 26 (1942): 371–381.

Buchli, Virginia, and W. Barnett Pearce. "Listening Behavior in Cooriential States." *Journal of Communication* 24 (Summer 1974): 62–70.

Buck, Ross, Robert E. Miller, and William F. Caul. "Sex, Personality, and Physiological Variables in the Communication of Affect Via Facial Expression." *Journal of Personality and Social Psychology* 30 (1974): 587–596.

Buerkel-Rothfuss, Nancy L., Anita M. Covert, Joanne Keith, and Christine Nelson. "Early Adolescent and Parental Communication Patterns." Paper presented at the annual conference of the Speech Communication Association, Chicago, IL, 1986.

Buffery, A. W. H., and J. A. Gray. "Sex Differences in the Development of Spatial and Linguistic Skills." *Gender Differences: Their Ontogeny and Significance*. Edited by C. Ounsted and D. C. Taylor. Edinburgh: Churchill Livingstone, 1972.

Bugental, Daphne E., Jacques W. Kaswan, Leonore R. Love, and Michael N. Fox. "Child Versus Adult Perception of Evaluative Messages in Verbal, Vocal, and Visual Channels." *Developmental Psychology* 2 (1971): 367–375.

Buhrke, R. A., and D. R. Fuqua. "Sex Differences in Same- and Cross-sex Supportive Relationships." *Sex Roles* 17 (1987): 339–352.

Burge, Penny Lee. "Parental Sex-Role Attitudes Related to Self-Concept and Sex Role-Identity of Pre-School Children." Ph.D. diss., Pennsylvania State University, 1979.

Burggraf, Cynthia S., and Alan L. Sillars. "A Critical Examination of Sex Differences in Marital Communication." *Communication Monographs* 54 (1987): 276–294.

Burgoon, Judee K., David B. Buller, W. Gill Woodall. *Nonverbal Communication: The Unspoken Dialogue.* New York: Harper and Row, Publishers, 1988.

Burgoon, J. K., D. B. Buller, J. L. Hale, and M. A. de Turck. "Relational Messages Associated with Immediacy Behaviors." Paper presented at the International Communication Association Convention, Boston, April 1982.

Burgoon, J. K., and S. B. Jones. "Toward a Theory of Personal Space Expectations and their Violations." *Human Communication Research* 2 (1976): 131–146.

Burgoon, Judee K., and Thomas Saine. *The Unspoken Dialogue: An Introduction to Nonverbal Communication.* Boston, Mass.: Houghton Mifflin Company, 1978.

Burke, Ronald J., Tamara Weir, and Denise Harrison. "Disclosure of Problems and Tensions Experienced by Marital Partners." *Psychological Reports* 38 (1976): 531–542.

Burr, Elizabeth, Susan Dunn, and Norma Farquhar. "Women and the Language of Inequality." *Social Education* 36 (1972): 841–845.

Busby, Linda J. "Sex Role Research on the Mass Media." *Journal of Communication* 25 (Autumn, 1975): 107–131.

Butler, Pamela E. *Self-Assertion for Women.* San Francisco: Harper & Row, 1981.

Butruille, S. "Women in American Popular Song: The Historic Image and the Reality." Paper presented at the annual conference of the Organization for the Study of Communication, Language, and Gender, New Brunswick, N.J., 1983.

Caffrey, J. "Auditing Ability at the Secondary Level." *Education* 75 (1955): 303–310.

Caldwell, George. "Feminist Considerations in Theatrical Design." *Empirical Research in Theatre* 8 (1982): 15–25.

Caldwell, M. A., and L. A. Peplau. "Sex Differences in Same-sex Friendship." *Sex Roles* 8 (1982): 721–732.

Campbell, Karlyn K. "Style and Content in the Rhetoric of Early Afro-American Feminists." *Quarterly Journal of Speech* 72 (1986): 434–445.

Cann, Arnie, and William D. Siegfried. "Sex Stereotypes and the Leadership Role." *Sex Roles* 17 (1987): 401–408.

Cano, L., S. Solomon, and D. Holmes. "Leak of Success: The Influence of Sex, Sex-role Identity, and Components of Masculinity." *Sex Roles* 10 (1984): 341–346.

Cargan, L., and M. Melko. "Is Marriage Good for Your Health?" *Family Perspective* 15 (1981): 107–114.

Cargan, L., and M. Melko. *Singles: Myths and Realities.* Beverly Hills, California: Sage Publications, 1982.

Carmichael, Carl W. "Frustration, Sex, and Persuasibility." *Western Speech* 34 (1970): 300–307.

Carns, Donald E. "Talking about Sex: Notes on First Coitus and the Double Sexual Standard." *Journal of Marriage and the Family* 35 (1973): 677–688.

Carroll, Lewis. *Through the Looking Glass.* New York: Random House, Inc., 1965.

Casciani, J. M. "Influence of Model's Race and Sex on Interviewees' Self-Disclosure." *Journal of Counseling Psychology* 25 (1978): 435–440.

Cash, Thomas F., and Deborah Soloway. "Self-Disclosure Correlates of Physical Attractiveness: An Exploratory Study." *Psychological Reports* 36 (1975): 579–586.

Cassata, Mary B., Thomas D. Skill, and Samuel Osei Boadu. "In Sickness and In Health." *Journal of Communication* 29 (Autumn 1979): 73–81.

Cate, Rodney, and Alan I. Sugarawa. "Sex Role Orientation and Dimensions of Self-esteem among Middle Adolescents." *Sex Roles* 15 (August 1986): 145–158.

Cathcart, Robert, and Gary Gumpert. "I Am a Camera: The Mediated Self." *Communication Quarterly* 34 (1986): 89–102.

Cegala, Donald J. "Interaction Involvement: A Cognitive Dimension of Communicative Competence." *Communication Education* 30 (1981): 109–121.

Cegala, Donald J., and Alan L. Sillars. "Further Examination of Nonverbal Manifestations of Interaction Involvement." *Communication Reports* 2 (1989): 39–47.

Centers, Richard. "The Completion Hypothesis and the Compensatory Dynamic in Intersexual Attraction and Love." *The Journal of Psychology* 82 (1972): 111–126.

Chandler, Theodore A., Bettyanne Cook, and David A. Dugovics. "Sex Differences in Self-reported Assertiveness." *Psychological Reports* 4 (1978): 395–402.

Chassler, Sey. "Men: Listening." *Ms.,* August 1984, 51–53, 98–100.

Chelune, G. J., L. B. Rosenfeld, and E. M. Waring. "Spouse Disclosure Patterns in Distressed and Nondistressed Couples." *American Journal of Family Therapy,* 85 (1986): 352–374.

Chesler, Phyllis. *Women and Madness.* Garden City, N.Y.: Doubleday, 1972.

Chronkite, Ruth. "The Determinants of Spouses Normative Preferences for Family Roles." *Journal of Marriage and the Family* 39 (1977): 575–585.

Cline, Rebecca J., and Karen E. Musolf. "Disclosure as Social Exchange: Anticipated Length of Relationship, Sex Roles, and Disclosure Intimacy." *Western Journal of Speech Communication* 49 (1985): 43–56.

Cohen, David. "The Avid Gazes of Strangers. *Psychology Today* 13 (October 1979): 40–115.

Coles, Ruth J. "Occupations in Regard to Ethnic Groups." *Journal of Vocational Behavior* 14 (1978): 43–45.

Colins, Michael, L. K. Waters, and Carrie Wherry Waters. "Relationships between Sex-role Orientation and Attitudes toward Women as Managers." *Psychological Reports* 45 (1979): 828–830.

Condry, J., and S. Condry. "Sex Differences: A Study of the Eye of the Beholder." *Child Development* 47 (1976): 812–819.

Conger, J. L., and K. A. Dindia. "A Functional Approach to Interruptions." Paper presented at the annual conference of the International Communication Association, Honolulu, Hawaii, May 1985.

Connor, J. M., M. Schackman, and L. A. Serbin. "Sex-related Differences in Response to Practice on a Visual-spatial Test and Generalization to a Related Test." *Child Development* 49 (1978): 24–29.

Connor, Jane M., and Lisa A. Serbin. "Children's Responses to Stories with Male and Female Characters." *Sex Roles* 4 (1978): 637–645.

Cook, Alicia S., Janet J. Fritz, Barbara L. McCornack, and Cris Visperas. "Early Gender Differences in the Functional Usage of Language." *Sex Roles* 12 (1985): 909–915.

Cooper, Pamela J. "Children's Literature: The Extent and Impact of Sexism on Adult Behavior—and Update." Paper presented at the annual Conference of the Organization for the Study of Communication, Language, and Gender, Washington, D.C., 1986.

Cordes, C. "Tent Tilt: Boys Outscore Girls on Both Parts of the SAT." *American Psychological Association Monitor* (1986): 30–31.

Cordua, Glenn D., Kenneth O. McGraw, and Ronald S. Drabman. "Doctor or Nurse: Children's Perception of Sex Typed Occupations." *Child Development* 50 (1979): 590–593.

Courtney, Alice E., and Thomas W. Whipple. "Women in T.V. Commercials." *Journal of Communication* 24 (Spring 1974): 110–117.

Courtney, Alice E., and Sarah Wernick Lockeretz. "A Woman's Place: An Analysis of the Roles Portrayed by Women in Magazine Advertisements." *Journal of Marketing Research* 8 (1971): 92–95.

Courtright, John A., Frank E. Millar, and L. Edna Rogers-Millar. "Domineeringness and Dominance: Replication and Expansion." *Communication Monographs* 46 (1979): 179–192.

Coyne, J. C., R. C. Sherman, and K. O'Brien. "Expletives and Woman's Place." *Sex Roles* 4 (1978): 827–835.

Craig, Jane M., and Carolyn W. Sherif. "The Effectiveness of Men and Women in Problem-solving Groups as a Function of Group Gender Composition." *Sex Roles* 14 (1986): 453–000.

Critelli, Joseph W., and Kathleen M. Dupre. "Self-Disclosure and Romantic Attraction." *The Journal of Social Psychology* 106 (1978): 127–128.

Critelli, Joseph W., and Karl F. Neumann. "An Interpersonal Analysis of Self-Disclosure and Feedback." *Social Behavior and Personality* 6 (1978): 173–177.

Crosby, Faye, and Linda Nyquist. "The Female Register: An Empirical Study of Lakoff's Hypotheses." *Language in Society* 6 (1977): 313–322.

Culbert, S. A. "Trainer Self-Disclosure and Member Growth in Two T-Groups." *Journal of Applied Behavioral Science* 4 (1968): 47–73.

Culley, James D., and Rex Bennett. "Selling Women, Selling Blacks." *Journal of Communication* 26 (1976): 160–174.

Culp, R. E., A. S. Cook, and P. C. Housley. "A Comparison of Observed and Reported Adult-infant Interaction: Effects of Perceived Sex. *Sex Roles* 9 (1983): 475–479.

Currant, Elaine F., Andrew L. Dickson, Howard N. Anderson, and Patricia J. Faulkender. "Sex Role Stereotyping and Assertive Behavior." *Journal of Psychology* 101 (1979): 223–228.

Dalto, C. A., I. Ajzen, and K. J. Kaplan. "Self-Disclosure and Attraction: Effects of Intimacy and Desirability on Beliefs and Attitudes." *Journal of Research in Personality* 13 (1979): 127–138.

Davidson, B., J. Balswick, and C. Halverson. "Affective Self-Disclosure and Marital Adjustment: A Test of Equity Theory." *Journal of Marriage and the Family* 45 (1983): 93–102.

Davidson, L. R., and L. Duberman. "Friendship: Communication and Interfactional Patterns in Same-sex Dyads." *Sex Roles* 8 (1982): 809–822.

Davis, John D. "Effects of Communication About Interpersonal Process on the Evolution of Self-Disclosure in Dyads." *Journal of Personality and Social Psychology* 35 (1977): 31–37.

Davis, John D. "When Boy Meets Girl: Sex Roles and the Negotiation of Intimacy in an Acquaintance Exercise." *Journal of Personality and Social Psychology* 36 (1978): 684–692.

Dawkins, Richard. *The Selfish Gene.* Oxford: Oxford University Press, 1976.

Dawson-Bailey, Cecilia. "Different Treatment for Eating Disorders Offered." *Second Edition* (July 24, 1989): 2.

Day, David R., and Ralph M. Stogdill. "Leader Behavior of Male and Female Supervisors: A Comparative Study." *Personnel Psychology* 25 (1972): 353–360.

Deaux, Kay. "Self-Evaluations of Male and Female Managers." *Sex Roles* 5 (1979): 571–580.

de Courcy, Anne. "Between Us." *Chicago Tribune,* (Jan. 3, 1988): Section 6, p. 4.

De Forest, C., and G. L. Stone. "Effects of Sex and Intimacy Level on Self-Disclosure." *Journal of Counseling Psychology* 27 (1980): 93–96.

De La Zerga, Nancy, and Robert Hopper. "Employment Interviewers' Reactions to Mexican American Speech." *Communication Monographs* 46 (1979): 126–134.

Densmore, Dana. *Speech Is a Form of Thought.* Pittsburgh, PA: KNOW, Inc., 1970.

Derlega, Valerian J., and Alan L. Chaikin. "Privacy and Self-Disclosure in Social Relationships." *Journal of Social Issues* 33 (1977): 102–115.

Derlega, V., B. Winstead, P. Wong, and S. Hunter. "Gender Effects in Initial Encounter: A Case Where Men Exceed Women in Disclosure." *Journal of Social and Personal Relationships* 2 (1985): 25–44.

Detroit Free Press. "We Tend to Be Attracted to Mates Most Like Us." April 20, 1981, sec. D, p. 1.

Deutsch, Francine M., Dorothy Le Baron, and Maury M. Fryer. "What Is in a Smile?" *Psychology of Women Quarterly* 11 (1987): 341–352.

Deutsch, Morton, and Robert M. Kraus. "Studies of Interpersonal Bargaining." *Journal of Conflict Resolution* 6 (1962): 52–76.

Dibble, Harold L. "More on Gender Differences and the Origin of Language." *Current Anthropology* 17 (1976): 744–749.

Dierks-Stewart, K. "The Effects of Protracted Invasion on an Individual's Action Territory." Unpublished Master's Thesis, Bowling Green State University, 1976.

Dierks-Stewart, K. "Sex Differences in Nonverbal Communication: An Alternative Perspective." In *Communication Language and Sex: Proceedings of the First Conference,* ed. Cynthia L. Berryman and Virginia A. Eman. Rowley, Massachusetts: Newbury House Publishers, Inc. 1979, pp. 112–121.

Dillard, J. P., and M. A. Fitzpatrick. "Compliance-gaining in Marital Interaction." *Personality and Social Psychology Bulletin* 11 (1985): 419–433.

Dimond, S. J. *Introducing Neuropsychology.* Springfield, Illinois: Charles C. Thomas, 1978.

Dindia, Kathryn. "The Effects of Sex of Subject and Sex of Partner on Interruptions." *Human Communication Research* (1987): 13, 345–371.

Dipboye, Robert L. "Women as Managers—Stereotypes and Realities." *Survey of Business* (May/June 1975): 22–26.

Dipboyle, Robert L. "Women as Managers—Stereotypes and Realities." *Survey of Business* (May/June 1975): 22–26. *Journal of Vocational Behavior* 13 (1978): 192–203.

Dobris, Catherine A. "In the Year of Big Sister: Toward a Rhetorical Theory Accounting for Gender." Paper presented at the annual conference of the Central States Speech Association, Cincinnati, OH., 1986.

Dohrmann, Rita. "A Gender Profile of Children's Educational T.V." *Journal of Communication* 25 (Autumn 1975): 56–65.

Dooley, D., C. K. Whalen, and J. V. Flowers. "Verbal Response Styles of Children and Adolescents in a Counseling Analog Setting: Effects of Age, Sex, and Labeling." *Journal of Counseling Psychology* 25 (1978): 85–95.

Dosey, Michael A. and Murray Meisels. "Personal Space and Self-Protection." *Journal of Personality and Social Psychology* 11 (1969): 93–97.

Downing, M. "Heroine of the Daytime Serial." *Journal of Communication* 24 (Spring 1974): 130–137.

Downs, Chris A., and Darryl C. Gowan. "Sex Differences in Reinforcement and Punishment on Prime Time Television." *Sex Roles* 6 (1980): 683–694.

Druley, Dawn, Dan Cassriel, and March H. Hollendar. "A Cuddler's Guide to Love." *Self Magazine* (May 1980): 96–100.

Drummond, R. J., W. G. McIntire, and C. W. Ryan. "Stability and Sex Differences on the Coppersmith Self-Esteem Inventory for Students in Grades Two to Twelve." *Psychological Reports* 40 (1977): 943–946.

Dubois, Betty Lou, and Isabel Crouch. "The Question of Tag Questions in Women's Speech: They Don't Really Use More of Them, Do They?" *Language in Society* 4 (1975): 289–294.

Duker, Jacob M., and Lewis R. Tucker. "Women Libbers' Versus Independent Women: A Study of Preferences for Women's Roles in Advertisements." *Journal of Marketing Research* 14 (1977): 469–475.

Duncan, Hugh Dalziel. *Symbols in Society.* New York: Oxford University Press, 1968.

Duncan, Starkey, Jr. "Nonverbal Communication." *Psychological Bulletin* 72 (1969): 118–137.

Duran, Robert, and Virginia Eman Wheeless. "Social Management: Toward a Theory Based Operationalization of Communication Competence." Paper presented at the Speech Communication Association Convention, 1982.

Eakins, Barbara, and Gene Eakins. "Verbal Turn-Taking and Exchanges in Faculty Dialogue." *Papers in Southwest English IV: Proceedings of the Conference on the Sociology of the Languages of American Women.* Ed. by Betty Lou Dubois and Isabel Crouch. San Antonio, TX: Trinity University, 1976.

Eakins, Barbara Westbrook, and R. Gene Eakins. *Sex Differences in Human Communication.* Boston, Mass.: Houghton Mifflin Co., 1978.

Efran, J. S., and A. Broughton. "Effect of Expectancies for Social Approval on Visual Behavior." *Journal of Personality and Social Psychology* 4 (1966): 103–107.

Eichorn, D. H., and N. Bayley. "Growth in Head Circumference from Birth Through Young Adulthood." *Child Development* 33 (1962): 257–271.

Eisenman, Russell, and Paul Johnson. "Birth Order, Sex, Perception and Production of Complexity." *The Journal of Social Psychology* 79 (1969): 113–119.

Ekman, Paul, and Wallace V. Friesen. "Head and Body Cues in the Judgment of Emotion: A Reformulation." *Perceptual and Motor Skills* 24 (1967): 711–724.

Ellis, Donald G., and Linda McCallister. "Relational Control in Sex-typed and Androgynous Groups." *Western Journal of Speech Communication* 44 (1980): 35–49.

Ellison, Craig W., and Ira J. Firestone. "Development of Interpersonal Trust as a Function of Self-Esteem, Target Status and Target Style." *Journal of Personality and Social Psychology* 29 (1974): 655–663.

Ellsworth, P., and L. Ross. "Intimacy in Response to Direct Gaze." *Journal of Experimental Social Psychology* 11 (1975): 592–613.

Ellsworth, Phoebe C., J. Merrill Carlsmith, and Alexander Henderson. "The Stare as a Stimulus to Flight in Human Subjects: A Series of Field Experiments." *Journal of Personality and Social Psychology* 21 (1972): 302–311.

Ellsworth, Phoebe C. and Linda M. Ludwig. "Visual Behavior in Social Interaction." *Journal of Communication* 22 (1972): 375–403.

Epstein, H. "Growth Spurts During Brain Development: Implications for Educational Policy and Practice." *Education and the Brain.* Ed. by J. S. Chall and A. F. Mirsky. Chicago, Illinois: University of Chicago Press, 1978.

Epstein, Norman, and Elizabeth Jackson. "An Outcome Study of Short Term Communication Training with Married Couples." *Journal of Consulting and Clinical Psychology* 46 (1978): 207–212.

Etaugh, C., and J. Malstrom. "The Effect of Marital Status on Person Perception." *Journal of Marriage and the Family* 43 (1981): 801–805.

Exline, Ralph, and L. C. Winters. "Affective Relations and Mutual Glances in Dyads." *Affect, Cognition, and Personality.* Ed. by S. S. Tomkins and C. E. Izard. New York: Springer Press, 1965.

Fabes, Richard A., and Mary R. Laner. "How the Sexes Perceive Each Other: Advantages and Disadvantages." *Sex Roles* 15 (1986): 129–143.

Falbo, Toni, and Letitia Anne Peplau. "Power Strategies in Intimate Relationships." *Journal of Personality and Social Psychology* 38 (1980): 618–628.

Farber, Gerald Mark. "Marital Satisfaction and the Topics of Self-Disclosure for Jewish Men and Women: A Correlational Study." Ph.D., diss., Boston University, 1979.

Farley, Jennie. "Women's Magazines and the ERA: Friend or Foe?" *Journal of Communication* 28 (Winter 1978): 187–193.

Farwell, M. "Women and Language." *Women on the Move.* Ed. by Jean R. Leppaluoto. Pittsburgh, PA: KNOW, Inc., 1973.

Feigenbaum, W. Morton. "Reciprocity in Self-Disclosure within the Psychological Interview." *Psychological Reports* 40 (1977): 15–26.

Feldman, Larry B. "Marital Conflict and Marital Intimacy: An Integrative Psychodynamic-Behavioral Systemic Model." *Family Process* 18 (1979): 69–78.

Ferrell, William Lyman. "A Comparison of Assertive Training and Programmed Human Relations Training in a Treatment Program for Problem Drinkers." Ph.D. diss., University of North Carolina at Chapel Hill, 1977.

Festinger, Leon, Stanley Schachter, and Kurt Back. *Social Pressures in Informal Groups.* New York: Harper, 1950.

Fillmer, H. Thompson, and Leslie Haswell. "Sex-Role Stereotyping in English Usage." *Sex Roles* 3 (1977): 257–263.

Fine, Marlene G. "Soap Opera Conversations: The Talk That Binds." *Journal of Communication* 31 (Summer 1981): 97–107.

Fiore, Anthony, and Clifford H. Swenson. "Analysis of Love Relationships in Functional and Dysfunctional Marriages." *Psychological Reports* 40 (1977): 707–714.

Fisher, B. Aubrey. "Differential Effects of Sexual Composition and International Context on Interaction Patterns in Dyads." *Human Communication Research* 9 (1983): 225–238.

Fisher, J. D., M. Rytting, and R. Heslin. "Hands Touching Hands: Affective and Evaluative Affects of Interpersonal Touch." *Sociometry* 39 (1976): 416–421.

Fisher, Jeffrey David, and Donn Bryne. "Too Close for Comfort: Sex Differences in Response to Invasions of Personal Space." *Journal of Personality and Social Psychology* 32 (1975): 15–21.

Fisher, Seymour. "Body Decoration and Camouflage." *Dimensions of Dress and Adornment: A Book of Readings.* Ed. by Lois M. Gurel and Marianne S. Beeson. Dubuque, Iowa: Kendall/Hunt Publishing Co., 1975.

Fishman, Pamela. "Interaction: The Work Women Do." *Language, Gender, and Society.* Ed. by Barrie Thorne, Cheris Kramarae, and Nancy Henley. Rowley, Mass.: Newbury House, 1983.

Fishman, Pamela M. "Interactional Shitwork." *Heresies: A Feminist Publication on Art & Politics* 2 (May 1978): 99–101.

Fitzgerald, Maureen P. "Self-Disclosure and Expressed Self-Esteem, Social Distance and Areas of the Self Revealed." *The Journal of Psychology* 56 (1963): 405–412.

Fitzpatrick, Mary Anne. *Between Husbands and Wives: Communication in Marriage.* Newbury Park, Calif.: Sage, 1988.

Fitzpatrick, Mary Ann, and Arthur Bochner. "Perspectives on Self and Others: Male-Female Differences in Perceptions of Communication Behavior." *Sex Roles* 7 (1981): 523–534.

Fitzpatrick, Mary Anne, and Julie Indvik. "The Instrumental and Expressive Domains of Marital Communication." *Human Communication Research* 8 (1982): 195–213.

Flanagan, Anna M., and William R. Todd-Mancillas. "Teaching Inclusive Generic Pronoun Usage: The Effectiveness of an Authority Innovation-Decision Approach Versus an Optional Innovation-Decision Approach." *Communication Education* 31 (1982): 275–284.

Flugel, J. C. *The Psychology of Clothes.* New York: International Universities Press, Inc., 1930.

Flynn, Elizabeth A. "Gender and Reading." *College English* 45 (1983): 236–253.

Fong, M. L., and L. D. Barders. "Effects of Sex Role Orientation and Gender on Counseling Skills Training." *Journal of Counseling Psychology* 32 (1985): 104–110.

Ford, J. Guthrie, Robert E. Cramer, and Gayle Owens. "A Paralinguistic Consideration of Proxemic Behavior." *Perceptual and Motor Skills* 45 (1977): 487–493.

Foreit, Karen G., Terna Agor, Johnny Byers, John Larue, Helen Lokey, Michael Palazzini, Michael Patterson, and Lillian Smith. "Sex Bias in Newspaper Treatment of Male-Centered and Female-Centered News Stories." *Sex Roles* 6 (1980): 475–480.

Forgionne, Guisseppi A., and Celestine C. Nwacukwu. "Acceptance of Authority in Female-Managed Organizational Positions." *University of Michigan Business Review* 29 (May 1977): 23–28.

Foss, Karen A., and Belle A. Edson. "What's in a Name?: Accounts of Married Women's Name Choices." Paper presented to the annual conference of the Organization for the Study of Communication, Language, and Gender, San Diego, Calif. 1988.

Foster, Lawrence W., and Tom Kolinko. "Choosing to be a Managerial Woman: An Examination of Individual Variables and Career Choice." *Sex Roles* 5 (1979): 627–634.

Fowler, Gene D., and Lawrence B. Rosenfeld. "Sex Differences and Democratic Leadership Behavior." *Southern Speech Communication Journal* 45 (1979): 69–78.

Frances, Susan J. "Sex Differences in Nonverbal Behavior." *Sex Roles* 5 (1979): 519–535.

Friedan, Barbara. *The Feminine Mystique.* New York: Dell, 1963.

Friedan, Barbara. *The Second Stage.* New York: Summit Books, 1981.

Friedley, Sheryl A., and Margery K. Nadler. "Perceptions of Gender Differences in Forensic Competition and Leadership." Paper presented at the annual conference of the Speech Communication Association, Washington, D.C., 1983.

Friedman, H. S. "The Interactive Effects of Facial Expressions of Emotion and Verbal Messages on Perceptions of Affective Meaning." *Journal of Experimental Social Psychology* 15 (1979): 453–469.

Friedman, Martha. *Fear of Success.* New York: Warner Books, 1982.

Frieze, Irene Hanson. "Nonverbal Aspects of Femininity and Masculinity Which Perpetuate Sex-Role Stereotypes." Paper presented at the Eastern Psychological Association, 1974.

Frieze, I. H., and S. J. Ramsey. "Nonverbal Maintenance of Traditional Sex Roles." *Journal of Social Issues* 32 (1976): 133–141.

Furnham, Adrian, and Anjali Singh. "Memory for Information about Sex Differences." *Sex Roles* 15 (1986): 479–486.

Gallagher, Margaret. "Communication, Control, and the Problem of Gender." Paper presented to the annual Conference of the International Association for Mass Communication Research, 1984.

Galvin, Kathleen M., and Bernard J. Brommel. *Family Communication: Cohesion and Change.* 2d ed. Glenview, Ill.: Scott, Foresman and Company, 1986.

Gardner, J. A. "The Effects of Body Motion, Sex of Counselor and Sex of Subject on Counselor Attractiveness and Subject's Self-Disclosure." Ph.D. diss., University of Wyoming, 1973.

Garland, H., K. F. Hale, and M. Burnson. "Attributions for the Success and Failure of Female Managers: A Replication and Extension." *Psychology of Women Quarterly* 7 (1982): 155–162.

Garrison, Laura. "Recognizing and Combatting Sexist Job Interviews." *Journal of Employment Counseling* 17 (1980): 270–276.

Gauthier, Joyce, and Diane Kjervik. "Sex-Role Identity and Self-Esteem in Female Graduate Nursing Students." *Sex Roles* 8 (1982): 45–55.

Geddes, Doreen. "Breaking Gender Communication Barriers in Management." Paper presented to the annual conference of the Speech Communication Association, Boston, Mass. 1987.

Gelman, Richard, and Hugh McGinley. "Interpersonal Liking and Self-Disclosure." *Journal of Consulting and Clinical Psychology* 46 (1978): 1549–1551.

"Gender Doesn't Matter in Managers, Survey Shows." *The Secretary,* May (1988): 5.

Gerson, J. M. "Women Returning to School: The Consequences of Multiple Roles." *Sex Roles* 13 (1985): 77–91.

Giesen, Martin and Harry A. McClaren. "Discussion, Distance and Sex: Changes in Impressions and Attraction During Small Group Interaction." *Sociometry* 39 (1976): 60–70.

Gigy, Lynn L. "Self-Concept of Single Women." *Psychology of Women Quarterly* 5 (1980): 321–340.

Gilbert, Shirley J. "Effects of Unanticipated Self-Disclosure on Recipients of Varying Levels of Self-Esteem: A Research Note." *Human Communication Research* 3 (1977): 368–371.

Gilbert, Shirley J., and David Horenstein. "The Communication of Self-Disclosure: Level Versus Valence." *Human Communication Research* 1 (1975): 316–322.

Gilbert, Shirley J., and Gale G. Whiteneck. "Toward a Multi-Dimensional Approach to the Study of Self-Disclosure." *Human Communication Research* 2 (1976): 347–355.

Giles, Howard, Janet Scholes, and Louis Young. "Stereotypes of Male and Female Speech: A British Study." *Central States Speech Journal* 34 (1983): 255–256.

Gilligan, Carol. *In A Different Voice: Psychological Theory and Women's Development.* Cambridge, Mass.: Harvard University Press, 1982.

Gilman, Charlotte P. *Herland: A Lost Feminist Utopian Novel.* New York: Pantheon Books, 1979.

Gitter, A. G., and H. Black. "Is Self-Disclosure Self-Revealing?" *Journal of Counseling Psychology* 23 (1976): 327–332.

"Progress in Prime-Time: TV Says Bye-Bye to Bimbos." *Glamour,* July, 1986.

Goffman, E. "The Nature of Deference and Demeanor." *American Anthropologist* 58 (1956): 473–502.

Goktepe, Janet R., and Craig E. Schneier. "Sex and Gender Effects in Evaluating Emergent Leaders in Small Groups." *Sex Roles* 19 (1988): 29–36.

Gold, Alice Ross, Lorelei R. Brush, and Eve R. Sprotzer. "Developmental Changes in Self-Perceptions of Intelligence and Self-Confidence." *Psychology of Women Quarterly* 5 (1980): 231–239.

Gold, Delores, and Charlene Berger. "Problem-Solving Performance of Young Boys and Girls as a Function of Task Appropriateness and Sex Identity." *Sex Roles* 4 (1978): 183–192.

Goldberg, C. N., C. A. Kiesler, and B. E. Collins. "Visual Behavior and Face-to-Face Distance During Interaction." *Sociometry* 32 (1969): 43–53.

Goldberg, P. "Are Women Prejudiced against Women?" *Transaction* 6 (1968): 28.

Goldhaber, Gerald M., and Carl H. Weaver. "Listener Comprehension of Compressed Speech When the Difficulty, Rate of Presentation, and Sex of the Listener are Varied." *Speech Monographs* 35 (1968): 20–25.

Goldman, Morton. "Effect of Eye Contact and Distance on the Verbal Reinforcement of Attitude." *The Journal of Social Psychology* 111 (1980): 73–78.

Golinkoff, Roberta Michnick, and Gail Johnson Ames. "A Comparison of Fathers' and Mothers' Speech with their Young Children." *Child Development* 50 (1979): 28–32.

Goodman, Ellen. "Among Winners in ERA Contest, Tyson gets Testosterone Special." *Milwaukee Sentinel* (Aug. 22, 1989): 8.

Gordon, William I., Craig D. Tengler, and Dominic A. Infante. "Women's Clothing Predispositions as Predictors of Dress at Work, Job Satisfaction, and Career Advancement." *The Southern Speech Communication Journal* 47 (1982): 422–434.

Gottman, John, Howard Markman, and Cliff Notarius. "The Typography of Marital Conflict." *Journal of Marriage and the Family* 6 (1970): 192–203.

Gouran, Dennis S. "Variables Related to Consensus in Group Discussions of Questions of Policy." *Speech Monographs* 36 (1968): 387–391.

Grant, T. *Being a Woman: Fulfilling Your Femininity and Finding Love.* New York: Avon Books, 1988.

Gray, Louis, Mervin White, and Roger W. Libby. "A Test and Reformulation of Reference Group and Role Correlates of Premarital Sexual Permissiveness Theory." *Journal of Marriage and Family* 40 (1978): 79–91.

Green, S. B., B. R. Burkhart, and W. H. Harrison. "Personality Correlates of Self-Report, Role-Playing and In Vivo Measures of Assertiveness." *Journal of Consulting and Clinical Psychology* 47 (1979): 16–24.

Greenberg, Bradley S., Robert Abelman, and Kimberly Neuendorf. "Sex on the Soap Operas: Afternoon Delight." *Journal of Communication* 31 (Summer 1981): 83–89.

Greenberg, Bradley, David Graef, and Charles Atkins. "Sexual Intimacy on Commercials and TV During Prime Time." *Journalism Quarterly Review* (1980): 410.

Greenblatt, Lynda, James E. Hasenauer, and Vicki S. Freimuth. "Psychological Sex Type and Androgyny in the Study of Communication Variables: Self-Disclosure and Communication Apprehension." *Human Communication Research* 6 (1980): 117–129.

Greenburg, S. "Educational Equity in Early Education Environments." *Handbook for Achieving Sex Equity Through Education.* Ed. by Susan Klein. Baltimore, Md.: Johns Hopkins University Press, 1985.

Haas, Adelaide. "Partner Influence on Sex-Associated Spoken Language of Children." *Sex Roles* 7 (1981): 225–234.

Haccoun, Dorothy M., George Sallay, and Robert R. Haccoun. "Sex Differences in the Appropriateness of Supervisory Styles: A Nonmanagement View." *Journal of Applied Psychology* 63 (1978): 124–127.

Hair, Stephanie. "Sexual Harassment: Subtle or Overt, Gnaws at Productivity." *Employee Assistance Quarterly* 3 (1987): 67–70.

Hacker, H. M. "Blabbermouths and Clams: Sex Differences in Self-Disclosure in Same-Sex and Cross-Sex Friendship Dyads." *Psychology of Women Quarterly* 5 (1981): 385–401.

Halberstadt, Amy G., Cynthia W. Hayes and Kathleen M. Pike. "Gender and Gender Role Differences in Smiling and Communication Consistency." *Sex Roles* 19 (1988): 589–604.

Haley, Elizabeth G. and Norejane J. Hendrickson. "Children's Preferences for Clothing and Hair Styles." *Home Economics Research Journal* 2 (1974): 179–193.

Hall, E. T. *The Hidden Dimension.* Garden City, N.Y.: Doubleday, 1966.

Hall, James R., and J. Diane Black. "Assertiveness, Aggressiveness, and Attitudes Toward Feminism." *The Journal of Social Psychology* 107 (1979): 57–62.

Hall, Judith A. *Nonverbal Sex Differences: Communication Accuracy and Expressive Style.* Baltimore, Md.: Johns Hopkins University Press, 1984.

Hall, K. "Sex Differences in Initiation and Influence in Decision-Making among Prospective Teachers." Ph.D. diss., Stanford University, 1972.

Hall, R. M., and B. R. Sandler. "Out of the Classroom: A Chilly Campus Climate for Women?" Report for the Association of American Colleges, Washington, D.C., 1984.

Halley, Richard D. "Distractibility of Males and Females in Competing Aural Message Situations: A Research Note." *Human Communication Research* 2 (1975): 79–82.

Halpern, Diane F. *Sex Differences in Cognitive Abilities.* Hillside, N.J.: Lawrence Erlbaum Associates, Publishing, 1986.

Hamilton, Mykol C. "Using Masculine Generics: Does Generic *He* Increase Male Bias in the User's Imagery?" *Sex Roles* 19 (1988): 785–799.

Hammen, C. L., and C. A Padesky. "Sex Differences in the Expression of Depressive Responses on the Beck Depression Inventory." *Journal of Abnormal Psychology* 86 (1977): 609–614.

Hampleman, R. S. "Comparison of Listening and Reading Comprehension Ability of Fourth and Sixth Grade Pupils." *Elementary English* 35 (1958): 49–53.

Hansen, Christine H., and Ronald D. Hansen. "How Rock Music Videos Can Change What Is Seen when Boy Meets Girl: Priming Stereotypic Appraisal of Social Interactions." *Sex Roles* 19 (1988): 287–316.

Harlow, H. F., M. K. Harlow, and E. W. Haesen. "The Maternal Affectional System of Rhesus Monkeys." *Maternal Behavior in Mammals.* Ed. by H. I. Rheingold. New York: Wiley and Son, Inc., 1963.

Harper, N., and R. Hirokawa. "A Comparison of Persuasive Strategies Used by Female and Male Managers 1: An Examination of Downward Influence." *Communication Quarterly* 36 (Spring 1988): 157–168.

Harrel, W. Andrew. "Physical Attractiveness, Self-Disclosure, and Helping Behavior." *Journal of Social Psychology* 104 (1978): 15–17.

Harrigan, Jinni A., and Karen S. Lucic. "Attitudes about Gender Bias in Language: A Reevaluation." *Sex Roles* 19 (1988): 129–140.

Harris, Laurilyn J. "Gender Difference, Perception, and the Artistic Process." Paper presented at the annual conference of the Speech Communication Association, 1984.

Harshman, R. A., E. Hampson, and S. A. Berenbaum. "Individual Differences in Cognitive Abilities and Brain Organization: Part I Sex and Handedness Differences in Ability." *Canadian Journal of Psychology* 37 (1983): 144–192.

Hart, R. P., and D. M. Burks. "Rhetorical Sensitivity and Social Interaction." *Speech Monographs* 39 (1972): 75–91.

Hart, R. P., R. E. Carlson, and W. F. Eadie. "Attitudes toward Communication and the Assessment of Rhetorical Sensitivity." *Communication Monographs* 47 (1980): 1–22.

Hartlage, L. C. "Identifying and Programming for Differences." Paper presented at Parent and Professional Conference on Young Children with Special Needs, Cleveland, Ohio, March 1980.

Haslett, Beth. "Communicative Functions and Strategies in Children's Conversations." *Human Communication Research* 9 (1983): 114–129.

Hattes, Joseph H., and Arnold Kahn. "Sex Differences in a Mixed-Motive Conflict Situation." *Journal of Personality* 42 (1974): 260–275.

Hawkins, Katherine. "Interruptions in Task-oriented Conversations: Effects of Violations of Expectations by Males and Females." *Women's Studies in Communication* (1988): 1–20.

Hayes, Daniel Truman. "Nonintellective Predictors of Public Speaking Ability and Academic Success in a Basic College-Level Speech Communication Course." Ph.D. diss., University of Missouri, 1977.

Hays, R. B. "A Longitudinal Study of Friendship Development." *Journal of Personality and Social Psychology* (1985): 909–924.

Hayt, Grimlin, ed. *The Women's Movement: Editorial Research Reports.* Washington, D.C.: Congressional Quarterly, 1977.

Heacock, D., and C. H. Spicer. "Communication and the Dual-career: A Literature Assessment." *Southern Speech Communication Journal* 51 (1986): 260–266.

Hecht, M., T. Shephard, and M. J. Hall. "Multivariate Indices of the Effects of Self-Disclosure." *Western Journal of Speech Communication* 43 (1979): 235–245.

Hegstrom, Timothy G. "Message Impact: What Percentage is Nonverbal?" *Western Journal of Speech Communication* 43 (1979): 134–142.

Heilbrun, A. B. "Measurement of Masculine and Feminine Sex Role Identities as Independent Dimensions." *Journal of Consulting and Clinical Psychology* 44 (1976): 183–190.

Heilman, Madeline E. "The Impact of Situational Factors on Personnel Decisions Concerning Women: Varying the Sex Composition of the Applicant Pool." *Organizational Behavior and Human Performance* 26 (1980): 386–395.

Heintz, Katharine E. "An Examination of Sex and Occupation-role Presentation of Female Characters in Children's Picture Books." *Women's Studies in Communication* 10 (1987): 67–78.

Heiss, J. "Degree of Intimacy and Male-Female Interaction." *Sociometry* 25 (1962): 197–208.

Helmich, Donald L. "Male and Female Presidents: Some Implications of Leadership Style." *Human Resource Management* (Winter 1974): 25–26.

Hendrick, S. "Self-Disclosure and Marital Satisfaction." *Journal of Personality and Social Psychology* 40 (1981): 1150–1159.

Henkin, Nancy Zimmerman. "An Exploratory Study of Self-Disclosure Patterns of Older Adults." Ph.D. diss., Temple University, 1980.

Henley, Nancy M. *Body Politics: Power, Sex, and Nonverbal Communication.* Englewood Cliffs, N.J.: Prentice-Hall, 1977.

Henley, Nancy M. "Status and Sex: Some Touching Observations." *Bulletin of the Psychonomic Society* 2 (1973): 91–93.

Henry, Celeste. "Feminists Seek Gender Changes in Religious Liturgies." *The Cincinnati Enquirer,* Oct 6, 1985.

Herek, G. M. "On Heterosexual Masculinity: Some Psychical Consequences of the Social Construction of Gender and Sexuality." *Changing Men.* Ed. by M. S. Kimmel. Newbury Park, Calif.: SAGE, 1987.

Hersey, Paul, and Kenneth H. Blanchard. *Management of Organizational Behavior: Utilizing Human Resources.* 3d ed. Englewood Cliffs, N.J.: Prentice-Hall, 1977.

Hess, Elizabeth P., Carol A. Bridgewater, Philip H. Bornstein, and Teresa M. Sweeney. "Situational Determinants in the Perception of Assertiveness: Gender-Related Influences." *Behavior Therapy* 11 (1980): 49–57.

Hickson, Mark L., and Don W. Stacks. *Nonverbal Communication: Studies and Applications.* Dubuque, Iowa: Wm. C. Brown Publishing, 1989.

Highlen, Pamela S., and Sheila F. Gillis. "Effects of Situational Factors, Sex, and Attitude on Affective Self-Disclosure and Anxiety." *Journal of Counseling Psychology* 25 (1978): 270–276.

Hilgard, Ernest R., and Richard C. Atkinson. *Introduction to Psychology.* 4th ed. New York: Harcourt, 1967.

Hill, Charles T., Letitia Ann Peplau, and Christine Dunkel-Schetter. "Self-Disclosure in Dating Couples: Sex Roles and the Ethic of Openness." *Journal of Marriage and the Family* 42 (1980): 305–317.

Hill, W. A. "Leadership Style: Rigid or Flexible." *Organizational Behavior and Human Performance* 9 (1973): 35–47.

Hillestad, Robert Christian. "A Schematic Approach to a Theoretical Analysis of Dress as Nonverbal Communication." Ph.D. diss., The Ohio State University, 1974.

Hillman, Judith Stevinson. "An Analysis of Male and Female Roles in Two Periods of Children's Literature." *Journal of Educational Research* 68 (1974): 84–88.

Hirschman, Lynette. "Female-Male Differences in Conversational Interaction." *Language and Sex: Difference and Dominance.* Ed. by Barrie Thorne and Nancy Henley. Rowley, Mass.: Newbury-House, 1975.

Hirst, Graeme. "An Evaluation of Evidence for Innate Sex Differences in Linguistic Ability." *Journal of Psycholinguistic Research* 11 (1982): 95–111.

Hoffman, Lois Wladis. "Effects of the Employment of Mothers on Parental Power Relations." *Journal of Marriage and the Family* 41 (1970): 27–35.

Hoffman, Martin L. "Sex Differences in Empathy and Related Behaviors." *Psychological Bulletin* 84 (1977): 712–722.

Hoffman, L., Richard Maier, and K. F. Norman. "Quality and Acceptance of Problem Solutions by Members of Homogeneous and Heterogeneous Groups." *Journal of Abnormal and Social Psychology* 62 (1961): 401–407.

Hollandsworth, J. G., Jr. "Self-Report Assessment of Social Fear, Discomfort, and Assertive Behavior." *Psychological Reports* 44 (1979): 1230.

Hollow, M. K. "Listening Comprehension at the Intermediate Grade Level." *Elementary School Journal* 56 (1956): 158–161.

Honeycutt, J. M., C. Wilson, and C. Parker. "Effects of Sex and Degrees of Happiness on Perceived Styles of Communicating In and Out of the Marital Relationship." *Journal of Marriage and Family Counseling* 44 (1982): 395–406.

Hoppe, Christiane M. "Interpersonal Aggression as a Function of Subject's Sex, Subject's Sex Role Identification, Opponent's Sex, and Degree of Provocation." *Journal of Personality* 47 (1979): 317–329.

Horn, Marilyn J. "Carrying It Off in Style." *Dimensions of Dress and Adornment: A Book of Readings.* Ed. by Lois M. Gurel and Marianne S. Beeson. Dubuque, Iowa: Kendall/Hunt Publishing Co., 1975.

Hosman, Lawrence A. "The Evaluative Consequences of Hedges, Hesitations, and Intensifiers: Powerful and Powerless Speech Styles." *Human Communication Research* 15 (1989): 383–406.

Hosman, Lawrence A., and Charles H. Tardy. "Self-Disclosure and Reciprocity in Short and Long-Term Relationships: An Experimental Study of Evaluational and Attributional Consequences." *Communication Quarterly* 28 (Winter 1980): 20–29.

Howell, William S. *The Empathic Communicator.* Belmont, Calif.: Wadsworth Publishing Company, 1982.

Hughes, Diana L., and Patricia L. Casey. "Pronoun Choice for Gender-unspecified Agent Words: Developmental Differences." *Language and Speech* 29 (1986): 59–68.

Hughey, Jim D. "Communication Responsiveness and Predictive Accuracy: Confirmation, Surprises, and Speculations." Paper presented to the annual conference of the International Communication Association, San Francisco, Calif., 1984.

Hurlock, Elizabeth. *The Psychology of Dress: An Analysis of Fashion and Its Motive.* New York: Ronald Press, 1929.

Hyman, Beverly. "Responsive Leadership: The Woman Manager's Asset or Liability?" *Supervisory Management* 25 (August 1980): 40–43.

Ickes, William, Brian Schermer, and Jeff Steeno. "Sex and Sex Role Influences in the Same-Sex Dyads." *Social Psychology Quarterly* 42 (1979): 373–385.

Illfelder, Joyce K. "Fear of Success, Career Salience and Anxiety Levels in College Women." *Journal of Vocational Behavior* 16 (1980): 7–17.

Inderlied, Sheila Davis, and Gary Powell. "Sex-Role Identity and Leadership Style: Different Labels for the Same Concept?" *Sex Roles* 5 (1979): 613–625.

Infante, Dominic A., and Jeanne Y. Fisher. "The Influence of Receivers' Attitudes, Audience Size, and Speakers' Sex on Speakers' Pre-message Perceptions." *Central States Speech Journal* 25 (1974): 43–49.

Irvin, C. E. "Evaluating a Training Program in Listening for College Freshmen." *School Review* 61 (1953): 25–29.

Jabes, Jak. "Causal Attributions and Sex-Role Stereotypes in the Perceptions of Women Managers." *Canadian Journal of Behavioral Science* 12 (1980): 52–63.

Jackson, Linda A. "The Influence of Sex, Physical Attractiveness, Sex Role, and Occupational Sex-Linkage on Perceptions of Occupational Suitability." *Journal of Social Psychology* 13 (1983): 31–44.

Jacobson, Marsha B., and Joan Effertz. "Sex Roles and Leadership: Perceptions of the Leaders and the Led." *Organizational Behavior and Performance* 12 (1974): 383–396.

Janofsky, A. Irene. "Affective Self-Disclosure in Telephone versus Face-to-Face Interviews." *Journal of Humanistic Psychology* 11 (1971): 93–103.

Jarvis, Jeff. " 'Kate & Allie' Aside, It's Far from Prime Time for Women on Television as Airheads Rule the Airwaves." *People Weekly,* May 7, 1984, 158–162.

Jespersen, Otto. *Language: Its Nature, Development and Origin.* London: Allen and Unwin, 1922.

Johannesen, Richard L. "The Emerging Concept of Communication as Dialogue." *Quarterly Journal of Speech* 57 (1971): 373–382.

Johnson, Fern. "Positions for Knowing about Gender Differences in Social Relationships." *Women's Studies in Communication* (1984): 77–82.

Johnson, P. J. "Personal Space as Reaction to Threat." Ph.D. diss., Catholic University of America, 1973.

Jolly, Eric J., and Charlotte G. O'Kelly. "Sex-Role Stereotyping in the Language of the Deaf." *Sex Roles: A Journal of Research* 6 (1980): 285–292.

Jonas, Doris F., and David A. Jonas. "Gender Differences in Mental Function: A Clue to the Origin of Language." *Current Anthropology* 16 (1975): 626–630.

Jones, Hardy. "Fairness, Meritocracy, and Reverse Discrimination." *Social Theory and Practice* 4 (1977): 211–226.

Jones, Stanley E. "Sex Differences in Touch Communication." *Western Journal of Speech Communication* 50 (1986): 227–241.

Jones, Tricia S., and Claire C. Brunner. "The Effects of Self-disclosure and Sex on Perceptions of Interpersonal Communication Competence." *Women's Studies in Communication* 7 (1984): 23–37.

Jorgensen, Stephen R., and Janis C. Gaudy. "Self-Disclosure and Satisfaction in Marriage: The Relation Examined." *Family Relations* 29 (1980): 281–287.

Jourard, Sidney M. *Self-Disclosure: An Experimental Analysis of the Transparent Self.* New York: John Wiley, 1971.

Jourard, S. M., and P. Lasakow. "Some Factors in Self-Disclosure." *Journal of Abnormal and Social Psychology* 56 (1958): 91–98.

Jourard, S. M., and J. E. Rubin. "Self-Disclosure and Touching: A Study of Two Modes of Interpersonal Encounter and Their Inter-relation." *Journal of Humanistic Psychology* 8 (1968): 39–48.

Judd, Larry R., and Carolyn B. Smith. "The Relationship of Age, Educational Classification, Sex, and Grade to Self-Concept and Ideal Self-Concept in a Basic Speech Course." *Communication Education* 26 (1977): 289–297.

Kaats, Gilbert R., and Keith E. Davis. "The Dynamics of Sexual Behavior of College Students." *Journal of Marriage and Family* 32 (1970): 390–399.

Kaess, Walter A., Sam L. Witryol, and Richard E. Nolan. "Reliability, Sex Differences and Validity in the Leaderless Group Discussion Technique." *Journal of Applied Psychology* 45 (1961): 345–350.

Kanungo, Rabindra N., and S. Jotindar Johar. "Effects of Slogans and Human Model Characteristics in Product Advertisements." *Canadian Journal of Behavioral Science* 7 (1975): 127–138.

Karpoe, Kelly P., and Rachel L. Olney. "The Effect of Boys' or Girls' Toys on Sex-Typed Play in Preadolescents." *Sex Roles* 9 (1983): 507–518.

Karre, I. "Stereotyped Sex Roles and Self-Concept: Strategies for Liberating the Sexes." *Communication Education* 25 (1976): 43–52.

Kelly, Eleanor, Caroline Daigle, Rosetta La Fleur, and Linda Wilson. "Adolescent Dress and Social Participation." *Home Economics Research Journal* 2 (1974): 167–175.

Kelly, Jeffrey A., Hal E. Wildman, and Jon K. Urey. "A Behavioral Analysis of Gender and Sex Role Differences in Group Decision Making and Social Interactions." *Journal of Applied Social Psychology* 12 (1982): 112–127.

Kemper, Susan. "When to Speak like a Lady." *Sex Roles* 10 (1984): 435–443.

Kennedy. C. W., and Carl T. Camden. "A New Look at Interruptions." *Western Journal of Speech Communication* 47 (1983): 45–48.

Kestenbaum, Linda V. "Decoding Inconsistent Communications: Importance of Body Versus Voice Cues and an Analysis of Individual Differences." Unpublished doctoral dissertation, City University of New York, 1977.

Key, Mary Ritchie. *Male/Female Language.* Mutuchen, N.J.: The Scarecrow Press, Inc., 1975.

Keys, David E. "Gender, Sex Role, and Career Decision Making of Certified Management Accountants." *Sex Roles* 13 (1985): 33–00.

Kidd, Virginia. "Happily Ever After and Other Relationship Styles: Advice on Interpersonal Relations in Popular Magazines, 1951–1973." *Quarterly Journal of Speech* 61 (1975): 31–40.

Kidd, Virginia. "A Study of the Images Produced Through the Use of the Male Pronoun as the Generic." *Moments in Contemporary Rhetoric and Communication* 1 (1971): 25–30.

Kiesler, C. A., S. B. Kiesler, and M. S. Pallak. "The Effect of Commitment to Future Interaction on Reactions to Norm Violations." *Journal of Personality* 35 (1967): 585–599.

Killarney, Jim, and Kathleen A. McCluskey. "Parent-Infant Conversations: Characteristics of and Differences Between Mothers' and Fathers' Speech to One-Year-Old Sons and Daughters." Paper presented at the Fourth Annual Communication, Language, and Gender Conference, Morgantown, West Virginia, 1981.

Kimmel, M. S. *Changing Men: New Directions in Research on Men and Masculinity.* Newbury Park, Calif.: SAGE, 1987.

Kimura, D. "Male Brain, Female Brain: The Hidden Difference." *Psychology Today* 19 (1985): 50–52, 54, 55–58.

King, W. H. "An Experimental Investigation into the Relative Merits of Listening and Reading Comprehension for Boys and Girls of Primary School Age." *British Journal of Educational Psychology* 29 (1959): 42–49.

Kinzer, N. S. "Soapy Sin in the Afternoon." *Psychology Today* (August 1973): 46–48.

Kirouc, G., and F. Y. Dore. "Accuracy and Latency of Judgment of Facial Expressions of Emotions." *Perceptual and Motor Skills* 57 (1983): 683–686.

Kleinke, Chris L. "Knowledge and Familiarity of Descriptive Sex Names for Males and Females." *Perceptual and Motor Skills* 39 (1974): 419–422.

Kleinke, Chris L., Armando A. Bustos, Frederick B. Meeker, and Richard A. Staneski. "Effects of Self-Attributed and Other Attributed Gaze on Interpersonal Evaluations Between Males and Females." *Journal of Experimental Social Psychology* 9 (1973): 154–163.

Klemesrud, Judy. "Speech Class Helps Women at the Podium." *New York Times* 11 Aug. 1983, 18Y.

Klos, Dennis S., and Diane F. Loomis. "A Rating Scale of Intimate Disclosure between Late Adolescents and Their Friends." *Psychological Reports* 42 (1978): 815–820.

Knapp, Mark L. *Essentials of Nonverbal Communication*. New York: Holt, Rinehart and Winston, 1980.

Koblinsky, Sally A., and Alan I. Sugawara. "Nonsexist Curricula, Sex of Teacher, and Children's Sex-role Learning." *Sex-Roles* 10 (March 1984): 357–367.

Koester, Jolene. "The Machiavellian Princess: Rhetorical Dramas for Women Managers." *Communication Quarterly* 30 (Summer 1982): 165–172.

Kohen, J. A. "The Development of Reciprocal Self-Disclosure in Opposite Sex Interaction." *Journal of Counseling Psychology* 22 (1975): 404–410.

Kohen, J. A. "Liking and Self-Disclosure in Opposite Sex Dyads." *Psychological Reports* 36 (1975): 695–698.

Kolleck, P., P. Blumstein, and P. Schwartz. "Sex and Power in Interaction: Conversational Privileges and Duties." *American Sociological Review* 50 (1985): 34–46.

Kopkind, Andrew. Review of "Second Serve," by . *The Nation,* June 1986, 800–802.

Kramarae, Cheris. "Informal Communication Networks: Who Is Listening to Women?" *Women and Language* 11 (1988): 46–50.

Kramarae, Cheris. *Women and Men Speaking*. Rowley, Mass.: Newbury House Publishers, Inc., 1981.

Kramarae, Cheris R. "Perceptions of Female and Male Speech." *Language and Speech* 20 (1977): 151–161.

Kramarae, Cheris R. "Sex Differences in Communication Behavior." Paper presented at the Speech Communication Association Convention, Houston, 1975.

Kramarae, Cheris R. "Sex Differences in Language." *Psychology Today* 8 (1978): 82–85.

Kramarae, Cheris R. "Wishy Washy Mommy Talk" *Psychology Today* 8 (June 1974): 82–85.

Kramarae, Cheris R. "Women's Speech: Separate But Unequal?" *Quarterly Journal of Speech* 60 (Spring 1974): 14–24.

Kramarae, Cheris, Barrie Thorne, and Nancy Henley. "Perspectives on Language and Communication." *Signs* 3 (1978): 638–651.

Kraut, Robert E., and Robert E. Johnston. "Social and Emotional Messages of Smiling: An Ethological Approach." *Journal of Personality and Social Psychology* 37 (1979): 1539–1553.

Krefting, Linda A. "Masculinity-Femininity of Job Requirements and Their Relationship to Job-Sex Stereotypes." *Journal of Vocational Behavior* 15 (1979): 164–173.

Krueger, Dorothy L. "Communication Strategies and Patterns in Dual-career Couples." *Southern Speech Communication Journal* 51 (1986): 274–284.

Krueger, Dorothy L. "Marital Decision Making: A Language-action Analysis." *Quarterly Journal of Speech* 68 (1982): 273–287.

Krueger, Dorothy L. "Communication Patterns and Egalitarian Decision Making in Dual-career Couples." *Western Journal of Speech Communication* 49 (1985): 126–145.

Kuhn, Deanna, Sharon Churnin Nash, and Laura Brucken. "Sex Role Concepts of Two- and Three-Year Olds." *Child Development* 49 (1978): 445–451.

Kuhn, Thomas. *The Structure of Scientific Revolutions*. 2d ed. Chicago: University of Chicago Press, 1974.

Kushell, Elliot, and Rae Newton. "Gender, Leadership Style, and Subordinate Satisfaction: An Experiment." *Sex Roles* 14 (February 1986): 25–36.

Labov, William. *Sociolinguistic Patterns*. Philadelphia: University of Pennsylvania Press, 1972.

Lafferty, J. C., and A. W. Pond. *The Desert Survival Situation*. Plymouth, Michigan: Human Synergistics, 1985.

LaFrance, Marianne, and Clara Mayo. *Moving Bodies: Nonverbal Communication in Social Relationships*. Monterey, Calif.: Brooks/Cole, 1978.

Lakoff, Robin. "Language and Woman's Place." *Language in Society* 2 (1973): 45–80.

Lakoff, Robin. *Language and Women's Place*. New York: Harper and Row, 1975.

Lakoff, Robin. "Language in Context." *Language* 48 (1972): 907–927.

Lakoff, Robin. "Women's Language." *Women's Language and Style*. Studies in Contemporary Language #1. U.S.: E. L. Epstein, 1978.

Lakoff, Robin "You Are What You Say." *Ms.* 3 (1974): 63–67.

Lane, Shelley D. "Empathy and Assertive Communication." Paper presented at the Western Speech Communication Association Convention, San Jose, California, 1981.

Lane, Terrance Scott. "Children's Task Performance on a Sex-Consistent or Sex-Inconsistent Game Following Social Comparison with their Peers." Ph.D. diss., University of Georgia, 1982.

Langner, Lawrence. *The Importance of Wearing Clothes*. New York: Hastings House, 1959.

Larche, Douglas W. *Mother Goose and Father Gander: Equal Rhymes for Girls and Boys*. Indianola, Iowa: Father Gander Press, 1979.

Larwood, Laurie, Marion M. Wood, and Sheila Davis Inderlied. "Training Women for Management: New Problems, New Solutions." *Academy of Management Review* 3 (1978): 584–593.

Lass, Norman J., Pamela J. Mertz, and Karen Kimmel. "The Effect of Temporal Speech Alterations on Speaker Race and Sex Identifications." *Language and Speech* 21 (1978): 279–290.

Lau, Sing. "The Effect of Smiling on Person Perception." *The Journal of Social Psychology* 117 (1982): 63–67.

Lavine, L. O., and J. P. Lombardo. "Self-disclosure: Intimate and Nonintimate Disclosures to Parents and Best Friends as a Function of Bem Sex-Role Category." *Sex Roles* 11 (1984): 735–744.

LaVoie, Joseph C., and Gerald R. Adams. "Physical and Interpersonal Attractiveness of the Model and Imitation in Adults." *The Journal of Social Psychology* 106 (1978): 191–202.

Lawick-Goodall, Jane van. *In the Shadow of Man*. Boston: Houghton-Mifflin, 1971.

Lebino, W. "No Way to Treat a Lady." *Channels* (Sept. 1986): 16.

Lemon, Judith. "Women and Blacks on Prime-Time Television." *Journal of Communication* 27 (Autumn 1977): 70–79.

Lesak, M. *Neuropsychological Assessment*. New York: Oxford University Press, Inc., 1976.

Leslie, Gerald R. *Marriage in a Changing World*. New York: John Wiley and Sons, 1977.

Leventhal, Gerald S., and Douglas W. Lane. "Sex, Age, and Equity Behavior." *Journal of Personality and Social Psychology* 15 (1970): 312–316.

Leventhal, Gloria, Marsha Lipshultz, and Anthony Chiodo. "Sex and Setting Effects on Seating Arrangement." *The Journal of Psychology* 100 (1978): 21–26.

Leventhal, Gloria, and Michelle Matturro. "Differential Effects of Spatial Crowding and Sex on Behavior." *Perceptual Motor Skills* 51 (1980): 111–120.

Lever, J. "Sex Differences in the Games Children Play." *Social Problems* 23 (1976): 478–487.

Levere, Jane. "Portrayal of Women in Ads Defended by Top Ad Women." *Editor and Publisher* (8 June 1974): 11.

LeVine, E., and J. N. Franco. "A Reassessment of Self-Disclosure Patterns among Anglo-Americans and Hispanics." *Journal of Counseling Psychology* 28 (1981): 522–524.

Levine, Lewis, and Harry J. Crockett, Jr. "Speech Variation in a Piedmont Community: Postvocalic," from *Explorations in Sociolinguistics,* ed. Stanley Lieberson. The Hague: Mouton, 1966.

Levine, Suzanne B. "TV's Race with Reality." *Ms.* (June 1987): 37.

Levinger, G., and D. Senn. "Disclosure of Feelings in Marriage." *Merrill-Palmer Quarterly of Behavior and Development* 13 (1967): 237–249.

Levy, J., and R. C. Gur. "Individual Differences in Psychoneurological Organization." *Neuropsychology of Left-handedness*. Ed. by J. Herron. New York: Academic Press, 1980.

Levy, J., and M. Reid. "Variations in Cerebral Organization as a Function of Handedness, Handposture in Writing, and Sex." *Journal of Experimental Psychology: General* 107 (1978): 119–144.

Levy, J. "Cerebral Lateralization and Spatial Ability." *Behavior Genetics* 6 (1976): 171–188.

Lewis, Lisa. "Form and Female Authorship in Music Video." *Communication* 9 (1987): 355–378.

Lewis, R. A. "Emotional Intimacy among Men." *Journal of Social Issues* 34 (1978): 108–121.

Lewittes, Hedva J., and Sandra L. Bem. "Training Women to Be More Assertive in Mixed-sex Task-oriented Discussions." *Sex Roles* 9 (1983): 581–596.

Libby, Roger W., Louis Gray, and Mervin White. "A Test and Reformulation of Reference Group and Role Correlates of Premarital Sexual Permissiveness Theory." *Journal of Marriage and Family* 40 (1978): 79–91.

Lichter, Robert, Linda S. Lichter, and Stanley Rothman. "From Lucy to Lacey: TV's Dream Girls." *Public Opinion* 9 (1986): 16–19.

Liebert, R. M., R. B. McCall, and M. A. Hanratty. "Effects of Sex-Typed Information on Children's Toy Preferences." *Journal of Genetic Psychology* 119 (1971): 133–136.

Lipmen-Blumen, Jean. *Gender Roles and Power*. Englewood Cliffs, N.J.: Prentice-Hall, 1984.

Lippa, Richard. "The Naive Perception of Masculinity-Femininity on the Basis of Expressive Cues." *Journal of Research in Personality* 12 (1978): 1–14.

Littlefield, Robert P. "Self-Disclosure Among Some Negro, White, and Mexican-American Adolescents." *Journal of Counseling Psychology* 21 (1974): 133–136.

Locksley, Anne, and Mary Colton. "Psychological Androgyny: A Case of Mistaken Identity." *Journal of Personality and Social Psychology* 37 (1979): 1017–1031.

Loeb, Roger C., and Leslie Horst. "Sex Differences in Self and Teachers' Reports of Self-Esteem in Pre-Adolescents." *Sex Roles* 4 (1978): 779–788.

Logue, Brenda J. "Male/Female Levels of Participation in Regional and National CEDA Debate Tournaments." Paper presented at the annual conference of the Speech Communication Association, Denver, Colorado, 1985.

Lombardo, John P., and M. D. Berzonsky. "Sex Differences in Self-Disclosure During an Interview." *Journal of Social Psychology* 107 (1979): 281–282.

Lombardo, John P., and Salverio Fantasia. "The Relationship of Self-Disclosure to Personality, Adjustment, and Self-Actualization." *Journal of Clinical Psychology* 32 (1976): 765–769.

Lombardo, John P., and Robert D. Wood. "Satisfaction with Interpersonal Relations as a Function of Level of Self-Disclosure." *Journal of Psychology* 102 (1979): 21–26.

Lomranz, J., and A. Shapira. "Communicative Patterns of Self-Disclosure and Touching Behavior." *Journal of Psychology* 88 (1974): 223–227.

Looft, William R., and Marc D. Baranowski. "Birth Order, Sex, and Complexity-simplicity: An Attempt at Replication." *Perceptual and Motor Skills* 32 (1971): 303–306.

Lott, Dale F. and Robert Sommer. "Seating Arrangements and Status." *Journal of Personality and Social Psychology* 7 (1967): 90–95.

Loy, Pamela Hewitt, and Lea P. Stewart. "The Extent and Effects of the Sexual Harrassment of Working Women." *Sociological Focus* 17 (January 1984): 31–43.

Luckey, Eleanore Braun. "Marital Satisfaction and Parent Concepts." *Journal of Counseling Psychology* 24 (1960): 195–204.

Lundsteen, Sara. "Teaching Abilities in Critical Listening in Fifth and Sixth Grades." Ph.D. diss., University of California, Berkeley, 1963.

Lundstrom, W. J., and D. Sciglimpaglia. "Sex Role Portrayals in Advertising." *Journal of Marketing* 41 (July 1977): 72–79.

Lurie, Alison. *The Language of Clothes*. New York: Random House, 1981.

Maccoby, Eleanor Emmons, and Carol Nagy Jacklin. "Myth, Reality, and Shades of Gray: What We Know and Don't Know about Sex Differences." *Psychology Today* 8 (December 1974): 109–112.

MacDonald, Kevin, and Ross D. Parke. "Parent-child Physical Play: The Effects of Sex and Age of Children and Parents." *Sex Roles* 15 (1986): 367–378.

MacDonald, Malcolm R. "How Do Men and Women Students Rate in Empathy?" *American Journal of Nursing* 77 (1977): 998.

Mackay, David C. and D. C. Fulkerson. "On the Comprehension and Production of Pronouns." *Journal of Verbal Learning and Verbal Behavior* 18 (1979): 661–673.

MacKay, Donald G. "Psychology, Prescriptive Grammar, and the Pronoun Problem." *American Psychologist* 35 (1980): 444–449.

Maier, Norman R. F. "Male versus Female Discussion Leaders." *Personnel Psychology* 23 (1970): 455–461.

Maier, Norman R. F., and Ronald J. Burke. "Response Availability as a Factor in the Problem-Solving Performance of Males and Females." *Journal of Personality and Social Psychology* 5 (1967): 304–310.

Maier, Richard A., and Robert C. Ernest. "Sex Differences in the Perception of Touching." *Perceptual and Motor Skills* 46 (1978): 577–578.

Malandro, Loretta A., Larry Barker, and Deborah A. Barker. *Nonverbal Communication.* New York: Random House, 1989.

Malone, Mary Jo, and Rebecca F. Guy. "A Comparison of Mothers' and Fathers' Speech to their 3-Year-Old Sons." *Journal of Psycholinguistic Research* 11 (1982): 599–607.

Mant, Andrea. "Media Images and Medical Images." *Social Science and Medicine* 9 (November–December 1975): 613–618.

Maples, Mary F. "Dual Career Marriages: Elements for Potential Success." *Personnel and Guidance Journal* 60 (1981): 19–23.

Marcum, Patricia J. "Men and Women on the Management Team." *University of Michigan Business Review* 28 (1976): 8–11.

Marecek, Jeanne, Jane Allyn Piliavin, Ellen Fitzsimmons, Elizabeth C. Krogh, Elizabeth Leader, and Bonnie Trudell. "Women as TV Experts: The Voice of Authority?" *Journal of Communication* 28 (Winter 1978): 159–168.

Mark, Elizabeth Wyner. "Sex Differences in Intimacy Motivation: A Projective Approach to the Study of Self-Disclosure." Ph.D. diss., Boston College, 1976.

Markel, Norman N., Joseph F. Long, and Thomas J. Saine. "Sex Effects in Conversational Interaction: Another Look at Male Dominance." *Human Communication Research* 2 (1976): 356–364.

Markel, Norman, Layne Prebor, and John Brandt. "Biosocial Factors in Dyadic Communication: Sex and Speaking Intensity." *Journal of Personality and Social Psychology* 23 (1972): 11–13.

Marshall, Joan E., and Richard Heslin. "Boys and Girls Together: Sexual Composition and the Effect of Density and Group Size on Cohesiveness." *Journal of Personality and Social Psychology* 31 (1975): 952–961.

Martin, Judith. "Sir, a Question Is in Order." *The Milwaukee Journal,* 23 July 1989, 7G.

Martin, Judith. "Birth Announcement . . ." *The Milwaukee Journal,* 7 Dec. 1988,

Martin, J. N., and R. T. Craig. "Selected Linguistic Sex Differences during Initial Social Interactions of Same-Sex and Mixed-Sex Student Dyads." *Western Journal of Speech Communication* 47 (1983): 16–28.

Martyna, Wendy. "What Does 'He' Mean? Use of the Generic Masculine." *Journal of Communication* 28 (Winter 1978): 131–138.

Mayo, Clara, and Nancy Henley. *Gender and Nonverbal Behavior.* New York: Springer Verlay Inc., 1981.

McAdams, Dan P., Renee M. Lester, Paul A. Brand, William J. McNamara, and Denise B. Lensky. "Sex and the TAT: Are Women More Intimate than Men? Do Men Fear Intimacy?" *Journal of Personality Assessment* 52 (1988): 397–409.

McAllister, H. A. "Self-Disclosure and Liking: Effects for Senders and Receivers." *Journal of Personality* 48 (1980): 409–418.

McAndrew, F. T., and J. E. Warner. "Arousal Seeking and the Maintenance of Mutual Gaze in Same and Mixed-Sex Dyads." *Journal of Nonverbal Behavior* 10 (1986): 168–171.

McArthur, L. Z., and B. G. Resko. "The Portrayal of Men and Women in American Television Commercials." *The Journal of Social Psychology* 97 (1975): 209–220.

McCall, Jr., Morgan W. "What Makes a Top Executive?" *Psychology Today* 26 (1983): 26–31.

McCarthy, W. J., M. C. Hamilton, C. Leaper, E. Pader, S. Rushbrook, and N. M. Henley. "Social Influences on What To Call Her: 'Woman,' 'Girl,' or 'Lady.'" *Advances in Language and Gender Research.* Symposium conducted at the meeting of the American Psychological Association, Los Angeles, Calif., (1985).

McCormick, Naomi B. "Come-ons and Put-offs: Unmarried Students' Strategies for Having and Avoiding Sexual Intercourse." *Psychology of Women Quarterly* 4 (1979): 194–211.

McCroskey, James C., and Virginia P. Richmond. "Communication Apprehension as a Predictor of Self-Disclosure." *Communication Quarterly* 25 (Fall 1977); 40–43.

McCroskey, James C., Timothy Simpson, and Virginia P. Richmond. "Biological Sex and Communication Apprehension." *Communication Quarterly* 30 (1982): 129–133.

McGhee, Paul E., and Terry Frueh. "Television Viewing and the Learning of Sex Role Stereotypes." *Sex Roles* 6 (1980): 179–188.

McKeever, W. F., and A. D. Van Deventer. "Visual and Auditory Language Processing Asymmetries: Influence of Handedness, Familial Sinistrality, and Sex." *Cortex* 13 (1977): 225–241.

McMillan, Julie R., A. Kay Clifton, Diane McGrath, and Wanda S. Gale. "Women's Language: Uncertainty or Interpersonal Sensitivity and Emotionality?" *Sex Roles* 3 (1977): 545–559.

McVicar, Pauline, and Al Herman. "Assertiveness, Self-Actualization, and Locus of Control in Women." *Sex Roles* 9 (1983): 555–562.

Mead, George Herbert, quoted in *Sociology: Human Society*, by Melvin DeFleur *et al.* Glenview, Illinois: Scott, Foresman & Company, 1977.

Meeker, B. F., and P. A. Weitzel-O'Neill. "Sex Roles and Interpersonal Behavior in Task-Oriented Groups." *American Sociological Review* 42 (1977): 91–105.

Megargee, Edwin E. "Influence of Sex Roles on the Manifestation of Leadership." *Journal of Applied Psychology* 53 (1969): 377–382.

Mehrabian, Albert. "Differences in the Forms of Verbal Communication as a Function of Positive and Negative Affective Experience." *Dissertation Abstracts* 25 (1965): 4818–4819.

Mehrabian, Albert. *Nonverbal Communication.* Chicago: Aldine-Atherton, 1972.

Mehrabian, Albert. *Silent Messages: Implicit Communication of Emotions and Attitudes.* Belmont, Calif.: Wadsworth, 1981.

Mehrabian, Albert. "Verbal and Nonverbal Interaction of Strangers in a Waiting Situation." *Journal of Experimental Research in Personality* 5 (1971): 127–128.

Mehrabian, Albert, and Susan R. Ferris. "Influence of Attitudes from Nonverbal Communication in Two Channels." *Journal of Consulting Psychology* 31 (1967): 248–252.

Mercer, G. William, and Paul M. Kohn. "Gender Differences in the Integration of Conservatism, Sex Urge, and Sexual Behaviors among College Students." *Journal of Sex Research* 15 (May 1979): 129–142.

Merritt, Sharyne, and Harriet Gross. "Women's Page/Lifestyle Editors: Does Sex Make a Difference?" *Journalism Quarterly* 55 (Autumn 1978): 508–514.

Milford, James T. "Aesthetic Aspects of Faces: A (Somewhat) Phenomenological Analysis Using Multidimensional Scaling Methods." *Journal of Personality and Social Psychology* 36 (1978): 205–216.

Miller, Casey, and Kate Swift. "Women and the Language of Religion." *Christian Century* 93 (1976): 353–358.

Miller, Casey, and Kate Swift. "De-Sexing the English Language." *Ms.,* Preview issue, Spring 1972.

Miller, Gerald R., and Michael McReynolds. "Male Chauvinism and Source Competence: A Research Note." *Speech Monographs* 40 (1973): 154–155.

Miller, Susan H. "The Content of News Photos: Women's and Men's Roles." *Journalism Quarterly* 52 (Spring 1975): 70–75.

Miller, T. W. "Male Attitudes toward Women's Rights as a Function of their Level of Self-Esteem." *International Journal of Group Tensions* 4 (1974): 35–44.

Mills, Judson, and Eliot Aronson. "Opinion Change as a Function of the Communicator's Attractiveness and Desire to Influence." *Journal of Personality and Social Psychology* 1 (1965): 173–177.

Miner, John B. "Motivation to Manage among Women: Studies of Business Managers and Educational Administrators." *Journal of Vocational Behavior* 5 (1974): 197–208.

Minnigerode, F. A. "Attitudes toward Homosexuality: Feminist Attitudes and Sexual Conservatism." *Sex Roles* 2 (1976): 347–352.

Minton, Henry L., and Arthur G. Miller. "Group Risk Taking and Internal-External Control of Group Members." *Psychological Reports* 26 (1970): 431–436.

Modleski, Tania. *Loving with a Vengeance: Mass-produced Fantasies for Women.* New York: Shoe String, 1982.

Molloy, John T. *Dress for Success.* New York: Peter H. Wyden, 1975.

Molloy, John T. *The Women's Dress for Success Book.* New York: Warner Books, Inc., 1977.

Money, John, and Patricia Tucker. *Sexual Signatures.* Boston: Little, Brown, 1975.

Montague, Ashley; ed. *Touching: The Significance of the Human Skin.* New York: Harper & Row, 1971.

Montgomery, Barbara M. "The Form and Function of Quality Communication in Marriage." *Family Relations* 30 (January 1981): 21–29.

Montgomery, Barbara M., and Robert W. Norton. "Sex Differences and Similarities in Communicator Style." *Communication Monographs* 48 (1981): 121–132.

Montgomery, Charles L., and Michael Burgoon. "An Experimental Study of the Interactive Effects of Sex and Androgyny on Attitude Change." *Communication Monographs* 44 (1977): 130–135.

Morgan, Brian S. "Intimacy of Disclosure Topics and Sex Differences in Self Disclosure." *Sex Roles* 2 (1976): 161–166.

Morgan, Marabel. *The Total Woman.* New York: Pocket Books, 1973.

Morganosky, M., and A. M. Creekmore. "Clothing Influence in Adolescent Leadership Roles." *Home Economics Research Journal* 9 (1981): 356–362.

Morris, William (Ed.). The American Heritage Dictionary of the English Language. Boston, Mass: American Heritage Publishing Company and Houghton-Mifflin Company, 1975.

Moss, Howard A. "Sex, Age, and State as Determinants of Mother-Infant Interaction." *Readings in Child Development and Personality.* 2d ed. Ed. by Paul Henry Mussen, John Janeway Conger and Jerome Kagan. New York: Harper & Row, 1970.

Moulton, Janice, George M. Robinson, and Cherin Elias. "Sex Bias in Language Use: Neutral Pronouns that Aren't." *American Psychologist* 33 (1978): 1032–1036.

Muirhead, Rosalind D. and Morton Goldman. "Mutual Eye Contact as Affected by Seating Position, Sex, and Age." *The Journal of Social Psychology* 109 (1979): 201–206.

Mulac, Anthony, James J. Bradac, and Susan K. Mann. "Male/Female Language Differences and Attributional Consequences in Children's Television." *Human Communication Research* 11 (1985): 481–506.

Mulac, A., C. R. Incontro, and M. R. James. "A Comparison of the Gender-linked Language Effect and Sex-role Stereotypes." *Journal of Personality and Social Psychology* 49 (1985): 1098–1109.

Mulac, Anthony, and Torborg Louisa Lundell. "Differences in Perceptions Created by Syntactic-Semantic Productions of Male and Female Speakers." *Communication Monographs* 47 (1980): 111–118.

Mulac, Anthony, and Torborg L. Lundell. "Linguistic Contributors to the Gender-linked Language Effect." *Journal of Language and Social Psychology* 5 (1986): 81–101.

Mulac, Anthony, Torborg L. Lundell, and James J. Bradac. "Male/Female Language Differences and Attributional Consequences in a Public Speaking Situation: Toward an Explanation of the Gender-linked Language Effect." *Communication Monographs* 53 (1986): 115–129.

Mulac, Anthony, Lisa B. Studley, John M. Wiemann, and James J. Bradac. "Male/Female Gaze in Same-sex and Mixed-sex Dyads: Gender-linked Differences and Mutual Influence." *Human Communication Research* 13 (1987): 323–343.

Mulac, Anthony, John M. Wiemann, Sally J. Widenmann, and Toni W. Gibson. "Male/Female Language Differences and Effects in Same-sex and Mixed-sex Dyads: The Gender-linked Language Effect." *Communication Monographs* 55 (1988): 315–335.

Mulcahy, G. A. "Sex Differences in Patterns of Self-Disclosure among Adolescents: A Developmental Perspective." *Journal of Youth and Adolescence* 2 (1973): 343–356.

Murray, J. "Male Perspective in Language." *Women: A Journal of Liberation* 3 (1973): 46–50.

Myers, Mildred S. "Mary Cunningham and the Press: Who Said What and How?" *Women's Studies in Communication* 6 (1983): 76–84.

Natale, M. "Social Desirability as Related to Convergence of Temporal Speech Patterns." *Perceptual and Motor Skills* 40 (1975): 827–830.

National Report on Human Resources (1989, February/March). "Adults Learn More from Women," p. 000.

Neer, Michael R., and David D. Hudson. "The Interactive Role Behaviors of Females and Males: How Differently Do the Sexes Really Communicate?" Paper presented at the Western Speech Communication Association convention, Albuquerque, New Mexico, February 1983.

Newcombe, Nora, and Diane B. Arnkoff. "Effects of Speech Style and Sex of Speaker on Person Perception." *Journal of Personality and Social Psychology* 37 (1979): 1293–1303.

Newport, E. "Motherese: The Speech of Mothers to Young Children." Ed. by N. Castellan, D. Pisoni, and G. Potts. *Cognitive Theory.* vol. 2 Hillsdale, New Jersey: Lawrence Earlbaum Associates, 1976.

Nichols, Ralph G. "Factors in Listening Comprehension." *Speech Monographs* 15 (1948): 154–163.

Nilsen, Alleen Pace. "The Correlation Between Gender and Other Semantic Features in American English." Paper presented at Linguistic Society of America, 1973.

Nilsen, Alleen Pace. "Sexism in English: A Feminist View." *Female Studies* VI. Ed. by Nancy Hoffman, Cynthia Secor, and Adrian Tinsley. Old Westbury, New York: The Feminist Press, 1972.

Noel, Richard, and Mary J. Allen. "Sex and Ethnic Bias in the Evaluation of Student Editorials." *Journal of Psychology* 94 (1976): 53–58.

Noller, Patricia, and Cynthia Gallois. "Understanding and Misunderstanding in Marriage: Sex and Marital Adjustment Differences in Structured and Free Interaction." *Perspectives on Marital Interaction* Ed. by Patricia Noller and Mary Ann Fitzpatrick. Clevedon: Multilingual Matters Ltd., (1988).

Noller, Patricia. "Sex Differences in Nonverbal Communication: Advantage Lost or Supremacy Regained." *Australian Journal of Psychology* 38 (1986): 23–32.

Norton, Robert W. "Foundation of a Communicator Style Construct." *Human Communication Research* 4 (1978): 99–112.

Norton, Robert, and Barbara Warnick. "Assertiveness as a Communication Construct." *Human Communication Research* 3 (1976): 62–66.

Nye, F. Ivan. *Family Relationships: Rewards and Costs.* Beverly Hills, Calif.: Sage Publications, 1982.

O'Donnell, Holly Smith. "Sexism in Language." *Elementary English* 50 (1973): 1067–1072.

O'Donnell, William J., and Karen J. O'Donnell. "Update: Sex-Role Messages in TV Commercials." *Journal of Communication* 28 (Winter 1978): 156–158.

Oser, O. A. "Experiments on the Abstraction of Form and Colour: Rorschach Tests." *The British Journal of Psychology* 23 (1932): 289–323.

Offermann, Lynn R. "Visibility and Evaluation of Female and Male Leaders." *Sex Roles* 14 (1986): 533–000.

O'Keefe, Eileen S. C., and Janet Shibley Hyde. "The Development of Occupational Sex-Role Stereotypes: The Effects of Gender Stability and Age." *Sex Roles* 9 (1983): 481–492.

Oliver, Linda. "Women in Aprons: The Female Stereotype in Children's Readers." *Elementary School Journal* 74 (1974): 253–259.

Oliveri, Mary Ellen, and David Reiss. "Social Networks of Family Members: Distinctive Roles of Mothers and Fathers." *Sex Roles* 17 (1987): 719–000.

O'Neill, Sylvia, Deborah Fein, Kathryn McColl Velit, and Constance Frank. "Sex Differences in Pre-adolescent Self-Disclosure." *Sex Roles* 2 (1976): 85–88.

O'Neill, W. L. *Everyone Was Brave: The Rise and Fall of Feminism.* Chicago: Quadrangle Books, 1969.

Orenstein, H., E. Orenstein, and J. E. Carr. "Assertiveness and Anxiety: A Correlational Study." *Journal of Behavior Therapy and Experimental Psychiatry* 6 (1975): 203–207.

Owen, William F. "The Verbal Expression of Love by Women and Men as a Critical Communication Event in Personal Relationships." *Women's Studies in Communication* 10 (1987): 15–24.

Palamatier, R. A., and G. McNinch. "Source of Gains in Listening Skill: Experimental or Pre-Test Experience." *Journal of Communication* 22 (March 1972): 70–76.

Paletz, David L., Judith Koon, Elizabeth Whitehead, and Richard B. Hagens. "Selective Exposure: The Potential Boomerang Effect." *Journal of Communication* 22 (March 1972): 48–53.

Paludi, M. A., and W. D. Bauer. "Goldberg Revisited: What's in an Author's Name." *Sex Roles* 9 (1983): 387–390.

Parlee, M. B. "Conversational Politics." *Psychology Today* 12 (May 1979): 48–56.

Parsons, Elsie Clews. *The Old-Fashioned Woman: Primitive Fancies about the Sex.* New York: G. P. Putnam's Sons, 1913.

Patterson, Miles, Sherry Mullens, and Jeanne Romano. "Compensatory Reactions to Spatial Intrusion." *Sociometry* 34 (1971): 114–121.

Patton, Bobby R., Kim Giffin, and Eleanor N. Patton. *Decision-making: Group Interaction,* 3d. edition. New York: Harper & Row, Publishers, 1989.

Patton, B. R., M. Jasnoski, and L. Skerchock. "Communication Implications of Androgyny." Presented at the Speech Communication Association convention, Washington, D.C., 1977.

Pearce, W. B., and S. M. Sharp. "Self-Disclosing Communication." *Journal of Communication* 23 (December 1973): 409–425.

Pearson, Judy C. "The Effects of Sex and Sexism on the Criticism of Classroom Speeches." Ph.D. diss., Indiana University, 1975.

Pearson, Judy C. "Evaluating Classroom Speeches: An Investigation of Speaker Sex, Sexism, and Sex Role Identification." International Communication Association convention, Minneapolis, Minnesota, 1981a.

Pearson, Judy C. "A Factor Analytic Study of the Items in the Rathus Assertiveness Schedule and the Personal Report of Communication Apprehension." *Psychological Reports* 45 (1979): 491–497.

Pearson, Judy C. "Gender, Similarity, and Source Credibility." Paper presented at the Western Speech Communication Association convention, Denver, Colorado, 1982.

Pearson, Judy C. "An Investigation of the Effects of Sexism and Sex Role Identification on the Criticism of Classroom Speeches." Paper presented at the Speech Communication Association convention. New York City, New York, November 1980.

Pearson, Judy C. "The Role of Psychological Sex Type in Rhetorical Sensitivity and Self-Disclosure." Paper presented at the Speech Communication Association convention, Anaheim, California, November 1981.

Pearson, Judy C. "Sex Roles and Self-Disclosure." *Psychological Reports* 47 (1980): 640.

Pearson, Judy C., and Paul E. Nelson. "The Basic Speech Communication Course: An Examination of Instructor Sex, Student Sex, and Type of Course on Grading." Paper presented at the Speech Communication Association convention, Anaheim, California, November 1981.

Pearson, Judy C., and Paul E. Nelson. *Understanding and Sharing: An Introduction to Speech Communication.* 2d ed. Dubuque, Iowa: William C. Brown Company, 1982.

Pearson, Judy C. and Spitzberg, Brian H. *Interpersonal Communication: Concepts, Components, and Contexts.* 2d ed. Dubuque, Iowa: William C. Brown Company, 1990.

Pedersen, Darhl M., and Kenneth L. Higbee. "Personality Correlates of Self-Disclosure." *Journal of Social Psychology* 78 (1969): 81–89.

Pedhauzur, Elazar, and Toby Tetenbaum. "Bem Sex Role Inventory: A Theoretical and Methodological Critique." *Journal of Personality and Social Psychology* 37 (1979): 996–1016.

Pellegrini, Anthony. "A Speech Analysis of Preschoolers' Dyadic Interactions." *Child Study Journal* 12 (1982): 205–215.

Pendleton, Linda. "Attraction Responses to Female Assertiveness in Heterosexual Social Interactions." *Journal of Psychology* 111 (May 1982): 57–65.

Peplau, L. A., Z. Rubin, and C. T. Hill. "Sexual Intimacy in Dating Relationships." *Journal of Social Issues* 33 (1977): 86–109.

Perry, M. O., H. G. Schutz, and M. H. Rucker. "Clothing Interest, Self-Actualization, and Demographic Variables." *Home Economics Research Journal* 11 (1983): 280–288.

Petersen-Perlman, Deborah. "Sitcom Husbands: Are They All They Can Be?" Paper presented to the annual conference of the Central States Communication Association, Kansas City, Mo., 1989.

Peterson, Eric E. "Media Consumption and Girls Who Want To Have Fun." *Critical Studies in Mass Communication* 4 (1987): 37–50.

Peterson, P. "An Investigation of Sex Differences in Regard to Non-verbal Body Gestures." Proceedings of the Speech Communication Association Summer convention, Austin, Texas, 1975.

Petronio, Sandra S. "The Effect of Interpersonal Communication on Women's Family Role Satisfaction." *Western Journal of Speech Communication* 46 (1982): 208–222.

Petronio, Sandra, Judith Martin, and Robert Littlefield. "Prerequisite Conditions for Self-Disclosing: A Gender Issue." *Communication Monographs* 51 (1984): 268–273.

Petty, M. M., and G. K. Lee, Jr. "Moderating Effects of Sex of Supervisor and Subordinate on Relationships between Supervisory Behavior and Subordinate Satisfaction." *Journal of Applied Psychology* 60 (1975): 624–628.

Petty, M. M., and Robert H. Miles. "Leader Sex-Role Stereotyping in a Female-Dominated Work Culture." *Personnel Psychology* 29 (1976): 393–404.

Pfeiffer, John. "Girl Talk, Boy Talk." *Science* 85 (1985): 58–63.

Pfister, Emil R. "A Study of the Influence of Certain Selected Factors on the Ratings of Speech Performances." Ed.D. diss., Michigan State University, 1955.

Phelps, S., and N. Austin. *The Assertive Woman.* San Luis Obispo, Calif.: Impact, 1975.

Philips, Gerald, and H. Lloyd Goodall, Jr. *Loving and Living.* Englewood Cliffs, N.J.: Prentice-Hall, Inc., 1983.

Phillips, J., and S. Cole. "Sex Differences in Triadic Coalition Formation Strategies." *Studies of Conflict, Conflict Reduction and Alliance Formation.* Report 70–1 of the Cooperation/Conflict Research Group. Ed. by J. Phillips and T. Connor. Michigan State University, 1970, pp. 154–176.

Pincus, A. R. H., and R. E. Pincus. "Linguistic Sexism and Career Education." *Language Arts* 57 (1980): 70–77.

Pingree, Suzanne. "The Effects of Nonsexist Television Commercials and Perceptions of Reality on Children's Attitudes about Women." *Psychology of Women Quarterly* 2 (1978): 262–277.

Pogrebin, Letty Cobin. "Can Women Really Have It All?" *Ms.* 6 (1978): 47–50.

Polhemus, Ted, and Lynn Procter. *Fashion and Anti-Fashion: Anthropology of Clothing and Adornment.* London: Thames and Hudson, 1978.

Porter, Natalie, Florence L. Geis, Ellen Cooper, and Eileen Newman. "Androgyny and Leadership in Mixed-sex Groups." *Journal of Personality and Social Psychology* (1984):

Post, Amy L., Bruce C. Wittmaier, and Mitchell E. Radin. "Self-Disclosure as a Function of State and Trait Anxiety." *Journal of Consulting and Clinical Psychology* 46 (1978): 12–19.

Powell, Gary N., and D. Anthony Butterfield. "A Note on Sex-Role Identity Effect on Managerial Aspirations." *Journal of Occupational Psychology* 54 (1981): 299–301.

Powers-Ross, Sally Jo. Ph.D. diss., prospectus. University of Minnesota, 1978.

Prerost, Frank. "The Effects of High Spatial Density on Humor Appreciation: Age and Sex Differences." *Social Behavior and Personality* 8 (1980): 239–244.

Press, Andrea L. "New Views on the Mass Production of Women's Culture." *Communication Research* 13 (1986): 139–149.

Price, Gayle B., and Richard L. Graves. "Sex Differences in Syntax and Usage in Oral and Written Language." *Research in the Teaching of English* 14 (May 1980): 147–153.

Prisbell, Marshall A., and Janis F. Andersen. "The Importance of Perceived Homophily, Level of Uncertainty, Feeling Good, Safety, and Self-Disclosure in Interpersonal Relationships." *Communication Quarterly* 28 (Summer 1980): 22–33.

Procter, Lynn. *Fashion and Anti-Fashion.* London: Cox and Wyman, 1978.

Purnell, Sandra E. "Politically Speaking, Do Women Exist?" *Journal of Communication* 28 (Winter 1978): 150–155.

Quina, Kathryn, Joseph A. Wingard, and Henry G. Bates. "Language Style and Gender Stereotypes in Person Perception." *Psychology of Women Quarterly* 11 (1987): 111–122.

Rachlin, Susan Kessler, and Glenda L. Vogt. "Sex Roles as Presented to Children by Coloring Books." *Journal of Popular Culture* 8 (1974): 549–556.

Ragan, Sandra L., and Victoria Aarons. "Women's Response to Men's Silence: A Fictional Analysis." *Women's Studies in Communication* 9 (1986): 67–75.

Ragolin, V. C., and J. C. Hansen. "The Impact of Equity or Egalitarianism on Dual-career Couples." *Family Therapy* 2 (1985): 151–162.

Rakow, Lana F. "A Paradigm of One's Own: Feminist Ferment in the Field." Paper presented at the annual conference of the International Communication Association, Honolulu, Hawaii, 1985.

Ramirez, Albert. "Social Influence and Ethnicity of the Communicator." *Journal of Social Psychology* 102 (1977): 209–213.

Rankin, Paul Tory. "The Measurement of the Ability to Understand Spoken Language." Ph.D. diss., University of Michigan, 1926.

Rawlins, William K. "Openness as Problematic in Ongoing Friendships: Two Conventional Dilemmas." *Communication Monographs* 50 (1983): 1–13.

Reeves, Byron, Annie Lang, Ester Thorson, and Michael Rothschild. "Emotional Television Scenes and Hemispheric Specialization." *Human Communication Research* 15 (1988): 493–508.

Restak, Richard M. *The Brain: The Last Frontier.* New York: Doubleday, 1979.

Rice, David G. *Dual Career Marriage: Conflict and Treatment.* New York: The Free Press, 1979.

Rich, Elaine. "Sex-Related Differences in Colour Vocabulary." *Language and Speech* 20 (1977): 404–409.

Richardson, Laurel. *The Dynamics of Sex and Gender: A Sociological Perspective.* New York: Harper and Row, 1988.

Richmond, Virginia P., Joan S. Gorham, and Brian J. Furio. "Affinity-seeking Communication in Collegiate Female-male Relationships." *Communication Quarterly* 35 (1987): 334–348.

Ridley, Carl A. "Exploring the Impact of Work Satisfaction and Involvement on Marital Interaction when Both Partners are Employed." *Journal of Marriage and the Family* 35 (1973): 229–237.

Ritter, Malcolm. "She Was a Woman, He Was a Man—and They Fought." *The Milwaukee Journal* 8 17 Sept. 1989, 6G.

Rivenbark, W. H., III. "Self-Disclosure Patterns among Adolescents." *Psychological Reports* 28 (1971): 35–42.

Robards, Brooks. "Venus Observed: The Stereotypic Image of Women in *Playboy* Magazine." Paper presented to the annual conference of the Speech Communication Association, Chicago, Ill., 1984.

Roberts, Helene. "The Exquisite Slave: The Role of Clothes in the Making of the Victorian Woman." *Signs* 2 (1977): 554–569.

Robison, Joan Tucker. "The Role of Self-Disclosure, Interpersonal Attraction, and Physical Attractiveness in the Initial Stages of Relationship Development within Single-Sex Female Dyads." Ph.D. diss., University of Georgia, 1975.

Roger, D. B. and R. L. Reid. "Small Group Ecology Revisited—Personal Space and Role Differentiation." *British Journal of Social and Clinical Psychology* 17 (1978): 43–46.

Roger, D. B., and A. Schumacher. "Effects of Individual Differences on Dyadic Conversational Strategies." *Journal of Personality and Social Psychology* 45 (1983): 700–705.

Rogers, Carl R. *Client-Centered Therapy.* Boston: Houghton Mifflin Company, 1951.

Rogers, L. E. and F. E. Millar. "Domineeringness and Dominance: A Transactional View." *Human Communication Research* 5 (1979): 238–246.

Rondal, J. "Fathers' and Mothers' Speech in Early Language Development." *Journal of Child Language* 7 (1980): 353–369.

Rose, S. "Same- and Cross-sex Friendships and the Psychology of Homosociality." *Sex Roles* 12 (1985): 63–74.

Rosegrant, Teresa J., and James C. McCroskey. "The Effect of Race and Sex on Proxemic Behavior in an Interview Setting." *Southern Speech Communication Journal* 40 (1975): 408–420.

Rosen, Bernard C., and Carol S. Aneshensel. "Sex Differences in the Educational-Occupational Expectation Process." *Journal of Social Forces* 57 (1978): 164–186.

Rosencranz, Mary Lou. *Clothing Concepts: A Social-Psychological Approach.* New York: MacMillan Co., 1972.

Rosencranz, Mary Lou. "Clothing Symbolism." *Journal of Home Economics.* 54 (1972): 22. *A Schematic Approach to a Theoretical Analysis of Dress as Nonverbal Communication,* by Robert Christian Hillestad. Ph.D. diss., Ohio State University, 1974.

Rosenfeld, Howard. "Effect of an Approval-Seeking Induction on Interpersonal Proximity." *Psychological Reports* 17 (1965): 120–122.

Rosenfeld, Howard M. "Approval-Seeking and Approval-Inducing Functions of Verbal and Nonverbal Responses in the Dyad." *Journal of Personality and Social Psychology* 4 (1966): 597–605.

Rosenfeld, L., and T. Plax. "Clothing as Communication." *Journal of Communication* 27 (1977): 24–31.

Rosenfeld, L. B. "Self Disclosure Avoidance: Why I Am Afraid to Tell You Who I Am." *Communication Monographs* 46 (1979): 63–74.

Rosenfeld, L. R., and V. R. Christie. "Sex and Persuasibility Revisited." *Western Speech* 38 (1974): 244–253.

Rosenfeld, Lawrence B., and Sharon M. Welsh. "Differences in Self-disclosure in Dual-career and Single-career Marriages." *Communication Monographs* 52 (1985): 253–263.

Rosenthal, Robert, Dane Archer, M. DiMatteo, Judith Hall Koivumaki, and Peter L. Rogers. "Body Talk and Tone of Voice: The Language without Words." *Psychology Today* 8 (September 1974): 64–68.

Rosenthal, Robert and Bella M. DePaulo. "Expectancies, Discrepancies, and Courtesies in Nonverbal Communication." *Western Journal of Speech Communication* 43 (1979): 76–95.

Rossi, Alice. "Gender and Parenthood." *American Sociological Review* 49 (1984): 1–19.

Rossi, Susan R., and Joseph S. Rossi. "Gender Differences in the Perception of Women in Magazine Advertising." *Sex Roles* 12 (1985): 1033–1039.

Rubin, Lillian B. *Intimate Strangers: Men and Women Together.* New York: Harper & Row, Publishers, 1984.

Rubin, Q., L. A. Peplau, and C. T. Hill. "Loving and Leaving: Sex Differences in Romantic Attachments." *Sex Roles* 7 (1981): 821–835.

Rubin, Zick. "Measurement of Romantic Love." *Journal of Personality and Social Psychology* 16 (1970): 265–273.

Rubin, Zick, Charles T. Hill, Letitia Ann Peplau, and Christine Dunkel-Schetter. "Self-Disclosure in Dating Couples: Sex Roles and the Ethic of Openness." *Journal of Marriage and the Family* 42 (1980): 305–317.

Rubin, Zick, and Stephen Shenker. "Friendship, Proximity, and Self-Disclosure." *Journal of Personality and Social Psychology* 46 (1978): 1–22.

Ruble, Diana N., and E. Tory Higgins. "Effects of Group Sex Composition on Self-Presentation and Sex-Typing." *Journal of Social Issues* 32 (1976): 125–132.

Ruch, Libby O., and Rae R. Newton. "Sex Characteristics, Task Clarity, and Authority." *Sex Roles* 3 (1977): 479–494.

Rucker, M. H., D. Taber, and A. Harrison. "The Effect of Clothing Variation on First Impressions of Female Job Applicants: What to Wear When." *Social Behavior and Personality* 9 (1981): 53–64.

Ruggiers, Josephine A., and Louise C. Weston. "Work Options for Women in Women's Magazines: The Medium and the Message." *Sex Roles* 12 (1985): 535–547.

Russell, John Hamilton, III. "Need for Achievement across Three Career Patterns of College Educated Mothers Compared with Participation in Marital Decision Making and Their Husband's Performance of Domestic Activities." Ph.D. diss., Ohio State University, 1975.

Ryckman, R. M., M. F. Sherman, and G. D. Burgess. "Locus of Control and Self-Disclosure of Public and Private Information by College Men and Women: A Brief Note." *Journal of Psychology* 84 (1973): 317–318.

Rytting, Marvin B. "Self-disclosure in the Development of a Heterosexual Relationship." Ph.D. diss., Purdue University, 1975.

Sachs, J. "The Adaptive Significance of Linguistic Input to Prelinguistic Infants." *Talking to Children.* Ed. by C. Snow and C. Ferguson. Cambridge: Cambridge University Press, 1977.

Sadker, Myra P., David M. Sadker, and Susan S. Klein. "Abolishing Misconceptions about Sex Equity in Education." *Theory into Practice* 25 (1986): 219–226.

Sadker, Myra P., and David M. Sadker. "Sexism in the Classroom of the '80s." *Psychology Today* (March 1985): 54, 56, 57.

Safilios-Rothschild, Constantina. "The Study of Family Power Structure: A Review 1960–1969." *Journal of Marriage and the Family* 32 (1970): 539–552.

Salter, Andrew. *Conditioned Reflex Therapy.* New York: Creative Age Press, 1949.

Saltiel, J., and J. Woelfel. "Inertia in Cognitive Processes: The Role of Accumulated Information in Attitude Change." *Human Communication Research* 1 (1975): 333–344.

Sanders, Janet S., and William L. Robinson. "Talking and Not Talking about Sex: Male and Female Vocabularies." *Journal of Communication* 29 (Spring 1979): 22–30.

Sayers, Frances, and John Sherblom. "Qualification in Male Language as Influenced by Age and Gender of Conversational Partner." *Communication Research Reports* 4 (1987): 88–92.

Schaef, Anne Wilson. *Women's Reality: An Emerging Female System in a White Male Society.* San Francisco: Harper & Row, 1985.

Schaninger, C. M., and W. C. Buss. "The Relationship of Sex-role Norms to Couple and Parental Demographics." *Sex Roles* 15 (1986): 77–94.

Scheibe, Cyndy. "Sex Roles in Television Commercials." *Journal of Advertising Research* 19 (1979): 23–27.

Scheidel, Thomas M. "Sex and Persuasibility." *Speech Monographs* 30 (1963): 353–358.

Schein, Virginia Ellen. "The Relationship Between Sex Role Stereotypes and Requisite Management Characteristics." *Journal of Applied Psychology* 57 (1973): 95–100.

Schein, Virginia Ellen. "Relationships between Sex Role Stereotypes and Requisite Management Characteristics among Female Managers." *Journal of Applied Psychology* 60 (1975): 340–344.

Scheinfeld, Amram. *Women and Men.* London: Chatto & Windus, 1944.

Scher, D. "Sex-role Contradictions: Self-perceptions and Ideal Perceptions." *Sex Roles* 10 (1984): 651–656.

Schiffenbauer, Allen and Amy Babineau. "Sex Role Stereotypes and the Spontaneous Attribution of Emotion." *Journal of Research in Personality* 10 (1976): 137–145.

Schmuck, Patricia A. "Deterrents to Women's Careers in School Management." *Sex Roles* 1 (1975): 339–353.

Schneider, Joseph W., and Sally L. Hacker. "Sex Role Imagery and Use of the Generic 'Man' in Introductory Texts: A Case in the Sociology of Sociology." *The American Sociologist* 8 (1973): 12–18.

Schneider, Kenneth C., and Sharon Barich Schneider. "Trends in Sex Roles in Television Commercial." *Journal of Marketing* 43 (Summer 1979): 79–84.

Schultz, Katherine, John Briere, and Lorna Sandler. "The Use and Development of Sex-typed Language." *Psychology of Women Quarterly* 8 (1984): 327–336.

Schulwitz, Bonnie Smith. "Coping with Sexism in Reading Materials." *The Reading Teacher* 29 (1976): 768–770.

Schwartz, Lori A., and William T. Markham. "Sex Stereotyping in Children's Toy Advertisements." *Sex Roles* 12 (1985): 157–170.

Schweickart, Patsy. Reading Ourselves: Toward a Feminist Theory of Reading. *Readers, Texts, Contexts: Essays on Gender and Reading.* Baltimore, MD: Johns Hopkins University Press, in press.

Scott, Kathryn P., and Shirley Feldman Summers. "Children's Reactions to Textbook Stories in Which Females are Portrayed in Traditionally Male Roles." *Journal of Educational Psychology* 71 (1979): 396–402.

Seegmiller, Bonni R. "Sex-Typed Behavior in Pre-Schoolers: Sex, Age, and Social Class Effects." *Journal of Psychology* 104 (1980): 31–33.

Seidner, Constance J. "Interaction of Sex and Locus of Control in Predicting Self-Esteem." *Psychological Reports* 43 (1978): 895–898.

Selnow, Gary W. "Sex Differences in Uses and Perceptions of Profanity." *Sex Roles* 12 (1985): 303–312.

Serafini, Denise, and Judy C. Pearson. "Leadership Behavior and Sex Role Socialization: Two Sides of the Same Coin." Paper presented at the International Communication Association convention, Dallas, Texas, 1983.

Sereno, Kenneth K., and Janet L. Weathers. "Impact of Communication Sex on Receiver Reactions to Assertive, Nonassertive and Aggressive Communication." *Women's Studies in Communication* 4 (Fall 1981): 1–17.

Sermat, V., and M. Smyth. "Content Analysis of Verbal Communication in the Development of Relationships: Conditions Influencing Self-Disclosure." *Journal of Personality and Social Psychology* 26 (1973): 332–346.

Sexton, Donald E., and Phyllis Haberman. "Women in Magazine Advertisements." *Journal of Advertising Research* 14 (Aug. 1974): 41–46.

Shaevitz, Marjorie Hansen, and Morton H. Shaevitz. "Making It Together as a Two-Career Couple. Boston: Houghton Mifflin, 1980.

Shanteau, James, and Geraldine F. Nagy. "Probability of Acceptance in Dating Choice." *Journal of Personality and Social Psychology* 37 (1979): 522–533.

Shear, Maria. "Finding the Ladies . . . er . . . Women's Room: Recent History of a Telling Detail." *Women and Language* 9 (1985): 40.

Sher, George. "Groups and Justice." *Ethics* 87 (1977): 174–181.

Sherman, Barry L., and Joseph R. Dominick. "Violence and Sex in Music Videos: TV and Rock 'n' Roll." *Journal of Communication* 36 (1986): 70–93.

Shimanoff, Susan B. *Communication Rules: Theory and Research.* Beverly Hills: Sage Publications, 1980.

Shimanoff, Susan B. "Degree of Emotional Expressiveness as a Function of Face-needs, Gender, and Interpersonal Relationship." *Communication Reports* 1 (1988): 43–53.

Shimanoff, Susan B. "Rules Governing the Verbal Expression of Emotions between Married Couples." *Western Journal of Speech Communication* 49 (1985): 147–165.

Shimanoff, Susan. "Types of Emotional Disclosures and Request Compliance between Spouses." *Communication Monographs* 54 (1987): 85–100.

Shuter, Robert. "A Study of Nonverbal Communication Among Jews and Protestants." *The Journal of Social Psychology* 109 (1979): 31–41.

Shuy, R. W. "Sex as a Factor in Sociolinguistic Research." Paper presented at the Anthropological Society of Washington meeting, Washington, D.C., 1969.

Shuy, Roger, Walter Wolfram, and William Riley. *Linguistic Correlates of Social Stratification in Detroit Speech,* Final Report, Project 6–1347, Washington, D.C.: U.S. Office of Education, 1967.

Siegel, Jeffrey, C. "Effects of Objective Evidence of Expertness, Nonverbal Behavior, and Subject Sex on Client-Perceived Expertness." *Journal of Counseling Psychology* 27 (1980): 117–121.

Siegler, David, and Robert Siegler. "Stereotypes of Males' and Females' Speech." *Psychological Reports* 39 (1976): 167–170.

Simkins Rinck. "Male and Female Sexual Vocabulary in Different Interpersonal Contexts." *The Journal of Sex Research* 18 (1982): 160–172.

Singer, Dorothy, and Diane Zuckerman. "What Every Parent Should Know about Television." *American Film* (Jan.–Feb. 1981): 32.

Skol, E., and Kaionzky. "Target Personality Characteristics and Self-disclosure: An Exploratory Study." *Journal of Clinical Psychology* 41 (1985): 14–21.

Slama, Katherine M., and Betty J. Slowey. "Gender-specific Common Nouns: Sex Differences in Self-Use." *Sex Roles* 18 (1988): 205–213.

Slater, Marty M., Deborah Weider-Hatfield, and Donald L. Rubin. "Generic Pronoun Use and Perceived Speaker Credibility." *Communication Quarterly* 31 (1983): 180–183.

Smith, A. "Nonverbal Communication among Black Female Dyads: An Assessment of Intimacy, Gender, and Race." *Journal of Social Issues* 39 (1983): 55–67.

Smith, Audrey. "Influence Differentiation in Family Decision Making." *Sociology and Social Research* 51 (1967): 18–25.

Smith, Dwayne M., and George D. Self. "The Influence of Gender Difference on Perceptions of Self-Esteem: An Unobtrusive Measure." *Resources in Education* (February 1978): 168.

Smith, M. Dwayne, and Marc Matre. "Social norms and Sex Roles in Romance and Adventure Magazines." *Journalism Quarterly* 52 (1975): 309–315.

Smith, Mickey C. "Rationality of Appeals Used in the Promotion of Psychotropic Drugs: A Comparison of Male and Female Models." *Social Science and Medicine* April 11 (1977): 409–414.

Smith, Philip M. *Language, the Sexes and Society.* Oxford, England: Basil Blackwood, Ltd., 1985.

Smythe, Mary-Jeanette, and David W. Schlueter. "Can We Talk? A Meta-analytic Review of the Sex Differences in Language of Literature. Paper presented at the annual conference of the Organization for the Study of Communication, Language, and Gender, Washington, D.C., 1986.

Snoek, Diedrick, and Ester Rothblum. "Self-Disclosure among Adolescents in Relation to Parental Affection and Control Patterns." *Adolescence* 14 (1979): 333–340.

Snow, C. "Mothers' Speech Research: From Input to Interaction." *Talking to Children.* Ed. by C. Snow and C. Ferguson. Cambridge: Cambridge University Press, 1977.

Snow, Margaret, Carol Jacklin, and Eleanor Maccoby. "Sex of Child Difference in Father-Child Interaction at One Year of Age." *Child Development* 54 (1983): 227–232.

Snyder, April. "The Impact of Women of Language [sic] in American Higher Education." *Women and Language* 10 (1986): 49.

Soares, Manuela. *The Soap Opera Book.* New York: Harmony, 1978.

Sollie, D. L., and J. L. Fischer. "Sex-role Orientation, Intimacy of Topic, and Target Person Differences in Self-disclosure among Women." *Sex Roles* 12 (1985): 917–929.

Solomon, Martha. "The Total Woman: The Rhetoric of Completion." *Central States Speech Journal* 32 (1981): 74–84.

Sommer, Robert. *Personal Space: The Behavioral Basis of Design.* Englewood Cliffs, N.J.: Prentice-Hall, 1969.

Sommer, Robert. "Studies in Personal Space." *Sociometry* 22 (1959): 247–260.

Sonnier, Isadore L. "Holistic Education: How I Do It." *College Student Journal* 16 (Spring 1982): 64–69.

Sorrels, B. D. *"The Nonsexist Communicator: Solving the Problems of Gender and Awkwardness in Modern English."* Englewood Cliffs, N.J.: Prentice-Hall, 1983.

Sote, G. A., and L. R. Good. "Similarity of Self-Disclosure and Interpersonal Attraction." *Psychological Reports* 34 (1974): 491–494.

Soto, Debbie Halon, Evelyn Florio Forslund, and Claudia Cole. "Alternative to Using Masculine Pronouns when Referring to the Species." Paper presented at the Western Speech Communication Association convention, San Francisco, Calif., November 1975.

South, Earl Bennett. "Some Psychological Aspects of Committee Work." *Journal of Applied Psychology* 11 (1927): 348–368.

Sparfkin, C., L. A. Servin, C. Deniek, and J. M. Connor. "Sex-differentiated Play: Cognitive Consequences and Early Interventions." *Social and Cognitive Skills.* Ed. by M. B. Liss. New York: Academic Press, 1983.

Sparks, G. G., and C. L. Fehlner. "Faces in the News: Gender Comparisons of Magazine Photographs." *Journal of Communication* 36 (1986): 70–79.

Spence, J. T., R. Helmreich, and J. Stapp. "Ratings of Self and Peers on Sex-role Attributes and Their Relation to Self-esteem and Conceptions of Masculinity and Femininity." *Journal of Personality and Social Psychology* 32 (1975): 29–39.

Spender, Dale. "Unprofessional Conduct in Language Research: Why Do Men Not Listen?" Speech delivered at the annual conference on Gender and Communication, Eugene, Oregon, 1989.

Spender, Dale. *Man Made Language.* London: Routledge and Kegan Paul, 1980.

Sprague, Jo. "The Reduction of Sexism in Speech Communication Education." *Speech Teacher* 24 (1975): 37–45.

Sprague, Jo A. "An Investigation of the Written Critique Behavior of College Communication Instructors." Ph.D. diss., Purdue University, 1971.

Stake, Jayne E., and Michael N. Stake. "Performance—Self-Esteem and Dominance in Mixed Sex Dyads." *Journal of Personality* 47 (1979): 71–84.

Staley, Constance. "Male-Female Use of Expletives: A Heck of a Difference in Expectations." *Anthropological Linguistics* 20 (1978): 367–380.

Staley, Constance. "Sex Related Differences in the Style of Children's Language." *Journal of Psycholinguistic Research* 11 (1982): 141–152.

Stanley, Julia P. "Paradigmatic Women: The Prostitute." Paper presented at South Atlantic Modern Language Association 1972.

Statham, Anne. "The Gender Model Revisited: Differences in the Management Styles of Men and Women." *Sex Roles* 16 (1987): 409–429.

Stericker, Anne. "Does the 'He or She' Business Really Make a Difference? The Effect of Masculine Pronouns as Generics on Job Attitudes." *Sex Roles* 7 (1981): 637–641.

Stericker, Anne B., and James E. Johnson. "Sex-role Identification and Self-Esteem in College Students; Do Men and Women Differ?" *Sex Roles* 3 (1977): 19–26.

Stern, Barbara B., Benny Barak, and Stephen J. Gould. "Sexual Identity Scale: A New Self-assessment Measure." *Sex Roles* 17 (1987): 503–519.

Stewart, Alan D. "Declarations of Independence: The Female Rock and Roller Comes of Age." Paper presented at the annual conference of the Organization for the Study of Communication, Language, and Gender, Washington, D.C., 1986.

Stewig, John Warren, and Mary Lynn Knipfel. "Sexism in Picture Books: What Progress?" *Elementary School Journal* 76 (1975): 151–155.

Stier, D. S., and J. A. Hall. "Gender Differences in Touch: An Empirical and Theoretical Review." *Journal of Personality and Social Psychology* 47 (1984): 440–459.

Stitt, Christopher, Stuart Schmidt, Kari Price, and David Kipnis. "Sex of Leader, Leader Behavior, and Subordinate Satisfaction." *Sex Roles* 9 (1983): 31–42.

St. John-Parsons, Donald. "Career and Family: A Study of Continuous Dual-Career Families." *Psychology of Women Quarterly* 3 (1978): 30–42.

Stochton, Nancy. "Sex Role and Innovative Major Choice among College Students." *Journal of Vocational Behavior* 16 (1980): 360–367.

Stokes, Joseph, Ann Fuehrer, and Laurence Childs. "Gender Differences in Self-Disclosure to Various Target Persons." *Journal of Counseling Psychology* 27 (1980): 192–198.

Stoner, Sue, and Lynn Kaiser. "Sex Differences in Self-Concepts of Adolescents." *Psychological Reports* 43 (1978): 305–306.

Stopes, Charlotte Carmichael. *The Sphere of "Man": In Relation to That of "Woman" in the Constitution.* London: T. Fisher Unwin, 1908.

Stotko, Vincent P., and Daniel Langmeyer. "The Effects of Interaction Distance and Gender on Self-Disclosure in the Dyad." *Sociometry* 40 (1977): 178–182.

Strahan, R. F. "Remarks on Bem's Measurement of Psychological Androgyny: Alternative Methods and a Supplementary Analysis." *Journal of Consulting and Clinical Psychology* 43 (1975): 568–571.

Strainchamps, Ethel. "Our Sexist Language." *Women in Sexist Society.* Ed. by Vivian Gorneck and Barbara K. Moran. New York: Basic Books, 1971.

Streicher, Helen White. "The Girls in the Cartoons." *Journal of Communication* 24 (Spring 1974): 125–129.

Strodtbeck, Fred L., and Richard D. Mann. "Sex Role Differentiation in Jury Deliberations." *Sociometry* 19 (1956): 3–11.

Stuteville, John R. "Sexually Polarized Products and Advertising Strategy." *Journal of Retailing* 47 (Summer 1971): 3–13.

Sullivan, Gary L., and P. J. O'Connor. "Women's Role Portrayals in Magazine Advertising: 1958–1983." *Sex Roles* 18 (1988): 181–188.

Summerhayes, Diana L., and Robert W. Suchner. "Power Implications of Touch in Male-Female Relationships." *Sex Roles* 4 (1978): 103–110.

Sundstrom, Eric. "An Experimental Study of Crowding: Effects of Room Size, Intrusion, and Goal Blocking on Nonverbal Behavior, Self-Disclosure, and Self-Reported Stress." *Journal of Personality and Social Psychology* 32 (1975): 645–654.

Sundstrom, Eric and Mary G. Sundstrom. "Personal Space Invasions: What Happens When the Invader Asks Permission?" *Environmental Psychology and Nonverbal Behavior* Vol. (Winter 1977): 76–82.

Swacker, Marjorie. "The Sex of the Speaker as a Sociolinguistic Variable." *Language and Sex: Difference and Dominance.* Ed. by Barrie Thorne and Nancy Henley. Rowley, Mass.: Newbury House Publishers, Inc., 1975.

Swanson, Cheryl and Karen Van Wagner. "From Machiavelli to Ms.: Differences in Male-Female Power Styles." *Business or Public Administration Review* 39 (1979): 66–72.

Switzer, Joy. "The Impact of Generic Word Choices: An Empirical Investigation of Age—and Sex-related Differences." Paper presented at the annual conference of the Central States Communication Association, Kansas City, Mo., 1989.

Szilagyi, Andrew D. "Reward Behavior by Male and Female Leaders." *Journal of Vocational Behavior* 16 (1980): 59–72.

Talley, Mary A., and Virginia Peck Richmond. "The Relationship between Psychological Gender Orientation and Communicative Style." *Human Communication Research* 6 (1980): 326–339.

Tan, Alexis S. "Television Use and Social Stereotypes." *Journalism Quarterly* 59 (Spring 1982), 119–122.

Tannen, Deborah. *That's Not What I Meant! How Conversational Style Makes or Breaks Your Relations with Others.* New York: William Morrow and Company, Inc., 1986.

Tan-William, Conchita. "Cerebral Hemispheric Specialization of Academically Gifted and Nongifted Male and Female Adolescents." *The Journal of Creative Behavior* 15 (Winter 1981): 276–277.

Tardy, C. H., L. A. Hosman, and J. J. Bradac. "Disclosing Self to Friends and Family: A Reexamination of Initial Questions." *Communication Quarterly* 29 (1981): 263–282.

Taylor, D. A. "Some Aspects of the Development of Interpersonal Relationships: Social Presentation Process." *Technical Report No. 1,* Center for Research on Social Behavior, University of Delaware, 1965.

Taylor, Ralph B., Clinton B. DeSoto, and Robert Lieb. "Sharing Secrets: Disclosure and Discretion in Dyads and Triads." *Journal of Personality and Social Psychology* 37 (1979): 1196–1203.

Telzrow, Cathy Fultz. "The Impact of Brain Development on Curriculum." *The Educational Forum* 45 (May 1981): 477–483.

Thase, M., and R. A. Page. "Modeling of Self-Disclosure in Laboratory and Non-Laboratory Interview Settings." *Journal of Counseling Psychology* 24 (1977): 35–40.

Thayer, S., and W. Schiff. "Observer Judgment of Social Interaction: Eye Contact and Relationship Inferences." *Journal of Personality and Social Psychology* 30 (1974): 110–114.

Thibaut, J. W., and H. H. Kelley. *The Social Psychology of Groups.* New York: Wiley, 1959.

Thorne, Barrie. Public speech at Michigan State University, East Lansing, Michigan, 1981.

Thorne, Barrie, Cheris Kramarae, and Nancy Henley (ed.). *Language, Gender and Society.* Rowley, Mass.: Newbury House Publishers, 1983.

Thorne B., and N. Henley. "Difference and Dominance: An Overview of Language, Gender and Society." *Language and Sex: Difference and Dominance.* Rowley, Mass.: Newbury House Publishers, Inc., 1975.

Thorne B., and N. Henley. "Sex and Language Difference and Dominance." *Language in Society* 6 (1977): 110–113.

Thornton, A., and D. Freedman. "The Changing American Family." *Population Bulletin* 38 (1983): 1–44.

Tibbetts, S. "Sex Role Stereotyping in the Lower Grades: Part of a Solution." *Journal of Vocational Behavior* 6 (1975): 255–261.

Tindall, J. H., L. Boyler, P. Cline, P. Emberger, S. Powell, and J. Wions. "Perceived Leadership Rankings of Males and Females in Small Task Groups." *Journal of Psychology* 100 (1978): 13–20.

Todd-Mancillas, William. "Evaluating Alternatives to Exclusive He." *Communication Research Reports* 1 (1984): 38–41.

Todd-Mancillas, W. R., and A. N. A. Rossi. "Gender Differences in the Management of Personnel Disputes." *Women's Studies in Communication* 8 (1985): 25–33.

Todd-Mancillas, William. "Masculine Generics = Sexist Language: A Review of Literature and Implications for Speech Communication Professionals." *Communication Quarterly* 29 (1981): 107–115.

Trenholm, Sarah, and William R. Todd de Mancillas. "Student Perceptions of Sexism." *Quarterly Journal of Speech* 64 (1978): 267–283.

Trenholm, Sarah, and William Todd-Mancillas. "The Effect of Sexist Language on Interpersonal Judgments." *Communication, Language and Sex.* Ed. by Virginia Eman and Cynthia Berryman. Rowley, Mass.: Newbury House, 1980.

Tsui, A. S., and B. A. Gutek. "A Role Set Analysis of Gender Differences in Performance, Affective Relationships, and Career Success of Industrial Middle Managers." *Academy of Management Journal* 27 (1984): 619–635.

Turner, Lynn H. "The Relationship between Communication and Marital Uncertainty: Is "Her" Marriage Different from "His" Marriage?" *Women's Studies in Communication.* In press.

Tuthill, Douglas M., and Donelson R. Forsyth. "Sex Differences in Opinion Conformity and Dissent." *The Journal of Social Psychology* 116 (1982): 205–210.

Tyler, Leona E. *The Psychology of Human Differences.* 3d ed. New York: Appleton-Century-Crofts, 1965.

Uesugi, Thomas K., and W. Edgar Vinacke. "Strategy in a Feminine Game." *Sociometry* 26 (1963): 75–88.

Uleman, James S., and Martha Weston. "Does the BSRI Inventory Sex Roles?" *Sex Roles* 15 (1986): 43–62.

Unger, Rhoda K. *Female and Male: Psychological Perspectives.* New York: Harper and Row, 1979.

Unitarian Universalist Women's Federation (1986). *Inclusive Language: An Issue of Social Justice.* (Program Guide). Boston, Mass.: Author.

U.S. Department of Commerce, "Civilian Labor Force and Participation Rates by Races, Hispanic Origin, Sex and Age." *Statistical Abstract of the U.S.,* Washington, D.C., 1989.

Vaden, Richard E., and Naomi B. Lynn. "The Administrative Person: Will Women Bring a Differing Morality to Management?" *University of Michigan Business Review* 31 (1979): 22–25.

Van Wagner, Karen, and Cheryl Swanson. "From Machiavelli to Ms.: Differences in Male-Female Power Styles." *Public Administration Review* 39 (1979): 66–72.

Verbeeck, Marcia A. "An Investigation of Sexual Harassment, Gender Orientation, and Job Satisfaction." Paper presented to the annual conference of the Organization for the Study of Communication, Language, and Gender, Washington, D.C., 1986.

Verna, Mary Ellen. "The Female Image in Children's T.V. Commercials." *Journal of Broadcasting* 19 (Summer 1975): 301–309.

Vieira, Kenneth G., and William H. Miller. "Avoidance of Sex-Atypical Toys by Five- and Ten-Year-Old Children." *Psychological Reports* 43 (1978): 543–546.

Vigliano, Barbara Murphy. "An Investigation of the Relationship Between the Sex of the Speaker and the Sex of the Listener on Message Comprehension and Judgment of Speaker Credibility." Ph.D. diss., New York University, 1974.

Vinacke, W. Edgar. "Sex Roles in a Three-Person Game." *Sociometry* 22 (1959): 343–360.

Vollmer, Fred. "Why Do Men Have Higher Expectancy than Women?" *Sex Roles,* 1986: 351–362.

Voss, F. "The Relationship of Disclosure to Marital Satisfaction: An Exploratory Study." M.A. thesis, University of Wisconsin–Milwaukee, 1969.

Wagner, Louis C., and Janis B. Banos. "A Woman's Place: A Follow-up Analysis of the Roles Portrayed by Women in Magazine Advertisements." *Journal of Marketing Research* 10 (1973): 213–214.

Walsh, K. *Neuropsychology.* London: Churchill Livingstone, 1978.

Walster, Elaine, Vera Aronson, Darcy Abrahams, and L. Rottman. "Importance of Physical Attractiveness in Dating Behavior." *Journal of Personality and Social Psychology* 4 (1966): 508–516.

Warfel, Katherine A. "Gender Schemas and Perceptions of Speech Style." *Communication Monographs* 51 (1984): 253–267.

Warmbrod, M. T. "Alternative Generation in Marital Problem Solving." *Family Relations* 31 (1982): 503–511.

Warren, James Frederick. "The Effects of Assertion Training on Self-Acceptance and Social Evaluative Anxiety of University Students." Ph.D. diss., University of Florida, 1977.

Warren, Mary Anne. "Secondary Sexism and Quota Hiring." *Philosophy and Public Affairs* 6 (1977): 240–261.

Watson, Neil. "A Theoretical and Empirical Study of Empathy and Sex Role Differentiation." Ph.D. diss., Harvard University, 1976.

Watzlawick, Paul, Janet Helmick Beavin, Don D. Jackson. *Pragmatics of Human Communication: A Study of Interactional Patterns, Pathologies, and Paradoxes.* New York: W. W. Norton and Company, 1967.

Weaver, Carl H. *Human Listening: Processes and Behavior.* New York: The Bobbs-Merrill Company, Inc., 1972.

Weinrauch, J. Donald, and John R. Swanda, Jr. "Examining the Significance of Listening: An Exploratory Study of Contemporary Management." *The Journal of Business Communication* 13 (February 1975): 25–32.

Wenige, Lynn Oliver. "Preschool Children's Classification of Adult Apparel as Related to Parents' Mode of Dress and Attitudes Toward Adult Gender Roles." Unpublished doctoral dissertation. The University of Tennessee, 1976.

Weisstein, Naomi. *Psychology Constructs the Female, or the Fantasy Life of the Male Psychologist.* Boston: New England Free Press, 1971.

Weitz, R. "Feminist Consciousness Raising, Self-concept, and Depression." *Sex Roles* 8 (1982): 231–241.

Weitz, S. "Sex Differences in Nonverbal Communication." *Sex Roles* 2 (1976): 175–184.

Welsh, M. Cay. "Attitudinal Measures and Evaluation of Males and Females in Leadership Roles." *Psychological Reports* 45 (1979): 19–22.

Werner, Elyse K. "A Study of Communication Time." M.A. thesis, University of Maryland—College Park, 1975.

Wexley, Kenneth N., and Peter J. Hunt. "Male and Female Leaders: Comparison of Performance and Behavior Patterns." *Psychological Reports* 35 (1974): 867–872.

Wheeler, Christopher, Judith Wilson, and Carol Tarantola. "An Investigation of Children's Social Perception of Child Speakers with Reference to Verbal Style." *Central States Speech Journal* 27 (1976): 31–35.

Wheeless, Lawrence R. "A Follow-up Study of the Relationships among Trust, Disclosure and Interpersonal Solidarity." *Human Communication Research* 4 (1978): 143–157.

Wheeless, Lawrence R. "Self-Disclosure and Interpersonal Solidarity: Measurement, Validation and Relationships." *Human Communication Research* 3 (1976): 47–61.

Wheeless, Lawrence R., and Janis Grotz. "The Measurement of Trust and Its Relationship to Self-Disclosure." *Human Communication Research* 3 (1977): 250–257.

Wheeless, Lawrence R., and Virginia Eman Wheeless. "Attribution, Gender Orientation, and Adaptability: Reconceptualization, Measurement, and Research Results." *Communication Quarterly* 30 (1981): 56–66.

Wheeless, Lawrence R., Virginia E. Wheeless, and Raymond Baus. "Sexual Communication, Communication Satisfaction, and Solidarity in the Developmental Stages of Intimate Relationships." *Western Journal of Speech Communication* 48 (1984): 217–230.

Wheeless, Virginia Eman, and Cynthia Berryman-Fink. "Perceptions of Women Managers and their Communicator Competencies." *Communication Quarterly* 33 (Spring 1985): 137–148.

Wheeless, Virginia Eman, Cynthia Berryman-Fink, and Denise Serafini. "The Use of Gender-Specific Pronouns in the 1980's." Paper presented at the Fourth Annual Communication, Language, and Gender Conference, Morgantown, West Virginia, 1981.

Wheeless, Virginia Eman, and Kathi Dierks-Stewart. "The Psychometric Properties of the Bem Sex-Role Inventory: Questions Concerning Reliability and Validity." *Communication Quarterly* 29 (1981): 173–186.

Wheeless, Virginia Eman, and Robert L. Duran. "Gender Orientation as a Correlate of Communicative Competence." *Southern Speech Communication Journal* 48 (1982): 51–64.

Wheeless, Virginia Eman, Donald C. Hudson, and Lawrence R. Wheeless. "A Test of the Expected Use of Influence Strategies by Male and Female Supervisors as Related to Job Satisfaction and Trust in Supervisor." *Women's Studies in Communication* 10 (Spring 1987): 25–36.

Wheeless, Virginia Eman, W. R. Zachai, and M. B. Chan. "A Test of Self-disclosure Based on Perceptions of a Target's Loneliness and Gender Orientation." *Communication Quarterly* 36 (Spring 1988): 109–121.

White, M. C., M. D. Crino, and G. L. DeSanctis. "A Critical Review of Female Performance, Performance Training and Organizational Initiatives Designed to Aid Women in the Work-role Environment." *Personnel Psychology* 34 (1981): 227–248.

White, James M. "Perceived Similarity and Understanding in Married Couples." *Journal of Social and Personal Relationships* 2 (1985): 45–57.

Whitehead, III, G. I., and S. L. Tawes. "Dogmatism, Age, and Educational Level as Correlates of Feminism for Males and Females." *Sex Roles* 2 (1976): 401–405.

Widgery, Robin Noel. "Sex of Receiver and Physical Attractiveness of Source as Determinants of Initial Credibility Perception." *Western Speech* 38 (1974): 13.

Wiebe, B., and T. B. Scott. "Self-Disclosure Patterns of Mennonite Adolescents to Parents and Their Perceived Relationships." *Psychological Reports* 39 (1976): 355–358.

Wiley, Mary G., and Arlene Eskilson. "Speech Style, Gender Stereotypes, and Corporate Success: What if Women Talk More Like Men?" *Sex Roles* 12 (1985): 993–1007.

Wiley, Mary Glenn, and Arlene Eskilson. "Coping in the Corporation: Sex Role Constraints." *Journal of Applied Social Psychology* 12 (1982): 1–11.

Williams, John E., and Deborah L. Best. *Measuring Sex Stereotypes: A Thirty Nation Study.* Beverly Hills, Calif.: Sage Publications, 1982.

Willis, F. N., C. M. Rinck, and L. M. Dean. "Interpersonal Touch among Adults in Cafeteria Lines." *Perceptual and Motor Skills* 47 (1978): 1147–1152.

Willis, F. N., and C. M. Rinck. "A Personal Log Method for Investigating Interpersonal Touch." *The Journal of Psychology* 113 (1983): 119–122.

Wilson, Allan, and Richard V. Krane. "Change in Self-Esteem and its Effects on Symptoms of Depression." *Cognitive Therapy and Research* 4 (1980): 419–421.

Wilson, Elizabeth, and Sik H. Ng. "Sex Bias in Visuals Evoked by Generics: A New Zealand Study." *Sex Roles* 18 (1988): 159–168.

Winstead, Barbara A. "Sex Differences in Same-sex Friendships." *Friendship and Social Interaction.* Ed. by Valerian Derlega and Barbara A. Winstead. New York: Springer-Verlag, 1986.

Winstead, B., V. Derlega, and P. Wong. "Effects of Sex-role Orientation on Behavioral Self-disclosure." *Journal of Research in Personality* 18 (1984): 541–553.

Winter, Clotilda. "Listening and Learning." *Elementary English* 43 (1966): 569–572.

Winther, Dorothy A., and Samuel B. Green. "Another Look at Gender-related Differences in Leadership Behavior." *Sex Roles* 16 (1987): 41–56.

Witelson, S. F. "Developmental Dyslexia: Two Right Hemispheres and None Left." *Science* 195 (21 January 1977): 309–311.

Witkowski, Terrence H. "An Experimental Comparison of Women's Self and Advertising Image." *New Marketing for Social and Economic Progress.* Ed. by R. C. Carham. Chicago: American Marketing Association, 1975.

Wittig, Michele Andrisia and Paul Skolnick. "Sex Differences in Personal Space." *Sex Roles* 4 (1978): 493–503.

Wittrock, M. D. "Education and the Cognitive Processes of the Brain." *Education and the Brain.* Ed. by J. S. Chall and A. F. Mirsky. Chicago: University of Chicago Press, 1978.

Wojahn, Ellen. "Why There Weren't More Women in This Magazine." *Inc.,* July 1986, 45–48.

Wolfe, Susan J., Cindy Struckman-Johnson, and Judy Flanagin. "Generic 'Man': Grammatical Distribution and Perception." Paper presented at the annual conference of the Speech Communication Association, Chicago, Ill., 1986.

Wolff, Florence I., Nadine C. Marsnik, William S. Tacey, and Ralph G. Nichols. *Perceptive Listening.* New York: Holt, Rinehart and Winston, 1983.

Wolpe, Joseph, and Arnold A. Lazarus. *Behavior Therapy Techniques.* New York: Pergamon Press, 1966.

Wolvin, Andrew D., and Carolyn Gwynn Coakley. *Listening.* Dubuque, Iowa: William C. Brown Company Publishers, 1982.

"Traditional Talk at Harvard." *Women and Language* 9 (1986): 8.

"The Work of Joan Barleycorn." *Women and Language* 9 (1985): 41.

"A Triumph of Reason." *Women and Language* 10 (1986), "Language Keeps Women in Their Place," 48.

Wood, Marion M. "The Influence of Sex and Knowledge of Communication Effectiveness on Spontaneous Speech." *Word* 22 (1966): 117–137.

Woodyard, Howard P., and David A. Hines. "Accurate Compared to Inaccurate Self-Disclosure." *Journal of Humanistic Psychology* 13 (1973): 61–67.

Woolf, Virginia. *A Room of One's Own.* New York: Harcourt Brace Jovanovich, 1957.

Wright, J. W., and L. A. Hosman. "Language Style and Sex Bias in the Courtroom: The Effects of Male and Female Use of Hedges and Intensifiers on Impression Information." *The Southern Speech Communication Journal* 48 (1983): 137–152.

Yamada, Elaine M., Dean Tjosvold, and Juris G. Draguns. "Effects of Sex-Linked Situations and Sex Composition on Cooperation and Style of Interaction." *Sex Roles* 9 (1983): 541–554.

Yerby, Janet. "Attitude, Task, and Sex Composition as Variables Affecting Female Leadership in Small Problem-Solving Groups." *Speech Monographs* 42 (1975): 160–168.

Yogev, S. "Marital Satisfaction and Sex Role Perceptions among Dual-earner Couples." *Journal of Social and Personal Relationships* 4 (1987): 35–46.

Yogev, Sara, and J. M. Brett. "Patterns of Work and Family Involvement among Single and Dual-earner Couples." *Journal of Applied Psychology* 70 (1985): 754–768.

Young, Jerald W. "Willingness to Disclose Symptoms to a Male Physician: Effects of the Physician's Physical Attractiveness, Body Area of Symptom and the Patient's Self-Esteem, Locus of Control and Sex." Paper presented to the International Communication Association Convention, Acapulco, Mexico, May, 1980.

Zahn, Christopher J. "The Bases for Differing Evaluations of Male and Female Speech: Evidence from Ratings of Transcribed Conversation." *Communication Monographs* 56 (1989): 59–74.

Zander, A., and A. Havelin. "Social Comparison and Interpersonal Attraction." *Human Relations* 13 (1960): 21–32.

Zeldin, R. Shepherd, Stephen Small, and Ritch Savin-Williams. "Prosocial Interactions in Two Mixed Sex Adolescent Groups." *Child Development* 53 (1982): 1492–1498.

Zeldow, P. B., D. Clark, and S. R. Daugherty. "Masculinity, Femininity, Type A Behavior, and Psychosocial Adjustment in Medical Students." *Journal of Personality and Social Psychology* 48 (1985): 481–492.

Zelko, Harold P., and Frank E. X. Dance. *Business and Professional Speech Communication.* New York: Holt, Rinehart, & Winston, 1965.

Zemach, Tamar, and Akiba A. Cohen. "Perception of Gender and Quality on Television and in Social Reality." *Journal of Broadcasting and Electronic Media* 30 (1986): 427–444.

Zimmerman, Don H., and Candace West. "Sex Roles, Interruptions and Silences in Conversation." *Language and Sex: Difference and Dominance.* Ed. by Barrie Thorne and Nancy Henley. Rowley, Mass.: Newbury House Publishers, 1975.

Zuckerman, Diana M. "Self-Esteem, Self-Concept and the Life Goals and Sex-Role Attitudes of College Students." *Journal of Personality* 48 (1980): 149–162.

Zuckerman, Miron, Richard DeFrank, Judith Hall, and Robert Rosenthal. "Encoding and Decoding of Spontaneous Facial Expressions." *Journal of Personality and Social Psychology* 34 (1976): 966–977.

Text and Visual Credits

Index

Self-image, 54–66
  biological explanations for, 56
  development of, 55–64
  effects on self-concepts, 64–66
  socialization as an explanation for, 56–66
Self-perceptions, 52–74
Sex, 8
Sexism, 8
Sexist practices, 92–96
Sexuality, 196–97
Sexual language, 110–11
Silence in conversations, 147–48
Similarity, 34
Small group interaction, 218–22
  coalition formation in, 219

gender composition of the group, 219–22
  risk taking in, 219
Stereotyped perceptions of language
  differences, 106–9

Tag questions, 115
Television, 259–64
Territoriality, 131–33
Topic control in conversations, 145–46

Verbal fillers, 112–13
Vocabularies, differences in men's and
  women's, 110–13

Women as managers, 240–47